# The Elusive Peace
# in the Middle East

Published under the auspices of the Arab-Israeli
Research and Relations Project, a program of
the International Peace Academy

# The Elusive Peace in the Middle East

Edited by Malcolm H. Kerr

State University of New York Press  Albany, 1975

*The Elusive Peace in the Middle East*

*First Edition*                327.569

*9 8 7 6 5 4 3 2*              E49

*Published by State University of New York Press*
*99 Washington Avenue*
*Albany, New York 12210*

*Printed in the United States of America*

*Library of Congress Cataloging in Publication Data*

*Main entry under title:*
*The Elusive peace in the Middle East.*
*Includes bibliographical references.*
*1. Jewish-Arab relations—1917—     —Addresses,*
*Essays, Lectures. I. Kerr, Malcolm H.*

*DS119.7.E54     327.5694'017'4927     75-15581*
*ISBN 0-87395-305-3*
*ISBN 0-87395-306-1 pbk.*
*ISBN 0-87395-307-X microfiche*

# Contents

# Introduction

**Malcolm H. Kerr**

THE best way to begin a book about peace in the Middle East is to acknowledge that this is not a promising subject. Everything in the historical record must encourage the most pervasive pessimism. While it is good to favor peace, comforting to suppose that peace is what the mass of ordinary people in the world desire, and tempting to ascribe the persistence of conflict to needless fears and misunderstandings, in the Middle East it is far too late for such simple-mindedness. Clearly we are contending with more fundamental difficulties, such that peace has been at best an intermediate objective for some and indeed a negative value for others. At key moments prolongation of the conflict has always been a tolerable price to pay, if it was a price at all, for the pursuit of other interests. This holds true not only for Israelis and Arabs but for the leading members of the United Nations as well, notably the United States.

Naturally enough, throughout the history of the Palestine conflict there have been periodic reassessments and flurries of diplo-

Malcolm H. Kerr is Dean of the Division of Social Sciences and Professor of Political Science at the University of California, Los Angeles. Born in Beirut, Lebanon, in 1931 and educated at Princeton, the American University of Beirut, Harvard, and the School for Advanced International Studies of the Johns Hopkins University, he taught at the American University of Beirut before joining the faculty of UCLA in 1962. In 1971–72 he served as President of the Middle East Studies Association of North America.

Kerr's books include *Lebanon in the Last Years of Feudalism, 1840–1868* (American University of Beirut, 1959); *Islamic Reform* (University of California Press, 1966); *The Arab Cold War* (Oxford University Press, third edition, 1971); and, coauthored with A. S. Becker and B. Hansen, *The Economics and Politics of the Middle East* (New York, Elsevier, 1975).

matic activity. From the first years of the British mandate up to the present day, these moments have typically come in the wake of major confrontations, as contenders and outside parties have probed the latest changes in the situation to determine how the patterns of interests and opportunities have been affected. Habitually, peace initiatives on these occasions have started up amidst optimism but have eventually led to renewed frustration for the would-be promoters of peace.

The research project that has led to this book took form a few years after the 1967 war, at a time when the initiatives and inquiries to which that war gave rise were still alive: Security Council Resolution 242, the Jarring Mission, the Rogers Plan, the proposed "interim settlement" at the Suez Canal, and President Sadat's "year of decision" of 1971. It was, however, becoming progressively clearer, in the two years that followed the failure of the "interim settlement" negotiations of spring and summer 1971, that although the Six-Day War had produced vast changes on the strategic chessboard, politically it had led to a deepening stalemate which all the initiatives mentioned above were not to break. The individual chapters of the book took form, to a large extent, as postmortems which linked the failures of post-1967 peace diplomacy to the chain of failures that had gone before.

As these chapters were being completed, the 1973 war arrived to introduce fresh and, conceivably, revolutionary changes in the patterns of the Middle Eastern conflict. The authors have each briefly taken note of this prospect, but essentially their studies stand as analyses of the cumulative record up to the most recent conflict. This is by no means an outdated contribution; on the contrary, it is crucially important in helping us to assess what the Yom Kippur-Ramadan War was all about and whether or not it really portends new and different prospects in the Middle East. For my own part, I confess that I find the answer much less encouraging than many others have lately done, and the material provided by the authors of this book deepens and confirms my skepticism.

Our authors have shown that whatever hopes for peace have been aroused in recent years, they need to be measured against a long historical record of similar hopes which ended in failure. We must consider not only the antagonisms that have pitted

Arabs against Jews in the Middle East but the whole tapestry of clashing perceptions of the most basic facts. What has happened over the past half century, what it has meant, what is at stake, and what needs to be done are questions that elicit very different answers, even from two reputable and professionally minded scholars such as Aharon Cohen and George Haddad, for whom these events have formed the personal experiences of their lifetimes. An uninitiated reader will find it difficult to believe that these two gentlemen are really both writing about the same subject; the initiated reader will find the disparities between them perfectly familiar, but will not thereby draw any greater hopes for the future.

Not only Arabs and Israelis have widely differing visions of the conflict between them, but outsiders too: statesmen, journalists, academics, men in the street. The disparities among statesmen's perspectives add to the difficulties of negotiation, and ultimately the same must be said about men in the street. Different men in different streets, conditioned in part by what their own political leaders and newspapers tell them, will have varying reactions to academic books such as this one. Within the normal spectrum of discussion in America, for instance, this is bound to be regarded as a pro-Arab book with a pro-Arab lineup of contributors, perhaps even including Aharon Cohen, who is known in Israel as a sharp critic of his government.

In other countries, however, the array of judgments is quite different. What passes for Arab propaganda in America is not necessarily accorded that compliment in Cairo or Beirut, nor for that matter in London, Paris, Tokyo, Delhi, Nairobi, or Buenos Aires. I would venture to predict that in such locations as these, many readers will dismiss the lot of us who have written in this book as a collection of foolish liberals unconsciously giving service to reactionary and oppressive interests. The important question, however, is not what label this book deserves, but how much progress toward peace in the Middle East can be made in an international atmosphere of such differing perspectives.

In the aftermath of the 1973 war it has been widely remarked that the war dispelled illusions and undermined policies that had prevailed the period since 1967—illusions and policies which had propped up the "no war, no peace" status quo quite plausibly at the time but had really stood in the way of a genuine settlement and which were bound sooner or later to fall victim to renewed violence unleashed by the pent-up force of Arab frustration. Among these illusions were the beliefs that superior Israeli military strength, backed by American support, could enforce the status quo on a long-term basis; that the Arabs, recognizing their military helplessness as time went by, would do nothing to shake the status quo and would either resign themselves to it, finding new ways to adjust to it, or eventually undergo a fundamental change of attitude and sue for peace; that the United States, thrust increasingly into the role of Israel's partner, patron, and arsenal, could not only afford politically to play this role on a long-term basis, despite Arab disapproval, but could turn this partnership into a positive asset, with Israel as its policeman in the Middle East; and, lastly, that the Soviet-American detente, symbolized by President Nixon's visit to Moscow in the spring of 1972 and by Secretary Brezhnev's return visit a year later, could be counted on to confirm the continued freezing of the Middle Eastern status quo.

These propositions made for an Israeli policy, increasingly acquiesced in by the United States, of great inflexibility and stubbornness. "An inch of territory is worth a thousand Arab assurances" became the byword. "I prefer Sharm el-Sheikh without a peace agreement to a peace agreement without Sharm el-Sheikh," declared Moshe Dayan. On the grounds that no Arab professions of readiness for peace could be trusted, a preference emerged in Israel for military advantage over any settlement such as might emerge from Resolution 242, the Jarring Mission, the Rogers Plan, etc. Concomitantly, there was a creeping annexation of the territory captured in 1967 through the establishment of Israeli settlements in these areas. This culminated in the Galili Document, adopted by the Labor Party in September 1973, which forecast an ambitiously expanded program. While some Israelis justified these moves primarily on the grounds of Biblical attachment, more widely the justification expressed itself in the slogan *ein breira,* or "no alternative"—an expression summing up the security argument. With Israel's very existence hanging in the balance, it was argued, it could not afford the luxury of compromise. Not only did *ein breira* allow for annexation with a good conscience, but it reflected confidence in Israel's ability to live with the results of permanent conflict with the Arabs.

The *ein breira* attitude was severely discredited by the Yom Kippur-Ramadan War, along with the whole bag of policy illusions referred to. It had seemed that Israel had no alternative to sitting tight, but sitting tight had not worked after all: Egypt and Syria had attacked, despite their supposed weakness, and inflicted very serious damage of the sort that Israel could not continuously sustain. "Sharm el-Sheikh without a peace agreement" and the complacent absorption of land from Kuneitra to El-Arish amidst Arab cries of outrage no longer looked so attractive. True, the "new territories" proved useful as a defensive buffer zone, but not altogether so, for obviously retaining them had helped stimulate the attack. In any case, Israel could no longer afford to stand still on the diplomatic front.

Not only Israel, but the Arab states, the United States, and the Soviet Union had suffered their own version of *ein breira,* and again, one would like to think that they were cured by the impact of the 1973 war. The two superpowers discovered that detente and the fear of escalation would not after all assure their clients' good behavior nor the stability of the stalemate between them. More particularly, for the United States, all the lessons the Israelis learned were her lessons also, only in some ways more so: not only did Israel's superior fighting capacity not obviate need for American intervention, but neither militarily nor politically could Israel deter assaults on American interests in the surrounding Middle Eastern region as a whole. Effective Arab use of the oil weapon against the United States underscored this. No longer could it be argued in Washington that in the face of Arab resentment and instability and Soviet competition, there was "no alternative" to standing fast with Israel.

The Arab version of *ein breira,* weakened significantly by the October war, includes the familiar reluctance to consider solutions entailing formal recognition of Israel or direct negotiations with it. Much ink has been spilt on this subject since the early days of the British mandate. Since 1967 commentators have focussed on the so-called "three noes of Khartoum" (no negotiations, no peace treaty, no recognition) declared by the Arab states in September 1967, the massive and rapid Egyptian rearmament the insistence on recovery of all territory lost in 1967, and the support for the Palestinian *fedayeen* organizations. In adopting these positions the Arabs have habitually argued that they had no choice, since otherwise they would be waiving their rights and rewarding Israeli aggression. Given the Arabs' military weakness and political disarray, their negotiating position was a poor one, and this circumstance strengthened the view that they must wait, play for time to turn the tide to their advantage, and meanwhile not make needless concessions. But the Arab "no choice" posture was moral as well as strategic, which prevented them from perceiving Israel's elementary motive of self-preservation.

To be sure, after 1967 Egypt and Jordan had repeatedly declared their acceptance of Resolution 242 and their willingness to settle for the return of the territories lost in the June war, plus a largely unspecified formula of justice for the Palestinians. Fundamentally, this position did not alter with the 1973 war. But generally among the Arabs as among others, the psychological atmosphere changed. What had been the diplomatic reflection of a defiant moral position—a refusal to accept what they saw as a dictated peace—now became a positive hope; and with it came the prospect of greater flexibility.

Regardless of the circumstances in which the fighting finally ended late in October, the general Arab military performance was so dramatically superior to any past occasion that it greatly boosted Arab morale. The unprecedented atmosphere of cooperation among the Arab states did likewise. Furthermore, the length of the war, the heaviness of Israeli (as well as Arab) material and human losses, Israel's dependence on rapid American resupply, and the success of the Arab oil cutback in making the rest of the world sit up and listen—all of these factors conspired to indicate that the future balance of bargaining power in the Middle East was likely to be quite different from what it had been. If so, then presumably the Arabs could afford to advance their case against Israel in a more relaxed, variable, imaginative, rational, moderate way, instead of clinging to a negative posture as their only recourse. Various events shortly after the October war lent support to such expectations—such as the willingness of Egypt and Syria to negotiate a disengagement with Israel, and the readiness of the Palestine Liberation Organization to participate in the Geneva peace conference.

Egypt's alacrity to restore diplomatic relations with the United States, and the euphoric atmosphere of reconciliation in which this was done, seem almost absurd when one remembers that Israel had fought the October war with hourly deliveries of American supplies and that it continues to depend on American financial and diplomatic help. But this reconciliation revealed an important consideration that lay dormant throughout the preceding six years: the abiding interest many Egyptians have in close relations with the United States, whose people and culture they instinctively like. Still more important, every conservative Arab regime (of which "revolutionary" Egypt is among the most important) requires a restored *modus vivendi* not only between the Arab world at large and the United States, but with Israel as well, if the established foundations of society are not to crumble under a tidal wave of frustration and nihilism. To achieve this *modus vivendi* the Arabs must obtain a good bargain from Israel in order to forestall more militant elements who continue to insist on all or nothing.

So far, so good for the prospects for peace. It has higher priority than ever before for all concerned, and the chances of real progress being made toward it appear unprecedented. To be sure, for many peace is still at best a contingent good, whose desirability depends on its terms. Others find it threatens to undermine cherished roles, attitudes, and careers. For some on the Arab side, peace with Israel automatically signifies injustice for the Palestinians, while in Israel there are those who view the continued conflict as the best means of maintaining Zionist morale and commitment. Nonetheless, for people who are fundamentally concerned with peace for its own sake, this has been a time for optimism.

Unfortunately, much of this optimism is based on short memory. After two generations of strife, often punctuated by abortive peace efforts, it behooves us to be cautious, not only about Israeli claims that 1967 created a radically new situation in the Middle East, but also about Arab claims that 1973 did so. The lessons supposedly provided since 1967 have been available for ten, twenty, even thirty years, as much of this book suggests.

Israel's obsession with security, its preoccupation with territorial possession and military advantage by *faits accomplis,* its great distrust of outside intermediaries, and its reluctance to take initiatives or show restraint for the sake of encouraging a softer Arab image of itself—all this has been clearly illustrated since the 1967 war; but it has also all been true for many previous years. In many respects the 1967 war and its aftermath constituted a replay of 1948–1949, when the Lausanne Protocol and the Conciliation Commission for Palestine (the forerunners of Resolution 242 and the Jarring Mission) were blocked by the seemingly instinctive Israeli conviction that mollification of the Arabs could not be worth sacrificing the material advantages Israel possessed, i.e., extra territory and the exclusion of Palestinian refugees. Both in 1948–49 and 1967–73, Israeli diplomacy was skillful enough to blur the lines of this policy and disguise it somewhat, but the reality was clear enough to those who cared to look. In short, there was nothing particularly new about Israeli policy after the June war.

Throughout these years, to be sure, voices were raised in Israel criticizing the wisdom and morality of this hard-line policy and insisting on the need to understand and come to terms with Arab (especially Palestinian) claims. In earlier times such voices came mainly from within the Zionist left and from independent intellectuals like Martin Buber and Judah Magnes; since 1967 dissent reflects a wider spectrum of diverse personalities such as Uri Avnery, Arie Eliav, Mattityahu Peled, Nahum Goldmann, Joseph Ben-Dak, Simha Flapan, Abie Nathan, and Shimon Shamir. Our colleague Aharon Cohen has been writing and speaking in the cause of Jewish-Arab conciliation since the 1930s.

Such critics as these have long made it clear that the government's confrontation tactics and mentality were by no means free of challenge within Israel. By condemning the authorities' penchant for retaliation, preemption, and *faits accomplis* through the years up to 1973, these critics can now be seen to have educated a crucial minimum sector of Israeli opinion. As the lessons of the Yom Kippur-Ramadan War began to sink in, the ideas of this group were available to a larger and newly receptive public.

The fact remains, however, that in the past these dissident voices were always those of a rather ineffectual minority, and the assumptions behind official policy were too deeply ingrained to be lightly repudiated even after the 1973 war—as the Israeli parliamentary elections of December suggested. Whatever concessions the government might entertain in subsequent international negotiations seemed likely to be spurred as much by a sober reassessment of Israel's bargaining power as by any newfound empathy with the enemy. By 1974, after all, Israel faced very serious prospects. Dependence on Arab oil might force the United States to join Europe in progressively withdrawing support from Israel and leaving it isolated and vulnerable, unable to replenish its armory or cover its mounting financial deficit. Once such a point were reached, Israel would have little choice but to accept whatever terms of settlement the United States, for the sake of an American detente with both the Arabs and the Soviets, saw fit to impose. It does not require an ideological or moral transformation in Israel to adjust to such a prospect, but only pragmatic realism on the part of the present establishment. Of course, the Israeli peace movement may contribute an essential supportive pressure on public opinion, and through it on the government, somewhat as the US antiwar movement from the late 1960s onward affected Nixon's foreign policy. But this is a secondary factor: what will influence the Israeli government most is the international situation it faces, including the strength and persistence of American pressure and the character of Arab demands.

There is no simple parallel between the domestic debate in Israel and that in the Arab world, for the two societies are very different, as are their historic circumstances. In the Palestine conflict from the Balfour Declaration onward, the Arabs have continuously been on the defensive, have lost ground time after time, and have always been the ones to cope with frustration. All this comes at a time when the Arabs already face a host of other crucial problems. Even if it were more a part of Arab tradition to conduct free and open debate on sensitive national questions, it would hardly be logical to expect a significant section of opinion to preach conciliation with those who sought to transform an Arab land into a Jewish state at the expense of its inhabitants. And once Israel was established, even if some in the Arab world thought it wisest to cut their losses and accept the new reality, there was little reason to invoke moral reasons for doing so. After all, they were aware that even those in the Israeli peace movement made no apology for the fundamental fact of Israel's existence, but considered the Jewish national home and its population to be in Palestine as a matter of right.

Therefore the Arab advocates of reconciliation have not been left-wing idealists and intellectuals, but conservative realists who feared the long-term social consequences that an ongoing conflict could bring to Arab society. Where we might choose Martin Buber as the classic peace advocate on the Israeli side, among the Arabs it would have to be King Abdullah. This disjuncture has not changed much in more recent times: what has changed since the October war is that diplomatic concessions in the name of realism seem to make more sense to a wider political spectrum in both Israel and the Arab world. If progress toward peace is made, it will not be negotiated between the likes of Martin Buber and King Abdullah but between such men as Yitzhak Rabin and Hafez Asad.

Nonetheless, in important respects the continuities of Arab attitude and conduct are more substantial than is sometimes realized. Despite what many Arabs themselves have been saying in the post-1973 euphoria, such dramatic hopes for a reversal of fortune have arisen before. Nasser in his early years produced great expectations; so did the Palestinian *fedayeen* between the battle of Karameh in March 1968 and Black September in September 1970. Nor have these upsurges of morale necessarily pointed toward greater Arab intransigence: it has always been plausible to argue that strengthened Arab confidence was a necessary basis for moderation and readiness to compromise.

In fact, the debate within Arab and even Palestinian society over the wisdom of compromise is a very old one, reaching back well into the years of the mandate. This debate has not usually been heard, for the militants speak loudly and directly, while the moderates cloak their message in euphemisms, when they speak publicly at all. The moderate view has always been a potentially important political factor, if favorable circumstances should arise. Thus there is nothing altogether surprising in Egypt's negotiation with Israel at Kilometer 101, nor in the enthusiasm of some Arab governments for Resolution 242, nor even in the wooing of Secretary Kissinger during an oil embargo against the United States. All of it has hung on the proposition—espoused over the years more or less wistfully by the moderates, eyed suspiciously or rejected outright by the militants—that the United States has an interest in ending the conflict on the basis of righting the wrongs in the Middle East and restoring legitimate Arab rights. This being in the American interest, sooner or later an American president will come to his senses and follow it; therefore, to give him a lead is always a plausible gamble. So the reasoning runs.

The Arab militants have always disparaged this view as naive, arguing that Israel and her supporters would wind up taking advantage of it. Thus, the militants argue, Israel secured its admission to the United Nations under the smokescreen of the Lausanne negotiations, while in 1970 it secured a desperately needed cease fire on the Suez front and Jordan's suppression of the Palestinian *fedayeen* under the smokescreen of the Rogers Plan—in each case, a western-sponsored diplomatic initiative that served as a trap. After the 1973 war, Arab skeptics viewed Kissinger's diplomacy in a similar light: it was a means of undermining the Arab oil boycott and buying time for Israel to reestablish the status quo. Where would Egypt and Syria find themselves a year or two later, after staking so much on compromise?

Whether the Arab moderates or militants were closer to the truth in their assessments of American interests and intentions, the pre-1973 record of American initiatives, much like the pre-1948 record of British inquiries, White Papers, and conferences, does lend credence to the militants' skepticism. It indicates a pattern of too little and too late, of grossly inadequate political support from the White House, and of a curiously persistent misconception that America must bring together Arab and Israeli governments that really want peace and successful negotiations, rather than that America should crack their heads together. Intended or not, the consistent effect has been to buy time in behalf of the status quo, which is to say, in behalf of the Israeli accumulation of *faits accomplis* and the Arab accumulation of resentment. This status quo has been of debatable value all along, but now, in light of the most recent hostilities and the oil crisis, it must be recognized as a sinking ship for American interest. Which is to say that Secretary Kissinger's frantic diplomacy after the October war will prove useless in the long run, if it is thought that separating the forces has bought time for peace and that the

United States can henceforth relax its pressure on Israel to withdraw from Arab territory and on the Arab governments to indicate reciprocal respect for Israeli security concerns.

With just what sort of arrangements this might eventually leave us, it is not our concern in these few lines to speculate. What settlement might be made on behalf of Palestinian self-determination? What formula for the city of Jerusalem? What reconciliation of Egyptian and Syrian sovereignty in Sinai and Golan with Israeli security claims? These have become widely familiar questions, however uncertain the answers; but our concern here is not with the substance of such concrete issues but with the spirit and process by which they are approached. With intermittent exceptions the American record until 1973 was one of nickel-and-dime diplomacy, in which a secretary of state was, at best, authorized by his president to broach various suggestions to the Middle Eastern parties and perhaps to argue heatedly behind closed doors, provided always that the political position of the president himself was not brought to the point of a domestically controversial commitment.

Nickels and dimes, by the mid-1970s, are no longer enough, if they ever really were: military disengagement along the cease-fire lines, if left at that, seems to promise a reengagement sooner or later. As the authors of this book implicitly suggest, time has never been on the side of peace in the Middle East. As this disturbing truth shows itself more clearly with each succeeding round of warfare, it may at last become obvious that seeking to buy time is fallacious. Just as peace is too important to be left to the combatants, so also is it too important to be left to the advocates of reconciliation. It must be imposed from the outside by those with the will and resources to do so.

To Israel and its friends the idea of an imposed peace has always seemed odious. At best, it smacks of the strong manipulating the weak; at worst, of a genocidal sellout. Israelis are understandably sensitive to the link between Munich and Auschwitz; they also recall that British policy in the last decade of the Palestine mandate sought to appease the Arabs at the expense of Zionist aspirations and that only the violence of the Haganah and the Irgun prevented it. The prospect of American support suddenly withdrawing has always fed a mood of suspicion, which bubbles beneath Israel's surface of pro-American sentiment.

Quite apart from any domestic considerations, American policy-makers have hesitated to press Israel into things it does not wish to do, for they are aware of Israeli sensitivities and fear the reactions in Israel that pressure might provoke. Most dramatically, they have feared that Israel may resort to nuclear weapons; less drastically, that Israel's political and military posture will stiffen just enough to frustrate current diplomatic initiatives. The large-scale arms shipments the Nixon administration supplied in the years prior to 1973 were accordingly justified in part by the argument that reassuring Israel of its security was a prerequisite for persuading Israel to soften its line. As matters turned out, it seems to have had the opposite effect, for the arms were the means by which the status quo was defended. On the other hand, the massive US resupply of Israeli equipment losses during the October war undoubtedly gave Secretary Kissinger important leverage in persuading Israel's leaders to accept a ceasefire and subsequently to yield territory in the disengagement agreements. It had become clear how heavily Israel would depend on American good will in the future, at a time when America faced a continuing dependence on Arab oil. Without the accompanying oil boycott, the implications would have been very different.

For Israel, the prospect of yielding to imposed peace terms is at once a simple and a difficult matter. It is simple in the sense that the requirement is unambiguous and material in character: Israel would presumably have to withdraw from certain territories, recognize a certain Palestinian national authority, grant residence permits to a certain number of Palestinian returnees according to a certain procedure, all of which would be clearly specified in the peace terms. In what spirit Israel did these things would be secondary; however grudgingly undertaken, a withdrawal would be a withdrawal. The difficulty would be for Israel to accept such terms at all, in the face of its fears that such a move might prove suicidal. Acceptance would simply signify that Israel thought defying American insistence would be still more dangerous.

For Arabs the idea of an imposed peace is much more complicated. Arab interests and aspirations are diverse, often masked by unfathomable modes of expression. Certainly the most militant Palestinians are as suspicious as the Israelis of being sold out, and certainly even the most moderate Arab governments are unwilling to yield control over their own decisions. For the Palestinians, what would be imposed would be a definitive settlement of their national claims outside the borders of Israel; for the Arab states, an equally definitive acceptance of Israel's legitimacy as a state, with the eventual development of some normal relations with it. On one psychological level, such an imposed settlement has some attractiveness to Arab minds, since it is Israeli military superiority and an Israeli status quo that would be negated by the great-power arbitration. It is Israel against whom the most tangible terms would be imposed, and the spectacle of this being done mainly by the United States would bring considerable satisfaction to many Arabs who have long believed that America's best interests in the Middle East should logically bring it to the Arab side. Furthermore, as we have already indicated, the more conservative forces in Arab society, and even some that are not so conservative, have a powerful practical interest in ending the disruptive effects of the conflict. For them, as long as the terms are minimally favorable, yielding to outside imposition may excuse them somewhat from charges of treason.

Still, on another level, there is no getting around the fact that any Arab recognition of Israel under any circumstances would engage a powerful and damaging symbolism of failure and dishonor. It would mean doing what many have long proclaimed should never be done; it would mean acknowledging formally in public what until now has only been spoken of guardedly in private. Perhaps worst of all, it would mean a bitter conflict amongst the Arabs themselves: between conservatives and radicals, between Arab governments and the Palestinian liberation movement, between those Palestinians who are ready to settle for half a loaf and those who are not.

Furthermore, Arab governments may find that to argue that they, like Israel, yielded reluctantly to *force majeure* is not worth very much. After all, in exchange for Israel's concessions, they would have to proclaim themselves satisfied with the bargain, and it would be difficult for them to point to any very tangible great-power threat, beyond mere disapproval. While they initially joined combat with Israel in 1948 for the sake of the Palestinians, they would now have to affirm that the Palestinians received adequate recompense in a truncated West-Bank state. Some Arab governments may be prepared to make such an affirmation; others perhaps not. With all of them, however, the crucial question would remain: how genuine would their assent prove to be under the stress of subsequent crises and charges of a sellout?

Only the Palestinian Liberation Organization would be yielding to *force majeure,* and that would be imposed primarily by the Arab states themselves. Like the Arab states, the PLO has nothing tangible to offer Israel in the bargain; and although the intangibles it can offer are of enormous importance, it is naturally impossible to make more than a calculated guess how they will turn out in the future. As Israelis are always quick to point out, a bargain of withdrawal in exchange for promises leaves all the risks on their side, and Arab promises, whether by sovereign states or by Palestinian spokesmen, may or may not turn out to be genuine and may or may not stick under future circumstances.

To Israel, pressure on the PLO from the Arab governments may carry more credibility than bargains accepted at the negotiating table by the Palestinians themselves, for Israel traditionally asserts that the "real" objective of the PLO is to destroy Israel, and hence any compromise arrangement would only become a springboard for further Palestinian claims. There appears to be no good prospect, however, of bringing about deals between Israel and the Arab states without PLO participation; and in any case the argument that the PLO cannot be a credible negotiator ignores two vital considerations.

In the first place, the maximalist posture habitually adopted by the Palestinian militants, like that of some of the Arab governments in the past, cannot simply be judged at face value. Until a minimally credible bargain is offered them, such as the chance to establish and govern an independent state of their own inside Palestine but outside Israel, they have no real incentive to water down their maximum demands. What they would really accept in the crunch remains to be seen. In the second place, even assuming the worst about the private intentions of PLO leaders who initially accept a compromise, it remains to be seen what effect the new political realities of a West-Bank state would have on those intentions—or on their continuing claims to leadership—as time went by. What was accepted for tactical purposes might, if given a chance, prove worth retaining.

Not only Israel and the Arabs but the great powers too have found their situation substantially affected by the 1973 war. Two old arguments have become obsolete. The first is that the very involvement of outside powers in the Middle Eastern conflict is artificial and unnecessary. The second is that since peace has been so elusive, wisdom dictates that if outsiders must be involved at all, they should restrict themselves to patchwork diplomacy aimed merely at keeping violence, misery, and anger at a tolerable minimum.

There will always be someone to argue that the great powers ought to keep out of the Middle East conflict, but given the facts of life of world politics, this is somewhat like arguing that gamblers ought to stay away from Las Vegas. Foreign involvement has assumed many forms and has had various effects on the course of the conflict. During the period between the two world wars it was Britain that held open the gates of Palestine to Jewish immigration over Arab protests and subsequently closed them over Jewish ones. Israel's creation as a state in 1947–49 was aided substantially by both the United States and the Soviet Union and consolidated in the 1950s with French help. The Arab states were able to maintain their defiance of Israel thanks largely to the support of the Soviet Union, after it reversed its policy. Since 1967 Israel has depended overwhelmingly on American money, arms, and diplomacy, and yet it is the United States to which several Arab states have turned since 1973 to seek pressure against Israel. Left to themselves, Israelis and Arabs would each find advantages and disadvantages that are not now so apparent: both would be deprived of advanced weaponry; Israel would enjoy an important technological superiority, but would also face crushing financial problems.

Obviously, then, the involvements of outsiders have had great effect on the course of the conflict. Indeed, without the support of Britain and the League of Nations it is hard to see how Zionism could have progressed far enough to cause more than a ripple in Palestine, let alone an international struggle. This is not to say that without the British on hand to arbitrate and irritate, or the Americans, the Russians, and the United Nations afterward, Arab nationalism and Zionism would somehow have been more compatible: between the two movements with their rival claims on the destiny of the territory of Palestine and the composition of its population, antagonism has been implicit since each of them arose a century ago, long before the arrival of the British. It is hardly surprising that in the interval, rival great powers have been drawn into the arena, considering the social ties and roots of Jews in eastern and western Europe and the United States, plus the strategic importance of the Arab world's geography and resources, and hence of its people.

The onset of the energy crisis and its linkage to Arab claims against Israel has altered the whole equation of international concerns in the Middle East, drastically but uncertainly. Of course, access to Arab oil has long been vitally important to the western European states—important enough, for instance, to help push Britain into war against Egypt in 1956—and there have always been Cassandras in European and American business and government circles warning that support for Israel would ultimately jeopardize the flow of oil. But few people were convinced. The Arabs were too weak and divided to make serious threats; they needed the oil companies to run the business, and they needed the money just as Europe needed the oil; there were plenty of alternate sources, and in fact for many years there was a glut of oil on the world market. The United States was self-sufficient in oil within the western hemisphere and thus immune from Arab pressure (although of course American companies operating in the Middle East were not).

All this has now changed. Most of the changes built up progressively, in the full light of day, and ought to have served as a warning: the rise in world consumption, the beginnings of American importation of Arab oil, the increase in Arab management capabilities, the improvement of political relations between Egypt and Saudi Arabia. Still, the impact of the measures the Arab producing countries took in the fall of 1973 surprised the world, just as Egypt's and Syria's launching of the October war had done. What had been consistently underestimated, especially in the United States, was the most fundamental political factor: the extent to which Arabs found the post-1967 status quo unacceptable, and the efforts they would make together to undo it.

With the precedent that was set by the Arab oil weapon in 1973, and with the enormous transfer of capital from consumers' to producers' hands caused by the rise in prices, there is no longer any prospect that Arab bargaining power will be so casually discounted in the calculations of the world's governments. Indeed, in much of Europe and in Japan the reaction seems to have bordered on panic, as if it were assumed that the passing of the age of gunboat diplomacy left them totally at the Arabs' mercy. Doubtless it will take time for the governments of the world to adjust their calculations of international relationships to this new and strange situation, in which desert sheikhdoms seem able to hold industrial giants up for ransom.

In time, it will become evident that the picture is more nuanced than this. Not all oil exporters are Arab; not all are primitive and underpopulated; many of the leaders are sophisticated and moderate men, preferring order and solvency to chaos and bankruptcy in the world at large and having much on their minds to negotiate about with the industrialized countries besides the Palestinian question.

In the United States particularly, we must hope for a growing recognition of such nuances and for acceptance of the idea that among Israel's survival, the territorial integrity of her neighbors, and the redemption of the Palestinian people there are and have always been legitimate questions for negotiation. Considering how unsuccessful the promotion of negotiations has always been in the past, it may not be a bad thing that the balance of bargaining power has now shifted markedly to the advantage of the previously almost impotent party.

In any case, the viability of patchwork diplomacy is now more than ever in question. Not only has the oil crisis drawn the industrialized and underdeveloped nations of the world alike into the web of the Middle East conflict, but the course of violence itself has charted an ominous upward pattern. Each war comes sooner, kills more people, and costs more money; in between, terror and counterterror have increasingly become part of the everyday scene. The net result is that the conflict has become too dangerous and costly for many nations of the world to tolerate. No doubt even the most comprehensive Arab-Israeli peace settlement that we might imagine today would leave room for a long train of difficulties in future years. Yet the overriding fact is that both the new possibilities of success and the risks of failure are too great to ignore.

# United Nations Peace Efforts

Fred J. Khouri

WHEN, on 2 April 1947, Britain placed the Palestine question in the hands of the United Nations, no one could have foreseen how difficult and long-lasting the problem would be or how crucial a role the fledgling world organization would ultimately play in trying to resolve it. Even less predictable was the degree to which widespread ignorance and misunderstanding of the essence of the problem, big-power rivalry and partisanship, the failure of the disputants to abide by UN decisions, and the inability of the UN to enforce its own resolutions would frustrate UN peacemaking efforts and turn a relatively localized dispute between Arabs and Zionist Jews into a complex and perilous Arab-Israeli dilemma of worldwide concern.

Although Arabs and Jews had, for many centuries, lived together throughout the Middle East in relative peace and harmony, once political Zionism and Arab nationalism began to develop in the nineteenth century and to lay claim to the same land, a political confrontation between the two Semitic peoples became virtually inevitable. Moreover, by making inconsistent promises to the Arabs and Zionists, by detaching the Palestine area from Syria and turning it into a separate political entity, by

Fred J. Khouri is Professor of Political Science at Villanova University. He was born and raised in New Jersey and was educated at Columbia University, where he received his B.A., M.A., and Ph.D. degrees. Following military service in World War II, he taught at the University of Tennessee and the University of Connecticut and moved to Villanova in 1951. He also taught at the American University of Beirut from 1961 to 1964.

Professor Khouri is the author of the book *The Arab-Israeli Dilemma* (Syracuse University Press, 1968); a monograph, *The Arab States and the UN* (Near Eastern Society, 1954); and numerous articles in journals and symposia.

failing to make determined efforts to bring the Palestine Arabs and Jews closer together, and by pursuing certain policies which served to widen the political and psychological gulfs between the two communities, Britain helped to create a Palestine Arab nationalism, to intensify the conflict between Arab nationalism and Zionism, and to make it even more difficult than ever to arrive at a peaceful resolution of the Palestine question.

In spite of the fact that its own policies had repeatedly proved inadequate and Arab and Jewish relations in the Holy Land were reaching the point of open hostility, Britain refrained from seriously seeking either advice or aid from the League of Nations, which had entrusted it with the Palestine mandate. In 1939 and again between late 1945 and early 1947, Britain tried to involve some Arab governments, the Jewish Agency, and the United States in the search for a solution, but none of these belated moves produced any favorable results.

### The UN and the Partition of Palestine

It was not until April 1947, when the situation in the Holy Land had further deteriorated and British efforts to achieve a solution had reached a dead end, that Britain, in desperation, dropped the Palestine question in the lap of the UN. Not only was the relatively new and untried UN seriously affected by growing cold war rivalries, but the world community had never had occasion—other than through the rather perfunctory deliberations of the League's Permanent Mandates Commission—to deal with the Palestine issue at an early stage: that is, before the positions of the adversaries had polarized and when a reasonable chance for promoting a peaceful settlement still existed. Moreover, it soon became apparent that neither the parties to the conflict nor the big powers were willing to provide sufficient cooperation to enable the UN to overcome those initial handicaps. All of this seriously undermined the ability of the world organization to grapple constructively with the Palestine problem from 1947 onward.

In the spring of 1947 the UN General Assembly met in its first special session to deal with the Palestine problem. During the session the USSR, as yet not particularly concerned with the Arab world, rather suddenly and unexpectedly switched its stand from strong opposition to Zionism, which it had previously condemned as being a "tool of Western imperialism," to strong support for Zionist goals in Palestine. The USSR attempted to exploit in its favor the unstable and explosive situation which had developed there. Since President Harry S. Truman and others in his administration already sympathized with Zionist efforts to establish a Jewish state, the Russian switch aligned the two superpowers, if only temporarily, on this particular issue.

After considerable debate, the General Assembly established a Special Committee on Palestine (UNSCOP) to investigate the problem and to offer recommendations for its solution. In September, after completing their investigations in Europe and the Middle East, the majority of UNSCOP recommended the partition of Palestine into Arab and Jewish states with an internationalized Jerusalem, while a minority offered a plan for a federal state for Palestine. The General Assembly *Ad Hoc* Political Committee then set up one subcommittee, composed wholly of pro-partition members (such as the United States and Russia), to consider the majority suggestion and a second subcommittee, originally composed of Colombia and a number of Arab and pro-Arab members,[1] to take up an Arab proposal for a unified Arab state with protection for minorities and for the Holy Places. No subcommittee was established to evaluate the federal plan or any other possible solution. A third subcommittee was set up to conciliate between the contending parties, but it made no significant attempt to carry out its mandate. Some states urged the General Assembly to delay any final decision until more serious efforts had been made to seek some kind of a compromise settlement. Ignoring this recommendation and Arab opposition and threats to resist partition by force, if necessary, under their alleged "right of self defense," the General Assembly passed the partition resolution on 29 November 1947.

Most UN members, led by the United States, voted for partition in the belief that it would somehow resolve the problem and that all parties would ultimately bow to the will of the world organization. However, the Arabs attacked the partition resolution as being unfair and contrary to the UN Charter. They contended that the UN had disregarded the rights of the Arab majority in Palestine by giving to the Palestine Jews, then representing one-third of the total population, more territory and resources than those allotted to the Arab state and by relegating well over 400,000 Arabs to minority status in the Jewish state.

While the Zionists were generally unhappy with the territorial boundaries given to them and with the internationalization of Jerusalem, most of them were nevertheless ready to accept the resolution because it provided them with a unique and early opportunity to establish a Jewish state. However, some extremists, led by the Irgun, considered the territorial provisions inadequate; and a very small number of Palestine Jews continued to support the idea of a binational state.

Passage of the partition resolution was followed quickly by an outbreak of serious fighting between the Arab and Jewish communities in Palestine. Arab leaders continued to insist that they would use force to prevent its implementation and Britain indicated it would not help to enforce partition. The United States therefore became increasingly concerned about the political dangers involved in the situation. In early 1948 the US started to move away from the concept of partition and to propose that the UN set up a temporary trusteeship in Palestine in order to provide the Arabs and Jews there further opportunity to reconcile their differences.

Another special session of the UN General Assembly was called in April 1948 to consider the American trusteeship proposal. Some Arabs supported this new move in the hope that it would bring about the repeal of the partition resolution. However, the Zionists, backed by Russia who continued to press for implementation of the partition resolution, opposed it because it could delay, if not kill, the chances for a Jewish state. Some Zionists insisted that they would use force, if necessary, to establish their state as soon as the Palestine mandate ended on 15 May 1948, regardless of what further action the UN might or might not take.

In the meantime, fighting between the Arabs and Jews in Palestine intensified and spread despite UN efforts to bring about a cessation of hostilities and a general truce. While in the earlier stages the Palestine Arabs, aided by some thousands of militarily trained "volunteers" from the neighboring Arab states, appeared to have the better of the fighting, by early April 1948 the Jews had gained a clearcut military superiority and began to expand their control in Palestine. Britain persisted in its refusal to help carry out the partition resolution and indicated that it would withdraw all of its troops from Palestine by 15 May.

Although Soviet-American agreement had helped the Zionists obtain the passage of the partition resolution, by late spring 1948 Soviet-American disagreement frustrated the new trusteeship proposal, which the United States finally decided to drop when it realized that implementation would probably require force. President Truman now renewed his support for partition, and the General Assembly Special Session ended on 15 May without repealing or replacing the partition resolution.

Meanwhile, on 14 May Palestine Jewish leaders proclaimed the existence of the state of Israel, which was quickly recognized by the United States, the Soviet Union, and a number of other UN members. On 15 May, armies from the neighboring Arab countries entered Palestine. This intervention precipitated a larger Palestine war and led to strong criticism of the Arabs by some UN Security Council members, including the two superpowers.

The General Assembly partition decision had not provided a permanent, peaceful solution and it made an Arab-Israeli military confrontation virtually inevitable. Moreover, the world organization soon discovered that it had merely exchanged a major Palestine problem for an even more explosive Arab-Israeli dilemma.

## The Palestine War and UN Mediation

### The Palestine War

After war broke out in Palestine on 15 May 1948, the UN was eventually successful in arranging ceasefires, then a permanent truce, and, finally, armistice agreements. But it soon discovered that the war had added new dimensions to the Palestine problem.

The Arabs' humiliating defeat had intensified their nationalism, shattered their pride and self-confidence, and added greatly to the already serious differences within the Arab world. In addition, the war uprooted hundreds of thousands of Palestinians, whose bitterness, militancy, and influence spread, with time, to many parts of the Arab world. These developments made it increasingly difficult for the non-Palestine Arabs and their leaders to accept, at least openly, the existence of Israel.

Israel's smashing victory and newly gained military supremacy, on the other hand, intensified nationalist feelings and aspirations and made Israel less willing to make those psychological, political, and territorial concessions which many outside observers, as well as some Israelis, felt were essential to the attainment of any lasting reconciliation and peace with the Arabs.[2]

### The UN Mediator for Palestine

The first serious effort to work out a peace settlement was made during the war by UN Mediator Count Folke Bernadotte of Sweden. On 14 May 1948 the UN General Assembly passed Resolution 186(S-2), providing for the appointment of a UN mediator, who was empowered, among other things, to "promote a peaceful adjustment of the future situation of Palestine." On 29 May the Security Council passed a resolution ordering a four-week ceasefire and truce to be supervised by the mediator. After arranging for the truce to begin on 11 June, Count Bernadotte sought, in separate discussions with Arab and Israeli officials, some common basis upon which peace negotiations could be undertaken.

On 27 June he submitted his first comprehensive proposal. This provided for a union of all Palestine with Transjordan; but it would comprise two sovereign members, one Arab and one Jewish. The Mediator also suggested some territorial changes from those set down in the partition resolution, limitations on Jewish immigration, the return of the refugees, and provisions for the protection of religious and other minority rights and of the Holy Places.[3]

Both sides rejected Bernadotte's proposal. Israel objected especially to any limitation on immigration and the placing of any great number of Jews in Arab-controlled areas. Bernadotte found that

the Jewish attitude had stiffened  . . . , that Jewish demands in the settlement would probably be more ambitious,
and that Jewish opinion was less receptive to mediation. A
feeling of greater confidence and independence had grown
out of Jewish military efforts during the interval between
the two truces. Less reliance was placed in the UN and
there was a growing tendency to criticize its shortcomings
with regard to Palestine.[4]

Israel began to modify its position on the UN partition resolution
and to insist upon direct negotiations with the Arabs, for this
would enable it to make maximum use of its superior bargaining
position and to disregard unwanted provisions of UN resolutions.

Bernadotte found the Arabs "considerably agitated" over the
Palestine issue and opposed to the partition resolution, to negotiations with Israel either directly or through the mediator, and
to the acceptance or recognition of the state of Israel. The Arabs
continued to propose a unitary state in the whole of Palestine—
with a government based on proportional representation. They
also insisted that a solution of the refugee question was fundamental to any settlement, while Israel, on security grounds, opposed dealing with the refugee problem separately from the negotiation of a final peace settlement.

In view of both Arab and Israeli opposition to his proposal,
Bernadotte decided to concentrate his efforts for the time being
on seeking a permanent truce, providing emergency help to the
refugees, and pushing for the demilitarization of Jerusalem, while
allowing for a cooling-off period.

Supported by a strong Security Council resolution calling for a
permanent truce, Bernadotte was finally able to obtain a ceasefire on 18 July. Once this went into effect, he revived his efforts
at mediation. He held that: the permanent truce should be followed as quickly as possible by either a peace settlement or at
least an armistice, which would also provide for demilitarized
zones under UN supervision; the Arabs should face reality and
resign themselves to the existence of Israel; it was now unrealistic
to consider setting up a unitary state for all of Palestine; "in the
interest of promoting friendly relations" with the Arabs, the Is-

raelis "would do well in defining their immigration policy to take carefully into account the basis of Arab fears" that unlimited Jewish immigration would lead ultimately to Israeli expansion; and "no settlement can be just and complete if recognition is not accorded to the right of the Arab refugee to return to [his] home," with proper safeguards being provided for Israeli security.

Bernadotte now proposed separate Jewish and Arab states, with the Arab state to be composed of Transjordan and the Arab part of Palestine. Realizing that it would be easier for the Arabs to accept Israel if a land bridge between the Asiatic and African parts of the Arab world were placed under Arab control, he proposed that the Arabs receive the Negev, while Israel would obtain all of Galilee. Haifa would become a free port for the Arabs and Lydda a free airport. The city of Jerusalem "should be placed under effective UN control with maximum feasible local autonomy for its Arab and Jewish communities" and with full safeguard for everyone's free access to the Holy Places. The Arab refugees should be allowed to return to their homes "at the earliest possible date" with "adequate compensation" for those not wishing to return.

Because he felt he had exhausted his usefulness, Bernadotte urged that the UN replace him with a conciliation commission to help promote "the peaceful adjustment of the situation in Palestine." He wanted a commission composed of uninstructed individuals, rather than of government representatives, and he wanted it authorized to conduct all negotiations, to patrol the truce lines, and to handle all other aspects of the Arab-Israeli problem. He also hoped that the UN would supply the commission with detailed guidelines and strong support for its decisions. While he was aware that Arab-Israeli feelings were still too intense to allow for an early, formal peace settlement, he nevertheless felt that if the General Assembly could "reach firm and equitable decisions" on the principal political issues and "strongly back them, there would be a reasonable prospect that a settlement could be achieved if not by formal at least by tacit acceptance." [5]

Unfortunately, the members of the UN—including the United States and Britain, who were then in the strongest position to exert pressure on the contending parties—were unable to agree on a "firm and equitable decision" and did not provide the strong backing required to implement even those decisions which were made. So from the start, both sides were encouraged to ignore the UN when it suited them, and this set a harmful precedent for future UN peace efforts in the Middle East and elsewhere. Moreover, by failing to act decisively at the beginning—before Arab and Israeli positions had fully hardened, before the spread of Russian influence into the area had brought new complications, and when potential opportunities for a political settlement still existed—the UN and the big powers allowed a golden opportunity to slip by.

Israel and the Arab states, except for Transjordan, strongly opposed the mediator's new plan. Israeli officials, claiming that the Arab "invasion" of their country on 15 May had invalidated the territorial provisions of the UN partition resolution, objected to those proposals which dealt with immigration, territorial changes, refugee repatriation, and the Holy City; and they began to criticize Bernadotte and the UN. Up to the end of the first truce, the Israelis had held the UN in relatively high esteem, for the partition resolution had helped Israel come into existence and the imposed truce in June 1948, when Israel was still seriously threatened by Arab armies, had helped it survive. However, Israel's attitude began to change because the Israelis felt that the UN had failed to come to their assistance when the Arab armies moved against them and because after Israel had attained a clear military superiority, the UN appeared to stand in the way of her interests. After July 1948, many Israelis became increasingly disillusioned with the UN and the Israeli government felt free, on a number of occasions, to disregard its decisions.[6] Some extremists, such as the Sternists, advocated ousting all UN officials from Israeli territory and on 17 September a group of Sternists assassinated Count Bernadotte. Even Prime Minister Ben Gurion began to belittle the UN and to contend "that the fate of Israel would be determined in Palestine either in battle or in peace negotiations between the Arabs and Israelis and not in the UN."[7]

King Abdullah of Transjordan found some value in the Bernadotte plan, for it coincided with his ambition to annex as much of Palestine as possible as a first step in achieving his goal of a Greater Syria under his leadership.

However, other Arab leaders, sympathetic to the idea of a

Palestine Arab state and concerned about King Abdullah's ambitions, objected to Transjordan annexing any part of Palestine. They also complained that Bernadotte's proposals represented "partition all over again" and a "surrender" to an Israeli *fait accompli*. They insisted that the Arab refugees be allowed to return home and expressed fear of Israeli expansion. They suggested that the UN set up a commission to study the situation and to come up with a plan for a single state of Palestine on a "cantonization or federal" basis. A Syrian move to have the UN General Assembly ask the World Court to rule on the legality of the partition resolution was defeated by a tie vote in the First Committee.

Because the Arabs were keenly aware of their own military weakness, they now expressed willingness to negotiate, but only through the UN.[8] Moreover, the Arab attitude towards the UN also started to change. Following the partition resolution in November 1947, the Arabs had become hostile to the UN and had disregarded its resolutions, for they felt the organization was acting contrary to their interests, as well as to its Charter. Once Israel had achieved clear military superiority and had occupied large areas beyond the boundaries the partition resolution set for the Jewish state, however, Arab need for the UN greatly increased just as Israeli need had decreased. Thus, the Arabs found it more and more to their advantage to cooperate with the UN and invoke those of its resolutions which would improve their position.

Britain backed the mediator's plan because it felt that it provided some benefits to the Arabs—especially to its ally, Transjordan. American Secretary of State George Marshall also endorsed it and informed the UN that he considered it to be "a fair and sound proposal."[9] It seemed that, at long last, the two major western powers had begun to find a common Palestine policy. However, influential pro-Israeli groups and individuals began to attack the Bernadotte proposals; a presidential election campaign was then in full swing; and on 28 October President Truman suddenly reversed the American position and announced that he would not approve of any changes in the UN partition resolution unless they were acceptable to Israel.[10] This action dealt a death blow to the Bernadotte Plan and to the newly founded Anglo-American accord on Palestine.

At the UN, only Britain, China, Denmark, and Brazil strongly favored the Bernadotte Plan, while the Soviet bloc and, after 28 October, the United States led opposition to it. The only proposal the General Assembly and Security Council finally accepted was that calling for a conciliation commission and for UN action to promote armistice negotiations. Russia and the Ukraine, still strongly pro-Israel, were the only Security Council members who urged bypassing the armistice stage and initiating direct peace talks between the parties. Meanwhile Israel, although calling for direct negotiations, had decided to ignore the truce and improve her territorial position by military offensives in October in the Negev and Galilee areas.[11]

### The Acting Mediator and the Armistice Agreements

On 4 November 1948 the Security Council passed a resolution which called upon Israel to withdraw its "forces which have advanced beyond positions held on October 14" in the Negev and upon Egypt and Israel "to establish . . . permanent truce lines . . . and neutral or demilitarized zones." On 16 November the Council passed another resolution which called upon the parties "to seek forthwith, by negotiations conducted either directly or through the Acting Mediator [Ralph Bunche] . . . , the immediate establishment of [an] armistice" in "all sectors of Palestine."

Early in December Egypt started seriously considering negotiating an armistice on the basis of the November resolutions. But as Egypt moved closer to accepting armistice negotiations, *The New York Times* noted, on 25 December, that Israel "raised the ante." On 31 December the *Times* further reported that the Israelis, in "no mood to wait for either world opinion or the UN to solve their problem," convinced that they could "win much more on the battlefield than at the peace table," and believing that "possession is nine points of the law," once again launched a major offensive in the Negev and gained considerably more territory.[12] Only after strong pressures were applied by the UN and especially by the United States did Israel halt its offensive and agree to early armistice talks with Egypt; but it refused to withdraw from the recently conquered areas.[13]

Armistice negotiations between Egypt and Israel began in January 1949, on the island of Rhodes with Ralph Bunche mediating. Bunche usually held separate talks with each delegation because Egypt opposed direct negotiations, but informal meetings were held when discussions reached an advanced stage on any important item, and the two delegations met to sign the final agreement on 24 February. Lebanon, Jordan, and Syria followed Egypt's lead and negotiated armistice agreements with the help of Bunche.

The armistice agreements went beyond the truces and cease-fires and represented the first formal agreements between the parties themselves. They provided for an end of military actions and, except in the Egyptian-Israeli case, for the termination of "acts of hostility" as well. Demarcation lines were established, but these were not to be "construed in any sense as a political or territorial boundary and [were] delineated without prejudice to the rights, claims and positions of [the Parties] as regards ultimate settlement of the Palestine question." The agreements were meant to "facilitate the transition from the present truce to permanent peace."

The armistice agreements also provided for important UN participation through a UN Truce Supervision Organization (UNTSO) and four Mixed Armistice Commissions (MACs). UNTSO, composed of UN officials headed by a chief of staff, and the MACs, composed of UN chairmen and UN observers plus an equal number of Arab and Israeli military representatives, were to supervise the armistices, investigate incidents, and report to the Security Council. While they were not directly involved in the peacemaking process, it was hoped that they would discourage incidents and keep the armistice lines quiet to provide a more favorable atmosphere for peace.

However, the armistice agreements did not end conflict and bloodshed or lead to peace. They did not deal effectively with the root causes for Arab-Israeli hostility; the contending parties failed to cooperate adequately with UN officials and organs; and the UN was unable to enforce the many resolutions it passed in support of the armistice agreements.

## UN Conciliation Commission for Palestine

### Origins and Functions

On the basis of recommendations from both Bernadotte and Bunche, the UN General Assembly, in Resolution 194(III) of 11 December 1948, set up a Conciliation Commission for Palestine (CCP). Bernadotte had preferred that the proposed commission be composed of uninstructed individuals and had hoped that it would be given clearcut and firm guidance and solid support by the UN. However, the General Assembly decided to have states compose the CCP, largely on the ground that this would more likely insure more effective political support for the body; and the only specific guidelines provided by the Assembly related to Jerusalem and the refugee issue. Resolution 194(III) called for the demilitarization of Jerusalem and asked the CCP to prepare "detailed proposals" for an internationalized Holy City, which would provide both "maximum local autonomy" for the Arabs and Jews living there and freedom of access for everyone to the Holy Places. After resolving that "the refugees wishing to return to their homes and live at peace with their neighbors should be permitted to do so at the earliest practicable date and that compensation should be paid for the property of those choosing not to return and for loss or damage to property," the resolution instructed the CCP "to facilitate the repatriation, resettlement and economic and social rehabilitation of the refugees and the payment of compensation" to them. However, the General Assembly did not establish specific guidelines on those other key issues, such as the crucial territorial one, that would be involved in any overall peace settlement. Thus, after calling upon the parties concerned to "seek agreement by negotiations conducted either with the Conciliation Commission or directly," the General Assembly merely instructed the CCP "to take steps to assist the governments and authorities concerned to achieve a final settlement."

In December 1948 all Arab UN members (Transjordan, as well as Israel, was not yet a UN member) voted against Resolution 194(III) and continued to oppose the 1947 partition resolution in its entirety, because these resolutions would ultimately require the Arabs to acknowledge the permanent loss of much of Palestine and to accept a state of Israel. Within a few months, however, they started to change their position. By early 1949 some Arab leaders realized that, at least for the near future and because of their military weakness, the Arabs would have more to gain from the implementation of these resolutions than they could possibly attain on their own. In fact, the Arabs soon began advocating that the UN implement the territorial and refugee provisions of these resolutions, while Israel became a leading opponent of them.

The United States, France, and Turkey were selected to serve as members of the CCP. The United States was at first reluctant, but Britain and other nations urged it to reconsider, because they felt that, since the United States was the most powerful and influential UN member, the United States should participate in any important CCP decisions and actions. As a Muslim country, Turkey was intended to be a bridge between the CCP and the Arabs; its *de facto* recognition of Israel would make it reasonably acceptable to the Israelis.

Believing that Turkey had betrayed them by recognizing the enemy and that the United States was pro-Israel, the Arabs were clearly unhappy with the commission's composition. In the mid-fifties, after France began to develop very close political and military ties with Israel, the Arabs became even more vehemently opposed to the CCP membership and they began to call for either a change in its membership or its enlargement to make it more "balanced." Yet, they strongly supported its continued existence, for some of its key guidelines favored them and, being weak relative to Israel, it was to their advantage to work through the UN.

While Israel had no complaints about CCP membership, it was very unhappy with the Jerusalem and refugee guidelines. Unable to alter them to its liking, Israel began, in the early 1960s, to press for the complete elimination of the CCP and for direct negotiations.

The CCP was actually organized in January 1949. While a number of lesser delegation officials and key members of the secretariat were able and energetic, some delegation heads proved to be generally inadequate for their important tasks.[14] The Turkish representative, H. C. Yalcin, was eighty years old, rarely said or did anything, and played an insignificant role. The French representative, M. Claude de Boisanger, although a young and able diplomat, was so convinced that his own efforts would be insignificant compared to those of the American member that he rarely took serious initiative on any matter, except Jerusalem. Moreover, the French and Turkish governments provided little help or guidance to their representatives.

In some ways, American CCP membership, especially during the first critical year, also proved unfortunate. After an unnecessary delay, Mark Ethridge was selected to represent the United States. Ethridge, a newspaper editor who had no experience in the Middle East, was so confident that the CCP could complete its mission without too much delay that he took the assignment on a "short term basis." [15] When he discovered how difficult and complex the problem was and that a quick solution was not forthcoming, he lost interest and resigned after serving only four months. He was succeeded by a Washington lawyer, Paul Porter, who also lacked the essential knowledge and experience and who was prevailed upon to take the job only after he too was convinced that the CCP could attain its goals fairly quickly. Two months later he too became disillusioned and resigned. After a temporary stint by Raymond Hare, an experienced and able diplomat, the United States finally selected another diplomat, Ely E. Palmer, as its representative. Although he remained on the CCP for over two years, he hesitated to take any action which might not be supported by the State Department. Moreover, American policy was uncertain and the American government, despite the urgings of Palmer and other CCP members, was generally reluctant to exert strong and persistent pressure on the parties, especially Israel. As the principal secretary of the CCP, Pablo de Azcarate, noted:

> The truth is that the government members of the Commission never had the slightest intention of putting . . . pressure on the parties as would, perhaps, have enabled the Commission to achieve positive results. . . . It was . . . obvious that without the decided and resolute support of the governments composing the Commission, in particular the American government, there was no chance of surmounting

the obstacles which blocked the path and it was equally becoming more and more obvious that this support was not
now, nor was it ever likely to be forthcoming.[16]

Even former Secretary of State Dean Acheson conceded that the
CCP was "without power, ideas or hope." [17]

Other CCP handicaps included inadequate transportation facilities in the earlier weeks, conflicts between the CCP secretariat
and the UN secretariat, lack of cooperation between the acting
mediator and the CCP and between UNTSO and the CCP, juris-
dictional and other disputes between the CCP and the UN Relief
and Works Agency for Palestine Refugees (UNRWA), and the
inadequate understanding and relative indifference American diplomats in the Arab world showed toward CCP work. The American ambassador in Israel even displayed "open and marked hostility." [18]

The CCP began with high hopes for early success. After holding discussions with Arab and Israeli officials, however, it soon
discovered that their views were so far apart that a final solution
of their differences would be considerably harder to achieve than
originally anticipated. At first, the Arabs insisted that the refugee
issue must be settled prior to holding other serious discussions.
Even after they agreed in the early spring to negotiate all outstanding issues, they still insisted that the refugee question should
be considered the most pressing one and that the CCP should implement the repatriation provisions of General Assembly Resolution 194(III) as quickly as possible. While rejecting direct talks,
they were ready to negotiate through the CCP on the basis of UN
resolutions, including the territorial provisions of the 1947 partition resolution. The Arabs also began to change their attitude on
Jerusalem, for by spring of 1949 many Arabs realized that internationalization would at least remove Israeli rule from most of
the Holy City. After this only Transjordan, who had occupied
and annexed East Jerusalem, continued to oppose internationalization.

Israel initially asserted that return of the refugees was contingent upon the completion of a formal peace treaty. Shortly after,
however, Israeli leaders—anxious to have as small an Arab minority as possible, concerned about security, and pressed to find

quickly many properties to house the large numbers of Jewish immigrants pouring into the country—began to oppose the whole idea of repatriation and to insist that, even with a peace settlement, the only solution they would accept would be resettlement of all the refugees in the Arab world. Having occupied and annexed the greater part of Jerusalem during the Palestine war, Israel also opposed internationalizing the Holy City. After moving most of its government from Tel Aviv in 1950, Israel proclaimed West Jerusalem the capital of the country. It argued that Arab military intervention in Palestine after the end of the mandate had nullified the territorial provisions of the UN partition resolution and that any territorial negotiations should be based only on the existing armistice lines. In short, Israel opposed any significant changes in the status quo.

### The Lausanne Conference, Summer 1949

Separate talks in early 1949 having proved fruitless, the CCP persuaded Israel, Egypt, Lebanon, Jordan, and Syria to attend a conference in Lausanne, Switzerland, to begin in April 1949. Although the Arabs opposed direct negotiations and insisted upon being treated as a single party, the CCP did, occasionally, discuss matters with individual Arab delegates, and informal, secret meetings took place between some Arab and Israeli delegates.

On 12 May the CCP succeeded in getting the Arabs and Israelis to sign two identical but separate protocols. These documents stated that the delegations would be willing to use an attached map, showing the 1947 partition boundaries, as the "basis for discussion with the Commission." The Israeli delegate signed with the reservation that its signature did not prejudice "the rights of his delegation to express itself freely on the matters at issue, on which it fully reserved its position." He also agreed, however, with the CCP's interpretation that this "meant simply that the Israeli delegation reserved its right to reject parts of the Partition Plan boundaries and propose others, but that the Partition Plan would be adhered to as a point from which to work." [19]

Since this was the first time that the Arab governments had officially expressed a willingness to accept the 1947 partition resolution, the Arab signature represented a major change of policy. Moreover, by accepting the partition boundaries as the "basis for discussion," the Arabs appeared willing to settle in the end for something less than that. By this time many Arab leaders realized that enforcement of the partition resolution—or something close to it—would be to their advantage, because it would require Israel to evacuate a considerable part of the territory it had occupied.

Israel's signature also appeared to indicate that it was now willing to make some significant boundary concessions, and CCP hopes were raised that at last they had reached a "point of departure and a basis for territorial discussion." [20] However, these hopes were dashed when, soon thereafter, Israel made it clear that it was not actually prepared to make more than minor territorial concessions; and the CCP ultimately had to give up trying to attain any agreement on the territorial issue.

The refugee question took up most of the time at Lausanne, and the CCP was convinced that this issue was the most pressing and a key to progress towards peace. The Arabs continued to insist on the implementation of paragraph 11 of Resolution 194(III), stressing its reference to the right of repatriation. In reply to CCP questions on 15 August, however, the Arabs began to concede that some resettlement would be necessary in any final solution. Syria and Jordan agreed to receive those refugees who did not want to be repatriated. Egypt and Lebanon, while not opposing the principle of resettlement, contended that their countries were too crowded already to enable them to absorb any refugees. [21] Again stressing fear for its security, Israel rejected any repatriation. So no progress was made on the refugee problem either.

According to David P. Forsythe, "to personnel on the CCP, including Ethridge, and to several others in the State Department, it seemed that a coherent UN policy on the Palestine question required a concerted effort to get Israel to agree to repatriation, at least in principle; and Israel's application [for UN membership] . . . seemed an obvious occasion to several US diplomats for the United States to exert some influence pursuant to that goal." [22] The United States, however, did not try to exert any pressure on Israel and continued to lead the move to admit it to the UN. But the United States may have been influenced, as many other UN members were, by formal assurances Israeli representatives made before the *Ad Hoc* Political Committee of the

General Assembly, which was debating Israeli's admission, that their government would pursue "no policies on any question which were inconsistent with . . . the resolutions of the Assembly and the Security Council." [23] Resolution 273(III) admitting Israel specifically recalled the "resolutions of 29 November 1947 and 11 December 1948" and took "note of the declarations and explanations made by the representative of the Government of Israel before the *Ad Hoc* Political Committee in respect of the implementation of the said resolutions."

When, after being admitted to the UN, Israel refused to abide by these resolutions, State Department officials and CCP members again urged the American government to apply pressures. In response, on 29 May President Truman sent a strong note to Prime Minister Ben Gurion in which, according to James McDonald, American ambassador to Israel, he

> expressed deep disappointment at the failure of Eytan at Lausanne to make any desired concessions on refugees or boundaries; interpreted Israel's attitude as dangerous to peace, and as indicating disregard of the General Assembly resolutions of 29 November 1947 and 11 December 1948; reaffirmed insistence . . . that tangible refugee concessions should be made now as an essential preliminary to any prospect for a general settlement. The "operative part" of the note was an implied threat that the United States would reconsider its attitude towards Israel.[24]

At that time the American government was pressing Israel to allow at least 200,000 to 300,000 refugees to return to their homes, and by late summer some State Department officials believed the Arab leaders would be willing to negotiate a peace treaty with Israel if it would agree to repatriate a substantial number of the refugees and to give up, in exchange for the Gaza Strip, sufficient territory in the southern Negev to restore direct land contact between the Arab states of North Africa and those in Asia.[25] But Israel rejected American suggestions.

However, in response to American pressures, Israel, in June 1949, expressed a willingness to accept the return of the refugees in the Gaza Strip if it obtained this area and if it received international financial assistance to help resettle the refugees in Israel. When this suggestion proved unacceptable to the CCP and the

Arabs, in August Israel offered to take back 100,000 refugees, but on the conditions that it could resettle them away from the borders and where they would best fit into its plans for economic development and that this be part of a general peace settlement. This proposal also proved "insufficient" and "unsatisfactory" to the United States, the CCP, and the Arabs.[26] Because most of Israel's political parties and public opinion generally opposed even this limited offer, Israeli officials began to back down from it and shortly after it was withdrawn. Only the Mapam Party, the Communists, and the Nazareth Democrats (an Arab group) supported any significant repatriation. In the end, following a CCP suggestion, Israel agreed to a limited reunion-of-families scheme, which provided for the return of some thousands of refugees, as well as allowing a much greater number of Arab refugees, who had illegally slipped back to their former homes, to remain in Israel.

President Truman, from the beginning favorably disposed toward Israel, refrained from applying any further pressures and did not repeat the "tough" threats and tone of the 29 May note. Although the American government continued to urge Israel to make some concessions, no serious effort was made to bring about compliance with any American or CCP suggestions. Nor did the United States press the Arabs to moderate some of their views, even though she was the only state which had considerable influence in both the Arab world and Israel. As for Russia, she still maintained her pro-Israeli position.

Without cooperation from the disputants or backing from the great powers, the CCP was unable to make significant progress. By the end of summer 1949, the CCP had achieved only three very limited successes: Jordan and Syria had agreed to accept those refugees who did not desire repatriation, Israel had accepted a limited reunion-of-families scheme, and the Arabs and Israelis had agreed to set up a mixed committee of experts to deal with the matter of blocked bank accounts in Israel belonging to Arab refugees.

### The UN Economic Survey Mission

Frustrated by its failure to make any serious headway through diplomatic and political means, in late August 1949 the CCP decided to try a new economic approach advocated by American representative Paul A. Porter. The CCP set up an Economic Survey Mission with Gordon Clapp, former director of the Tennessee Valley Authority, as chairman and instructed it to

> examine the economic situation arising from the recent hostilities in the Near East and  . . . recommend to the Conciliation Commission means of overcoming resultant economic dislocations, of reintegrating the refugees into the economic life of the area, and of creating economic conditions which will be conducive to the establishment of permanent peace.[27]

At first, the Economic Survey Mission had hoped that it would be able to recommend several large development projects and that these, by bringing about the economic reintegration of the refugees, would help promote a situation more conducive to a final peace settlement. The mission soon discovered, however, that there were many political and emotional, as well as economic, obstacles to economic development of the region. For example, the most important projects on the Jordan River and its tributaries would require Arab-Israeli cooperation—demonstrating, as Clapp put it, the "inseparability of political and engineering planning of a major water resource." [28] The mission warned in its final report (A/AC.25/6) on 28 December 1949 that

> the region is not ready, the projects are not ready, the people and governments are not ready for large-scale development of the region's basic river systems or major undeveloped areas. To press forward on such a course is to pursue folly and frustration and thereby delay sound economic growth.

Because of the "realities" of the situation, the mission proposed that stress be placed on creating a series of "pilot demonstration projects" in the hope that these would provide immediate employment for some refugees and set the stage for larger future projects. The mission also suggested that the UN set up a special agency to carry out a relief and works program.

At first, the Arabs distrusted the mission, for they feared that it was an American scheme to force refugee resettlement and recognition of Israel in return for economic assistance. But it was not long before Arab hostility subsided—and some Arabs even began to praise the mission. The Israelis, never enthusiastic about it, generally condemned its report, especially because it did not emphasize that resettlement was the only feasible solution to the refugee problem.

In response to the mission's suggestions, the United States, France, Britain, and Turkey submitted a resolution to the General Assembly which, after reaffirming paragraph 11 of Resolution 194(III), provided for a $54,900,000 relief and works program to be administered by a new agency, UN Relief and Works Agency for Palestine Refugees (UNRWA). The passage of this resolution, on 8 December 1949, indicated that many UN members continued to support the American contention that an economic approach—by resettling some refugees and giving employment to others—could help open the way for solving other Arab-Israeli issues. Many others voted for the resolution because they felt any action, even if it offered little hope for success, was better than none. Although UNRWA was set up, the the CCP remained the primary organ responsible for implementing paragraph 11, as well as other parts of Resolution 194(III).

The CCP met informally with the Arabs and Israelis in late 1949 and early 1950. On 29 March it suggested setting up mixed committees, which would combine in a single procedure Arab wishes for CCP mediation and Israeli insistence on direct negotiations, to discuss questions submitted by the CCP. The Arabs stated that if Israel accepted the UN resolutions dealing with the refugees, they would be willing to sit on the same committee with it for the purpose of implementing these resolutions. On the other issues, they wanted principles agreed on before the mixed committees could be established. Israel, however, continued to call for direct negotiations and contended that the CCP should provide good offices only and not try to act as a mediator.[29]

During 1950 the CCP, still convinced that Israeli concessions on the refugees could break the deadlock on the other matters in dispute, concentrated its efforts in this area, but it was unable to make significant progress. At the end of the summer it reported that it had received "the impression" that the Arab governments were "inclining more and more to the view that the problem cannot be fully solved by the return of the refugees to their homes" and that, consequently, the resettlement of some refugees "must also be contemplated." [30] The Arabs also remained willing to meet jointly with Israeli delegates on the refugee topic, but only if Israel accepted the repatriation provisions of UN resolutions.

In 1949 and 1950 there were some indications that leaders in Jordan and Egypt were willing to consider peace settlements with Israel if they could receive enough of the face-saving concessions on the refugee and territorial issues. They felt they needed these before daring to make peace in the face of the strong anti-Israeli feelings and the growing instabilities and rivalries in the Arab world. King Abdullah, who had been negotiating secretly with Israel off and on since 1948, was apparently prepared to consider making a separate peace—but Ben Gurion refused to offer the necessary territorial concessions.[31] There were also more indirect and circumspect contacts, especially in February 1950, between Israel and Egypt, where hostility to Israel was not as intense as in some other Arab states and where the ruling Wafd Party was freer to negotiate than other Egyptian parties because it had not been in power when Egypt was defeated in 1948 and because it enjoyed long-standing and widespread popular support. Egypt not only wanted Israeli concessions on the refugee question, but, as it aspired to the leadership of the Arab world, it especially wanted a land bridge through the Negev connecting with Jordan and the other Arab states of Asia.[32] An Israeli official acknowledged, as *The New York Times* reported on 19 December 1950, that "their strong statements to the contrary notwithstanding," some Arab leaders wanted peace, but their main problem, because of the aroused emotions and rivalries in the Arab world, was "to discover a formula to allow them to begin negotiations with Israel." In the opinion of one Israeli scholar, because Israel was unwilling to take the essential "first step" and to make the required concessions in return for possible peace, a "golden opportunity for arriving at a final settlement in the Middle East had been lost for a long time to come." [33]

The Arab states brought the entire Arab-Israeli problem before the Fifth Session of the General Assembly in fall 1950. At this session, however, neither the Arabs nor the Israelis revealed any important policy changes, so the deadlock remained unbroken. The Soviet Union unsuccessfully advocated abolishing the CCP and calling upon the parties to negotiate directly, two proposals which the Arabs firmly opposed and the Israelis warmly welcomed.

In December 1950, the General Assembly passed a resolution which, after reiterating paragraph 11 of Resolution 194 (III), noted "with concern" that the parties had not reached any agreement "on the final questions outstanding between them" and that "repatriation, resettlement, economic and social rehabilitation of the refugees and payment of compensation have not been effected"; urged the Arabs and Israelis to seek agreements by negotiations conducted either with the CCP or directly; and directed the CCP to set up a Refugee Office to study the compensation issue, work out arrangements for dealing with the objectives of paragraph 11, and consult with the Arabs and Israelis regarding measures to be taken "for the protection of the rights, property and interests of the refugees." It was hoped that the new Refugee Office might somehow make headway on the refugee issue and thus open the way to progress on other matters. All it was able to do, however, was handle such narrow technical issues as estimating the value of refugee properties.

By early 1951, as the principal secretary of the CCP concluded, "the commission had become an instrument that neither the governments composing it nor the UN knew how to use; it seemed to me that the French and Turkish members openly waited for the American colleague [Palmer] to take the initiative and, that, as the latter was without instructions or directives from his government and was unsuited by temperament and professional habit to take the initiative or to accept responsibility on his own, the Commission fell into a state of what can without exaggeration be called atrophy"—and since whatever limited negotiations that took place were often conducted by individual CCP members, there was an "organic disintegration" and an "incoherence and lack of unity in its work." [34]

*The Paris Conference, 1951*

James Barco, a senior member of the United States delegation on the CCP, had grown impatient with its diplomatic inactivity during the first six months of 1951 and felt that it should make one final attempt to carry out its mandate. Backed by the State Department, he was finally able to overcome the hesitation of Palmer and the other representatives and it was arranged to hold a conference in Paris.

After the conference opened on 13 September 1951, the United States pressed for a preamble to a CCP peace plan, which would ask the parties to refrain from "any use of force or act of hostility." This wording was consistent with that in the armistice agreements between Israel and Lebanon, Jordan, and Syria. But the Egyptian-Israeli armistice agreement had forbidden only military actions. Not only did Egypt oppose the wording of the preamble, since it went beyond its own armistice obligations and threatened to undermine Egypt's contention that it had the legal right to close the Suez Canal to Israeli shipping until a final peace settlement had been reached, but all the Arab states rejected the wording, since they feared that it could support Israel's demand for an end to their economic boycott and blockade of Israel and thus deprive them of two of their few bargaining weapons. The Arabs proposed to change the wording so only military actions would be precluded, but Israel rejected this. After lengthy and heated discussions on the preamble issue, the CCP decided to drop the matter—but not until feelings had been further exacerbated.

The CCP then submitted its own peace plan in two parts. The first provided for an immediate agreement on mutual cancellation of war-damage claims, an agreement to repatriate a "specific number of Arab refugees in categories which can be integrated into the economy of the State of Israel and who wish to return and live in peace with their neighbors," an Israeli compensation payment of a global sum based upon a study of refugee property in Israel and Israel's ability to pay, and the unfreezing of blocked Arab refugee bank accounts. The second part provided for a new conference under UN auspices, which would consider revising armistice agreements relating to territorial adjustments along the demarcation lines and in the demilitarized zones, disposition of the Gaza Strip, creation of an international port at Haifa, creation of an international water authority for the Jordan-Yarmouk river systems, action to provide free access to the Holy Places, and arrangement for the economic development of the area.[35]

Although the Arabs and Israelis each accepted those parts of the plan which served their purposes, they rejected the rest. The Arabs particularly criticized the CCP for proposing major alterations in existing UN resolutions on the refugee and Jerusalem issues, and they insisted that the CCP's mandate was to implement existing resolutions, not to undermine them. They also insisted that the UN partition resolution boundaries, not the armistice lines, should be used as the basis for any territorial changes. Israel, on the other hand, held that the only solution for the refugee problem was resettlement, not repatriation, and that its ability to pay compensation to the refugees had been gravely affected by the Arab boycott and blockade, by the influx of large numbers of Jewish refugees from Arab lands, and by Iraqi seizure of the properties of those Iraqi Jews migrating to Israel.

To add to the difficulties, the Paris Conference was held at an unpropitious time. Developments related to the exodus of Iraqi Jews, a border dispute between Israel and Syria in the Lake Huleh area, and the bristling differences between Israel and Egypt over use of the Suez Canal by Israeli ships had dragged Arab-Israeli relations to their lowest level since the Palestine war. Moreover, the situation in Jordan was tense as a result of King Abdullah's assassination on 20 July 1951; Britain was trying to resolve its dispute with Egypt over the Sudan and the Suez Canal Zone, and its relations with Iraq and Jordan were also strained; the Iranian oil crisis was at its climax; anti-western sentiment was running high in the Middle East; and although the CCP asked the United States to exert strong pressures on the parties, the American government did not comply, nor did any other government. Without Arab-Israeli willingness to modify their positions and without pressures from the major powers, the CCP decided to discontinue discussions at Paris. The conference was terminated on 19 November and the CCP turned the problem back to the UN General Assembly with a report of its failure to carry out its mandate. It urged, however, that some competent body be kept available for the day when both parties proved to be really ready to resolve their differences and to make peace.

On 25 January 1952 the UN General Assembly passed Resolution 512(VI), which attempted to give some accommodation to both the Arabs and the Israelis. For example, it recalled "all" prior General Assembly resolutions on Palestine; it considered that the governments concerned had "the primary responsibility for reaching a settlement of their outstanding differences in conformity with the resolutions of the General Assembly"; and it urged these governments to seek agreement "with a view to an early settlement of their outstanding differences in conformity with [UN] resolutions." While Israel interpreted the resolution as emphasizing direct negotiations, the Arabs contended that it emphasized both a settlement achieved in conformity with earlier resolutions and CCP responsibility to implement these earlier resolutions. Some Arab delegates said that they were willing to enter even direct negotiations, provided they were held on the basis of past resolutions.[36]

Resolution 512(VI) also provided that the CCP should continue its efforts. However, the UN secretary general, "in agreement, no doubt, with the American delegation, confronted the Commission with a *fait accompli . . .* by practically dissolving the Commission's secretariat and abolishing the post of its Principal Secretary"; and, in April 1952 the CCP decided to stay in New York City and the states composing it, "instead of being represented by specially appointed delegates, were to be represented by members of their permanent delegations to the UN." [37] These developments seriously weakened CCP prestige and its ability to act. In fact, after this the CCP made no serious effort at conciliation and merely waited for either the parties concerned or the UN General Assembly to take the initiative. The CCP did, however, continue its work on the technical aspects of the refugee question and it was able to make some headway.

The Palestine question came up in fall 1952 before the Seventh Session of the UN General Assembly at Arab request.

Eight states jointly sponsored a draft resolution (A/AC.61/L.23) which reaffirmed the principle that the governments concerned had primary responsibility for reaching a settlement and urged them to enter into "direct negotiations," "bearing in mind" prior resolutions. This was strongly supported by the Israelis, who offered their own proposals for a solution. These included binding mutual guarantees against aggression, elimination of all demilitarized zones and only minor border rectification, resettlement of all refugees outside of Israel and talks on their compensation, an end to all boycotts and blockades, regional cooperation in economic, health, communications, and related fields, and an end to the state of war.[38]

The Arabs attacked the draft resolution. They claimed that it repudiated earlier UN decisions and that it proposed the UN "wash its hands" of the Palestine dispute. They again agreed to negotiate through mixed committees on the refugee, Jerusalem, and territorial issues, but only on the basis of UN resolutions.[39] Most Asian and some Latin American and African states also opposed the draft resolution on the ground that it disregarded earlier resolutions. Catholic members were especially concerned about the fate of the resolution calling for Jerusalem's internationalization. Opposition also was encouraged by Prime Minister Ben Gurion's poorly timed statements that there could be "no cession of territory, but there could be minor adjustments of pieces of land to straighten out the frontier"; that Israel would "not under any conditions" allow any repatriation; and that Jerusalem "cannot be an issue for negotiations." [40] These statements so antagonized Catholic and other delegations that despite strong backing from the United States, France, and some other western members, the resolution was defeated. While Russia supported most elements in the draft, it voted against the resolution because it would continue the existence of the CCP, which Russia considered an American "agency" for pushing US "imperialistic" interests in the Middle East.[41]

Having nearly suffered a major defeat by bringing up the Palestine question, the Arabs refrained from placing this question on the General Assembly agenda until 1959, when they sought to revive the role of the CCP. In the meantime, each year the General Assembly passed a resolution dealing with the refugee question, in which reference was made to paragraph 11 of Resolution 194(III) and, starting with Resolution 818(IX) passed on 4 December 1954, each resolution reiterated the CCP's responsibility for implementing this paragraph. But for many years after 1952, the only serious moves to bring about a peace settlement were made, especially in 1954 and 1955, by the United States and Britain outside of the UN. However, starting in December 1959, the General Assembly revived its request that the CCP "make further efforts to secure the implementation of paragraph 11."

*The Johnson Mission, 1961–1963*

The Kennedy administration was also anxious to make another attempt to deal with the Arab-Israeli question through the CCP. Considering that the refugee problem remained the key, the United States obtained the agreement in May 1961 of the other CCP members to employ a UN special representative on this. By working through the UN, the United States felt that it could draw other nations into the effort and would not be risking its own prestige alone if the representative failed. At the same time, President John F. Kennedy sent letters to important Arab leaders to reassure them that the United States still supported the CCP and UN resolutions on the refugee problem.[42]

On 21 August 1961, the CCP appointed Dr. Joseph E. Johnson, president of the Carnegie Endowment for International Peace, "to undertake a visit to the Middle East to explore with the host governments and with Israel practical means of seeking progress on the Palestine Arab refugee problem, pursuant to Resolution 1604(XV) of the UN General Assembly," which had called for the implementation of paragraph 11 of Resolution 194(III). This meant that he was to involve himself primarily with the refugee issue, not with the whole Arab-Israeli question.

Although Johnson was appointed by the CCP, his mission was based largely upon an American initiative. Both France, which held very close political and military ties with Israel, and Turkey were hesitant about supporting the Johnson undertaking, for they feared that it might somehow work against their own interests in the Middle East. While Johnson made his own decisions and developed his own views, he was aware that American support was vital to the success of his efforts. Consequently, he spent considerable time discussing matters with his own government.

After visiting the Middle East and holding discussions with Arab and Israeli officials, Johnson concluded, in his first report (A/492/Add 1), written in November 1961, that: (1) all parties generally wanted peace as a long-term goal even though they were not yet ready to make the necessary concessions and their public positions had hardened with time; (2) substantial mistrust, suspicion, and fear on both sides provided a "serious barrier to progress on any issue that divides the parties" and this must be taken into consideration in any solution; (3) an overall political settlement was essential for the full solution of the refugee problem; and (4) any refugee settlement would require considerable international assistance over a long period of time. While Johnson believed that there was no prospect for an early resolution of the Palestine question, he felt that, since the Arabs and Israelis were willing to "consider the possibility of a step-by-step process" to resolve the refugee issue "without prejudice to positions on other related issues," the CCP should continue its efforts.

In March 1962 Johnson was reappointed by the CCP, who asked this time for specific recommendations on how to resolve the refugee problem. In the meantime the situation in the Middle East had worsened, making his task more difficult. In late March a Syrian-Israeli border crisis had developed and inter-Arab rivalry and hostility (especially between Syria and Egypt) were in full swing. Jordan's attitude apparently had hardened. While the American government worked closely with Johnson, it did not provide him with any meaningful support.

In the summer of 1962, after both Arabs and Israelis had turned down his suggestion for setting up a small pilot project to ascertain refugee views as to their ultimate residence, he formulated and quietly submitted the following proposals: (1) the wishes of the refugees must be given priority and each refugee should be given an opportunity, free from all external pressures and with UN help, to express whether he preferred repatriation or resettlement in any Arab state or elsewhere;

(2) the refugees should be clearly informed as to what their choice would entail for their future, especially in case they chose Israel, and that they might not be able to get their first choice; (3) the legitimate security interests of the states concerned must be safeguarded—thus Israel and the Arab states would be allowed to reject individual refugees as security risks, subject to UN review; (4) repatriation and resettlement would be started slowly and handled in a gradual, step-by-step process; (5) a special fund, to which Israel would be expected to make a substantial contribution, would be set up by the UN to pay for Arab properties left in Israel, as well as to help the resettled Arabs become self-supporting; (6) the UN would play a vital role in setting up any needed organizations and in supervising all aspects and stages of the program; and (7) any state involved could withdraw from the process at any time if its security became endangered.[43]

Israel quickly but quietly expressed to Johnson and the United States its opposition to the proposals, especially since they envisaged significant repatriation. While some Arabs were not especially hostile to the Johnson proposals, since they came closer to Arab than Israeli views, other Arabs privately criticized them as not providing a "suitable framework for a fruitful discussion." Each side waited for the other to express open opposition so that it would be blamed for the failure of the Johnson Plan. This Syria, to the surprise of other Arab states, was the first to do. After that, Israeli officials and the Knesset felt free to announce their own disapproval.[44]

The American government decided to put off pressing the Johnson Plan. Both the United States and the CCP even agreed not to publicize the Johnson proposals, partly in the hope that they might be revived at some more favorable time. Johnson, disappointed in the failure of both the United States and the CCP to give him adequate support throughout his mission, resigned. The American government offered to make quiet diplomatic efforts to see if the parties might accept some aspects of the proposals; but these efforts were not pushed to any extent.

Despite the failure of Johnson's mission, on 3 December 1963, the UN General Assembly, by a vote of eighty-two to one (Israel) with fourteen abstentions, passed Resolution 1912

(XVIII), which again called upon the CCP "to continue its efforts for the implementation of paragraph 11 of Resolution 194(III)." The CCP, however, agreed to let the United States try dealing quietly with the problem through normal diplomatic channels—but this move also failed.

By the early 1960s the CCP position had further weakened. Both the USSR and Israel worked to terminate its mandate; and Israel pressed for direct negotiations and succeeded in persuading a number of UN members to submit resolutions calling for them. While the Arabs had lost much of their enthusiasm for the CCP, they still urged its continued existence, largely because the terms of the CCP's mandate favored them. But they persisted in trying to change or enlarge the CCP membership and to pass resolutions calling for a UN-appointed custodian of refugee properties in Israel who would collect the income from these properties and turn it over to the refugees. Fearing that all these conflicting resolutions would merely exacerbate the situation, the United States opposed them and they failed to pass.

The CCP members were now even more convinced that it would be futile to press for a final settlement before the Arabs and Israelis were more psychologically and politically prepared and before the great powers were ready to provide the required pressures. So the CCP confined its activities to such technical matters as completing the release of refugee blocked accounts, finishing the evaluation of refugee property in Israel, and preparing an index of names of the property owners.

The June 1967 war further weakened the CCP, as well as making all the issues more complicated. Nevertheless, the General Assembly continued in its annual resolutions on the refugee issue to note "with regret" that the CCP was "unable to find a means of achieving progress in the implementation of paragraph 11" and to request it "to exert continued efforts towards implementation thereof." But the CCP never tried to reactivate its conciliation efforts, even on the refugee matter alone, because the situation which had prevented all progress in the past remained essentially unchanged. Moreover, when the Security Council set up the Jarring Mission in late 1967, it effectively bypassed the CCP and its original mandate.

## The 1956 Suez-Sinai War and the UN

While in the early years after the 1949 armistices, border incidents were relatively minor in scope, with time they became
much more serious, as the Palestine Arab refugees grew more
frustrated and as governments and military commando forces
became increasingly involved. Serious conflicts developed over
the Syrian-Israeli and Egyptian-Israeli (El-Auja) demilitarized
zones, with Israel ultimately appropriating most of the former
and all of the latter, despite UN and Arab protests. Tensions
also arose over use of Jordan River waters and over Egypt's
closing of the Suez Canal—despite Security Council Resolution 95(1951) criticizing this action—and the Gulf of Aqaba
to Israeli ships.[45]

Moreover, by the middle 1950s Russia had switched its support from Israel to the Arabs and had begun to spread its influence into the Arab world after making a major arms deal with
Egypt in September 1955. France, aroused over Arab efforts to
help the Algerians attain independence, had developed close
political and military ties with Israel. The intrusion of cold-war
rivalry into the area and the partisan policies followed by Russia,
the United States, and France obstructed UN peace efforts, for
they fostered an arms race, heightened Arab-Israeli distrust and
insecurity, and encouraged greater intransigence on both sides.

When President Nasser nationalized the Suez Canal Company
on 26 July 1956 and refused to accept western proposals for the
canal's internationalization, France, Britain, and Israel secretly
agreed to a joint, but phased, military attack on Egypt. France
and Britain hoped to overthrow Nasser and seize the Suez Canal,
while Israel welcomed the opportunity to destroy Arab commando bases and Egyptian military power, to force open the
canal and Gulf of Aqaba to its ships, and to compel Egypt to
stop depending on the UN as an intermediary and to enter into
direct peace negotiations.[46] On 29 October Israel invaded the
Sinai area and on 31 October Britain and France, alleging that
they were intervening merely to protect the canal, began military
operations against Egypt.

Considering the Israeli invasion a serious violation of the UN
Charter, the United States called for an urgent Security Council

meeting and introduced a strong resolution (S/3710) which directed Israel to withdraw her forces behind the armistice lines "immediately" and urged all UN members to "refrain from giving military, economic or financial assistance" so long as it "had not complied with the resolution." When Britain and France vetoed the American proposal, the United States pressed the Security Council to request an emergency session of the General Assembly.

By 1 November when the General Assembly had convened, Anglo-French air and sea attacks on Egypt had already started and Russia began to demand strong action against the invaders. While he had grown increasingly distrustful of Nasser, President Eisenhower firmly believed in the UN, and he considered the Anglo-French-Israeli invasion an illegal and ill-advised adventure, which would undermine UN authority and world law, as well as the position of the West in the Middle East. The United States, therefore, again took the lead in introducing a resolution (A/3526) which urged all parties involved in the hostilities to "agree to an immediate ceasefire" and called for a "prompt withdrawal" of Israeli forces behind the armistice lines. It passed on 2 November by an overwhelming vote—only Australia, Britain, France, Israel, and New Zealand voted against it. When only Egypt agreed to abide by this resolution, nineteen Afro-Asian states submitted a more strongly worded ceasefire and withdrawal proposal (A/3275) and this was easily adopted on 4 November.

A few members suggested that the UN should consider the overall Arab-Israeli problem. On 2 November Canada suggested that once a ceasefire had been arranged, the UN should set up an international police force to man the lines between the Israeli and Egyptian armies until an attempt was made to reach a final political settlement of their differences. The next day the United States introduced a draft resolution (A/3272) which would terminate the CCP and set up a new committee to consult with the contending parties and to submit recommendations to the General Assembly for solving the Arab-Israeli problem. While Israel found some aspects of this proposal to her liking, the Arabs opposed it on the grounds that it would undermine existing UN resolutions and reward aggression.

Acknowledging that it would set a bad precedent for the UN

to allow Israel to achieve political gains from the use of force,[47] the United States decided to withdraw its resolution and to concentrate on trying to get a ceasefire and complete Israeli withdrawal before actively seeking ways to promote a final peace settlement through UN auspices. Consequently, the United States and most other UN members voted for a Canadian resolution (A/3276) which provided for the "setting up, with the consent of the nations concerned, of an emergency international UN force to secure and supervise the cessation of hostilities in accordance with the [withdrawal] terms" of the 2 November resolution. Firm pressure by the UN, the United States, and Russia finally compelled Britain and France (on 6 November) and Israel (on 8 November) to agree to a ceasefire. In the meantime, UN Secretary General Dag Hammarskjold had quickly organized a UN Emergency Force (UNEF) composed of Asian, Scandinavian, and Latin American troops. UNEF units were hurriedly stationed along the west bank of the Suez Canal, facilitating the withdrawal of British and French forces and providing a buffer between the Egyptian and Israeli armies.

Israel, however, refused to honor UN withdrawal demands and contended that it first must have international guarantees that Egypt would agree to negotiate a final peace settlement and that Israeli ships would be ensured freedom of passage through the Suez Canal and the Gulf of Aqaba.

While many UN members wanted to promote an Egyptian-Israeli peace, they still insisted that the territorial situation which existed before the Sinai war must first be restored; and they passed a series of resolutions (A/3385/Rev. 1 on 24 November, A/3501/Rev. 1 on 16 January, and A/3517 on 2 February) which again demanded an immediate and unconditional Israeli withdrawal. To encourage compliance, American officials assured Israel that they would insist that UNEF be stationed in the Gaza Strip and at Sharm el-Sheikh overlooking the Straits of Tiran; that they considered the Gulf of Aqaba to be an international waterway legally open to the ships of all nations; and that they were prepared to exercise the American right of free navigation through the Straits of Tiran and to join with other nations to secure general recognition of this right. Although Israel was not wholly satisfied with these assurances, increasingly strong calls for sanctions in the UN and determined American pressures compelled Israel to agree to a withdrawal. However, it refused to give up the El-Auja Demilitarized Zone; it held that it would no longer recognize the continued validity of the Egyptian-Israeli armistice agreement; it warned that if the Egyptians ever tried to close the Gulf of Aqaba to Israeli ships, it would feel free to take whatever action deemed necessary; and it contended that it was withdrawing only on the basis of its own interpretation of the American assurances. American spokesmen took note of Israel's interpretation, but they still considered the withdrawal to be unconditional.[48]

UNEF troops were stationed along the demarcation lines in the Sinai and Gaza Strip areas and at Sharm el-Sheikh. It had been hoped that UNEF would be allowed to operate on both sides of the Egyptian-Israeli border, so that it could be more effective in preventing incidents and large-scale armed conflicts. Israel, however, refused, claiming UNEF units would infringe upon Israeli sovereignty. Even though UNEF remained on only one side, it proved very effective in keeping the Egyptian-Israeli demarcation lines and the Gulf of Aqaba area quiet for ten years.

No one ever followed through the suggestion made by some UN members that once the ceasefires and withdrawals had been attained, the UN should revive its efforts to promote an overall Arab-Israeli peace settlement. This was unfortunate, because for several years the relatively quiet borders considerably reduced Arab-Israeli tensions. Apparently while the calmer atmosphere in the Middle East provided a more favorable basis for a peace offensive, it also lessened the pressures on the UN and the big powers to deal with the Arab-Israeli question as a whole. For the next few years UN efforts were largely confined to the Arab refugee problem, the continuing nature of which made it hard to ignore.

## Other UN Efforts Before June 1967

### The UN Relief and Works Agency for Palestine Refugees (UNRWA) and Peace

As mentioned earlier, the UN General Assembly had responded to recommendations of the UN Economic Survey Mission by establishing UNRWA; it was authorized to spend $54,900,000 on a relief and works program for an eighteen-month period. The General Assembly allotted another $50,000,-000 in December 1950 for one year and then $250,000,000 in January 1952 for three years. Thus the UN decided, despite warnings from the Economic Survey Mission about the major political and psychological obstacles to peace, to try a wholly economic approach once again. Not only did the belief persist that the refugee question could be effectively handled apart from the other Arab-Israeli issues, but the conviction remained that if some action could resolve the refugee problem or at least reduce its scope, this would open the way to settling the other issues.

Israel did not oppose these resolutions. However, it continued to reject the principle of repatriation for security and other reasons and, in later years, it urged the UN to turn over the whole refugee problem to the Arab states, so that they could start looking at it more "realistically" and start planning to resettle all the refugees.

At first the Arabs saw the works program as a devious attempt to resolve the problem through refugee resettlement alone. Arab leaders felt that they could not be expected to give up, unilaterally, the right of refugee repatriation, since even the CCP and UNRWA had reported that the refugees continued to display "invariably . . . an extremely emotional and deep-seated desire to return to their homes," [49] since the influence of the refugees had grown and spread among the Arab masses, and especially since the overwhelming majority of UN members had voted repeatedly in favor of the principle of repatriation. Only after they were assured that their cooperation would not jeopardize the right of repatriation did the Arab governments agree to participate in UNRWA's work projects. Indeed, by the end of the summer of 1950 UNRWA and the CCP also reported that the Arab governments were "inclining more and more to the view" that the Arab refugee problem could "not be fully solved by" repatriation and that "the settlement of a considerable number of refugees in the Arab countries must also be contemplated." [50]

The works program did not succeed very well, primarily because there were sparse natural resources and only limited funds. Whereas the UN resolution called for $200,000,000 for a works program, only about $37,000,000 were actually made available to UNRWA and only $18,743,150 had been expended, mostly on small-scale projects, by June 1955. Thus, relatively few refugees were resettled and/or became self-supporting through this program, while their total number mounted by at least 25,000 each year as a result of natural increase. Nevertheless, by providing food, housing, and essential services, UNRWA at least helped to alleviate refugee misery.

The high hopes once held that UNRWA could somehow greatly reduce the scope of the refugee problem and thus help pave the way to a final solution of all major Arab-Israeli differences proved to be unfounded. Moreover, with time the refugee problem grew not only in scope and complexity, but also in its dangerous consequences. Refugee pressures on the host governments intensified and, as the refugees moved into all parts of the Arab world in search of jobs, they spread their hatred and militancy wherever they went. In fact, many Arabs might have forgotten the Palestine question and the humiliation of the Palestine war defeat, had it not been for the goading Palestinian in their midst. The festering refugee problem also produced many border incidents, commando raids, and Israeli retaliatory assaults; and it was the refugees who exerted the greatest and most persistent pressure against any Arab peace with Israel, at least until their right to repatriation or compensation as provided by UN resolutions had been reasonably satisfied. Failing to obtain satisfaction by peaceful means, the refugees and their supporters have felt they had no alternative but force.

*The UN Secretaries General and Peace*

With one possible exception, the UN did not officially authorize the secretaries general to seek and recommend an Arab-Israeli peace settlement. Nevertheless, all of them have been deeply concerned about the situation and, at times, have sought opportunities, either through quiet personal talks or through the UN mediator and the CCP, to promote a settlement. Dag Hammarskjold in spring 1956 and U Thant in May 1967 went to the Middle East in belated attempts to bolster the armistice agreements and head off wars. During these missions they discussed some of the broader issues, but conditions were too unfavorable to spur any serious peace efforts. Instead, they found their most pressing task was trying to prevent war.

In fall 1958, the General Assembly sought some new procedure which might help to break the deadlock at least on the refugee question. Secretary General Hammarskjold agreed to look into the "technical operations of UNRWA" and prepare proposals for the next General Assembly session.

Following a trip to the Middle East, Hammarskjold submitted a report (A/4121) on 5 June 1959. After analyzing in some detail various technical operations of UNRWA, he discussed several major aspects of the refugee problem. He indicated that the political and psychological aspects constituted the most serious impediments to progress. The refugees still yearned to return to their homes and felt that the only way that the "wrong" done to them could be righted was to allow them a real choice between repatriation and compensation. They also feared that large-scale development projects could jeopardize their rights under UN resolutions. The secretary general held, however, that a *"de facto* economic integration" need not prejudice any rights established by such resolutions. The refugees did "welcome opportunities to become self-supporting as individuals"; but here activities suffered from lack of funds. He warned that the refugees could not be forcibly resettled against their will without further aggravating the "economic and political stability" in the area. Despite his stress on political and psychological refugee obstacles, he still believed that refugee economic reintegration was "perfectly within reach provided that the area be developed through sufficient capital formation." Only a vast economic development program for the area as a whole, with large-scale outside financial support (from \$1.5 to \$2 billion by 1965 alone), could possibly enable the indigenous population to raise its already low standard of living, while allowing at the same time for reintegration of the refugees as well. In brief, he recommended a general economic development program to be started as quickly as possible in the hope that solving the area's economic difficulties might help improve the possibilities of peace.

While the Arabs were pleased that the secretary general had stressed refugee desire to return home and the political, psychological, and humanitarian aspects of the problem, they generally criticized the report as a whole because it appeared to them to emphasize economic development and refugee "reintegration" instead of refugee "repatriation." After he had assured them that he recognized the continued validity of pertinent UN resolutions, the Arabs decreased their attacks. The Israelis reacted more favorably, although they had some reservations; and they claimed that by calling for the "reintegration" of the refugees, Hammarskjold was backing resettlement and not repatriation. In any case, the General Assembly took no action on the secretary general's report.

## The June 1967 War and UN Peace Efforts

### The May 1967 Crisis and the UN

In May 1967 the UN faced another grave Middle East crisis. In late 1966 and early 1967 incidents involving the Syrian-Israeli demilitarized zone, stepped-up Palestine Arab commando activities (which had started in early 1965 with the aid of Syria), and Israeli military retaliations increased Arab-Israeli tensions. Major assaults by Israel on as-Samu in Jordan on 13 November 1966 and on military positions and villages in Syria on 7 April 1967 both inflamed Arab hostility further and provided opportunities for those Arabs who had begun to challenge President Nasser's leadership in the Arab world to accuse him of fearing Israel, timidly hiding behind UNEF, and failing to help even his ally, Syria. During the first two weeks of May, Israeli leaders began to make unusually strong threats against Syria on the grounds that Syria was primarily responsible for Arab guerrilla attacks and that Syrian officials were making bellicose speeches.[51] In the middle of May Syria and Russia claimed, despite Israeli and UN denials, that Israel was mobilizing its army on the Syrian border, and Syria appealed to Egypt for military support.

In response Nasser decided to take a big gamble. He began to mobilize his forces, asked on 16 May that UNEF units be withdrawn from part of the Egyptian-Israeli demarcation lines, and warned Israel that he would go to Syria's aid if it were attacked. Since Secretary General U Thant insisted that UNEF must either stay in all areas or leave completely, Nasser decided to request a complete UNEF withdrawal. Its departure not only opened the entire Egyptian-Israeli frontier to potential conflict, but also compelled Nasser, because of rising Arab pressures, to close the Straits of Tiran to Israeli ships, despite repeated Israeli warnings that it would consider such a move an act of war.

Increasingly concerned, the secretary general tried to halt the trend towards war. He urged Israel to allow UNEF to take up positions on its side of the demarcation lines, because he believed that a neutral buffer was essential to prevent a military conflict and that UNEF could operate as effectively from Israeli territory as it had for ten years from Egyptian territory. Israel replied that this would be "completely unacceptable." [52] By 19 May UNEF ceased to exist as an active peacekeeping force. U Thant then pressed Egypt and Israel to reactivate fully the Egyptian-Israeli armistice machinery [53] in order to provide some kind of effective UN presence along their borders. Egypt accepted this proposal, but Israel, who had denounced the Egyptian-Israeli Armistice Agreement during the Sinai war, rejected it. On 19 May U Thant made a general plea to Israel and the Arabs for restraint. Then, on 22 May he flew to Cairo, where he exhorted Nasser to lift the Gulf of Aqaba "blockade" temporarily. Since the UN General Assembly had insisted after the Sinai war that Israel should not benefit in any way from its aggression, Nasser claimed the right to restore prewar conditions at the Straits of Tiran and so he refused to comply with U Thant's suggestion.[54]

Unfortunately, even though the Arab-Israeli situation had become extremely grave, neither the governments directly concerned, nor the secretary general, nor any UN member requested that the Security Council meet to deal with the situation before it deteriorated still further. As too often in the past, it was not until matters had become extremely dangerous—that is, until both sides had begun to mobilize their armies and threaten war—that the Security Council belatedly met. It held two sessions on 24 May but took no positive action, for its members decided to await U Thant's return from Cairo and his report before seriously considering any action. Even though U Thant presented his report on 26 May, the Security Council did not meet until 29 May and only on 31 May were any substantial draft resolutions submitted. Apparently, most Security Council members continued to believe that they had adequate time to deal with the situation, but they were wrong.[55]

In his report (S/7906), the secretary general stated that the situation had become so grave that a "peaceful outcome [would] depend upon a breathing spell," which would "allow tensions to subside." He pressed "all the parties concerned to exercise special restraint, to forego belligerence and to avoid all other actions which could increase tension [in order] to allow the [Security] Council to deal with the underlying causes of the . . . crisis and to seek solutions." He indicated that he had expressed his "deep concern" to Egyptian leaders about the closing of the Gulf of Aqaba and that they had "assured" him that the "UAR would not initiate offensive action against Israel." He recommended that the UN reaffirm the validity of the Arab-Israeli armistice agreements and revitalize the armistice machinery to help relieve the crisis.

Although some Security Council members maintained that the UN must do something about resolving the overall Arab-Israeli problem, it was obvious that the Security Council must first defuse the explosive situation and prevent a war. Therefore, on 31 May the United States submitted a draft resolution (S/7916) which called upon the parties concerned, "as a first step," to comply with the secretary general's appeal to "exercise special restraint" and avoid hostile actions in order to provide a "breathing spell." It also encouraged the "pursuit of international diplomacy in the interests of pacifying the situation and seeking reasonable, peaceful and just solutions." While the United States generally supported Israel's views—especially on the Straits of Tiran—it exhorted Israel, as well as Egypt, not to use force and it supported U Thant's recommendation on the armistice machinery, despite Israel's opposition. The United States interpreted this resolution to require the rescinding of Egypt's "blockade" of the Gulf of Aqaba, at least for the time being.

The Arabs, generally supported by the Soviet Union, indicated a readiness to accept a resolution calling for a cooling-off period as long as it did not require reopening the Gulf of Aqaba to Israeli ships. On 31 May Egypt submitted a draft resolution (S/7919) which reiterated the validity of the Egyptian-Israeli General Armistice Agreement and which would strengthen and enforce it.

While most Security Council members favored an appeal along the lines of the American draft resolution, much valuable time was taken up trying to agree on its precise terms. The Security Council met on 3 June and then adjourned to 5 June (the day war started) without having made any other significant move.

Meanwhile, the United States initiated diplomatic efforts outside the UN. Although President Johnson urged Israel to give him enough time to try to organize a western naval test of the Gulf of Aqaba "blockade" and to negotiate quietly with Egypt on the gulf issue (Egyptian Vice President Zahariya Mohieddin was due to consult with Johnson),[56] Israel decided not to wait any longer, but to take the military initiative against Egypt.

### The June 1967 War and the UN

By forcing the more moderate Arab leaders to face up to the reality of its existence and the need for an overall political settlement, Israel's overwhelming victory made possible a major breakthrough in the Arab-Israeli impasse. At the same time, however, Israel's victory and occupation of large parts of Egypt, Syria, and Jordan containing more than a million Arabs created fresh problems. Israeli feelings of superiority and the Arabs' sense of humiliation were stimulated; and Israel developed an interest in retaining portions of the occupied territories, while Egypt, Syria, and Jordan now held irredentist claims to those same lands. The war aggravated the refugee problem by causing more than 200,000 Palestinians to flee the West Bank of Jordan, more than 100,000 Syrians and Palestinians to leave the Golan Heights, and over 300,000 Egyptians to evacuate the Sinai and the Suez Canal's west bank areas. Israel's victory also intensified Palestinian nationalism and militancy and expanded Palestinian influence throughout the Arab world. Commando activities, border conflicts, and retaliations accelerated. Jerusalem became one of the most serious and irreconcilable issues. The partisanship of Russia and the United States grew sharper. During the 1956 Suez-Sinai crisis the two superpowers had usually voted together in the UN and this enabled the world organization to enforce its will, but in 1967 they took opposing sides, thus making it practically impossible for the UN to act effectively. In many ways, therefore, the 1967 war added greatly to the complexities of the Arab-Israeli problem.

Shortly after the war had begun, the Security Council hurriedly convened. Israel claimed that the Arabs, by "illegally" closing the Gulf of Aqaba, mobilizing their armies, and calling for its "extermination," were the aggressors and that Israel was merely exercising its "right of self-defense," as provided by Article 51 of the UN Charter. It announced that it no longer recognized the validity of the armistice agreements with Jordan, Syria, and Lebanon. In addition, it warned that it would reject any UN ceasefire proposal which required Israel to withdraw its troops unconditionally and before the Arabs agreed to negotiate a final peace settlement. Israel argued that the UN demand for an unconditional withdrawal after the 1956 Sinai war had been a mistake which should not be repeated.

The Arabs, in turn, contended that Israel was the aggressor and that it deliberately started the war in disregard of UN obligations, despite Egypt's assurances that Egypt would not initiate any offensive military action, and while the UN and the United States were still actively trying to resolve the crisis. They held that Article 51 provided for the right of self-defense only in case of an "armed attack," and no such attack had been made against Israel. They insisted that the UN should, as it had done during the Sinai war with American support, order an immediate and complete withdrawal of Israeli troops from all occupied areas as part of any ceasefire resolution and also make it clear that no state would be allowed to benefit in any way from the use of force contrary to the UN Charter.

While all Security Council members favored an early ceasefire resolution, they disagreed as to whether the ceasefire should be conditional or not. The Soviet Union strongly supported Arab arguments on the withdrawal issue. The United States, on the other hand, backed Israel's insistence on an unconditional ceasefire. As soon as it was obvious that the Arab military position was deteriorating and continuing the armed conflict would merely bring about greater Arab losses, Russia decided, despite Arab opposition, to vote for a draft resolution (S/233) which merely called for an "immediate ceasefire" without specifically mentioning withdrawal. It passed unanimously on 6 June. It was not until the Arabs had lost even more territory and the Security Council had passed another unconditional ceasefire resolution (S/234) on 7 June that Jordan, the UAR, and finally Syria reluctantly agreed to a ceasefire which did not provide for an Israeli withdrawal. Despite the nominal adherence of all parties to the ceasefire by 9 June, Israeli forces subsequently pushed into the Golan Heights and occupied the town of Kuneitra.

*Early Postwar UN Peace Efforts*

Once the ceasefire had gone into effect on all fronts, the Arab states and the USSR again tried in vain to persuade the Security Council to condemn Israel for starting the war and to order an immediate and unconditional withdrawal of Israeli forces from all occupied areas. The Soviet bloc, France,[57] and various Asian and African states agreed with the Arab contention that it would set a dangerous precedent for the UN to allow Israel to benefit in any way from its military actions and that Israel must first withdraw its forces before any progress could be made on the overall question. However, backed by some western European and Latin American nations and especially by the United States, Israel blamed the Arabs for the war and held that, unlike the action taken after the Sinai war, this time a final peace settlement must precede any withdrawal. It also reserved its position on future frontiers and insisted that the Arabs should be encouraged to negotiate directly.

The outcome of the war stunned the Arabs and left them, for a few months, uncertain but unyielding. At first they insisted upon an unconditional withdrawal and refused to negotiate a peace settlement with Israel. By rushing desperately needed economic and military aid to Egypt and Syria, the Soviet Union strengthened Arab reluctance to accept Israel's peace demands; at the same time, however, Russia urged the Arabs to seek a political rather than a military solution. The more moderate Arab leaders, aware that it would take years before they were strong enough to attempt retrieving their "rights" and lands by force, soon began to think seriously of some permanent political settlement, as long as it was neither a direct nor a humiliating one and as long as it provided for the return of all occupied territories.

Failing to obtain the passage in the Security Council of a resolution calling for an unconditional Israeli withdrawal, the USSR requested an emergency session of the General Assembly in the hope it would fare better in that larger body.

At this session Yugoslavia and sixteen Afro-Asian nations introduced a draft resolution (A/L.522/Rev. 3) which called for an Israeli withdrawal to positions held before 5 June and asked the Security Council to consider all aspects of the Arab-Israeli problem and to seek a peaceful solution for them. The United States, in turn, encouraged some Latin American members to submit a draft resolution (A/L.523/Rev. 1) which, while requiring an Israeli withdrawal and reaffirming that there should be no recognition of the occupation or acquisition of territories through force, also asked the parties to end the state of belligerency and requested the Security Council to ensure Israeli withdrawal, an end to the state of belligerency, freedom of transit for all states in international waterways, a full solution of the refugee problem, and the establishment of demilitarized zones.

The United States submitted a draft proposal of its own which referred only vaguely to an Israeli withdrawal and which appeared to stress direct negotiations. This received so little backing that it was ultimately dropped without a vote. Britain and Canada suggested that the UN should dispatch a high-level mediator to the Middle East to seek some common ground between the opponents and that it should make a greater effort to prevent the rising number of incidents which were erupting along the ceasefire lines. The two members, however, did not put their suggestions into any formal resolution, and no action was taken on them.

The Arabs supported the Yugoslav draft and opposed the Latin American one, because they were still pressing for an unconditional Israeli withdrawal before accepting further measures. Israel not only attacked the Yugoslav proposal but also objected to the Latin American draft, because it did not require direct negotiations and because it called for a greater UN role than Israel wanted it to assume in arranging a settlement. Since neither draft resolution received the required two-thirds vote, the Russian and American delegates started working on a compromise proposal. This called for an Israeli withdrawal to positions held prior to 5 June, representing a significant change in the American position, as well as for Israel's right to exist in peace and security and as an independent nation free from any state of belligerency. However, Arab opposition, led by Algeria and Syria, prompted Russia to withdraw its support, and thus ended a very brief, but hopeful, period when the two powers were trying to work together. Meanwhile, the General Assembly passed a resolution calling upon Israel to rescind its annexation of East Jerusalem; and, eventually, it requested that the Security Council resume its considerations of the Middle East situation "as a matter of urgency."

Because the two superpowers had reverted to their more partisan positions, the Security Council was unable to break the deadlock. In fact, it had to turn its most urgent attention to the escalating violence—the revival of Arab commando activities, Israeli retaliatory attacks, and shooting across the Suez Canal.

In the meantime, Israel was consolidating its position in the occupied areas and its diplomatic position was hardening. While in the past Israel might have been relatively satisfied with an Arab declaration ending the state of belligerency, it now insisted before the UN that it would accept nothing less than a complete and final peace treaty which not only would terminate the state of war but would also formally acknowledge Israel's existence and right to live in peace and security and would provide for demilitarized zones in Arab territories along the more exposed parts of its eventual borders. Moreover, while Israeli leaders stated at the outbreak of the war that Israel had no territorial claims,[58] with time such claims surfaced. At first, Israel made definite claims only to East Jerusalem; it then grew increasingly evident that many Israelis were determined to retain the Golan Heights, portions of the West Bank, the Gaza area, and, finally, a strip of Sinai territory along the Gulf of Aqaba to include the Sharm el-Sheikh sector. In addition, Israel began to speak of the need for "secure" borders and to maintain that Israel, not the UN, should determine what these would be. The Herut Party and other ultra-nationalists, strongly opposed to the UN and its resolutions, even called for the retention of all occupied areas. Israel also insisted that it would depend only upon itself and never upon the UN, which it still considered biased and undependable, or upon any outside power for its security; that the ceasefire arrangements could be "superseded" only by final peace treaties; and that each Arab state involved must negotiate a separate peace treaty with Israel. Israeli leaders felt that if they retained an overwhelming military superiority and all conquered areas, then the Arabs would be forced to develop a more "realistic" attitude. They would stop looking to the UN for support and make peace with Israel, even if it were largely on Israel's own terms and not on those in the UN resolutions. A number of Israeli liberals, including some members of Mapam, criticized this view and urged the government to comply more fully with the UN resolutions. They contended that lasting peace and security for Israel would depend more on achieving true reconciliation and friendly relations with the Arabs than on mere military power and territorial expansion, and that it was up to Israel, the victor with undiminished pride, to take the initiative in beginning a process of gradual reconciliation.[59] But these liberals were relatively few in number and had little political influence.

While nearly all Arabs whose voices were heard continued to oppose recognizing and negotiating directly with Israel, there was a wide divergence of opinion as to what policies they should follow in order to eliminate the serious consequences of their military defeat. The more aggressive Arabs, led by the Palestine commando groups, Syria, and Algeria, rejected any effort to achieve a compromise political settlement through the UN and insisted that the only solution should be the overthrow of the Israeli state, through guerrilla actions and ultimately war, and the establishment of a "democratic Palestine."

However, recognizing that the Arabs were and would remain for many years too weak to defeat Israel, the more moderate Arab leaders, such as King Hussein and President Nasser, concluded that they had to view the situation more pragmatically and try to salvage as much as possible from the recent disaster by diplomatic and political means. This would naturally require some major and unpopular concessions in exchange for an Israeli return of all captured areas and a "just" solution of the refugee question. Therefore, Nasser and Hussein arranged for a summit conference in Khartoum in August 1967. Opposing any compromise with the hated enemy, the Syrian and Algerian presidents refused to attend and the Palestine representative refused to accept its decisions. On 1 September, the leaders who did attend passed various resolutions. While they found it necessary to try to placate the aroused Arab masses with words—they therefore stated that they would not make any peace agreement with or extend recognition to Israel and would work for the "rights" of the Palestinians—they nevertheless also called for efforts at the diplomatic level to eliminate the "consequences of aggression."

The Egyptian and Jordanian governments now felt free to submit the whole Arab-Israeli question to the fall 1967 session of the General Assembly. They considered it imperative that the UN act quickly, because they feared that the longer Israel held on to the occupied areas, the more difficult it would be to extricate them from its control. Since it was evident that the Assembly would not accept any resolution calling for an unconditional Israeli withdrawal, they realized that they would have to soften their position. So they sought to revive the Latin American proposal which had been submitted during the Emergency Session and they began to speak of accepting a peace settlement with Israel through the UN. Newspaper accounts indicated that King Hussein had actually been dealing secretly with the Israelis in an attempt to work out a peace agreement and that he, Nasser, and other Arab leaders were showing a more "realistic" and "flexible" approach. Nasser was reported as being prepared to negotiate a final settlement through the UN or some other third party which would end the state of belligerency, concede the right of Israel to exist in peace and security, renounce the use of force, and recognize the political independence and territorial integrity of all countries and their right to use international waterways in return for a "just" solution of the refugee problem and a complete Israeli withdrawal from all occupied areas.[60] But as some Arab leaders were becoming more flexible, Israel's position was hardening.

In fall 1967 the UN, encouraged by the more temperate attitude of some key Arabs and pressed by the secretary general, initiated intensive behind-the-scenes diplomatic talks. Since these talks made no significant progress, many UN delegates began to support a move to send a special representative to the Middle East. However, neither the Arabs, the Israelis, nor their respective supporters could agree on the functions and powers of such a representative, and Israel also continued to insist on direct negotiations without the interference of any intermediary of any kind. The Arabs and Russia backed a draft resolution (S/8227), submitted by India, Mali, and Nigeria, which called for an Israeli withdrawal to positions held on 4 June and a just solution of the refugee problem, as well as the end of the state of belligerency; respect for the sovereignty, territorial integrity, and political independence of all states; the right of all states to security and to freedom of navigation in all international waterways; and the appointment of a special representative to implement the resolution. Israel and the United States led the opposition to this proposal. The United States submitted its own draft (S/8229), which called for "armed forces" to withdraw "from occupied territories" —without specifying what forces were involved and whether they were to withdraw from all territories or not—and for "territorial inviolability," to be guaranteed through demilitarized zones and "secure and recognized" borders. It also specified that the UN should send a representative to the Middle East "to establish and maintain contacts with the states concerned with a view to assisting them in the working out of solutions"—a provision which appeared to encourage direct negotiations. The Arabs and their supporters strongly objected to this draft and labelled it pro-Israeli. Several Latin American delegations attempted a compromise plan based on the draft resolution they had submitted in June. The Arabs favored this move, but Israel opposed it; and the Latin Americans abandoned their effort.

With the General Assembly deadlocked, Britain, who was then trying harder than any other big power to maintain a relatively balanced position, introduced a compromise draft resolution in the Security Council, where it passed by a unanimous vote on 22 November. This resolution (242), after "emphasizing the inadmissibility of the acquisition of territory by war" and the need to work for a just and lasting peace in which "every state" in the Middle East could "live in peace and security," affirmed that a just and lasting peace required the "withdrawal of Israeli armed forces from territories occupied in the recent conflict" and the "termination of all claims or states of belligerency and respect for and acknowledgment of the sovereignty, territorial integrity and political independence of every state in the area and their right to live in peace with secure and recognized boundaries free from threats or acts of war." It also asserted the "necessity" for "guaranteeing freedom of navigation through international waterways in the area," "achieving a just settlement of the refugee problem," and "guaranteeing the territorial inviolability and political independence of every state in the area, through measures including the establishment of demilitarized zones." The resolution also requested the secretary general "to designate a Special Representative to proceed to the Middle East to establish and maintain contacts in order to promote agreement in accordance with the provisions in this resolution."

While most Arab states accepted Security Council Resolution 242, others, led by Syria, Algeria, and Palestinian leaders, denounced it especially on the ground that it failed to make any reference to the national rights of the Palestinians, whom they considered a primary party in the Arab-Israeli question. Israel was unhappy with the resolution, for it preferred to bypass the UN and deal directly with the Arabs, using its formidable bargaining position—based on its superior military power and control over Egyptian, Syrian, and Jordanian territories—to compel the Arabs to make peace largely on its own terms.

After the resolution passed, the Arabs and Israelis lost no time in disagreeing on the interpretation of key provisions. Israel claimed that the resolution did not require a complete withdrawal from all occupied areas; that it required Israel to withdraw only to "secure" borders and only after a final peace settlement had been achieved and had provided Israel with assured security; and that it provided only a basis for negotiations and not a definitive plan for a final peace agreement. The United States was then generally sympathetic to these views. The Arabs, on the other hand, quoted the preamble, which emphasized "the inadmissibility of the acquisition of territory by war," and contended that not only the resolution but also the principles and purposes of the UN Charter, as stated in Article 2, required a complete Israeli withdrawal. They held that the resolution set down specific guidelines for a peace settlement and instructed the special representative to implement them. Russia and France generally supported Arab views on the resolution.

The overwhelming preponderance of the UN members revealed a great degree of agreement on the general principles enunciated in Resolution 242 and on the need for the UN to play an active and essential role in the whole affair. Israel was nearly alone in claiming the right to substantial border changes. While the United States held that some changes were valid, these should, as Secretary of State William P. Rogers stated on 9 December 1969, "not reflect the weight of conquest and should be confined to insubstantial alterations." [61] Since the Security Council and the General Assembly passed a number of resolutions (S/252[1968], S/267[1969], S/271[1969], and A/2628(XXV) [1970], A/2799(XXVI)[1971]) which reaffirmed "that the acquisition of territories by force is inadmissible," most members apparently considered that the UN Charter and Security Council Resolution 242 required a virtually complete Israeli withdrawal and that territorial changes should be made only by voluntary agreement between the parties. Most members also apparently considered that Israel had the right to use the Suez Canal and Gulf of Aqaba and to exist in peace and security and that there must be a "just" solution to the refugee problem.

### The Jarring Mission

On 23 November 1967 Secretary General U Thant appointed Dr. Gunnar Jarring, Swedish ambassador in Moscow, as special representative. Ambassador Jarring had held diplomatic posts in several countries in the Middle East, had been a Swedish delegate to the UN from 1948 to 1964, and had been sent on a UN peace mission in 1957 to deal with the Kashmir dispute. Thus, for the first time the UN selected someone to deal with the Arab-Israeli question who already had significant experience with both the Middle East and UN peacemaking efforts.

During 1968 and early 1969 Ambassador Jarring held numerous discussions both in the Middle East and in New York. Because Syria had rejected Resolution 242, Jarring made no attempt to meet with her officials; but he probably hoped that she would ultimately go along, even though reluctantly, with any peace settlement which proved acceptable to Egypt. Lebanon had backed the resolution and made it clear that it would accept any agreement Egypt and Jordan made with Israel. Lebanon held, however, that since it had not participated in the June war and since it considered its armistice agreement with Israel still valid,[62] it preferred not to get involved in any peace negotiations through the special representative for the present. Consequently, Jarring concentrated on Egypt and Jordan for the Arab side.

Dr. Jarring first tried to obtain from the Israelis a more precise formulation of their acceptance of Resolution 242, since Israel had not clearly and directly accepted it *in toto*. At the same time, he urged the Arab states to hold meetings with Israel under his auspices. He soon discovered that the contending parties still disagreed over the resolution's interpretation and implementation. In March 1969 he submitted specific questions to both sides to ascertain their latest attitudes in a more formal and explicit manner.

By this time, the positions of Egypt and Jordan had softened on some key points. They dropped their demand that an Israeli withdrawal must precede any discussions on other issues and they were now willing to implement Resolution 242 in its entirety as a "package deal" and to accept a phased Israeli withdrawal simultaneous with implementation of other parts of the resolution.[63] Jordan even appeared willing to make some border rectifications.[64] However, they continued to oppose any direct negotiations and any formal recognition of Israel and to insist that the resolution provided a "plan for settlement of the Middle East dispute" and that Jarring should set a "timetable" for implementing this "plan"; that Israel must accept the resolution as a whole and the principle of complete withdrawal from occupied areas; that the refugee question must be resolved on the basis of earlier UN resolutions; and that any demilitarized zones that would be set up must be placed "astride the boundaries" and supervised by the UN.[65] They also condemned Israeli activities, including the establishment of Jewish settlements, in the occupied areas. Especially after the large-scale Israeli attack on the Karameh refugee camp and *fedayeen* base in East Jordan in March 1968, the Palestinian commando movement gained momentum and its militant influence spread rapidly throughout the Arab world. This naturally tended to limit Arab flexibility.

Israel continued to insist that the resolution represented only a statement of principles "for the promotion of agreement . . . to be reached by negotiation" with each Arab country separately; that the Arabs must specifically renounce belligerency with and accept the existence of "Israel" and not merely refer to it as just a "state in the area"; that Arab governments should not allow commando groups to operate from their territories and should openly commit themselves to prevent any further operations of this kind; that the refugee issue must be resolved by "regional and international cooperation" rather than by repatriation; and that Israel would not withdraw from all occupied areas but only to "secure and recognized" borders, and then only after final peace agreements had been attained.[66] Israel also expressed concern about the rising intensity of commando attacks and, because Palestinian, Syrian, Iraqi, and some other Arab leaders continued to oppose any compromise settlement, it questioned the sincerity of any proclaimed Arab readiness to agree to a peace which would require acceptance of a state of Israel.

Unable to make any headway, Jarring returned to his post in Moscow to await further developments. U Thant then urged the big powers to become more actively involved, past experience having demonstrated that the UN was unable to act effectively without the cooperation of the major states.

On 3 April 1969 the permanent representatives of the United States, Russia, Britain, and France began a series of meetings, which continued intermittently into 1971, in an effort to break the deadlock and strengthen Jarring's hand. The big four especially sought ways to assure Israel's security, by means of big-power and UN guarantees and by the establishment of demilitarized zones and UN peacekeeping forces (possibly including big-four participation) along its borders, in the hope that Israel would then be encouraged to accept the principle of withdrawal.

The Egyptian and Jordanian governments hoped big-power intervention, especially that of the United States, would compel Israel to comply with the withdrawal and refugee provisions of Resolution 242 and that this intervention would make it easier for the Arab leaders to justify accepting Israel and making peace to their own peoples. In addition, they welcomed UN and big-power efforts to provide effective guarantees for the security of "all" states in the area, since they considered that Israel's present military superiority made them far more vulnerable than Israel.

Israel, however, objected to any outside intervention, even from the United States, despite the generally pro-Israeli positions of the American government and most Americans. Various Israeli leaders frankly stated that they had little confidence in Arab promises, big-power or American guarantees, and UN peacekeeping forces and that, regardless of UN resolutions, they would not give up those territories which they considered to be strategically essential to their security, even in return for a peace settlement.

Neither the special representative nor the big four could break the deadlock. Meanwhile, commando activities, Egyptian artillery barrages across the Suez Canal, and Israeli retaliatory attacks and deep air penetrations over Egypt had greatly aggravated Arab-Israeli relations and had brought increased Russian military involvement into the area. Accordingly, in June 1970 the United States took the initiative to obtain a standstill ceasefire between Egypt and Israel. In August both sides finally accepted a ninety-day ceasefire and military standstill in the Suez Canal area.

Encouraged by this development, Jarring returned to New York on 25 August to renew his peace efforts. Shortly after, however, Israel refused to participate any further in the Jarring talks until Egypt not only halted movement of Russian-supplied ground-to-air missiles into the canal zone area contrary to the standstill agreement, but also restored the military conditions there to their "original situation." Since Egypt did not comply with these conditions, Israel declined to meet with Jarring, although Egyptian and Jordanian representatives continued to confer with him.

In fall 1970 the UN once again attempted to deal with the impasse. On 4 November the General Assembly passed Resolution 2628(XXV) which: reaffirmed that "the acquisition of territories by force is inadmissible and that, consequently, territories thus occupied must be restored"; reiterated the withdrawal, security, and other provisions of Security Council Resolution 242; recognized that "respect for the rights of the Palestinians is an indispensable element in the establishment of a just and lasting peace"; called upon the parties concerned to "resume contact" with Jarring "to enable him to carry out, at the earliest possible date, his mandate for implementation of the Security Council Resolution (242) in all its parts"; and recommended that the ceasefire be extended for three more months. The resolution passed by a vote of fifty-seven (including France, Russia, Egypt, Jordan, Lebanon, Libya, Morocco, Sudan, and Tunisia) in favor, with sixteen (including Israel and the United States) against and thirty-nine (including Britain) abstaining. Algeria, Iraq, Kuwait, Saudi Arabia, South Yemen, Syria, and Yemen did not participate in the vote, because they felt that this resolution, like Security Council Resolution 242, failed to take into adequate consideration Palestinian rights and interests. Nevertheless, most Arabs were particularly pleased that the General Assembly resolution considered the Palestinians not merely as refugees but as a people whose rights had to be respected. The resolution also made it easier for Egypt to extend the ceasefire and it required Jarring to renew his efforts to bring Israel back to the stalled talks. In response to UN and American urgings and to American promises to sell Israel more Phantom planes and other military equipment, to provide badly needed loans, and to increase American political commitments to its security, Israel finally indicated on 30 December 1970 that it was ready to resume the talks.

A number of important developments had provided a slightly more favorable climate for Jarring's mission. The extended cessation of hostilities had helped to abate Israeli-Egyptian tensions somewhat. Russia and the United States had begun to intensify their own diplomatic pressures on the parties to seek a political settlement. King Hussein was in a stronger position to make peace and the influence of the Palestine commando groups had diminished in the Arab world as a result of their major defeat by the Jordanian army in late 1970. Anwar Sadat, who had succeeded Nasser as president and indicated a willingness to seek a political settlement, had consolidated his position; increasing numbers of Egyptians were more psychologically prepared to make peace with Israel if the terms were attractive enough. Also more moderate and realistic leadership had taken over in Syria. However despite these relatively favorable developments, despite the urgings of some American, western European, and UN officials, and despite the efforts of a growing number of Israeli "doves," Israel's official position remained unyielding, especially on withdrawal.[67]

After written exchanges of views between the parties through Jarring had taken place in January 1971 and had revealed no changes, Jarring concluded that the only procedure now left would be to seek from each party parallel and simultaneous commitments on what seemed to him the "inevitable prerequisites of an eventual peace settlement." Thus, on 8 February in identical aide-memoires, which had the approval of the big four,[68] he requested Israel to give a commitment to withdraw its forces from all occupied UAR territory with the understanding that satisfactory arrangements would be made for establishing demilitarized zones along the final borders, for providing "practical security arrangements" at Sharm el-Sheikh to ensure freedom of all shipping through the straits and the Suez Canal. Egypt, in turn, was asked to commit itself to a peace "agreement with Israel" and to make explicit therein to Israel, on a reciprocal basis, the termination of all belligerency, respect for and acknowledgment of each other's independence and right to live in peace within secure and recognized boundaries, responsibility to prevent acts of belligerency or hostility from originating in one state against the other and noninterference in each other's domestic affairs.

In its reply, Egypt welcomed Jarring's move and agreed to accept all the commitments which he had requested and which were contained in Security Council Resolution 242, "if Israel would give, likewise, commitments covering its own obligations under the Security Council resolution, including commitments for the withdrawal of its armed forces from Sinai and the Gaza

Strip and for the achievement of a just settlement for the refugee problem in accordance with UN resolutions." (Having already indicated on earlier occasions that it no longer insisted on any immediate or even prior Israeli withdrawal, Egypt was apparently requesting primarily an Israeli commitment to accept the "principle" of an ultimate and complete withdrawal.) In return, Egypt indicated that it was now prepared to make some unprecedented concessions. It formally stated its readiness to "enter into a peace agreement with Israel" (referring specifically for the first time to Israel by name), to assume responsibility for preventing commando activities against Israel from Egyptian territories, to accept an international peacekeeping force, with big-power participation if necessary, at Sharm el-Sheikh and along the final borders, and to agree to the establishment of demilitarized zones, provided they were "astride the borders." Some UN and American officials now felt that Egypt had made all the important concessions required by Resolution 242.[69]

Israel, on the other hand, refused to give the main commitment sought by Jarring, as well as by the United States, even though this meant accepting complete withdrawal from Egyptian territory only and did not require a withdrawal from any other area, including the Gaza Strip. Not only did Israel refuse this specific commitment, but in spite of strong American pleas, Israel insisted on stating formally and bluntly that it would "not withdraw to the pre-June 5, 1967 lines." [70] Israel also indicated opposition to any refugee repatriation. Israeli officials criticized Jarring's questions and procedures and claimed that he was only expressing his own "personal views and proposals" for a settlement and that, by doing this, he had "overstepped his mandate." But, according to *The New York Times* of 13 February 1971, "Western diplomats and United Nations officials . . . did not share the Israeli interpretation of the nature of Jarring's initiative." [71] Moreover, Israel's stubbornness, especially when compared to Egypt's more flexible posture, was criticized both at home [72] and abroad and served to weaken, at least for the time being, Israel's diplomatic position in the UN and in many parts of the world, including the United States.[73]

With the special representative at another impasse, the big four intensified their own discussions. When these also reached a dead

end, the United States again took the initiative. Having decided
to try a new "step-by-step" approach, American officials began
to press Egypt and Israel to work for a Suez Canal agreement in
the hope that this would ultimately facilitate Jarring's mission to
attain an overall peace settlement. But this American initiative—
as well as a later one whose aim was to get "proximity talks"
started between Egypt and Israel—also proved unsuccessful.

By late summer 1971 Egyptian leaders had become increasingly concerned about Israel's persistent efforts to strengthen its
control over and claims to substantial parts of the Sinai and other
occupied areas—especially by establishing more new Jewish settlements in these areas—and about American inability to moderate the Israeli stand on withdrawal. In addition, they were wor-
ried about the reactions of their own people to their failure to
show any progress in fulfilling their pledge to free their lands
from alien occupation. Consequently, they once again felt it necessary to submit the Arab-Israeli question to the General Assembly in the hope that it would pass another, even stronger resolution calling for an Israeli withdrawal and that this action would
further bolster Egypt's international political position, would encourage the United States to apply more effective pressures on
Israel, and would make it easier for the Egyptian leaders to maintain the ceasefire without too much loss of face.

On 13 December 1971 the General Assembly passed Resolution A/2799(XXVI), which reaffirmed all the principles set
down in Security Council Resolution 242; requested reactivation
of the Jarring Mission, expressed "full support" to Jarring, and
invited the parties to give him "full cooperation"; and noted
"with appreciation the positive reply by Egypt" to Jarring's February 1971 questionnaire and called upon Israel as well "to respond favorably."

On 6 December 1971 the General Assembly had passed another resolution (2792D[XXVI]) by a vote of seventy-nine (including Britain, France, Russia, Egypt, Jordan, Kuwait, Saudi
Arabia, Sudan, and Tunisia) in favor with only seven (including
Israel) against and thirty-six (including Algeria, Libya, Morocco,
Syria, Yemen, and the United States) abstaining. Iraq had refused to participate in the voting, for it felt that the resolution
did not sufficiently favor the Palestinians. While in 1969 and

1970 General Assembly resolutions 2535 (XXIV), 2628 (XXV), and 2672 (XXV) had referred rather vaguely to the need to "respect" the "rights" of the Palestinians as Palestinians and not merely as refugees, the new resolution more specifically stated that the "people of Palestine are entitled to the right of self-determination" and that "full respect" for this right was "an indispensable element in the establishment of a just and lasting peace." This and the earlier resolutions offered some satisfaction to those Arabs who had criticized Security Council Resolution 242 on the ground that it failed to provide in any way for the national aspirations of the Palestine Arabs. They also showed that most UN members had finally become convinced that the Palestinians could no longer be ignored in any Middle East peace settlement.[74] Even in Israel, increasing numbers of intellectuals and others felt it was necessary to provide some satisfaction for Palestinian national aspirations before there could be any real hope of a lasting Arab-Israeli peace.[75]

As requested by General Assembly Resolution 2799 (XXVI), Ambassador Jarring made a trip to the Middle East in February 1972 in an attempt to reactivate his mission. He suggested to Egypt and Israel that, as a means of getting around the deadlock, the parties should exchange, through him, clarifications of their positions on the various subjects dealt with in Security Council Resolution 242 with a view to formulating provisions for inclusion in a peace treaty. The Egyptian authorities, while insisting that progress towards a settlement lay through a complete Israeli withdrawal, "were prepared to take part in the process of clarification" in an effort "to break the impasse." [76]

Israel, in turn, insisted that it would not cooperate with the new proposal until Jarring gave "assurances . . . that he would be guided solely by Security Council Resolution 242 . . . and that he did not consider himself bound by his aide-memoire of 8 February 1971 and General Assembly Resolution 2799 (XXVI)," which endorsed the aide-memoire. Ambassador Jarring held that he had to consider General Assembly Resolution 2799 (XXVI) as representing "the constitutionally adopted judgement of a major organ of the UN" and that as a UN official he could not disregard it. He also indicated, however, that Israel's acceptance of the resolution "was not a condition for the clarification procedure that had been suggested." [77] Israel apparently did not reply positively to his suggestion for initiating a process of clarification. Jarring nevertheless made occasional trips from his post in Moscow to New York in order to confer with Arab and Israeli delegates at the UN and he kept himself otherwise available to the disputants.

In a speech in Damascus on 8 March 1972, President Hafez Asad of Syria stated for the first time that Syria would accept Security Council Resolution 242, provided that Israel gave up all Arab lands conquered in 1967 and that the "rights" of the Palestinians were recognized. As the *Christian Science Monitor* put it on 10 March 1972, this statement "apparently" brought "Syria at least formally into line with the policy of Egypt." Despite this relatively significant softening in Syria's official position, the impasse remained as great as ever.

As soon as UN Secretary General Kurt Waldheim took office at the beginning of 1972, he indicated that he intended to play an even more active role than U Thant had in the area of international diplomacy and peacemaking. Consequently, he not only sought to bolster the Jarring Mission, but he also held numerous discussions with Arab and Israeli diplomats in New York and traveled to the Middle East in the hope that he could help promote progress toward a settlement by means of quiet and personal diplomacy—but he too failed to break the deadlock.

When in July 1972 Egypt caused the withdrawal of Soviet armed forces from its territory, its weakened military position and political bargaining power vis-à-vis Israel made it even more imperative than before for Egypt to obtain greater UN, as well as American and western European, support, if it were ever to regain its lost lands. Egypt therefore requested another discussion of the Middle East situation at the autumn 1972 session of the General Assembly. On 8 December the Assembly passed a stronger resolution than usual and by a larger majority than in the past. Eighty-six members (including Britain, France, Russia, and most Arab states) voted for it, while seven (including Israel) voted against and thirty-one (including the United States) abstained. Algeria, Iraq, Libya, Syria, and Yemen again did not participate in the voting, for they felt the resolution was not strong enough. This resolution  (2949[XXVII]) reaffirmed past resolutions; held that Security Council Resolution 242 "must be implemented in all its parts"; deplored Israel's continued rejection of Jarring's February 1971 proposal calling for mutual commitments by Egypt and Israel; declared that "changes carried out by Israel in the occupied Arab territories in contravention of the Geneva Conventions of 1949 are null and void"; called "upon all states not to recognize any such changes and measures carried out by Israel" and invited "them to avoid actions, including actions in the field of aid, that could constitute recognition of that occupation"; and transmitted "the present resolution to the Security Council for its appropriate action." On 13 December by a vote of sixty-seven in favor and twenty-one against, the General Assembly passed Resolution 2963-E(XXVII) reaffirming that "the peoples of Palestine are entitled to equal rights and self determination."

Egypt and most of the other Arab states welcomed both resolutions and the growing number of favorable votes. Israel, on the other hand, criticized the resolutions and again claimed that the UN was biased in favor of the Arabs. Bolstered by continued American political, economic, and military support, Israel felt it could safely continue disregarding General Assembly resolutions. Moreover, it continued to do what it could to play down the roles of Jarring and the UN.

Since the Arabs were unable to obtain any effective UN action either to implement these and earlier resolutions or to bring new life to the Jarring Mission, in April 1973 Egypt suggested to the Security Council, while it was debating a Lebanese complaint against Israel, that it request the secretary general to submit as soon as possible a comprehensive report giving a full account of UN efforts since June 1967 pertaining to the Middle East situation. Egypt also suggested that the Security Council meet and examine the entire situation following receipt of the secretary general's report. On 20 April the Security Council passed Resolution 331 to carry out Egypt's two suggestions.

On 18 May the secretary general submitted his report (S/10929), which outlined the relatively well-known developments that had taken place since the June 1967 war. He indicated that the basic deadlock remained and urged the Security Council to make a "new appraisal of the possibilities and procedures of the Council itself for conciliation."

The Security Council held a series of meetings during the second week of June. Egypt pressed it to pass a strong resolution which would clearly call upon Israel to withdraw from all conquered territories, condemn the continued occupation of Arab lands, and proclaim the right of the Palestinians to a political entity of their own. As a result of a resolution passed at a meeting of the Organization of African Unity (OAU) in May, two African foreign ministers attended Security Council meetings as spokesmen for the OAU and supported Egypt's position. Israel, whose views were generally backed only by the United States, opposed any changes in the substance or interpretation of Security Council Resolution 242(1967) and urged the Council to recommend negotiations between the parties.

Since they were unable to agree on a common course of action and a big-two summit meeting was to be held in the latter part of June, Council members decided to recess for a month for further study and private consultations. Disappointed that the lengthy communiqué issued at the conclusion of the Nixon-Brezhnev talks had contained only thirty-five words devoted to the Middle East situation and had made no mention of either Security Council Resolution 242 or the Jarring Mission, the Arabs pressed for a strong resolution when the Council reconvened on 20 July.

After extensive consultation with other Council members, Guinea, India, Indonesia, Kenya, Panama, Peru, Sudan, and Yugoslavia submitted an amended draft resolution which deeply deplored Israel's continued "occupation of the territories occupied" in 1967; expressed both "serious concern at Israel's lack of cooperation with Jarring" and also support for his 8 February 1971 aide-memoire; expressed "the conviction that a just and peaceful solution" could "be achieved only on the basis of respect for national sovereignty, territorial integrity, the rights of all states in the area and for the rights and legitimate aspirations of the Palestinians"; declared that "in the occupied territories no changes which may obstruct a peaceful and final settlement or which may adversely affect the political and other fundamental rights of all the inhabitants in these territories should be introduced or recognized"; and requested the secretary general and Jarring "to resume and to pursue their efforts" and called upon the parties to extend full cooperation to them. Although the Arab, Russian, Chinese, and African members preferred a more strongly worded resolution, it was generally supported by all Council members except the United States, who sought unsuccessfully to amend it in substantial ways.

Claiming that the eight-power proposal would seriously alter Security Council Resolution 242, Israel warned that its passage would result in Israel's refusal to cooperate further with UN efforts to implement the 1967 resolution and would make "futile" a planned visit by Secretary General Waldheim to the Middle East.

On 26 July Australia, Austria, Britain, France, and the Soviet Union joined the eight sponsors in voting for the draft resolution. China did not participate in the voting, because it felt that the proposal was too weak. The United States vetoed the resolution on the grounds that it was "unbalanced" and that it would have "undermined" and done "irrevocable and permanent damage" to Resolution 242, which was "the one agreed basis on which a settlement in the Middle East could be constructed." [78] Thus, the Security Council terminated its discussions without having taken any action.

On 26 August, after conferring with Jarring in Geneva, Secretary General Waldheim began an eight-day visit to the Middle East. He met with the leaders of Syria, Lebanon, Egypt, Jordan, and Israel in an attempt to encourage greater flexibility on all sides and to discover some new ideas or approaches which might help break the deadlock. After concluding his trip, he reported that while he "found everywhere a strong desire for peace," "deep divisions persisted regarding the nature of the peace and how to achieve it." [79] Even though he achieved no breakthrough, Waldheim nevertheless insisted that because of the great dangers involved in a continued Arab-Israeli conflict both Jarring and the UN must remain actively involved in seeking a final Arab-Israeli peace settlement.

Disappointed at making no progress toward regaining their lost territories, the Arabs placed the Middle East situation on the agenda of the fall 1973 General Assembly Session. However, on 6 October, before the General Assembly had a chance to discuss this item, Syria and Egypt initiated a war with Israel in the hope that this action would compel the superpowers to make more determined efforts to implement the UN resolutions.

The Security Council held four meetings between 8 and 12 October, but it was unable to take any action to end the fighting, because its members, and especially the superpowers, were seriously divided over the terms of a ceasefire resolution. The United States and Israel pressed for one which would call for a return of the combatants to the pre-6 October lines. Since in the early stages of the war Egypt and Syria held the military initiative and their armies had made territorial gains, the Arabs and their Russian and Afro-Asian supporters on the Security Council insisted that any ceasefire resolution should call for an Israeli withdrawal to the 5 June 1967 lines.

After the USSR and then the United States had begun to send large-scale arms aid to the warring parties, the secretary general and some European governments urged the Security Council to take prompt action to end the fighting; but Council members remained as disunited as ever. Once Israeli forces had taken the offensive, had crossed to the west bank of the Suez Canal, and were threatening to surround the Egyptian armies on the east side of the canal, Egypt appealed to Russia for direct military assistance. Faced now with a growing danger of being dragged into the war, the superpowers decided to cooperate to end the fighting as quickly as possible. On 22 October they jointly submitted Security Council Resolution 338, which called upon the belligerents to terminate all military activity within twelve hours and "to start immediately after the cease-fire the implementation of Security Council Resolution 242(1967) in all of its parts" and which decided that negotiations between the parties concerned should start immediately "under appropriate auspices aimed at a just and durable peace in the Middle East." With the United States and the Soviet Union now working together, the resolution passed the same day. Israel and Egypt agreed to the ceasefire on 22 October, while Syria delayed its acceptance until 23 October.

Despite the ceasefire order, Israeli forces continued to advance southward until they encircled Suez City and the Egyptian Third Army. On 23 October the superpowers jointly sponsored Security Council Resolution 339, which called for a return of all military units to their 22 October positions and requested the secretary general to dispatch UN observers to supervise the ceasefire between Egypt and Israel. When Israel refused to withdraw its forces, Egypt urgently appealed for American and Soviet armed intervention to enforce the resolutions they had sponsored. As Russia appeared to be preparing to send troops to Egypt and the United States responded by ordering a military alert, eight non-permanent Security Council members acted speedily to defuse the situation by submitting a draft resolution which passed on 25 October with both US and USSR support, for they were anxious to avoid military confrontation. This resolution (340) not only demanded compliance with the ceasefire and withdrawal provisions of Resolutions 338 and 339, but also increased the number of UN observers on both sides of the ceasefire lines and called for the immediate establishment of a UN Emergency Force. A new UNEF was established quickly by the secretary general and sent to the Suez Canal area in order to implement the earlier resolutions and to separate the Egyptian and Israeli armies. UNEF also supervised the agreement Egypt and Israel made through the mediation of Secretary of State Kissinger, which permitted Egypt to send nonmilitary supplies to Suez City and its Third Army. These developments decreased the danger of a superpower military intervention and confrontation.

Because the UN could not get Israeli forces back to the 22 October lines, there were frequent incidents between Israeli and Egyptian troops, and more large-scale fighting threatened in the Suez Canal area, the United States, with Soviet cooperation, initiated an Arab-Israeli conference in Geneva. This was first to press for Arab-Israeli military disengagement agreements on all fronts and then to try formulating a final Arab-Israeli peace settlement. The Arabs urged that the UN play a major role at the conference; but Israel, with American support, succeeded in limiting it. By the end of 1973 the United States, through Dr. Kissinger, with the consent of the contending parties, had clearly assumed unchallenged leadership in trying to negotiate Arab-Israeli disengagement and peace agreements.

Nevertheless, the UN remained very much in the overall picture. UN officials participated in the signing of the Egyptian-Israeli and Syrian-Israeli disengagement agreements on 18 January and 31 May 1974 respectively. These agreements provided for the active participation of UN peacekeeping forces in their implementation and stated that the agreements were to constitute a first step toward a final "peace according to the provisions of Security Council Resolution 338"—which, in turn, had referred to the implementation of Security Council Resolution 242. The Security Council passed resolutions formally recognizing the agreements and authorizing the setting up of the required UN forces for six-month periods. On 23 October and 29 November 1974, the Security Council renewed the mandate of these forces for six more months and called upon "the parties concerned to implement immediately Security Council Resolution 338." Secretary General Waldheim continued his own active interest in the Arab-Israeli problem and he held discussions with Arab and Israeli officials in New York and the Middle East.

Moreover, on 22 November 1974, the UN General Assembly, after allowing PLO leader Yasir Arafat to address it on 14 November, passed two resolutions involving the Palestinians. Resolution 3237 (XXIX) gave UN observer status to the PLO and Resolution 3236 (XXIX) declared that the "Palestinian people" had the right to attain "national independence and sovereignty" and "to return to their homes and property." On 17 December the Assembly passed resolutions (3331A and 3331D) reiterating the right of Arab refugee repatriation and requesting the CCP to continue its efforts to implement paragraph 11 of Resolution 194 (III). In order not to complicate Dr. Kissinger's diplomatic efforts, the Arabs agreed not to press for Assembly debate on the item "The Situation in the Middle East" which they had originally placed on the Assembly's agenda. However, they obtained the consent of the other UN members to suspend, not formally end, the Assembly session so that it could be quickly reconvened to discuss this item if this became necessary.

In the early months of 1975, there was increasing discontent— especially on the part of the Syrians, Palestinians, and Russians —with Kissinger's step-by-step procedure and growing pressure to revive the Geneva Conference. Whether Kissinger's mission to the Middle East in March 1975 succeeded or not in bringing about another Egyptian-Israeli disengagement agreement, it appeared inevitable that, sooner or later, there would be a reconvening of the Geneva Conference, where the UN would have a significant, if limited, role to play. If the Geneva Conference were to fail, the UN would probably once more be faced with primary responsibility for dealing with the unresolved Arab-Israeli problem, which had been made more potentially dangerous to world peace than ever before by the October war, by the enhanced political role óf Arab oil and oil money, and by the massive rearmament of the contending sides by the superpowers. In fact, if another Arab-Israeli war were to break out—as could happen following the premature removal of UN peacekeeping forces from the area—the UN would again be faced with the tremendous responsibility, not only to bring such a war to a quick end, but also to prevent the superpowers from being drawn into the military conflict.

## Conclusion

### The Failure of UN Peace Efforts

Despite the fact that since 1947 the UN has devoted more time and effort to the Arab-Israeli problem than to any other international dispute, the world organization has not been able to resolve it. There are a number of reasons for this.

To begin with, the UN is not a superstate with power to act on its own, but only an instrument set up by sovereign countries to promote international cooperation. In the final analysis, its effectiveness depends mainly upon either the voluntary compliance of the disputants with its decisions or the willingness of the major powers to enforce its will. When both the Arabs and Israelis felt it to their advantage to work with the UN, or when the United States and the USSR were adequately united and determined in their support of the UN, its decisions were usually implemented. For example, during the 1956 Sinai-Suez war, Russia and the United States compelled not only Israeli, but also British and French, military forces to withdraw from Egyptian territory as called for by UN resolutions; and during the 1948, 1967, and 1973 wars, the big powers were ultimately able to bring about Arab and Israeli compliance with UN-supported truces and/or ceasefires.

However, on many occasions, and especially since the June 1967 war, the superpowers have not been united and determined enough to persuade the contending parties to live up to all of their UN obligations. Moreover, the Soviet Union and the United States often assumed partisan and conflicting positions and firmly backed their "clients," despite the fact that these moves encouraged disregard of the UN and its resolutions.

There have also been occasions, as in 1949 and 1953 and at times after the June 1967 and October 1973 wars, when the United States was in a strong enough position to exert considerable pressures of her own on both Israel and some Arab states. In October 1953, by threatening to suspend all economic aid, the Eisenhower administration was able to bring about Israeli compliance with a UN request to stop work, at least temporarily, on a canal project in the Syrian-Israeli demilitarized zone. On a few occasions in 1949, in support of the CCP, and after 1968, in support of Gunnar Jarring, the United States applied its own pressures on Israeli and some moderate Arab leaders to encourage them to cooperate more fully with UN peacemaking efforts and hopes had been raised that these moves would prove successful.[80] However, emotional ties, internal political considerations, and other factors prevented America from exerting sufficient pressure, especially on Israel, to produce a decisive effect.[81] After the October 1973 war, the United States successfully exerted pressure to bring about disengagement agreements between Israel and Egypt and Israel and Syria and to initiate a step-by-step negotiating procedure aimed at bringing about a complete resolution of the Arab-Israeli problem in stages. But it remains to be seen whether the United States, as well as the UN, will ultimately be willing and/or able to apply the far greater pressure needed to overcome all those formidable differences between the contending parties which still stand in the way of a final peace settlement.

Rarely over the years did the UN receive adequate cooperation from both the Arabs and Israelis at the same time; and the posture each side assumed was determined by what it considered its own self interest. In the beginning, the Arabs were less cooperative than the Israelis because they firmly objected to UN efforts to partition Palestine, while the Israelis considered it essential to work with the world organization in order to establish and then preserve their state. After Israel had attained a clear-cut military superiority during the 1948 Palestine war, the attitudes and policies of the opposing parties towards the UN were largely reversed. Some Arabs felt it to their advantage to work with the UN and to encourage its involvement in any peacemaking process, while many Israelis began considering various UN resolutions unfair and any significant UN peacemaking role contrary to their own interests. After the 1967 war this was especially true, for the more moderate Arab leaders became convinced that it was now imperative to accept the reality of Israel's existence and military superiority and that only with UN, as well as big-power, help could they attain a peace settlement which would return those territories occupied in June 1967. Consequently, the more moderate Arabs, as well as some Israeli liberals, showed greater readiness to cooperate with UN peacemaking efforts than did the more militant Arabs and the most influential Israeli leaders. UN peace efforts failed, therefore, largely because there was inadequate voluntary compliance on the part of the more uncompromising Israeli and Arab elements, as well as because the big powers would not exert the required pressure.[82]

Another major reason for UN peacemaking ineffectiveness was aptly explained by Secretary U Thant in a speech on 16 September 1971.

> Great problems usually come to the UN because governments have been unable to think of anything else to do about them. This applies equally to the Middle East and to the environment. The UN is a last-ditch, hard-core affair, and it is not surprising that the organization should often be blamed for failing to resolve problems which have already been found insoluble by governments.[83]

Britain waited until the Palestine question became virtually insoluble before she considered turning it over either to the League of Nations or to its successor, the UN. Obviously, the conflict would have been more susceptible to a solution at a much earlier stage in its development.

Although the Palestine question was already extremely complex when it was first placed on the UN agenda, member states, through their misunderstanding of the problem's true nature, actually added new dimensions to it. For example, by not attempting conciliation to lessen the existing psychological and political gulf between Arabs and Jews, the partition resolution of November 1947 merely precipitated a bloody conflict and widened that gulf still further. From the beginning not only was the entire problem often oversimplified, but inadequate consideration was given to the more basic human aspects. For instance, until very recently UN members have failed to take into adequate account the nationalist feelings of the Palestine Arabs and sought to deal with them only as displaced persons. As a result, the UN as a whole and the major powers in particular have generally failed to come to grips with some of the most important psychological, as well as political, obstacles that obstruct an Arab-Israeli reconciliation; and they wasted invaluable time searching vainly for some quick, easy political or, especially, economic panacea. This was particularly unfortunate, because a final solution could have come more easily in 1948 and 1949, when Arab-Israeli antipathy was not so deeply rooted, when positions had not yet polarized, when both the UN and the West still had relatively strong influence in the Middle East, and when the cold war had not yet spread to the area.

Before June 1967 UNEF, UNTSO, and the Arab-Israeli MACs were able, at times, to stop border strife and encourage periods of relative calm along the demarcation lines. But neither the UN and the major powers nor Israel and the Arab states made determined efforts to try to resolve the fundamental issues during those periods when emotions had abated and when leaders were in the most favorable position to make those concessions essential to peace. Only when a major crisis had erupted would the UN and the big powers suddenly bestir themselves and revive their efforts to deal with the overall problem; but in the meantime Arab and Israeli emotions would have again become so acute that outside attempts at conciliation had little chance to succeed.

Moreover, UN efforts were also hindered by the fact that during the first critical years, the chief CCP delegates lacked some of the most essential qualifications for their formidable assignment; they were inadequately supported by their home governments and the UN; and they did not cooperate effectively with those other UN officials and agencies which dealt with important phases of the Arab-Israeli problem.

### The Role of the UN in Any Peace Settlement

The UN will have to continue playing an important role in any peacemaking process. This role will remain rather limited as long as the United States retains the sole leadership it assumed shortly after the October war in working for an Arab-Israeli peace settlement. But even so, UNTSO observers and the new UN peace-keeping forces are essential to the successful implementation of both the disengagement and any future peace agreements. In addition, Security Council Resolution 338 of 22 October 1973 reiterated the validity of Security Council Resolution 242 in "all" of its "parts" as the basis for any peace settlement, and the UN has an official status at any reconvened Geneva Conference. Moreover, if Secretary of State Kissinger's personal diplomatic efforts were to fail to bring about a final peace settlement, then the Arabs may feel that they had no peaceful alternative but to press the UN to resume leadership in the peacemaking process.

In either eventuality, because ignorance has tended to obstruct progress towards peace in the Middle East, UN members, especially the superpowers, need to develop a deeper understanding of all facets of the problem. It is especially important to recognize that the Arab-Israeli conflict is primarily a complex human problem which, as the last several decades have demonstrated, cannot be resolved quickly and easily, but which will require a step-by-step process of education and reconciliation for its ultimate solution. Only then will the UN, the big powers, and the contending parties be finally able to deal effectively with the fundamental causes of the conflict.

If the UN should resume its leadership in the search for an Arab-Israeli peace, it should work particularly hard during periods of relative calm in the Middle East. Moreover, it should, as in the past, employ quiet diplomacy in dealing with the most sensitive issues and work through an able, experienced mediator or special representative, such as Ambassador Jarring. Since probably not all the disputants will cooperate adequately on their own initiative with UN and other peacemaking efforts, sufficient pressure must come from the two superpowers—especially the United States, who alone has the means to exert considerable influence on both Israel and some key Arab countries. The big powers must set aside partisan attitudes, provide concerted backing to the UN, and exert determined pressure directly on the antagonists. The larger nations of Western Europe could also make an important contribution to peace in the Middle East, if they would effectively coordinate their policies, pool their resources, exert their own potentially significant influence, and, in general, play a more prominent role by themselves, as well as in concert with Russia and the United States, in trying to break the Arab-Israeli deadlock. In short, all the big powers should make the requisite efforts and sacrifices, not only because of their obligations under the UN Charter and their natural concern about the fate of the peoples in the Middle East, but also because another Arab-Israeli war could lead to disastrous military confrontation. The October war alerted the world to this danger, because only quick action by the Security Council and by the superpowers helped prevent such a confrontation during the latter stages of that conflict.

In the meantime, to improve the climate for peace in the Middle East, the UN should continue aiding the Arab refugees for as long as is necessary so as to prevent the refugee problem from exacerbating the already explosive situation. The UN must also continue providing UNEF units and military observers—and even increase their number whenever possible—in order to discourage incidents, promote further military disengagement, and enhance feelings of security on the part of Israel and the Arab states. In addition, the UN must press the parties to maintain the ceasefire and prevent acts of terrorism and retaliation, and it must exploit every area of compatibility that may develop between the opposing sides.

Through various UN resolutions—such as General Assembly Resolution 194 (III) providing for the right of refugee repatriation or resettlement with compensation; Security Council Resolution 242 providing for an Israeli withdrawal from occupied areas and the right of all states in the Middle East to live in peace and security and to use the Suez Canal and Gulf of Aqaba; and Assembly Resolutions 2628 (XXV) and 2672 (XXV) recognizing the need to "respect . . . the rights of the Palestinians"— a large majority of the members have set down those basic principles which they felt were consistent with the UN Charter and were essential to peace between the Arabs and the Israelis. The principal reason for establishing the UN was to provide some organized means and universally accepted principles, on the basis of which reasonably just and lasting solutions to international disputes could be reached. Imperfect as this procedure may sometimes be, it is still the fairest and best that man has devised to date. The alternative, reverting to the rule of brute force, would return the world to a far more insecure and unstable situation than presently exists—a situation in which whatever nations happened to have the greatest military might at a given time would determine what is "right."

If and when the Arabs and Israelis do finally agree on a peace settlement, the UN will still have a vital role to play. Peacekeeping forces, such as the UNEF which was set up after the Sinai war and those UN forces established by the Egyptian-Israeli and Syrian-Israeli disengagement agreements, could provide a stabilizing influence,[84] first by interposing their presence between the antagonists during the future stages of Israeli troop withdrawals and then by being stationed along the final borders and in strategic areas, such as Sharm el-Sheikh, for as long as their presence is needed. UNEF units could be recruited not only from the smaller and more neutral countries, but from the big powers as well, if any one of the parties directly involved desired this and felt that it could more effectively insure its security. Each party could even be permitted to determine what nations should contribute to the UNEF elements stationed on its own soil, so that it would not be compelled to accept troops from any state considered unfriendly and unreliable. Safeguards could also be provided to assure that UNEF would have adequate long-term financing and legal authority [85] and that it could not be removed by unilateral action.

If peacekeeping units could be placed on both sides of the ultimate boundaries, they would be better able to prevent incidents, as well as wars. Moreover, in the event that one party forced a total UN troop withdrawal from its territory, the situation could remain stable, because UN units would still continue to operate on the territory of the other party. Besides, if there is to be any real hope of maintaining UNEF in the Middle East for any considerable period, then all parties must be dealt with on a reasonably equal basis. The same reasoning applies to the setting up of demilitarized zones, which were specifically referred to in Security Council Resolution 242 as necessary to "guaranteeing the territorial inviolability and political independence of every state in the area." As professor N. Bar-Yaacov of the Hebrew University of Jerusalem concluded after making a thorough historical study of demilitarized zones:

> It is generally recognized that, in order to be effective, an agreement on demilitarization should be based on the principles of reciprocity, relativity, and free consent. The principle of reciprocity entails the location of the demilitarized zone on both sides of the frontier  . . . between the contracting parties. . . . It is futile to create security on one side of the frontier if apprehension and mistrust exist on the other. Relativity implies that, in delimiting the zone and formulating its regime, account should be taken of the relative circumstances of a geographical, strategic, political or ethnic nature, with a view to avoiding inequality of treatment.[86]

Past experience has shown that sooner or later, unequal treatment would arouse strong nationalist resentment against the continued presence of such zones or of UNEF forces on one side of the border only. The UN Security Council and the big five, either individually or collectively, could also provide formal guarantees of the territorial integrity and security of all states in the area as part of a final peace settlement.

While UN peacekeeping forces, demilitarized zones, and formal guarantees cannot ensure absolute security for any party in the Middle East, reliance on one's own power alone cannot, in the long run, ensure this either. Throughout its entire history, the shifting and unreliable balance of power system has never, on its own, provided permanent peace and security for any state, no matter how strong it was. It is a system which always had the built-in weakness of giving greater security to one side only at the expense of greater insecurity for the other, and the other side, if it had the potential, would then strive to shift the balance in its own favor. It would therefore be to everyone's long-range benefit to accept the best guarantees presently available and to cooperate with the world community's efforts to attain a peace settlement in the

Middle East. In the final analysis, only by promoting meaningful reconciliation between antagonists and by working to develop more effective international law and organization can there be any hope that, someday, man will be able not only to prevent the outbreak of war, but also to provide lasting peace and equal security for both the Arabs and Israelis, as well as for all peoples everywhere.

In the nuclear age, a serious threat to world peace anywhere is a potential threat to the very survival of mankind. Consequently, to the extent that an international conflict—such as the one between Arabs and Israelis—can endanger world security, its peaceful defusing, with the UN's essential help, clearly serves the vital interest of all nations.

## Notes

1. Colombia resigned from the second subcommittee when her proposal that uncommitted states should also be assigned to the first and second subcommittees was not acted upon.

2. See the statement by Moshe Sharett in *The Israel Digest at the 28th World Zionist Congress,* 21 January 1972, II, III; UN Mediator's Report A/648; *The New York Times,* 4 July 1948; Edgar O'Ballance, *The Arab-Israeli War* (New York: Praeger, 1957), p. 139.

3. This and the following five paragraphs are largely based on the UN Mediator's Report, A/648.

4. *Ibid.,* p. 11.

5. *Ibid.*

6. See quotations from Bernadotte's report (A/648) given earlier and from *The New York Times* of 31 December 1948. See also S/1023, 3 October; 1948; S/1040, 18 October; S/1071, 6 November; S/1152, 27 December 1948; *The New York Times,* 30 July, 8, 14, 15 August, 17–20, 29 September, 3, 15, 16, 20–31 October, 4–17 November 1948, 6 January 1949; Jon Kimche, *Seven Fallen Pillars* (New York: Praeger, 1953), pp. 242ff; Harry Sacher, *Israel and the Establishment of a State* (London: G. Weidenfeld and Nicolson, 1952), pp. 295, 303; Robert St. John, *Ben Gurion* (Garden City, N.Y.: Doubleday, 1959), pp. 163, 168ff; Rony E. Gabbay, *A Political Study of the Arab-Jewish Conflict* (Geneva: E. Droz, 1959), p. 155; Maj. Gen. Carl Van Horn, *Soldiering for Peace* (New York: D. McKay, 1967), pp. 61, 64, 80, 83, 126, 239ff, 283; Kenneth W. Bilby, *New Star in the East* (Garden City, N.Y.: Doubleday, 1950), pp. 161, 277; George Eden Kirk, *Survey of International Affairs: The Middle East, 1945–1950* (London: Oxford University Press, 1954), p. 227; O'Ballance, *Arab-Israeli War,* pp. 166, 175; Walter Eytan, *The First*

*Ten Years* (New York: Simon and Schuster, 1958), p. 24; James Grover McDonald, *My Mission to Israel* (New York: Simon and Schuster, 1951), p. 47; *Time,* 16 August 1948; Fred John Khouri, *The Arab-Israeli Dilemma* (Syracuse, N.Y.: Syracuse University Press, 1968), pp. 80–90.

7. *The New York Times,* 29 September 1948.

8. UN, *Official Records of the Security Council,* 380th Meeting, 15 November 1948, pp. 4ff; 381st Meeting, 16 November, p. 55; 383rd Meeting, 2 December, pp. 1ff; 386th Meeting, 17 December, p. 23; 392nd Meeting, 24 December, p. 47.

9. Harry S. Truman, *Memoirs* (Garden City, N.Y.: Doubleday, 1955–56), vol. 2, p. 166.

10. *The New York Times,* 22–26 September; 1, 22, 25, 28–30 October; 5, 9 November 1948; Jacob Coleman Hurewitz, *The Struggle for Palestine* (New York: Norton, 1950), pp. 322ff; Truman, *Memoirs,* pp. 166ff.

11. *The New York Times,* 10, 15, 16, 18, 19, 20, 31 October; 1, 2, 7 November 1948; Jon and David Kimche, *A Clash of Destinies: the Arab-Jewish War and the Founding of the State of Israel* (New York: Praeger, 1960), pp. 206, 236, 255ff; Sacher, *Israel,* p. 295; St. John, *Ben Gurion,* p. 48; O'Ballance, *Arab-Israeli War,* p. 177; S/1042, 18 October 1948; S/1071, 6 November 1948; Khouri, *Arab-Israeli Dilemma,* pp. 85–91.

12. Also see: St. John, *Ben Gurion,* pp. 168ff; Sacher, *Israel,* pp. 304ff; S/1152, 27 December 1948; Bilby, *New Star,* p. 171.

13. *The New York Times,* 4, 7, 8 January 1949; O'Ballance, *Arab-Israeli War,* p. 201; Sacher, *Israel,* p. 307; St. John, *Ben Gurion,* p. 171.

14. Data on the members of the delegations had been taken largely from David P. Forsythe, *United Nations Peacemaking: The Conciliation Commission for Palestine* (Baltimore: Johns Hopkins University Press, 1972), pp. 37ff; and Pablo de Azcarate, *Mission in Palestine, 1948–1952* (Washington, D.C.: Middle East Institute, 1966), pp. 136ff.

15. Forsythe, *United Nations Peacemaking,* p. 38.

16. de Azcarate, *Mission,* pp. 145ff and 135ff.

17. Dean Acheson, *Present at the Creation: My Years in the State Department* (New York: Norton, 1969), p. 396.

18. de Azcarate, *Mission,* p. 164; see also Forsythe, *United Nations Peacemaking,* p. 45 (note 25).

19. A/1367, 22 September 1950, pp. 9ff.

20. *Ibid.,* pp. 45, 49.

21. A/992, 22 September 1949.

22. Forsythe, *United Nations Peacemaking,* p. 50 (note 43).

23. UN, *Official Records of the General Assembly,* Third Session, Part II, 191st Plenary Meeting, 13 April 1949, pp. 38ff; 217th Plenary Meeting, 11 May, p. 330; *Ad Hoc* Political Committee, 42nd Meeting, 3 May, pp. 186ff; 45th Meeting, 5 May, pp. 227ff.

24. McDonald, *My Mission,* pp. 181, 184. See also: Bilby, *New Star,* pp. 231, 239; Don Peretz, *Israel and the Palestine Arabs* (Washington, D.C.: Middle East Institute, 1958), p. 41; Gabbay, *Political Study,* pp. 253ff.

25. Peretz, *Israel,* p. 64.

26. A/927, 21 June 1949; A/992, 22 September 1959, pp. 3ff; Gabbay,

*Political Study,* pp. 244ff; Peretz, *Israel,* p. 43; Kirk, *Middle East,* p. 303; Bilby, *New Star,* p. 240.

27. A/992, pp. 9, 13.

28. Gordon Clapp, "An Approach to Economic Development," *International Conciliation* (April 1950): 211ff.

29. A/1255, 29 May 1950, pp. 1ff; A/1288, 17 July 1950, pp. 3, 9.

30. A/1367, 22 September 1950, p. 44; see also A/1451, 19 October 1950, p. 20.

31. Kirk, *Middle East,* pp. 309ff; Gabbay, *Political Study,* pp. 318, 325, 339; Aqil H. H. Abidi, *Jordan, A Political Study* (New York: Asia Publishing House, 1965), pp. 29–38, 71, 77; Eytan, *First Ten Years,* p. 41; McDonald, *My Mission,* pp. 210ff; John Bagot Glubb, *A Soldier with the Arabs* (New York: Harper, 1957), p. 341; *The New York Times,* 1, 15, 25 March, 15 October, 28 November 1950.

32. *The New York Times,* 13 February, 19 March 1950; 15 April 1951; Gabbay, *Political Study,* pp. 317ff.

33. Gabbay, *Political Study,* p. 322; A/1367, p. 43.

34. de Azcarate, *Mission,* pp. 166, 168.

35. A/1985, pp. 2ff.

36. UN, *Official Records of the General Assembly,* Sixth Session, *Ad Hoc* Political Committee, 33rd Meeting, 7 January 1952, pp. 176ff; 34th Meeting, 8 January, pp. 181ff; 35th Meeting, 9 January, pp. 187ff; 36th Meeting, 10 January, pp. 196ff; 37th Meeting, 11 January, pp. 201ff; 38th Meeting, 11 January, pp. 209ff; 40th Meeting, 14 January, pp. 220ff; 364th Plenary Meeting, 26 January, pp. 392ff; 365th Plenary Meeting, 26 January, pp. 402ff.

37. de Azcarate, *Mission,* p. 179. Also see Forsythe, *United Nations Peacemaking,* p. 96.

38. UN, *Official Records of the General Assembly,* Seventh Session, *Ad Hoc* Political Committee, 29th Meeting, 1 December 1952, pp. 165ff; 36th Meeting, 8 December, p. 213.

39. *Ibid.,* 25th Meeting, 26 November 1952, p. 155; 28th Meeting, 29 November, p. 159; 29th Meeting, 1 December, pp. 171ff; 30th Meeting, 1 December, pp. 173ff; 31st Meeting, 2 December, pp. 178ff; 32nd Meeting, 3 December, pp. 183ff; 33rd Meeting, 4 December, pp. 192ff; 35th Meeting, 8 December, p. 210; *The New York Times,* 6 December 1952.

40. *The New York Times,* 8, 15 December 1952.

41. UN, *Official Records of the General Assembly,* Seventh Session, 405th Plenary Meeting, 18 December 1952, pp. 393ff; 406th Plenary Meeting, 18 December, pp. 408ff.

42. *The New York Times,* 26, 27 June 1961.

43. Joseph E. Johnson, "Arab vs. Israeli: A Persistent Challenge," *Middle East Journal* (Winter 1964): 2ff; Forsythe, *United Nations Peacemaking,* pp. 133ff.

44. Forsythe, *United Nations Peacemaking,* pp. 135ff.

45. On 29 March 1954, Russia, now fully committed to a pro-Arab policy, vetoed a resolution which called upon Egypt to abide by the 1951 resolution. After this, Israel began to contend that, since no resolution opposed by the Arabs could pass the Security Council because of the Russian veto, the Security Council had become one-sided and unfair to

it. Egypt, in turn, held that it was unfair for the Security Council to insist upon its compliance with Security Council Resolution 95 (1951) while Israel was allowed to disregard many UN resolutions on the refugee, Jerusalem, and other issues. Egypt claimed that it would be willing to abide by Security Council Resolution 95 if Israel lived up to the other UN resolutions and that it would agree to a world court test of its refusal to allow Israeli ships to use the Suez Canal and the Gulf of Aqaba. (UN, *Official Records of the Security Council,* 661st Meeting, 12 March 1954, p. 21; 663rd Meeting, 25 March, pp. 11f; 549th Meeting, 26 July 1951, pp. 14ff; 556th Meeting, 29 August, p. 2; 682nd Meeting, 14 October 1954, pp. 22ff.)

46. See Israel's communication to the UN Secretary General, A/3320, 8 November 1958.

47. In an address on TV on 20 February 1957, President Eisenhower said: "Should a nation which attacks and occupies foreign territory in the face of UN disapproval be allowed to impose conditions on its own withdrawal? If we agree that armed attack can properly achieve the purpose of the assailant, then I fear we will have turned back the clock of international order. . . . If the UN once admits that international disputes can be settled by using force, then we will have destroyed the very foundation of the organization and our best hope of establishing a world order. That would be a disaster for us all. . . . The UN must not fail. I believe that in the interests of peace the UN has no choice but to exert pressure upon Israel to comply with the withdrawal resolutions." (*The New York Times,* 21 February 1957).

48. UN, *Official Records of the First Emergency Session of the General Assembly,* 563rd Plenary Meeting, 3 November 1956, p. 61; 567th Plenary Meeting, 7 November, p. 126; UN *Official Records of the General Assembly,* Eleventh Session, 638th Plenary Meeting, 17 January 1957, pp. 886ff; 639th Plenary Meeting, 17 January, pp. 897ff; 640th Plenary Meeting, 18 January, pp. 919ff; 651st Plenary Meeting, 2 February, p. 1072; 666th Plenary Meeting, 1 March, p. 1275; 668th Plenary Meeting, 8 March, p. 1314; A/3389/Add 1, 24 November 1956; A/3500, 1 December; A/3512, 24 January 1957; A/3527, 11 February; A/3568, 8 March; S/3410, 1 December 1957; *The New York Times,* 7, 9, 15 December 1956; 1, 15, 17, 23, 27 January; 6–27 February; 4–10, 21 March 1957.

49. A/1255, 29 May 1950, p. 2; A/1288, 17 July 1950, p. 13.

50. A/1367, 22 September 1950, p. 44; A/1451, 19 October, p. 20.

51. *The New York Times* reported on 13 May 1967 that Israeli leaders had "decided that the use of force against Syria" might be "the only way to curtail increasing terrorism. . . . The comments being heard [in Israel] in recent weeks, and especially since last weekend [have been] stronger than those usually heard in responsible quarters." Also see: *The New York Times,* 17 May; S/7880, Annex 1; Charles W. Yost, "The Arab-Israeli War: How it Began," *Foreign Affairs* (January 1968): 307.

52. A/PV.1527, 20 June 1967, p. 6.

53. The Egyptian-Israeli Mixed Armistice Commission (MAC) continued to exist even after Israel declared in 1956 that it would no longer recognize and cooperate with it. The MAC continued to operate, but only

on Egyptian territory and with only Egyptian and UN members participating in its activities.

54. S/7896, 19 May 1967; S/7906, 27 May.

55. See Arthur Lall, *The UN and the Middle East Crisis, 1967* (New
York: Columbia University Press, 1968), pp. 2–10, 38ff.

56. Lyndon Baines Johnson, *The Vantage Point: Perspective of the
Presidency* (New York: Holt, Rinehart & Winston, 1971), pp. 293–297;
*The New York Times*, 27–30 May; 2–6, 12 June, 10 July 1967.

57. Franco-Israeli political and military relations had been very close
in the middle and late 1950s. After the Algerian war had ended, France
sought friendlier relations with the Arab world; but it still retained
fairly close ties with Israel until the 1967 war. President De Gaulle was
greatly annoyed because Israel had disregarded the advice he had given
it in late May 1967 not to be the first to initiate large-scale military hostilities. Consequently, Franco-Israeli relations cooled off considerably and
France almost completely stopped selling Israel planes and other weapons
and it stopped providing Israel with political support at the UN.

58. See the statements made by Prime Minister Levi Eshkol and Defense Minister Moshe Dayan as reported by *The New York Times*, 6 June
1967.

59. In the last week of March 1969, the Editorial Board of *New Outlook* (Tel Aviv) and the Israeli Movement for Peace and Security held an
International Symposium on Inevitable War or Initiatives for Peace in an
attempt to publicize these "liberal" views and to try to mobilize Israeli
public opinion against the establishment of Jewish settlements in the occupied areas. Many leading Israeli "liberals," as well as non-Israelis, including the writer, participated in the symposium. See *To Make War or
To Make Peace: Symposium on the Middle East* (Tel Aviv, 1969). *New
Outlook*, originally set up by Mapam in the middle 1950s, has published
numerous articles since the 1967 war by such Israeli "doves" as Yehoshua
Arieli, Simha Flapan, Amnon Kapeliuk, Victor Cygielman, Haim Darin-
Drabkin, and others who criticized the "inflexible" and annexationist poli-
cies of their government and pressed for action to achieve "reconciliation"
with the Arabs. For example, see: Yehoshua Arieli, "What is 'Realistic
Politics?'—a Survey of the Past Year," *New Outlook* (August 1971): 8ff;
Simha Flapan, "The Difficult Dialogue," *New Outlook* (May 1972): 30ff;
Victor Cygielman, "Israel's Illness: The War," *New Outlook* (November 1971): 2. Even David Ben Gurion, some of whose views had, at least
for several years, become more flexible with time, stated in an interview
in the spring of 1971: "Peace, *real* peace, is now the great necessity for
us. It is worth almost any sacrifice." "Sinai? Sharm el-Sheikh? Gaza? The
West Bank? Let them go. Peace is more important than real estate." "As
for security, militarily defensible borders, while desirable, cannot by themselves guarantee our future. *Real* peace with our neighbors—mutual trust
and friendship—that is the only true security." *The Saturday Review*,
3 April 1971, pp. 14, 16.

60. *The New York Times*, 7, 22 October; 1, 6–11, 16 November 1967;
*U.S. News and World Report*, 18 September 1967, p. 67; UPI and AP
Dispatches of 6, 16 October 1967.

61. This remained American official policy at least into 1972. See US Congress, House of Representatives, Ninety-Second Congress, Second Session, 14–23 March 1972, *Foreign Assistance Act of 1972: Hearings Before the Committee on Foreign Affairs,* 14–23 March 1972, p. 96.

62. S/10070, 4 January 1971, Annex I, p. 12.

63. *Ibid.,* p. 8.

64. Personal interviews with Jordanian officials in Amman in the summer of 1969. See also: Edward R. F. Sheehan, "A Visit with Hussein, The Palestinians and Golda Meir," *The New York Times Magazine,* 27 August 1972; and Ahmed Barham, "Amman's Twisted Logic," *New Middle East,* August 1971, p. 23.

65. S/10070, pp. 8, 10; Annex I, pp. 10f, 15ff.

66. *Ibid.,* pp. 4f; Annex I, pp. 5ff.

67. Former American Ambassador to the UN Charles W. Yost wrote in an article ("Last Chance for Peace in the Mid-East") in the 9 April 1971 issue of *Life:* "It has been my strong impression, growing out of the Four Power talks . . . , that the Arabs have in fact been ready for a year and a half to make such a peace and undertake such commitments [as Israel had been demanding 'for more than 20 years']. It is wholly unrealistic for Israel to say . . . that it will not return to the pre-war line even with Egypt. . . . To insist upon . . . extensive territorial demands, and others, is simply to refuse to make a peace settlement on the only terms on which it can be made. . . . " Simha Flapan wrote: "Most objective observers of Israeli policy are drawn to the conclusion that Israel is more interested in gaining time than in winning peace." ("Middle East Brinkmanship," *New Outlook* [December 1971]: 4.) History Professor Yehoshua Arieli contended: "Israel has been less flexible than Egypt in seeking the path to peace" and "no Israeli-Arab peace can be based on annexation and on the refusal to recognize the right of the Palestinians to shape their own destiny." ("What is 'Realistic Politics'?" pp. 8, 11.) Also see: Arieh Yaari, "Peace, Dayan and the Shadow Cabinet," *New Outlook* (March–April 1972): 10; Amnon Rubinstein, "Give Peace a Chance," *New Outlook* (January 1972): 23; S/10070, Annex 1, pp. 6f; *The New York Times,* 23 January 1971. There then were important differences between various Israeli leaders and officials over the territorial issue. In the summer of 1970, the right-wing Gahal party left the government coalition because it opposed any territorial concessions to the Arabs. Reports indicated that some Israeli officials (such as Foreign Minister Abba Eban and Finance Minister Pinhas Sapir) and members of the government coalition (especially from the Mapam party) had been readier to give up much of the occupied territories in return for a peace settlement than Prime Minister Golda Meir, Defense Minister Moshe Dayan, and others had been. (For example, see: *Time,* 21 August 1972, p. 16; Victor Cygielman, "A Disquieting Convention," *New Outlook* (May 1971): 51f; Cygielman, "Hussein's Proposal and the West Bank Municipal Elections: A Post Mortem," *New Outlook* (March–April 1972): 41, 45f; Haim Darin-Drabkin, "Dayan's Moment of Truth," *New Outlook* (5 September 1971): 5ff.

68. See the answer by Secretary General Waldheim (S/PV.1725,

14 June 1973, p. 7) to a question raised by Egypt (S/PV.1721, 11 June, p. 23).

69. Ambassador Yost wrote in *Life* that Egypt had "accepted" the commitments requested by Jarring, while the "Israelis have not." According to Amnon Kapeliuk, "Secretary of State William Rogers had told Sadat during his visit to Cairo last year that in his opinion Egypt had done everything it was obliged to do in order to promote a Near East settlement." ("Student Unrest in Egypt," *New Outlook* [February 1972]: 29, 31.) See also: A/10070/Add 2, 5 March 1971, p. 4.

70. A/10070/Add 2, 5 March 1971, p. 4.

71. Also see: S/PV.1721, 11 June 1973, p. 23; S/PV.1723, 12 June, pp. 18ff; S/PV.1725, 14 June, p. 7; S/PV.1728, 15 June, p. 42.

72. According to Simha Flapan ("Middle East Brinkmanship," p. 4), "the fact remains that the Israeli Government is held responsible by nearly everybody, including her friends, for the failure of Dr. Jarring's Mission." Also see: Rubinstein, "Give Peace a Chance"; Mordechai Bentov, "Israel Must State Its Proposals Now," *New Outlook* (February 1972): 9.

73. It was reported in *Newsweek,* 6 December 1971, p. 43, that "the Nixon Administration regards Israeli inflexibility as the main cause of the diplomatic stalemate that has afflicted the Middle East for the last four years." *The New York Times,* 13 February, 1 December 1971; *Newsweek,* 26 April 1971, p. 39; Yost (*Life* article). Also see *The New York Times* editorials of 8, 20 April; 8, 18 October 1971.

74. Even American officials began to concede the need to take the Palestine Arabs into consideration. For example, Assistant Secretary of State Joseph E. Sisco stated in an interview on 8 June 1972: "We don't see how a peace agreement that is stable and will stick can be achieved unless the legitimate concerns of the Palestinians have been met." *The New Middle East* (July 1972): 5.

75. Israeli historian Arieli held: "No Israeli-Arab peace can be based . . . on the refusal to recognize the right of the Palestinians to shape their own destiny." ("What Is 'Realistic Politics'," p. 11.) See also: Yaari, "Peace, Dayan and the Shadow Cabinet," pp. 11ff; Nahum Shur, "The King, the Palestinians and Ourselves," *New Outlook* (September 1971): 19ff; Kurt Kanowitz, "Back to Jarring," *New Outlook* (January–February 1971): 42; Rosh Hashana, "Editor's Notes," *New Outlook* (September 1971): 3; Nissim Rejwan, "Voices from the West Bank," *New Outlook* (September 1971): 4ff. In an interview in early 1971, even former Prime Minister Ben Gurion "repeated again and again": "Remember, this land belongs to two peoples—the Arabs of Palestine and the Jews of the world." He also believed that "the refugees clearly have rights which have been far too long denied and must be justly and promptly dealt with." *The Saturday Review,* 3 April 1971, pp. 14f.

76. See the report of the UN Secretary General, S/10929, 18 May 1973, pp. 37f.

77. *Ibid.,* p. 38.

78. S/PV.1735, 26 July 1973, pp. 57–61.

79. *UN Weekly News Summary* (WS/624), 14 September 1973, p. 2; *The New York Times,* 5 September 1973.

80. On the basis of an interview with Ralph Bunche, former Acting Mediator for the UN in the Middle East, Forsythe stated: "No less an expert on this [Arab-Israeli] conflict than Bunche believes that a settlement was possible in the early months of 1949 if governmental pressure had been brought to bear in support of the CCP." Forsythe, *United Nations Peacemaking*, p. 159.

81. Despite the urgings of the CCP, the American government applied serious pressure only on one occasion, and even this was so "hastily withdrawn" that it "impaired future United States influence," weakened the CCP "since it discredited the Commission's most powerful member," and encouraged Israel to continue to refuse making significant concessions because she became convinced that the United States would refrain from applying truly effective and persistent pressures on her. (*Ibid.*, p. 53. See also de Azcarate, *Mission*, p. 164.)

82. UN Secretary General Kurt Waldheim noted in the introduction to his annual report to the 1972 session of the General Assembly that, since the UN was not an independent sovereign organization with independent powers of its own but was an association of sovereign states, "its failure was their [member states'] failures." *The New York Times*, 4 August 1972.

83. *Ibid.*, 21 September 1971.

84. After the October 1973 war, even Israel began to recognize the very helpful role UN peacekeeping forces can play.

85. The UN resolution of 25 October establishing UNEF did not indicate how long this force would remain in existence and who had the authority to terminate its existence. Egypt had reserved her sovereign rights while admitting UNEF to be stationed on her territory. On 27 October the Security Council approved a "Report of the Secretary General on the Implementation of Security Council Resolution 340 (1973)" (S/11052/Rev.1) which estimated the cost of UNEF at "approximately $30,000,000 for a Force of 7,000, all ranks, for a period of six months" and which stated that the "costs of the Force shall be considered as expenses of the [UN] Organization to be borne by the Members in accordance with Article 17, paragraph 2, of the Charter." There is uncertainty as to what would happen to UNEF if a big power were to veto another appropriation at the end of the six months. There would appear to be a far better chance of ensuring a long term life for UNEF once a final peace settlement had been reached. Until then, UNEF's future could remain uncertain.

86. N. Bar-Yaacov, *The Israeli-Syrian Armistice: Problems of Implementation, 1949–1966* (Jerusalem, Magnes Press, Hebrew University, 1967), pp. 319f. See also pp. 286 and 337.

# Israel and Jewish-Arab Peace

*Governmental and Nongovernmental Approaches*

**Aharon Cohen**

THE overall picture of Jewish-Arab relationships is one of unsual complexity. The very structure of this book is, to an extent, indicative of this. Is it mere coincidence that the Arab viewpoint is represented here only by a single author? Anybody in the least familiar with the situation is aware that the political views of Egypt, Jordan-Palestine, Syria, and Lebanon are by no means identical. Is it only for technical reasons that the "Arab" chapter says so little about Arab efforts for peace before 1967?

In Israeli public life, the issues of peace and security, like all other political issues, are the subject of open and endless discussion. This is one expression of Israel's democratic character. The internal discussion on the issues of war and peace helps to determine the country's social and moral image. This is what

Aharon Cohen was born in Russia in 1910. Settling in Palestine in 1929, he was a founder-member of Kibbutz Sha'ar Ha'amakim, where he still lives and works. He served in various positions in the kibbutz movement, the Histadrut, and the Jewish national movement, both in Palestine and abroad. He was a founder, and longtime head, of the Arab Department of the left-Zionist Hashomer Hatzair Movement (later the Mapam Party) and from 1941 to 1948 was secretary of the League for Jewish-Arab Rapprochement and Cooperation.

Since the midfifties Mr. Cohen has concentrated on research, writing, and teaching on the Arab world and Jewish-Arab relations. His publications include: *Culture and Education in the Arab World* (Hebrew, 1944); *The Jewish Question and the Problem of Palestine* (Arabic, 1945); *The Arab Workers Movement* (Hebrew, 1947); *The Arab East* (Hebrew, 1955; Arabic edition, 1970); *The Contemporary Arab World* (Hebrew, 1958); *Political Developments in the Arab World* (Hebrew, 1959); *Our Arab Neighbors* (Hebrew, 1969); and *Israel and the Arab World* (Hebrew, 1964; English edition, New York, Funk & Wagnalls, 1970).

enables us to deal in the following pages with both official and nongovernmental Israeli peace efforts.

We intend to deal with them on three levels. First we discuss the historical background to the conflict. Then follows an explanation of the situation as seen through official Israeli eyes and expressed in government policy, which set out from the assumption that "there is no partner on the other side for peace efforts," "there is therefore no realistic alternative policy to replace that which the Israelis were forced to adopt," etc. Finally we evaluate Israeli circles (and their Jewish supporters abroad) who criticize the lack of bold peace initiatives on Israel's part and who, rejecting the fatalistic attitude on both sides, believe in a practical and progressive alternative Israeli peace policy.

## It Did Not Begin in June 1967

In order to leave no room for error (which is often common in Arab and other circles), it should be emphasized that the British rule did not bring the Jews to Palestine, nor did they "create" the problem under discussion. Indeed they used and "developed" it for their own ends. Since what is known as the Destruction of the Second Temple in the year 70 A.D., the living connection between the Jewish people and its historical homeland was not severed. For hundreds of years—in fact, up to the Crusade massacres—the Jews constituted a considerable part of the country's population, enjoying autonomy as a religion and as a people. Whenever this was possible, waves of Jewish immigration reached Palestine. The organized modern return of the Jews to their ancestral home began several decades before British rule in Palestine. Historically, it can be said that the British arrived in Palestine and imposed their rule over it at a time when the Jewish national movement, one of the historical claimants to the country, had already become an indisputable element there. British policy exploited the movement, giving it limited support, in the same way as it supported other national movements (including the Arab national movement), using them for its own ends.

It cannot be overlooked that at least from the end of the nineteenth century there were *two* historically substantive claims to Palestine. The *Arab* claim asserted that after the Islamic conquests in the seventh century, the country became part of their heritage and that at the end of the nineteenth century over half a million Arabs lived in the areas on both sides of the Jordan included in the British mandate after World War I. The *Jewish* claim arose from the fact that for almost two thousand years they never ceased to regard the country as the land of their national-cultural past and as the place to which they hoped to return, the place where they would gain their national and social freedom, in the same way as other nations strive toward these ends.

On the eve of World War I there were almost 700,000 Arabs in the country (on both sides of the Jordan). The number of Jews, whose population had doubled in the last quarter of the nineteenth century to 40,000, had redoubled by the beginning of World War I, to 85,000. In Jerusalem the Jews had constituted a majority since the middle of the nineteenth century.

### The Third Encounter Between the Two Peoples

The Jews and Arabs did not meet for the first time at the end of the nineteenth century. The *first encounter* of these two ancient peoples took place 3,000 years ago, 1,500 years before the western European states came into being and 2,000 years before the eastern European states crystallized.

When the Islamic empire was established and the far-flung Arab empire expanded after the death of Muhammad to include the vast majority (80–90 precent) of the Jewish people at that time within its borders, this marked, in a way, the beginning of the *second encounter* between the two peoples. The second encounter between the Jews and the Arabs was, in the main, a relatively better and more fruitful relationship than most in Jewish diaspora history. Jewish-Arab cooperation was particularly productive, for example, in the Jewish centers in Babylon and Egypt and especially during the "Andalusian period," when Arab culture in Spain reached its peak and Hebrew culture attained heights unequalled for over a thousand years. The golden age of the Jewish-Arab symbiosis not only contributed most significantly to the development of the two peoples themselves, but also provided a strong stimulus to general cultural advancement. The Jews were not confined to helping create a greater Arab culture; they also served as the intermediaries between the Arabs and the rest of Europe. By translating the wealth of Arab scientific and philosophical works into Latin and other European languages, they played a vital role in the awakening and rise of Europe. When Muslim rule in Spain ended with the conquest of Granada, both Jews and Muslims shared a common fate: expulsion (1492).

With the degeneration of the Ottoman empire (from the seventeenth century), the countries of the Middle East sank into a period of cultural sterility. Arab creativity withered and Jewish-Arab cooperation declined. For several centuries the Arabs virtually vanished from the world scene, while the center of Jewish life shifted to Europe. The Jews in the Islamic countries were left on the byroads of history.

The encounter between these two peoples, who were at the time the most important in the "East," [1] and whose cooperation had contributed so much to the cultural development of all mankind, was to be renewed during their awakening many years later, when each aspired, in its own way, subject to its own new historical circumstances, to regain its national independence and restore its former glory. Unfortunately, this *third encounter* also took place at a time of imperialism and chauvinism, which marked this encounter and to a large extent determined its development and consequences.

## Background to the Poisoned Relations in Recent Generations

Progressive elements in the Arab world (and they are not the only ones) lose a great deal by seeing the Jewish national movement (or, by its short name, "Zionism") in the light of superficial, and often, therefore, demagogic propaganda, without really becoming acquainted with it. However, every thinking person should consider this. We are dealing with the national movement of a relatively small people, scattered over the four corners of the earth—a movement that began from almost nothing, without a territorial base, with no framework of national organization, with no recognized status in the international arena, no means, no political or land settlement experience. How did such a movement reach within two or three generations an achievement like the sovereign state of Israel, an equal member in the family of nations?

This phenomenon cannot be understood without appreciating the historical roots of this movement, created by a people with an ancient civilization, a movement that was the fruit of qualities nurtured and augmented through pain and suffering during continual wanderings among the various cultures. It is necessary to appreciate its high idealism, exemplary dedication, devotion, and readiness for self-criticism. Special importance should be attributed to the avoidance of laying failures at someone else's door, as well as to the practical talents which blessed the movement at its start. Possibly its characteristics were such because of the very fact that the movement did not yet have any material or territorial base, and these had to be created from scratch.

At all events, forty years passed between the arrival of the first Jewish immigrants in Palestine in the last quarter of the nineteenth century, as the pioneers of the Palestine-oriented Jewish national movement, and the start of British rule in Palestine (1918). Research into Jewish-Arab relations before British rule, as well as at the beginning of the mandate, may provide sufficient material to confirm the assumption that had the Arabs and Jews encountered one another *by themselves,* as they had earlier in history, they might have been able to come to an understanding and might have managed to cooperate. The Jewish revival in Palestine could have then integrated peacefully with the movement for the revival and freedom of the whole area. There is a great deal of evidence (which cannot be even briefly presented here) [2] to show that the return of the Jews to Palestine was initially well received by many local Arabs and important contemporary Arab leaders. Although it sounds fantastic today, it is an historical fact that a representative of the Zionist Bureau, which was then situated in Istanbul, participated in the first Arab

National Congress in Paris in June 1913 as an invited guest. A joint Zionist-Arab conference was due to meet in Lebanon in summer 1914, but World War I intervened. We know not only of the Faisal-Weizmann Agreement of 1919 but also that in 1922, after the mandate had taken effect, serious negotiations were held in Egypt between Jewish and Arab representatives. The negotiations were on the threshold of success, when last-minute British intervention set them at nought.[3] Similar endeavors over the years show that these were not merely isolated instances. Unfortunately, therefore, Jewish-Arab relations were poisoned in recent generations by national hatred which external elements fostered for their own interests.

This had already begun under Turkish rule. The growing Arab national movement (similar movements were also on the increase among the other nations in the Ottoman empire) was set on seceding from the Ottoman empire or at least gaining a measure of cultural and administrative autonomy for the Arab provinces. The Ottoman rulers attempted to block it by developing the notorious "fasad." [4]

The Turks carried out the task fairly primitively, but the superb professionalism of the British turned it into an art.[5] It is interesting that despite the differences of opinion between the Jews and the Arabs in Palestine, both communities were united in their opinion that "British policy—both in what it did and did not do in Palestine—had a large share in exacerbating the national conflict in the country." [6]

A close analysis of Palestine policy during British rule indicates that the policy and conduct of Jewish and Arab leaders at the time was, to a large extent, a function of British policy and its basic tendencies. And when the British mandate ended and the state of Israel was established in the late 1940s, the cold war had begun, so Israel-Arab relations increasingly became a function of that.

The vital historical interests of the reborn state of Israel and the Jewish people, scattered throughout the countries of both the superpower blocs, made it necessary for Israel to adopt a policy of scrupulous neutrality and nonalignment. This was, indeed, the declared policy of the first Israeli government (the provisional government that took office when the state of Israel was declared on 14 May 1948). However, it did not take long for the government, under Ben Gurion, to deviate from this position (over the Korea issue in the summer of 1950). In its search for security in the guise of military guarantees and alliances, the government started consistently to join the western powers. While opposition in the neighboring Arab states to being drawn into the global confrontation grew, the orientation of Israeli policy became decidedly pro-western. This orientation was to lead to the links with France and Great Britain in the Suez-Sinai campaign in autumn 1956, the failure of which removed Britain and France as the dominating elements in the area. They were replaced by the United States. The growing international polarization drew Israel ever closer to the United States, while the leading Arab states established closer links with the USSR, and the rest of the Communist bloc. This total divergence in the international arena could only lead to deteriorating relations between Israel and Egypt, Syria, and the other Arab countries which adopted a similar policy. A similar difference in orientation between Egypt and such other Arab states as Nuri as-Sa'id's Iraq led to severe tension, which is still far from being forgotten. Yet Nuri as-Sa'id was not a Zionist Jew, but a Sunni Muslim, one of the standard-bearers of the Arab national movement as early as Turkish times.

## A Chapter of Vital Significance

After much conflict in the Jewish-Arab-British triangle, the Palestine issue reached the highest international forum, the United Nations General Assembly, in 1947. A representative UN commission held investigations for several months in Palestine, the neighboring Arab countries, and Europe, where they saw the results of the Nazi holocaust, and submitted a well-founded and reasoned report. The General Assembly heard the Arab and Jewish representatives and discussed all aspects of the problem at length. It delivered its recommendations on 29 November 1947: by a majority of thirty-three votes for (including the USA, and the USSR), thirteen against, and ten abstentions, the supreme international organ resolved that the country would be partitioned into two independent states, one Jewish and the other Arab, and that Jerusalem would be internationalized, with all three units enjoying a degree of economic unity. Of the 27,000 square kilometers of territory west of the Jordan, 15,850 square kilometers were allocated to the Jews (of which over 9,500 square kilometers, almost two-thirds, were in the Negev wastes). According to Jewish Agency sources, of the 865,000 population in the area allocated to the Jewish state, there were about 515,000 Jews and about 350,000 Arabs (including about 40,000 Bedouins, 92,000 urban residents, and about 200,000, or 70 percent, rural residents). The area of the planned Jewish state was divided into three regions, linked only by two narrow strips, and it had to bear the burden of giving financial assistance to the planned Arab state. For the sake of finding a way out of the dead end that faced Palestine policy, the Jews—all political groupings—accepted the United Nations resolution as the binding decision of the highest international moral and political authority. No responsible Jewish leader considered changing these difficult and unfavorable conditions by force. Had the Arabs adopted a similar position, the Palestine question would have been well on the way to a constructive solution and the Arab-Jewish rupture could have been healed. The proposed economic links between the Jewish and Arab states could have served as a bridge to the reunification of the country as the common homeland of the Jews returning to their homeland and the Arab people living in it. The continual struggle could have thus been replaced by potentially fruitful cooperation for the benefit of the two peoples and the entire region.

What did the partition plan mean to the Arab world? Of the 11.5 million square kilometers covered by the Arab countries (a million square kilometers more than Europe up to the Urals), 16,000 square kilometers (0.7 percent) were set aside for the Jewish state. Of the 50–60 million Arabs at that time, 350,000 (a little more than 0.5 percent) were to be a national minority in a Jewish state, which, surrounded by Arab countries, would need to live in peace with them. However, the Arab leaders rejected the UN Resolution outright and without waiting for the judgment of history it can be fairly stated that they made a fateful political error.

When Jewish representatives tried, at the eleventh hour, to take the matter up with the secretary general of the Arab League in an effort to prevent bloodshed and war and to reach a peaceful solution, he replied: "The proposed plan may be logical, but the fate of nations is not decided by rational reasoning. . . . For us there is only one test, the test of strength. . . . the problem can apparently only be solved by force of arms. . . . We will try to rout you." [7] In his speech in Philadelphia on 2 December 1947, a few days after the UN resolution, Professor Chaim Weizmann said: "Bombs and threats from the neighboring countries will not frighten us; we stretch our hand out to the Arabs in peace, and suggest that they think hard before they reject it." *Al Wahda,* the newspaper of the Husseini Party (the dominant Palestinian Arab party), responded to the UN resolution as follows: "What was written in black at Lake Success will be erased in red in Palestine." [8]

The Arab leaders were encouraged by Britain's open opposition to the resolution and by the equivocal American policy—the US had voted for the partition plan in November 1947, but immediately afterwards began to withdraw its support and by the General Assembly session in April 1948 even went so far as to try frustrating the resolution.[9] (The US later imposed an arms embargo on Israel at the most critical time, while the Arabs were receiving a plentiful supply.) Refusing to accept the judgment of the nations, the Arabs elected to go to war. The Jews, irrespective of their political persuasion, had therefore no alternative but to fight in self-defense for their very survival, which embodied the hopes and aspirations of the whole Jewish people.

The armed conflict up to the end of the British mandate (15 May 1948) proved that the Jews of Palestine would not submit to threats and were firmly resolved to implement the UN resolution, come what may. When the British mandate ended, the Jews held most of the territories allocated by the General Assembly to the Jewish state. The Arab leaders and their foreign supporters could still have accepted partition, which had become a reality, thus settling the issue peacefully on the basis of the UN resolution. However, the Arab Higher Committee, led by the former mufti Haj Amin al-Husseini, and the rulers of the Arab states were seduced by the assurances of British experts that there was no possibility that the Jewish irregular forces, lacking heavy military equipment, could hold out against the regular Arab armies for longer than two weeks at most. Even two weeks struck some "experts" as an exaggerated estimate.[10]

On 12 April 1948, the Arab League decided to invade Palestine with the regular armies of the Arab states on the day the mandate ended. Abd-er-Rahman Azzam, the Arab League secretary, announced on 15 May 1948, at a press conference recorded by the BBC, that "this war will be a war of annihilation, and the slaughter taking place will be remembered like the Mongol invasion and the Crusades." [11]

The next few months were to prove that when full-scale warfare began, with the intervention of the Arab regular armies and involving the political and strategic interests of world powers, it was no longer an exclusively Arab-Jewish affair. The Palestine war became part of the international political scene, in which the Arab supporters were no longer the only deciding factors. The kings of Egypt, Jordan, and Iraq, who were known to be amenable to British influence, were the prime movers behind the Arab armies' invasion of Palestine. Paralleling the help that the Arabs received directly from Britain, was help coming to the Jews from another direction.

War has its own laws, and he who declares war should not think that death and destruction will be visited only on the other side. Self-defense and self-preservation dictate that the defenders must obtain help from any possible source and must go from defense to offense as soon as possible, must beat the invaders in battle and drive them as far as possible from the defenders' boundaries. In view of the international alignment after World War II, Israel was not abandoned to its fate. Seven years before the well-known Egyptian-Czech arms deal in fall 1955, the newborn state of Israel received arms from Czechoslovakia (in the spring of 1948), which played a vital role in maintaining the state of Israel. In the diplomatic sphere, the Soviet Union provided a bulwark for Israel as it fought for its life. During the Security Council session on 29 May 1948, the Soviet representative, Andrei Gromyko, declared that "what is happening in Palestine can only be defined as a military campaign organized by a number of states against the new Jewish state," and that "this is not the first time that the Arab states, the organizers of the invasion, have alienated themselves from a UN Security Council or General Assembly resolution." Aid from the Communist bloc enabled Israel to defend its life in the decisive test, strengthened it by a flow of Jewish immigrants (including men with important military experience) from eastern Europe, while the Communist spokesmen defended the young state's vital interests within the United Nations.

All this is now a thing of the past. Much has changed in Israel, in the Arab world, and on the international scene. The means used to resolve the imbroglio were, and still are, filled with bloodshed and suffering. However, any discussion of possible solutions to current problems must take this period into account as background for subsequent problems and developments.

### The Facts About the Beginning

Whether in terms of "à la guerre comme à la guerre" or in terms of declared (and practiced) Arab policy, it will not be easy to deny the course of official Israeli policy.

The absence of an open and militant opposition to governmental policy in the Arab countries vis-à-vis Israel makes it difficult to point to a practicable alternative policy in Israel. The vast majority of the Israeli public regards their government's policy as the only realistic one that can be adopted. Moreover, without a complete acceptance by the Arab countries of Israel as a permanent part of the regional fabric, their understanding of Israel's social and political structure, and of its internal struggles, must remain limited. If they are even partially aware of the existence of forces opposed to official policy in Israel, their own experience in the Arab countries makes it difficult for them to understand the workings of Israeli political democracy and the scope that exists in a democratic society for influencing government policy. Just as individuals judge others in terms of their own natures, so they frequently gauge political life elsewhere by their own local experience. Furthermore, while extremists in Israel are supported by the declarations of their counterparts in

the Arab countries (and vice versa), there is no similar cooperation between people genuinely seeking peace and understanding
on both sides of the front. The lack of possibilities for direct contact between Israelis and the residents of the neighboring countries is a primary cause of this state of affairs. Both parties to the
conflict have to bear the heavy cost of the "asymmetry" in the
political struggle. No purpose can be served by detailing the
endless and hated controversy, based on legal, historical, moral,
and logical arguments with which both sides have equipped themselves so fully over the years. Arguments and counterarguments
cannot refute hard, unequivocal facts, which from the Israeli
point of view formed the real framework for the conflict, at least
during the twenty-year period 1947–1967.

First, the independent state of Israel was declared in May 1948
in conformity with the UN partition resolution. The Declaration
of Independence included the following paragraph: "We extend
the hand of peace and good neighborliness to all the states around
us and to their peoples, and we call upon them to co-operate in
mutual helpfulness with the independent Jewish nation in its
land. The state of Israel is prepared to make its contribution in a
concerted effort for the advancement of the entire Middle
East." [12] The invasion of Palestine by the regular Arab armies,
and their assault on the state of Israel the day after its establishment, forced Israel, in self-defense, to deviate from the borders
laid down by the United Nations in November 1947.

Second, the letter by the Israeli Foreign Minister Moshe
Sharett, on 6 August 1948, to the United Nations mediator,
Count Bernadotte, requested him to transmit to the Arab governments "our offer that their representatives should meet with
the representatives of the provisional government of Israel for the
purpose of peace negotiations," [13] but the offer went unheeded.

And third, in the first (Political) Committee of the UN General Assembly on 15 November 1948, the Israeli foreign minister
repeated this offer: "We are ever ready to negotiate, just as we
are ready to withstand any hardship and burden of continued warfare if it is forced upon us." He added that "Israel would be willing to negotiate, at a general peace conference, the future of the
Arab refugees, whom their leaders had incited to decamp." [14]
This call, too, went unanswered by the Arab governments.

The war continued, with truces, until the armistice agreements, which were signed on the same essential basis between Israel and Egypt (24 February 1949), Lebanon (23 March 1949), the kingdom of Jordan (3 April 1949), and Syria (2 July 1949). "It is not the fault of the Jews," stated J. Malik, the Soviet delegate to the UN Security Council during the second debate on accepting Israel as a member nation, "that the area held by Israel is not according to the map" (made up by the United Nations in their decision to partition Palestine). Further, concerning the question of Arab refugees, he said that "the responsibility for their condition is to be borne by those who incited war between Jews and Arabs."

On 11 May 1949, the UN General Assembly voted to admit Israel as a member nation, thereby, as it were, actually confirming the comments of the Soviet delegate.

The armistice agreements were designed as a first step toward peace. Their preamble stated their primary function: "to facilitate the transition from the present truce to permanent peace in Palestine." Article I (3) provides that "the rights of each of the parties to security and freedom from fear and attack by the armed forces of the other party" will be fully respected. Articles II and III provide that "no element of the land, sea or air military or para-military forces of either party, including non-regular forces, shall commit any warlike or hostile act against the military or para-military forces of the other party, or against civilians in territory under the control of that party."

When the Conciliation Commission for Palestine (CCP), which was constituted by the UN General Assembly on 11 December 1948, called the Lausanne Conference in April 1949, the government of Israel submitted a memorandum calling for real peace between Israel and its neighbors, respect for the security, freedom, and sovereignty of each state, and for the agreements to be regarded as a springboard to normal diplomatic relations and general cooperation between the parties, in the spirit of the UN Charter.[15] The Israeli delegation made several goodwill gestures during the conference, which lasted until September 1949: it expressed Israel's readiness to allow members of certain families who had been cut off from their relatives during the war to return to the country; it agreed to pay compensation for abandoned Arab lands that had been cultivated prior to the hostilities; it declared itself willing to discuss the release of Arab refugee accounts frozen in Israeli banks; and finally, the Israeli delegation announced the government's willingness to repatriate to Israel up to 100,000 Arab refugees as a contribution to the solution of the problem (their number was estimated at the time as approximately 600,000).

Addressing the UN General Assembly on 11 May 1949, following Israel's admission to the United Nations, the Israeli foreign minister voiced Israel's conviction that "despite the Arab attack on Israel that followed the Arab rejection of General Assembly Resolution of 29 November 1947, there are no problems between Israel and the Arab states which cannot be resolved by peaceful negotiations." In a letter to the chairman of the CCP on 8 May 1950, the Israeli foreign minister reiterated Israel's position on peace negotiations: "The government of Israel requires no concessions or undertakings in advance of such negotiations, it being understood that any party having claims to make will be entitled to put them forward in the course of the negotiations." [16]

The Israeli foreign minister renewed this offer in the Political Committee of the General Assembly on 30 November 1950 and before the General Assembly itself on 14 December 1950. On the second occasion, he added: "It is the firm conviction of my government that peace can be attained only by direct negotiations, but they have been emphatically rejected by the Arab governments concerned. We, for our part, have found it impossible to conceive that a government which refuses to talk to its neighbor, even to sit with him at one table, should be in a mood to reach a peace settlement with him. Needless to say, the mere adoption of a procedure of direct negotiations does not, in itself, guarantee success. Negotiations may prove futile. Yet the absence of negotiations, nay, the expressed refusal to negotiate, certainly predetermines failure." [17]

Similar Israeli statements were made in the years that followed. It was disastrous for *both* sides to the conflict that objective circumstances now frustrated any joint efforts to break the ice by understanding, tolerance, and far-sightedness. This pushed both parties towards the conviction that the imbroglio could be resolved only by the sword, whether it belonged to the party involved or was supplied by others. There were three main circumstances involved.

The first was that the Arab representatives signed the Protocol of 12 May 1949, in which their delegations in Lausanne agreed that the document attached to the Protocol—the map of Palestine attached to the UN General Assembly Resolution of 29 November 1947, indicating the areas allocated to the Jewish and Arab states in Palestine—should serve as a basis to the CCP's discussions with the two parties. In so doing they recognized in principle the partition of Palestine on the basis of the UN resolution and the existence of the state of Israel. However, they did not have the courage to go any further towards solving the practical problems created by partition and the establishment of the state of Israel, by recognizing Israel and opening negotiations with her.

The real reason the Arab world could not discuss the borders of Israel seriously was that the Arab states disagreed among themselves on the fate of those areas of Palestine that were beyond the borders of the Jewish state. In their heart of hearts, the Arab leaders did not accept the existence of Israel, but after first rejecting the UN resolution by force of arms in an attempt to prevent its implementation, they then appeared as its upholders and proponents in all aspects unfavorable to Israel's position. This was the Arabs' weak point.

The second circumstance was that the state of Israel was reborn, so to speak, on the edge of an abyss, only a hairsbreadth away from destruction. The powerful forces that gave rise to the feeling of back-to-the-wall (or sea) self-defense, with the pendulum swinging for the Jewish people between the hopes of generations on the one hand, and the fear of destruction on the other, could not change the objective facts: it was a country with 0.05 percent of the world's population, with few natural resources, and surrounded on all its land borders by neighbors (with more than fifty times the population) who openly declared their intention of wiping it out.

The third circumstance was the outbreak of the cold war in the international arena. The major world powers, while claiming laudable humanitarian aims, were only too ready to exploit the conflict for their own ends, with all the implications this involved for the peoples of the area.

For the government of Israel these were the circumstances which in a large measure dictated its policy. Israel's security problems, in contrast to other countries, were not questions of territory, borders, or sovereignty, but the issue of sheer physical existence. Not only Israel's existence was at stake, but, in Israeli eyes, the future hopes of the Jewish people throughout the world. Experience had taught this ancient, much-afflicted people, which had only just emerged from the most terrible holocaust in its history, that it dare not show weakness, as weakness invites disaster.

## The Israeli Government's Policy Towards Peace

The government of Israel claims that it made repeated attempts to reach an understanding first of all with Egypt. On 18 August 1952, shortly after the July coup in Egypt, Ben Gurion welcomed the new regime there and expressing the hope for "a free, independent, progressive Egypt," he stated: "There was not at any time, nor is there now, any reason for strife between Egypt and Israel . . . no occasion for political, economic or territorial conflict between the two neighbors." The government of Israel has more than once stated its conviction that "the only hope of achieving the purpose of the armistice agreements lies in giving effect to their central provision—namely, the effecting of a transition to permanent peace." [18] "A permanent peace depends on [our neighbors] alone—on our part we are always ready for it." [19] When the Arab states accused Israel of wanting "total peace or nothing," Moshe Sharett, the prime minister and foreign minister replied: "On a number of occasions, both in public statements and by direct contact, Israeli representatives expressed readiness to explore the possibilities of partial advance towards final peace, but Arab reaction—where there was any reaction—was negative. Israel has always expressed readiness to pay compensation for lands abandoned by Arabs, without setting as an absolute condition the attainment of final peace; we offered to conclude a nonaggression treaty as an improvement on the armistice agreements and a prelude to peace. Has there ever been a response?" [20]

On 30 June 1954 Sharett promised Egypt to solve its problems of communications with other Arab countries through Israel.[21] Israel would have been willing to "grant Jordan free port facilities at Haifa as part of a general peace settlement as soon as the Jordanians stop the boycott and open their country to trade with Israel. . . . Such an arrangement was even possible in the absence of a formal peace settlement." [22]

"The original position of the government of Israel was that the question of compensation for abandoned Arab lands was one aspect of the larger problem, i.e., a general Israel-Arab settlement. Subsequently, because of the humanitarian nature of the refugee problem, my government announced that it was prepared to enter into discussion on compensation with any appropriate United Nations organ, in advance of any general settlement." [23]

Whatever the arguments put forward against the government of Israel, such direct, public statements were unheard of from the Arab leaders at the time. Page after page could be filled with statements by national leaders, prime ministers, ministers, editors, and other prominent personalities from the Arab countries who almost seemed to compete with each other in expressing hostility and threats towards Israel. It is true that not all of them went so far as King Saud, who declared that "the Arab nations must be prepared to sacrifice up to 10 million out of their 50 million human beings, if necessary, in order to wipe out Israel. . . . It must be uprooted like a cancer." [24] Even a man like Faris al-Khouri, who held office several times as Syria's prime minister, foreign minister, and ambassador to the United Nations, declared that "Syria, Iraq, and Egypt must agree among themselves upon a united plan that will enable them to bring about the annihilation of Israel." [25] Unable to implement these threats, the Arab leaders tried to undermine Israel by an economic boycott and blockade, economic isolation, "cold war," and harassment through sending marauders into Israel to undermine its internal security.

In the face of its neighbors' policy, the government of Israel felt that the security of the state could be best guaranteed by strengthening the Israel Defense Forces (Zahal). It set out to make Zahal an army of the people, especially deeply rooted in the border settlements and outstanding as regards its organization, training, dedication, and resourcefulness. As far as possible, the government also made sure that if the army had to fight, it would not do so empty-handed.

In general, the government of Israel did not respond to its neighbors' provocation by using the same indiscriminate methods against the civilian population, but chose "deterrent retaliation." When complaints to the United Nations observers proved fruitless, a localized military response followed, whose force was much greater than the extent of the provocation. The reprisal frequently took the form of dramatic incidents (for which Israel was repeatedly censured by the Security Council): the Qibya incident in Jordan, 14 October 1953; Gaza, 28 February 1955; east of the sea of Galilee, 11 December 1955; Kalkiliyah, in the kingdom of Jordan, not far from Tel Aviv, 10 October 1956; Tawafik in Syria, 1 February 1960; Nuqaib, on the Syrian border, 16 March 1962; Almagor, 14 July 1966; Samo'a, in Jordan, 13 November 1966. The reprisal raids, some of which aroused strong criticism in Israel, not only fanned the flames of Arab hostility towards Israel, but also spurred the Arabs to increase their armaments, which in turn forced Israel to step up its own unending efforts to fortify its military strength. This chain reaction led in due course to the Sinai operation.

In fall 1956, the Sinai campaign took place. It is no secret that this war led to marked differences of opinion in Israel. However, the government of Egypt had no justification for complaint. It is a fact that Egyptian representatives in the UN General Assembly and Security Council had expressly stated (Mahmud Fawzi, on 16 July 1951; Abd-ul-Hamid Galeb, on 16 December 1954; Mahmud Azmi, on 13 March 1955) that Egypt still regarded itself at war with Israel, despite the outspoken resolution by the Security Council on 1 September 1951 that a state of war was inimical to the armistice agreements.

The Security Council, in its resolution of 1 September 1951, specifically called on Egypt to end its restrictions on the passage of commercial vessels and their cargoes via the Suez Canal, whatever their destination might be, and to refrain from all interference with the movements of ships, apart from measures necessary for the safety of the ships themselves in the canal, and to preserve the existing international agreements.

Egypt ignored the Security Council resolution and continued to prevent Israeli shipping from using the canal. It maintained that the armistice agreements, though marking a *pause* in the acts of belligerency, did not bring to an end the existing state of war between the parties, which could be ended only by a peace treaty. There would be no peace treaty, the Egyptians maintained, so long as Israel did not implement the United Nations Assembly resolutions (of 11 December 1948) concerning the repatriation of the refugees and the payment of compensation to those who preferred not to return. Egypt not only sealed off the Suez Canal to Israeli shipping, but for seven years it stopped Israeli ships from leaving and entering the Israeli port of Eilat via the Red Sea.

The government of Israel often showed great forbearance in the face of the provocations from across the border and the attacks on civilians. However, as the border situation worsened, the government declared that "it is prepared to faithfully observe every jot and tittle of the armistice agreements, both their letter and spirit, but the other side is also obliged to do so. An agreement breached by the other side will not be binding on us. If the armistice lines across the border are opened to terrorists and killers, they will not remain closed to the defenders at the gates. If our rights are infringed by violence on land or at sea, we shall preserve our freedom of action to defend our rights in the most effective way." [26]

In this respect, Egypt could complain only that it was not permitted to forestall Israel. When the late Abd ul-Hakim Amir was Egyptian chief of staff, he declared (in Alexandria on 11 June 1956) that "the Israeli danger no longer exists. The Egyptian army is strong enough to wipe Israel off the map of the country." On 24 October 1956 Egypt, Jordan, and Syria announced the formation of a joint command under Abd ul-Hakim Amir. The commander of the Jordanian Arab Legion, Ali Abu Nawar, declared that "the time has come when the Arabs can choose the correct moment to begin an offensive to destroy Israel." On 29 October 1956 Israeli forces began the Sinai campaign. This was coordinated with the French and British governments who, in response to Nasser's nationalization of the Suez Canal, decided to overthrow his government.

Whatever motivations are ascribed to the government of Israel, it cannot be overlooked that in the six years before October 1956, official figures show that there were 1,843 cases of armed robbery and theft from Egyptian territory, 1,339 armed clashes with Egyptian forces, and 172 acts of sabotage committed by the *fedayeen* and units of the Egyptian army, resulting in the killing of 364 Israelis, with many more wounded.[27]

Nevertheless, as a result of Israeli collusion with England and France, whom the Arabs had hated ever since their long rule over and repression of the Arabs, the Sinai campaign widened the chasm between the Arabs and Israel. This point of view was forcibly expressed by various political circles in Israel.

The relaxation of military tension between Egypt and Israel after the Sinai campaign was the result of the stationing of the United Nations Emergency Force in the Gaza Strip and the Straits of Tiran. When it seemed that the storm over Sinai had died down (though the Syrian border was still far from quiet), Israel again tried the niceties of diplomacy. On 21 January 1958, replying to a note from the Soviet Union, Israel declared: "It is Israel's desire to base its relations with the neighboring Arab countries on the proposal put forward by the government of the USSR at the 12th session of the United Nations General Assembly, namely, in respect for the territorial integrity and sovereignty of Israel and of its neighbors, on abstention from attack and from interference in its internal affairs as well as theirs, and the main-tenance of coexistence on the basis of amicable cooperation, with the purpose of the fruitful development of the entire region as well as strengthening world peace." [28]

In addressing the United National General Assembly on 11 October 1960, then Foreign Minister Golda Meir said: "We are not impressed by lofty speeches on world disarmament and peace by leaders who do not practice at home what they preach abroad. . . . I ask the president of the United Arab Republic: Is he pre-pared to do as he advises President Eisenhower and Chairman Khrushchev to do—namely, to meet and negotiate? Is he prepared to meet Mr. Ben Gurion, the prime minister of Israel, for negotia-tion of peace or at least an agreement on nonaggression? And we put the same question to the king of Jordan, the prime minister of Lebanon and all other Arab leaders. On behalf of my prime minister, I say that he is prepared for such a meeting without any preconditions, immediately, here or at any other place proposed to him." [29]

When Levi Eshkol succeeded Ben Gurion as prime minister, he declared on 26 June 1963 in the Knesset: "The government will strive by all possible means for such a peace, which will be based on mutual respect and preservation of the independence and territorial integrity of all states in the area. . . . Peace has become an essential condition for the very survival of mankind, and the endeavor to achieve it is the primary imperative of the world's governments. We believe that it will come, and we on our part will do all in our power to bring it nearer." On 19 July 1963, replying to a question in a BBC interview as to the likelihood of Israel taking some new initiative for negotiations, the new prime minister said: "We have taken the initiative in the past, without publicity, whenever it seemed that there might be some possibility of establishing contact with a view to initiating negotiations. We shall continue to do the same in the future. We have responded to any initiative that might bring us into contact with Arab leaders. Our willingness to talk peace is public knowledge. We have been carrying on a monologue about peace for the last fifteen years and before. I wish it were in our power to turn it into a dialogue." [30]

After several years of relative quiet following the Sinai campaign, the acts of provocation were renewed in the mid sixties with the appearance of al Fateh, a Palestinian military organization. Some Arab states permitted it to organize, train, and equip itself on their territory, which it used as a springboard for sabotage, murder, and forays into Israel whenever possible.

The Arab summit conferences (January 1964 in Cairo, September 1964 in Alexandria, September 1965 in Casablanca) continued the saber-rattling. The skies darkened once again with the establishment of a joint Arab command to plan "a showdown with Israel"; the formation of a "Palestine Liberation Army" from among the Arab refugees; and the plan to divert the Jordan River headwaters (an operation to commence at the beginning of 1965) in order to deprive Israel of the small enough quantities of water at her disposal. From the beginning of 1965 al Fateh groups began to appear, infiltrating Israel in order to sabotage the National Water Carrier project, to lay mines along the roads, and to sow violence and destruction wherever they could. Syrian outposts along the Golan Heights once again began to shell the Israeli settlements in the Huleh and Jordan valleys. Only people with the strength and character of the Jewish settlers in the area (mostly kibbutzniks) could stand living for so many years under the barrels of artillery pieces, bringing up a generation of children for whom underground shelters were an organic part of their daily existence.

The political influence of the confrontation between the members of NATO and the Warsaw Pact grew progressively stronger. NATO members tried to use Israel against the left-leaning Arab regimes, while their rivals increasingly restricted their reservations about the revanchist Arab policy towards Israel. Although openly recognizing Israel's right to exist in principle, the USSR and its allies evaded the problems of Israel's existence, security, and sovereignty. The constant stress on Israel's actions against its neighbors took no note of the provocations that invited such action, which could not be tolerated by any sovereign country. At the same time the Soviet Union exercised her veto at the United Nations Security Council when there was any possibility of rebuking or condemning Arab provocations against Israel. It no longer served any purpose for Israel to lodge a complaint there; the results of any debate were a foregone conclusion.

Instead of acting as a neutral peacemaker the Soviet Union took an increasingly one-sided position in support of the Arab governments, which forced Israel to depend increasingly on those whose interests were opposed to the Arabs'. This, in turn, served as a pretext for further denunciations and threats. The continual oversimplified identification of Israel with reaction and imperialism and of the Arab countries with progress and anti-imperialism was in itself enough to enflame the Arab enmity and to vindicate the chauvinistic policies of the Arab leaders towards Israel.

There was no let-up in the warlike statements Arab leaders made. The government of Israel could not regard them as empty threats at a time when large quantities of arms were flowing into the neighboring countries. When the Soviet Prime Minister Nikita Khrushchev proposed in 1964 that the nations of the world refrain from the use of force in territorial conflicts, Israel responded favorably. Egypt, however, in accepting the proposal, made an exception of the use of force against Israel.

It is an undeniable fact that Israel continued to propose joint efforts to make peace with its neighbors. In the Knesset on 17 May 1965, the late Prime Minister Eshkol once again appealed to the Arab governments to replace the armistice agreements with peace accords, based on full respect for the independence, sovereignty and territorial integrity of all the states in the region. In stating Israel's readiness to help financially in the rehabilitation of the Arab refugees in the countries in which they had settled, he emphasized the advantages in making the Middle East an "open area" as a bridge to Asia and Africa. The countries of the Middle East would benefit from unhindered land transport by road and rail, free ports in Israel for Jordan, the growth of tourism and free access to holy sites, normal processes of trade and economic cooperation, joint development of arid areas and research in water desalination methods, and restraint in the arms race, in which reliable arrangements could be sought for the limitation of armaments under reciprocal control.

These words went unheeded; and ultimately events led to the Six-Day War. Once again the Arab leaders complained bitterly about "the treacherous attack by Israel" which did not leave them free to implement their hostile declarations. But those very leaders have never abandoned their claim that they are in a state of war with Israel and are waiting for the right moment to settle accounts. Nasser announced, for example, over Radio Cairo on 24 February 1964, that "the prospects are for war with Israel. It is we who will dictate the time. It is we who will dictate the place." On the other hand, Israeli threats against Syria cannot be overlooked. It was these threats which moved Egypt to express solidarity with Syria and the Soviet Union to goad the Arabs against Israel.

The sequence of events is well known. On 14 May 1967 Egypt began moving 90,000 troops and a large tank force into Sinai, close to the Israeli border. Four days later Nasser ordered the United Nations Emergency Force out of Egypt and replaced it along the borders of the Gaza Strip, Sinai, and at Sharm el-Sheikh with Egyptian forces. On 19 May the Egyptian commander of the Israel front announced: "The Egyptian forces have received into their hands the positions of the Emergency Force and are ready to carry the campaign beyond the borders of Egypt." Three days later the Egyptian president announced the closure of the Gulf of Aqaba to Israeli shipping: "The Gulf of Aqaba is Egyptian territorial waters and we will under no circumstances allow the flag of Israel to pass in the Gulf of Aqaba." On 27 May Nasser made his intentions clear: "Our basic objective will be the destruction of Israel. The Arab people want to fight." Other Arab states joined Egypt. On 30 May King Hussein signed a military pact with Nasser in Cairo, placing his army under the command of the Egyptian chief of staff. On 2 June King Hussein declared: "Our increased cooperation with Egypt and other Arab states both in the east and the west will enable us to march along the right road which will lead us to the erasure of the shame, and the liberation of Palestine." President Aref of Iraq was equally frank on 31 May: "The existence of Israel is an error which must be rectified. This is our opportunity to wipe out the ignominy which has been with us since 1948. Our goal is clear—to wipe Israel off the map."

Even as the Israeli reserves were being called up and the country was preparing itself for the coming test, Israel began an energetic diplomatic compaign. On 23 May Prime Minister Eshkol, in addressing the Knesset, called on the powers to act without delay to maintain freedom of navigation through the Tiran Straits. "The Egyptian action constitutes a gross violation of international law, a blow at the sovereign rights of other nations, and an act of aggression against Israel." The Israeli foreign minister and Israeli ambassadors met urgently with the leaders of the great powers and other states in an effort to find a last-minute diplomatic solution. None of the powers was prepared to do anything concrete to preserve the freedom of Israeli shipping in the Straits and to reinstate the previous situation on the border between Egypt and Israel. Full-scale hostilities began on 5 June 1967, when Israel set out to ward off the Egyptian threat on the southern front and to put the Egyptian air force out of action. Within six days the armies of Egypt, Jordan, and Syria were routed and ceasefires were arranged with the resulting new demarcation lines.

After the war, the Arabs argued that in order to justify its attack, "the Israelis exploited ill-considered statements by certain Arab leaders." But in the words of a Russian saying: "What the pen writes, the ax cannot erase."

Even those who assumed that Nasser's provocations were not

intended to start a war, but that he was only carrying out these acts in the belief that Israel would reconcile herself to the new situation without going to war, would have to admit that he was playing with fire. And, indeed, the end of such a dangerous game could only be the igniting of a huge conflagration with all its consequences. Those who caused it and those who provided political encouragement (even if from behind the scenes they may have had reservations about one or another of the moves) must bear responsibility for the results.

### Another View of Israeli Policy

Anybody even a little familiar with the history of the Zionist movement and the political history of Palestine is aware that important segments of the Jewish national movement sought over a long period to settle the Jewish-Arab question not by partition, but on the basis of an equal national status (political parity) for the two peoples in an undivided Palestine and, when the time would be ripe, for federal links with the neighboring countries. Only after it became apparent at the end of the 1940s that such a solution was impracticable under the circumstances, did all agree to the only possible solution, embodied in the UN General Assembly resolution of 29 November 1947, the partition of the country.

Since the establishment of the state of Israel, these circles— parties, groups, and public figures—have not abandoned their struggle for a policy of active Jewish-Arab understanding and cooperation. The Jewish-Arab issue has become a kind of watershed in Israeli political life. The argument has revolved around the attitude towards the Arab minority in Israel (10–12 percent of the population) and its rights and status, as well as the orientation of Israeli foreign policy in the international arena, with its implications for the region's problems and Jewish-Arab relations.

Although Israel could indicate to the outside world—the Arab world, the great powers, and smaller states with an interest in the troubled region—that its policy was far more geared towards making peace than that of the Arab states, the internal political struggle had to meet a more stringent test. Here it was judged not by statements only, but by the relationship between the words and deeds, some of them public, some kept quiet, but which in a democratic country such as Israel cannot be completely hidden from interested eyes. Conduct that would be passable in comparison to the Arabs' policy was far from satisfactory when compared to the traditional basic principles of the Jewish national movement, and this related both to morality of international relations and to the obligations which the state of Israel took upon itself according to the Declaration of Independence of 1948. The search for peace, like the search for justice, must be seen as well as heard.

Between the establishment of the state and David Ben Gurion's final resignation from the helm in June 1963, the internal political struggle polarized between the "Ben Gurion policy" and its opponents. Neither formed a monolithic ideological-political bloc, but rather, wide coalitions of parties, groups, and public figures, sharing more or less common ground on Israel-Arab relations.

Ben Gurion played such a decisive role in shaping the country's image and the direction of its development, that Israeli policy towards the Arabs cannot be considered without taking his influence into account.

Ben Gurion's opponents on this subject disputed the claim that his policy was only a response to the situation that had come into being; they thought his policy was largely responsible for creating the situation. Ben Gurion's successors did not have his powers of leadership and lacked his charisma. Although their approach to the Jewish-Arab problem differed from Ben Gurion's, they were too weak to turn the state from the course Ben Gurion had set—a fatal course in a large degree. Israeli policy should have worked to heal the wounds caused by the 1948–9 military confrontation; but instead of balm, it often rubbed salt into them. Instead of patient face-to-face political confrontation with the complicated and delicate problem of Jewish-Arab relations, Israeli policy set its mind towards attempting a military solution. Instead of gradually bridging the gap between the two peoples, they widened it. Instead of bringing nearer the desired peace, they pushed it even further away. The ideological education Ben Gurion gave the Israeli public and, in particular, his followers and protégés in the government apparatus, as well as his aides in the formulation and execution of foreign policy, became in time an influential objective factor.

"Deep down Ben Gurion does not believe that peace is possible. If he ever permitted himself to hope for the normalization of relations with the Arabs, he meant only future generations." This view was expressed by Dr. Nahum Goldmann,[31] who knew Ben Gurion closely for decades. It should, however, be added that Ben Gurion never got to know the Arab world, far less to understand it. It is no coincidence that since his arrival in the country (1906), he learned Turkish, English, and, at a later stage, Greek and Spanish, but never Arabic, the language of the whole area of which Israel forms a part. Ben Gurion died on 1 December 1973. His remoteness from the problems of the Arab world is very noticeable in his writings.

Jon Kimche, a man well-versed in Israeli affairs, once noted that from 1953 onward "the main emphasis [in Israeli affairs] was placed on the military side of the problem" and that "a new rule was determined according to the assumption that Israel must be prepared for war and not for peace." [32] Nonetheless, since the establishment of the state of Israel, Israeli spokesmen have taken every opportunity to offer peace and friendly cooperation to the Arabs from every international platform. However, Ben Gurion himself expounded many years ago (in a speech to the representative body of Palestinian Jewry in 1926) that the test for the Jews in their relations to the Arabs is not "high-sounding statements, promises, and declarations, delivered solemnly from this or that platform" but that "our attitude will be tested by what we do and not what we say." The deeds, both in regard to the Arabs inside Israel and to the surrounding Arab world, did not match the words and often contradicted them.[33] The actual policy the government of Israel pursued towards the Arab world was based on unfounded assumptions which would inevitably lead them to miss the target. If the qualities of a real statesman involve understanding the course of history and anticipating what is in store, then those into whose hands a solution of the Jewish-Arab problem was committed were not outstanding for these qualities. Prejudice, blinding emotions, and mistaken political orientation prevented them from seeing the great world picture of the anticolonialist liberation movement. It was within these turbulent streams that the Arab peoples progressed towards their longed-for political independence.

Understanding history was and is a prerequisite for understanding the present developments in the area known as the Middle East. A mistaken evaluation of political developments all around them not only led Israeli policy to cast its lot with powers in deep disfavor with the Arabs, but it has often seemed "more Catholic than the Pope." Apart from its moral and historical aspects, this policy also revealed an incorrect assessment of the situation. Not only were firm warnings issued from within against this policy, but they were also heard from a large number of different Israeli sympathizers abroad.

In a lecture delivered in Jerusalem in spring 1953, Jon Kimche, then editor of the London *Jewish Observer,* said: "The policy of, as it were, 'policing' the Middle East will not only cause Israeli policy and aims to fail, but will widen the gulf between Israel and the Arab states and confirm the opinion prevalent in the Arab countries that Israel is a 'foreign body' in the Middle East and 'the agent of Western imperialism.' " [34]

Siding with Britain and France in their struggle against the freedom movements of the peoples in the region did not bear the hoped-for fruit, namely Arab acceptance of Israel. Israel's ideological identification with the colonialist viewpoint, in contradiction to the outlook of the region's inhabitants, only served to widen the gap. While the neighboring countries increasingly opposed being included in the system of military-political alliances the western powers planned in the early 1950s (the Arab countries then wished to remain neutral and free to cooperate with either side on the basis of equality and mutual benefit), the Israeli government increasingly sought a military alliance with opponents of the Arabs and even tried to "assist" them in imposing their schemes on the Arabs (the Baghdad Pact of 1955 is the outstanding example). Ben Gurion's dramatic appeal to General Naguib after the July 1952 coup in Egypt and the offer of cooperation between Israel and the new Egypt were in fact also part of the "Middle East defense plans," then proposed by the western powers, that Israel intended to be part of. The Arabs refused to be drawn into them. Even at a time when relations were relatively tranquil, on the day Egypt and Britain signed the agreement for the British evacuation of the Suez Canal, Nasser declared: "The Egyptian position towards Israel depends on Israel's behavior toward her and toward the Arab people." [35] In fact, this was a repetition of what General Naguib said on other occasions, namely that a prime condition for peace between the Arabs and Israel was that Israel should see herself as a state belonging to the area and not as a European bridgehead, foreign in essence to the Middle East.[36]

On his return from a visit to Egypt, Marshal Tito declared that the basis of his talks with Nasser was that "the Egyptian people want to live in peace," and emphasized "the identical positions of Yugoslavia and Egypt on the need for a way to solve every disputed issue by peaceful means." [37]

Most discreditable of all was the Sinai campaign in 1956, about which so much has been written. The foreign minister of a friendly state like Sweden said that "Israel perpetrated an act of madness, which is within the realm of catastrophe." [38] It was Hugh Gaitskell, the British Labor Party leader who issued "a warning to my many friends in Israel": "Israel must continue to live among the peoples of the area and if they will see her as an ally of imperialism, then all hope for the chance of a peace agreement between Israel and the Arabs will go." [39] Leaders of the Italian Socialist Party (then led by Pietro Nenni) voiced their understanding of Israel's position during discussions in Rome with Israeli representatives and justified Israel's demand for free navigation and security, but expressed the view that "the Sinai campaign was not the right way for Israel to achieve its just aims," and that in their view, "Israel must take care not to be lumped together with Anglo-French neocolonialism." [40]

In Israel, those who disagreed fundamentally with Ben Gurion's policy included leading figures like Moshe Sharett, who felt himself obliged to resign from the government in June 1956 (about four months before the Sinai campaign). He had served without a break for twenty-three years, conducting foreign affairs before the state existed and as foreign minister after it was established. When Ben Gurion resigned in December 1953 "for personal reasons" (in fact due to differences of opinion within the leadership of his party), he retired to Sdeh-Boker in the Negev. Moshe

Sharett became prime minister and served until Ben Gurion returned to office in November 1955. In 1954–5 at least four serious attempts were made to mediate between Israel and the Arabs, two by the British Members of Parliament Richard Crossman and Maurice Orbach; one by the Maltese Labor Party leader (now prime minister), Dom Mintoff; [41] and the fourth was during a face-to-face meeting between Israeli and Egyptian representatives in Paris. This last was very close to a positive conclusion, when it came to nought as a result of what became known as the Lavon Affair [42] in Israel. In an exclusive interview Maurice Orbach gave to the London *Jewish Chronicle* on 29 July 1965, it was revealed that Nasser sent a goodwill message to Moshe Sharett, who was then prime minister of Israel, addressed to "my brother Sharett" (Sharett knew Arabic and "my brother" in Arabic is the equivalent of "colleague").

Jom Kimche explained Sharett's resignation succinctly in 1957, when he wrote that "the neorealists advocating the new Israeli policy appeared to be exploiting a moment of opportunity, but in fact tended to ignore the real problem." When these neorealists took over, "the foreign office was asked to surrender completely to security needs and since Sharett did not surrender easily, he was forced to go." [43]

Sharett was in Delhi at the time of the Sinai campaign. After reading the Israeli newspapers on the events of the campaign, he made some surprised comments in his diary about "the extent to which emotion dominates our political thinking, leading to the belief that it is possible to reach peace through coercion." [44] He, along with many others in Israeli political circles, did not share this view. Sharett's evaluation of the Sinai campaign was voiced in his Knesset speech of 6 March 1957, which, in spite of its careful diplomatic language, contained severe criticism of Ben Gurion's policies. "Security," said Sharett, "is the first and primary condition for the existence of the state, and this is an axiom; but narrow-minded and shortsighted concentration on security problems, along with the diversion of attention from seemingly different considerations, is likely to have direct consequences on security itself." On one occasion he spoke of the Sinai campaign as "Eden's adventure, which bore no fruit." [45]

Sharett's removal from power [46] did not end the argument over

Ben Gurion's policy. It often continued, for example, as an indirect exchange between the prime minister and the president of the World Zionist Organization, Dr. Nahum Goldmann, which Dr. Goldmann aptly termed "not a personal, but rather an ideological-political argument." The whole involved issue can be summed up by one question: does the way to genuine security for Israel lie only in reliance upon military force—both of Israel and of its supporters abroad—or in a farsighted, long-term, patient, and enterprising political approach? Ben Gurion was the victor in this argument, and it was his stand which guided Israeli policy, both in its military and diplomatic operations.

British Labour leader Richard Crossman, an old friend of Israel, wrote at the time of the Sinai campaign: "Ben-Gurion is indeed an inspiring leader in war, but unless Israel wants to lose the peace, she needs a completely different leadership." [47] Almost seven years passed before Ben Gurion handed over the reins of government to his colleagues and protégés. During this time a fateful course was set, which his successors subsequently did not change.

When Moshe Sharett left the Foreign Office in June 1956, he was succeeded by Mrs. Golda Meir. Israeli policy during her term of office (1956–1965) can be summed up in a single short sentence: "Israel can do nothing; there is nothing to be done to bring peace closer." When the opponents of this passive, fatalistic approach criticized it, pointing to its sterility and demanding that the government adopt a frank and bold peace policy, the response was often: "Peace is closer now than it ever was." [48] This, of course, cannot be denied, for if peace comes in a hundred years' time, every passing moment brings "peace closer than it ever was. . . ." At all events, instead of positive efforts to gain the Arabs' confidence and prepare the ground for a *rapprochement,* Israel staked its policy on a peace imposed by a third party. The western powers were once seen as that third party, but as they lost influence in the region, similar hopes were placed in the Asian and African peoples, with some of whom (particularly those with western-leaning governments) Israel established diplomatic and other links.

In the late 1950s, after the Sinai campaign had failed to justify hopes "to reach peace through coercion" (in Moshe Sharett's critical phrase), new and interesting ideas came to the fore. In time, an attempt was even made to give them some kind of ethnographic basis: "The Middle East is not solely an Arab region. On the contrary, the majority of the inhabitants are not Arabs," "they are more numerous than the Arabs in the Middle East" (? ! A.C.) and "it may be that by establishing relations with the peoples on the outer areas of the Middle East, we will establish friendly relations with the peoples of the inner area, our neighbors on the borders of Israel." [49]

A different view on this matter pointed out that "with all the importance of bridgebuilding, even partial bridgebuilding, between Israel and the peoples of Asia and Africa, it is wrong to regard these efforts as a *substitute* for direct efforts to bring peace between Israel and the Arab world closer. In an emergency, even the most roundabout of ways should not be dismissed, but it should not be forgotten for a moment that the *natural* route from Israel to Asia and Africa lies via Damascus and Baghdad to Burma, and via Cairo and Tunis to Ghana, and not the other way around. This very issue of opening this natural route, together with security and the Ingathering of the Exiles, is Israel's *main problem* today." [50]

The same line was taken by Mapam Knesset member Y. Hazan, during the Knesset foreign policy debate at the end of March 1959. "The Foreign Office," said Hazan, "may claim credit for recent noteworthy achievements, which have created opportunities to strengthen our links with Africa and Asia, but we must not fall prey to the illusion that by indirect means we shall solve our main problem—making peace in our region. We have to make the world and the Arab masses aware that we want peace, are ready for peace, and that we have real peace proposals." [51] Recent developments in Israel's relations with African states would appear to provide food for thought as to the validity of these conceptions.

Two basic approaches crystallized in Israel on questions of war and peace: the first, the majority view, feels that there is, unfortunately, no real chance of ending the conflict in the foreseeable future; the second approach regards the continuation of the conflict as a tragedy which cannot be accepted as inevitable.

## The Struggle Over the Direction of Israeli Policy

The internal struggle in Israel over Arab-Jewish relations has not let up since the state's establishment. It takes place both on parliamentary and extraparliamentary levels. In the Knesset various political factions have taken up the struggle, with the Arab-Jewish problem and the critical attitude to it forming main party planks. These include Mapam,[52] the Israel Communist Party,[53] and after 1965, the Haolam Hazeh-Koach Hadash.[54] There were, and still are, leading personalities and even groups with the Israel Labor Party (Israel's largest party), the National Religious Party, and sometimes even in Gahal (a rightist parliamentary bloc) who, in one way or another, from time to time support certain aspects of this struggle. Party discipline, however, has sometimes prevented them from expressing their support in public. Many public figures have taken part in the struggle outside the Knesset. Some are people who were active before the establishment of the state in various societies and organizations working for Jewish-Arab cooperation and understanding, such as the *Brit Shalom* (Peace Alliance) in the twenties, which contained people like Professor Martin Buber and Professor Ernest Simon, *Kedma Mizracha* ("Eastward") in the thirties, the "League for Jewish-Arab Rapprochement and Co-operation," and the *Ihud* (Unity) Association formed by Dr. J. L. Magnes in the forties. Others—members of the university staffs, writers and journalists, artists, active Histadrut members, etc.—are people who entered political life after the establishment of Israel. On certain issues, such as the long drawn-out struggle to abolish military government in Arab areas in Israel, and everything relating to the status and implementation of the rights of the Arab minority in the country, they have acted in unison. On international issues, such as the anticolonialist struggle, opposition to weapons of mass destruction, and the encouragement of peaceful coexistence in the world, some have taken joint action in the framework of the Israeli Peace Committee and other political groups such as the Vietnam Committee.

As early as 1954, the Israeli Peace Committee organized a referendum in Israel. Its main demands were a negotiated peace between Israel and the Arab world which would set no prior conditions, safeguard the rights of all the peoples in the region, convene great-power meetings to reduce tension, etc. Four hundred and one thousand men and women over the age of eighteen (43 percent of Israel's adult population at the time) supported these demands, which were presented to the Knesset. The peace movement has also attempted to reduce tension in the area by a campaign to declare the Middle East a nuclear-weapons-free zone and to eliminate foreign bases there.

When the Peace Council convened in the early 1950s, representatives of the Israeli Peace Committee met delegates from the Arab countries, including several prominent Arab figures. They met in Rome (September 1951), Berlin (July 1952), and Peking (October 1952) and worked together in committee and the plenum. In the 1951 Rome meeting, all the resolutions were passed unanimously, including one calling for the British evacuation of the Suez and another which provided for convening in Cairo. Although it was considered unlikely that an Israeli delegation would be admitted to Cairo, the decision was based on the consideration that if the Egyptian authorities would permit the peace movement to convene a regional conference in their land, the peace-movement leaders in Egypt would demand that it be made possible for the delegation from Israel's peace movement to participate. These resolutions were esentially the work of three men: the late engineer Antoun Tabet of Beirut, the late attorney Joseph Hilmi, secretary of the Egyptian Peace Committee, and the writer, member of the Israeli delegation.[55] Israeli delegates were not invited to the November 1953 meeting of the Committee of Middle Eastern Peoples in Beirut, nor was the Israeli Peace Committee consulted. This was seen in Israel, on the one hand, as a sign of increased Arab chauvinism with which the peace-movement members in the Arab countries did not dare contend and, on the other, as a response to the Israeli reprisal raid on the Jordanian village of Qibya (14 October 1953). Public meetings of the Peace Council ceased after 1953, but a series of personal contacts continued in an effort to discuss reducing tension, despite the often bitter exchanges on the public platform of the world peace movement.

Israelis took part in the Mediterranean Discussions (Colloques méditerranéens), initiated by the mayor of Florence, Giorgio la Pira, in October 1958, October 1960, May 1961, June 1963, and June 1964. They provided an opportunity for intellectuals and leading political figures from Mediterranean countries to hold unofficial discussions on problems that led to tension and conflicts in the region, including of course, the Israel-Arab conflict. These meetings opened the way for subsequent meetings with prominent Arabs in Britain, France, Italy, and the United States.

The English-language monthly *New Outlook* was founded in 1957 (after the Sinai campaign) as a forum for circles supporting Arab-Jewish reconciliation and peace in the Middle East. It is one of the few platforms bringing together in its pages Jews, Arabs, and people from Asian and African countries who are concerned over the problems of this region. The editors' main hope was an accommodation between the national movement of the Jewish people returning to its homeland and building its state there and the national movement of the Arab peoples. Articles in the magazine deal with problems of Israel and Arab society and their development, with questions of education and political life, with Israel's relations with the Arab world, etc. Among the more than fifty names on the editorial council and executive (which includes Israeli Arabs), there are leading figures from Israel's universities, Knesset members from five parties, research workers, writers and poets, editors and journalists, church leaders, business-men, etc. The monthly has initiated international symposia: the first, in Israel in January 1963, in which Jewish and Israeli Arab public figures and overseas guests participated (including An-thony Wedgwood Benn of the British Labour Party, Claude D'Ester of the French socialists, Bishop James Pike and the economist Abba Lerner of the United States), ended with a call for the revision of Israeli foreign policy and the abolition of mili-tary government in Arab areas in Israel, etc. This led to heated arguments in the Israeli press and in the Knesset. The second symposium, in March 1969 ("Inevitable war or an initiated peace") had almost fifty participants, including guests from abroad like Professor Fred Khouri and Paul Jacobs from the United States, Professor Giorgio la Pira from Italy, and Dreyfus-Schmidt from France.

The visit of Jean-Paul Sartre and Simone de Beauvoir to Egypt and Israel in early 1967 deserves special mention, for it was intended to clarify the possibilities of a dialogue between the Arab and Israeli left. A special edition of *Les Temps Modernes,* edited by Sartre and published in June 1967, was devoted to the Arab-Israel conflict. In it, for the first time, Arabs and Israelis put their views and proposals alongside each other. The visit of Sartre and de Beauvoir, as guests of the Egyptian *Al-Taliyah* and the Israeli *New Outlook,* was to have initiated a dialogue, but this highly significant development was interrupted by the Six-Day War. It was revived, however, by the Conference for Peace and Justice, which took place in Bologna in May 1973. An Israeli delegation took part both in the preliminary discussions in Rome and in the conference in Bologna itself. Although the Israeli and Arab delegations have not yet sat at the same table in these discussions, the Rome talks were regarded as recognition by leading personalities in the Arab world of the existence and status of the Israeli peace forces and of the need to talk to each other and together so as to seek a way to peace at the Bologna conference and beyond it. And at the World Conference of Peace Forces in Moscow at the end of October 1973, an Israeli delegation, composed solely of Rakah and its supporters, participated.

## The Six-Day War and its Consequences

Faced by the uncompromising Arab stand, which refused to accept Israel's existence, whatever its borders, and the efforts by the Arab states to destroy it, Israel could not accept Egypt's arbitrary blockade of the Gulf of Aqaba, which had been open to Israeli shipping since 1957 under UNEF supervision. The logic of the situation was that had Israel acceded to this arbitrary measure, Egypt could not have stopped there, and Israel would have been subjected sooner or later to further similar trials. The concentration of a large Egyptian force on the long border from the Gaza Strip to Eilat, a border with no natural obstacles, forced Israel to call up its forces to defend the border, while Syria and Jordan threatened its other borders. The Israeli army consists primarily of reserves, and calling them up involves paralyzing the economy, the educational system, and various vital services. Israel could not bear such a burden for long. To make certain of victory and limit its casualties, Israel had to take the initiative and strike first. It did so on the morning of 5 June 1967.

On 10 June 1967, the day the ceasefire took effect, Israel held three times as much territory as it had six days earlier. The new ceasefire lines included the Sinai Peninsula, the Gaza Strip, the West Bank of the Jordan, and about 1,250 sq. km. in the Syrian Golan Heights. According to a report published by the United Nations secretary general on 18 August 1967, 325,000 people fled from the areas taken by Israel, while more than a million Arabs remained in the areas.[56]

## The Situation in 1972

The results of the Six-Day War came as an astounding shock to the Arab world and as a great surprise to Israel. Both were perplexed. The Arabs did not know what to do in the light of their defeat; Israel was uncertain what it would do with its victory. The Arabs demanded an Israeli withdrawal from all the conquered territories as a prerequisite for any accommodations and that Israel declare its willingness to do so as a first step. In the first days of the war, the prime minister and the minister of defense had declared that Israel's objective was peace and security, not territorial conquest. Now Israel refused to commit itself to anything in advance of direct negotiations, a position to which the Arabs did not agree.

The Six-Day War allowed Israel to breathe freely insofar as current security was concerned, but the political problem remained as acute as ever. The issues that had existed before the war had not been solved. Some of them were now more severe (the addition of many more refugees) and new problems had been added, which, in the long run, were likely to prove even more complicated than the old ones. This would seem to indicate that problems which are basically political cannot be solved by military means. And so long as the Arab and Israeli leaders are unable to find a way out of the deadlock by their own resourcefulness, the leading role will pass to the giants of the international arena, while those directly involved will play increasingly diminished roles.

The well-known Security Council decision of 22 November 1967 (Resolution 242) was in no way the result of an agreement between the belligerent parties, but a great power modus vivendi. It was accepted unanimously and Dr. Gunnar Jarring was chosen as the special representative. Dr. Jarring left for the Middle East "to promote agreement and assist efforts to achieve a peaceful and accepted settlement in accordance with the provisions and principles in this resolution." However, the contradictions which the Security Council resolution had hoped to resolve reappeared with the Jarring Mission. The United States, Israel's advocate, did not accept the interpretation that Israel had to withdraw from *the territories* occupied in June 1967 (according to the French text), while the USSR, the advocate of Egypt and Syria (and in effect Jordan as well), rejected the interpretation that Israel had to withdraw from *territories* it occupied (according to the English text), i.e., not from all the territories, but from those agreed by negotiations. The contrasts between the parties were also reflected in procedural stumbling blocks. Israel demanded "direct negotiations between the belligerent parties" to achieve "a written and signed peace treaty" in the *spirit* of the Security Council resolution; the Arabs held that it must be a "peaceful and accepted settlement," i.e., indirect negotiations through Dr. Jarring, according to the letter of Resolution 242.

Discussions were held by representatives of the US and the USSR (the two-power talks); the four-power talks involved Britain and France as well. Bargaining, pressures, and counter-pressures continued with Arab threats to renew the war and Israeli deterrent declarations, and "proximity talks" were suggested for a partial settlement on the Suez Canal. All these in theory revolved around the area of the conflict, but in practice they involved the interests and positions of the superpowers. Every so often their negotiations were held in the fiery language of the parties in the Middle East—the war of attrition initiated by Egypt and the bombardments and commando actions by Israel deep inside Egypt. When events threatened to draw the superpowers into war, a ceasefire was again arranged (8 August 1970) and negotiations through Dr. Jarring resumed. His efforts again failed when on 8 February 1971 Israel refused to give an affirmative answer to his questions whether Israel was willing to undertake to withdraw to the old international borders of 4 June 1967. Egypt replied favorably to the question of whether "it would sign a peace treaty with Israel," though the reply included several reservations which in the opinion of the Israel government emptied it of all real content. Israel's reason for its refusal was that "Dr. Jarring's demand ignored the Israeli position on the issue of borders and by submitting this demand he cut the ground from under free negotiations and identified himself with the claim of one party [Egypt]." [57]

Israel's basic approach embodied "secure and recognized boundaries," in the language of Resolution 242, i.e., "defensible borders," which the government of Israel wanted to determine together with Egypt, Jordan, and Syria in the framework of peace treaties. In an unequivocal clarification of its view that the previous demarcation lines were not defensible borders and of its intention to obtain new borders, the government of Israel made a public announcement of principle: Israel would not return to the 4 June boundaries, which exposed it to the temptation of aggression and, in different sectors, gave an aggressor decisive advantages.[58] Israel also opposed the American Rogers Plan (of 9 December 1969), "because this plan ignores Israel's desire to determine new and secure borders with Egypt and Jordan" (Syria was not mentioned, as it then rejected Resolution 242 on principle). The Israeli reply to King Hussein's proposals in March 1972 was primarily that "the territorial basis of the plan is in direct contrast to Israel's intention of achieving new, secure, and recognized boundaries." Nevertheless, Israel did state that "the positions it has taken on the borders are not prior conditions for negotiations, but guidelines laid down by the government of Israel, which will provide the basis for negotiation by the Israeli representative. All matters at issue, including the territorial question, are open to discussion in negotiations." The Israeli experience in the period before the Six-Day War, and experience in other areas of the world (particularly the Indo-Pakistan war in 1971), show that it is impossible to rely on international guarantees. Secure and recognized boundaries to be determined by negotiation are essential to prevent another war.[59]

In the Israel government's basic policy lines (approved by the Knesset on 15 December 1969), it is stated: "Israel will persist in its readiness to conduct negotiations—without prior conditions by any party—with each of its neighbors, for the purpose of concluding a peace treaty. Without a peace treaty, Israel will continue to maintain the situation as it was at the time of the ceasefire and will strengthen its position, according to the essential requirements of its security and development." Israel has acted accordingly.

With the approach of the Soviet-American summit meeting at the end of May 1972, Israel and Egypt requested their respective great-power advocates not to take any fateful step without first consulting them. Their request was granted. According to the official communiqué released at the close of the summit talks, both sides affirmed their support for a peace settlement in the Middle East in accordance with Resolution 242 of the Security Council, indicated the importance of joint constructive action by the parties concerned with Ambassador Jarring, affirmed their desire to contribute to the success of his mission, and announced their readiness to fulfill their roles in achieving a peace settlement in the Middle East. This concurred in a general way with the Rogers Plan, which early in the summit talks was said to be in deep freeze, but not dead.[60] This also conformed to the following section of Security Council Resolution 242, which Egypt and Jordan had accepted some time before, and Syria later showed a tendency to support.[61]

> "Termination of all claims or states of belligerency and respect for and acknowledgment of the sovereignty, territorial integrity and political independence of every state in the area and their right to live in peace with secure and recognized borders free from threats or acts of force."

During the summit conference, official American spokesmen declared that "a settlement in the Middle East is primarily the concern of the parties directly involved," and that "both sides should assist Dr. Jarring's [renewed] mission." Many people in Israel understood this as an attempt by America to gain time until after the fall 1972 elections and felt that the Soviet leaders were willing to accede to it. Meanwhile, the wounds remained open, while the game continued according to the accepted rules.


## Foreign Policy and Internal Alignments in Israel

The June 1967 war and the continuing confrontation brought about sharp changes in the political landscape of the area. Against the background of a wait-and-see foreign policy, polarization within the Israeli public on the issues at hand increased and new alignments came about. On the one hand, the Land of Israel movement, claiming that all the conquered territories belonged to an undivided Eretz Israel, was established. When the government responded favorably to the American peace initiative in August 1970 (including agreement in principle to a withdrawal in return for peace), the Gahal ministers resigned from the government and the Land of Israel movement established a "nonparty committee to prevent withdrawal." Labor Party members who had associated with the Land of Israel movement (mainly *Kibbutz Hameuhad* and former *Ahdut Haavoda* members) did not join the committee, due to its opposition character, but formed a separate group with the same aims inside the Labor Party.

The movement and the committee attracted the chauvinistically inclined political and intellectual circles in Israel, and sections of the Israeli press which enjoy a large circulation supported them. Some of these speak for the vested interests of certain Israeli groups as regards the administered areas. Their slogans include: "The Jews have the sole right to the whole Land of Israel" (meanwhile, up to the Jordan River . . .); "not one inch" (of withdrawal); "the liberated areas must not be returned," etc. Their propaganda, sometimes couched in religious or Biblical terminology, have increased chauvinistic tendencies and helped deepen the gulf of hatred between Arabs and Jews.

At the other end of the spectrum, the Movement for Peace and Security was established. It brought together professors, students, kibbutz members, political activists, etc., both within and outside party political groupings, among whom are also members of religious circles. They are united in their belief that the Six-Day War was a justified war of defense, but that the country's central goal must be persistent and active efforts to make peace, which will ensure the existence and security of the state of Israel.

At the movement's founding meeting on 1 July 1968, the following demands were made of the government. It was to state clearly that Israel had not adopted an annexationist course and that it adopted the principle of withdrawal from the occupied areas following a peace treaty based on recognized and secure borders; to stop civilian Jewish settlement in the occupied areas, aimed at creating facts in the occupied areas, and to cease the expropriation of land for this purpose; to announce a plan for the rehabilitation of the Arab refugees, as part of the peace treaty, to take the first steps without delay towards implementing the plan, and to prevent any actions likely to increase the number of refugees; to incorporate the residents of the occupied areas as a factor in and party to the efforts to achieve peace, while recognizing the right of the Palestinian Arab people to self-determination.

The activities of the Movement for Peace and Security have been aimed at putting pressure on the government to declare explicitly that it accepts the whole of the November 1967 Security Council resolution—this document, recognized by the nations of the world, calls for a just and lasting peace based on secure and recognized boundaries—and to assist in the full implementation of its letter and spirit. The movement works towards the immunization of the Israeli public against chauvinist tendencies. It is campaigning against attributing a political character to the military consequences of the Six-Day War, whether *a priori* or *a posteriori*. The movement has always opposed a do-nothing policy and the "no-alternative" slogans, demanding instead a peace initiative, both to give the lie to Israel's image as a country with aspirations for territorial expansion rather than peace and to prevent an imposed settlement. It pressed the government to welcome Dr. Jarring's mediation and to assist him. It stressed that obstacles should not be placed in the way of Resolution 242's implementation. It persistently demanded that rigidity be avoided which could stop the Jarring Mission and the political negotiations, thereby creating a political vacuum in which the armed conflict between Israel and its neighbors could well be renewed. The movement called on the government not to reject the possibility of a third party helping to break the ice and bring the two parties to indirect negotiations.

The tense struggle over the questions of war and peace made a deep impression on party alignments, which the 1969 Knesset elections reflected. One development was that the majority in Rafi (Israel Workers List), led by Moshe Dayan, rejoined the Labor Party. (Under Ben Gurion, Rafi had broken away from Mapai in 1965, receiving ten seats in the elections that year.) The remainder, including Ben Gurion, campaigned on their own and won four seats. Subsequently, Ben Gurion resigned from active political life and toward the end of his life expressed "dove-ish" opinions on the problems of peace and Jewish-Arab relations. In the elections to the seventh Knesset, Mapam decided for the first time in its history and over the objections of about one-third of its members, not to appear as a separate list. It formed an alignment with the Labor Party, with the proviso that it could maintain its own party framework and dissent on certain defined issues ("partnership within struggle").[62]

The dissenting Mapam members formed two new political groupings. The Independent Left Zionist-Socialist Alliance, led by Yaakov Riftin (a founder and leading member of Mapam, who had served in the Knesset since Israel's establishment) advocated a more radical line in the class struggle and in the area of Jewish-Arab peace, as well as efforts to improve relations with the Soviet Union and the Communist bloc. *Siah,* the Israeli New Left, is not a party organization, but an activist group that aims at fostering radical political ideas and especially extraparliamentary action. It has some hundreds of members, mostly university students, kibbutz members, and young urban intelligentsia, some of whom had left Maki because of political and tactical differences with that party. These two groups are active in the Movement for Peace and Security, together with Mapam members (with the approval of their party) and other nonparty people.

The polarization over war and peace has left its mark on other parties as well (there are many doves in the various coalition parties, several holding important political posts), but this is not at present expressed in organizational forms.

In order to understand the internal political alignments in Israel after the Six-Day War, it should be noted that the anti-annexationist position (as expressed, for example, by the slogan "security-yes; annexation-no" of the Movement for Peace and Security) has a double significance. Not only is it against undermining the rights of Israel's Arab neighbors, but it also takes into account the possible implications that an annexationist policy has for and in the state of Israel itself. Many Israelis of various political persuasions think that to "digest" more than a million Arabs from the occupied areas would endanger the democratic character of the state of Israel and its moral essence.

## Again a Major War

After an extended  period of sabre-rattling which went hand in hand with violence on the part of belligerent Palestinian units and Israeli reactions-in-force, the fear that a political vacuum would inevitably lead to another outbreak of war was amply substantiated. Official Israeli policy had mistakenly assumed that the Arabs had no military option and therefore diplomatic initiative was not urgent.

The balance struck between maintaining the status quo and refraining from total use of power was again undermined. This time Egypt and Syria caught Israel off guard, for Israel, since 1967, had tended to underestimate Arab military capability and daring. The government of Israel did not adequately appreciate the Arab need—especially Egypt's—to restore their honor, lost on the battlefield. Nor did Israel appreciate the oil factor. The Arab oil states, and particularly Saudi Arabia, were interested in a new war as justification for their offensive over oil prices. The sudden joint military attack by Egypt and Syria, coordinated to some degree with Jordan, on 6 October found Israel less prepared than it might have been, had not its leadership thought that Israel was constantly forging ahead, while the Arabs remained stagnant.

During the first days of the war, until the reserves were mobilized and the necessary equipment brought up to the front lines, Israel suffered heavy losses. The few Israeli soldiers in the advanced positions, generally from the Israeli regular army, staved off bravely at great cost the Egyptian and Syrian assaults. The Arabs outnumbered the Israelis ten to one, were massively equipped, and on this occasion enjoyed the additional factor of surprise. The Egyptians succeeded in crossing the Suez Canal and capturing a strip of some consequence (about 700 square kilometers eastward), while the Syrian assaults brought them at some points up to the pre-1967 Israeli boundaries. However, as the battles continued, the qualitative superiority of the Israel Defense Forces came to the fore. Not only were the assaults repulsed, but Israel succeeded in driving them back beyond the 1967 ceasefire lines. When the new ceasefire went into effect after eighteen days of battle, the IDF had in its possession about 600 square kilometers of additional Syrian territory and about 1500 square kilometers west of the canal in Egypt. Yet, as the IDF reached the peak of its drive, the full political pressure of the two superpowers was brought into play. The United Nations Security Council, which met in urgent session on 22 October at the request of the United States and the Soviet Union, passed a resolution (Resolution 338) which called upon all parties to remain in their present positions and terminate all military activity no later than twelve hours after the resolution was adopted; urged the implementation, immediately after the ceasefire, of Security Council Resolution 242 (1967) in all of its parts; and decided that immediately and concurrently with the ceasefire, negotiations should start under appropriate auspices between the parties concerned, which were aimed at establishing a just and durable peace in the Middle East.

With the exception of the Chinese delegate, who did not participate in the voting, the remaining fourteen members of the Security Council supported the American-and-Soviet-sponsored resolution. China was opposed to the US-USSR policies but did not want to jeopardize a suggestion which Egypt and Syria agreed upon and wanted to put into effect. Between 22 and 24 October (between the Security Council's Resolution 338 and 339), when it looked as if one or both sides would not carry out Resolution 338, a dramatic confrontation was reached between Washington and Moscow. The US declared a state of atomic preparedness, a fact that emphasized the grave global background of the dispute.

The ceasefire went into effect on 24 October under the supervision of UN observers and emphasis shifted to the diplomatic negotiations on consolidating the ceasefire and paving the way for the implementation of Resolution 338.

On 12 November, after intensive negotiations in which Dr. Kissinger acted as an intermediary, representatives of Israel and Egypt met at Kilometer 101 on the Suez-Cairo Road and signed a six-point agreement covering scrupulous observance of the ceasefire, the exchange of prisoners, free passage of supplies to the city of Suez, free passage of nonmilitary supplies to the Egyptian Third Army, the staffing of observation points on the Suez-Cairo Road by UN troops, and the opening of negotiations on the separation of forces. Between 14–22 November the prisoners of war were exchanged between Israel and Egypt. Since the negotiations between the representatives of both armies on Kilometer 101 encountered difficulties, it was agreed to refer them to the Israeli-Arab Peace Conference which was about to convene in Geneva.

In a flurry of press and television coverage, the conference convened on 21 December in the Palace of Nations in Geneva, with delegations from Egypt, Israel, and Jordan participating. UN Secretary General Kurt Waldheim chaired the opening session. After both sides and the initiating powers had exchanged views, the session closed with the acceptance of a decision to set up an Egyptian-Israeli military work-group to deal with the separation of their respective forces. This work-group began its deliberations on 26 December under the chairmanship of General Ensio Siilasvuo, commander of the UN Emergency Force. When it, too, struck a snag, the American secretary of state on 11 January commenced alternate talks with President Sadat and his chief advisers in Egypt and in Jerusalem with Prime Minister Golda Meir, several senior cabinet members, and the Israeli commander-in-chief. An agreement was finally signed at Kilometer 101 on 18 January and the separation of forces took effect in various stages ending 5 March. As published in Israel, the agreement included provisions in writing, plus secret provisions, and provisions agreed upon orally. Among the latter was the abolition of the Egyptian shipping blockade in the Bab El Mandeb Straits, which had been imposed without prior announcement and was similarly rescinded.

In accordance with the agreement, the Israeli forces withdrew from the west bank of the canal and also from its occupied areas on the east bank to a line twenty to twenty-five kilometers east of the canal. Parallel to this, between the Israeli and the Egyptian line east of the canal, a strip of eight to ten kilometers was created, to be occupied by the UN Emergency Forces. As agreed, the Egyptians thinned out their forces east of the canal; and apart from thirty tanks and thirty artillery pieces, all weaponry, especially missiles and heavy artillery, was evacuated to a distance of about twenty kilometers west of the canal. Israel retained, in the area it held, forces of parallel strength. Similar agreements were to be worked out and signed between Israel and Syria and between Jordan and Israel, and in due course, the Geneva Conference would reconvene. The concluding article of the Egyptian-Israeli agreement stated: "This agreement shall not be regarded by Egypt and Israel as a final peace settlement. It constitutes a first step towards a final, just and enduring peace, according to the articles of the Security Council Resolution 338 and within the framework of the Geneva Conference."

From the strategic point of view, despite Israeli military achievement, Egypt succeeded in winning back, by military means, the east bank of the canal and the possibility of reopening the canal and reconstructing the cities on the west bank, without giving up political options as regards the rest of the occupied areas.

The situation as regards Syria was more complicated. On the Syrian front a more or less clear line divided the armies, but while an exchange of POW's was immediately effected between Egypt and Israel, for several months Syria refused to supply a list of prisoners or allow the Red Cross to visit them. Syria shamelessly exploited the prisoners as a bargaining point in the negotiations over disengagement of forces, even though the number of Syrian prisoners in Israel was much larger than that of Israeli prisoners in Syria.

An entirely different issue was the prospect of "disengagement" of forces between Israel and Jordan, whose armies were in effect wholly disengaged. This could become a respectable Jordanian method of legalizing the secret negotiations with Israel which had gone on in different forms for some time. The matter became urgent in view of the possibility that the Palestinian organizations would be brought into the Geneva peace talks, in accordance with the decisions of the Algiers Conference and later of the Muslim Summit Conference in Lahore, Pakistan at the end of February 1973.

The October 1973 war has been compared in Israel to an earthquake. Indeed, it is hard to find a more descriptive term for the shock that shook Israel and affected its sense of security, its economic life, its internal social problems, and its political problems in the international arena.

At the beginning of September 1973, a month before the Egyptian-Syrian attack, the conference of nonaligned nations in Algiers gave the green light for severing relations with Israel, which brought about the imminent collapse of its remaining diplomatic positions in Africa. Several African chiefs of state pointedly emphasized that they were taking such action because and as long as Israel refused to return the territories it captured in June 1967. On 6 November, under pressure and boycott from the oil countries, the foreign ministers of the European Common Market nations issued a joint declaration calling upon Israel to withdraw from all the territories it captured in June 1967. This declaration also expressed support for the "legitimate rights of the Palestinians." Indeed, in addition to the military shock, Israel suffered an equal political one. "The lightning-like action of the powers to halt the hostilities in the region descended upon Israel with almost meteoric speed. It seemed that in the political sphere we were confronted by a surprise no less formidable than that which overtook us on Yom Kippur in the military sphere," observed the newspaper *Haaretz* on 25 October. At that very hour when "veteran government Middle East experts believed that considerable time would elapse before both sides in the conflict would get a call from the superpowers and the UN for a cease-fire, time enough for Israel to gain control of the canal" (*Haaretz*, 22 October), the Kissinger-Brezhnev Moscow agreement was on its way to becoming Security Council Resolution 338.

After the Israeli forces had overcome the effects of surprise and taken the offensive, Israel was forced to accept a ceasefire within twelve hours. The proposal was one "which must not suffer rejection." The giant American transport planes which had delivered to Israel urgently needed arms and ammunition (parallel to those Egypt and Syria got from the USSR) were impressively timed to arrive in Israel simultaneously with Kissinger's plane. Kissinger's conversation with Mrs. Meir and her cabinet, held during his fleeting visit on 22 October was cordial and President Nixon's broadcast to her was also friendly in tone, but Knesset member Meir Yaari thought its contents were essentially a directive requiring a response within four hours.[63]

Indeed, Israel's government could only accept "America's counsel," if it wished to continue receiving necessary aid. The right-wing Likud leader, Knesset member Begin, voiced severe displeasure: "Why wasn't the opposition consulted at such a fateful hour?" But his criticism of the government provided him with his own answer: "The government of Israel itself was not asked to express its opinion on the decision [of Kissinger and Brezhnev in Moscow]." Defense Minister Moshe Dayan explained that "to refuse the ceasefire in such fashion as to cause a breach with the Americans, could only be described as an excessive risk." [64]

In the face of the decision of the Likud [65] and its constituent parties in the Knesset, that "they reject the government's decision to respond to the Security Council in the matter of the ceasefire . . . and denounce the government's sense of obligation to begin the immediate fulfillment of Security Council Resolution 242," Knesset member Zadok, chairman of the Knesset Committee on Foreign Affairs and Security, clarified beyond a doubt that "one could not reject the American initiative and at the same time expect its help." As for the critical query of the opposition—why had the government permitted Israel to be taken by surprise—Mr. Dayan countered that "in the course of his intimate conversation with Kissinger during the latter's visit to Israel at the time, he learned from him that if Israel had started a deterrent offensive, we would not have received the American aid flowing into the country." [66]

The digestion of these sobering facts by the Israeli public is likely to exercise an important influence. More and more are beginning to understand that under the prevailing international political conditions, even military victory on the battlefield is not identical with a political settlement. Military successes sometimes fall short of achieving their purpose.

## The Price of War

War, with its harvest of death and destruction, is the greatest of tragedies for a people. A situation of "no war and no peace," of sporadic outbursts and endless tension, is only slightly better.

In the first five years after the Six-Day War 817 Israelis were killed (637 soldiers and 180 civilians). The number of Israeli wounded in this period is 3,109 (2,193 army personnel and 916 civilians).[67] In proportion to population, these figures would be about 81,700 and 310,900 respectively for the United States. The reckoning does not begin from 1967; over the preceding twenty years over 9,000 Israelis have died and the number of war invalids was over 15,000! [68] Proportionally, these figures would be about 900,000 and 1,500,000 in the United States. The statistics cannot, of course, convey the awful human suffering behind the figures. Is it any consolation to Israel that the Arab casualties are much greater?

According to the report issued on 8 December 1973 by the chief of manpower of the IDF General Staff, a total of 2,412 Israelis were killed in the October war. In addition about 400 were declared missing. "The number of Israelis who fell in this war," remarked Mrs. Golda Meir, "was proportionately two and a half times as great as the number of all the American soldiers killed in Indochina during the past ten years." [69] In addition to the fatalities and those missing in action, several thousand have been crippled for life, and many will require prolonged hospitalization. Israeli broadcasts placed the number of IDF casualties who were crippled since 1948 at 20,000.

The continued state of war prevents the government from overcoming worsening social problems in Israel: the disparity in income level and standard of living; the problems of social integration within Israeli society (between those who came from Europe and America and those of Asian or African origin); the decline of the social and moral values that are the main source of strength and the raison d'être of the reborn state of Israel. War, whether active or latent, is wreaking havoc on the spiritual and moral heritage of an ancient people which suffered torture and bloodshed for centuries in order to preserve it. In any case, there are far more vital needs for the resources required to continue the war.

The Jewish national movement set out to express the finest ideals of a generation: an authentic nationalism; social constructivism; the redemption and rehabilitation of the individual; the brotherhood of nations; and the consummation of all the highest ideals in the humanistic heritage of Judaism and mankind. How tragic it is that due to this long and awful war, the Jewish state is becoming a kind of "Prussia of the East"; that a people with the moral heritage of the prophets and the martyrology of the Jewish people, a people of refugees and persecuted minorities, should make other people refugees; that it should banish public figures from their homeland for their political views, blow up houses as "collective punishment," hold hundreds of people in administrative detention, confine people to their homes or settlements, and on occasion, treat the neighboring people in the same way as their enemies treated them in their exile.[70] People of thought and feeling among the Arabs must also be pained by the same social and moral problems which war conditions breed.

Unless both peoples are cured of their traumatic fear of each other (which is not without foundation), further perverted development and disaster are unavoidable. "Those who think the price of peace is too high should remember the cost of war"—these words were contained in a booklet for kibbutz members completing their army training. The author was one of Israel's finest young men who struggled unremittingly for peace, Major Mula Agin, a member of Kibbutz Shuval. He wrote them seven years before the Six-Day War. Along with many more of the cream of Israeli youth he fell in the line of duty during the war.

In an interview with Nathan Yalin-Mor (the former commander of the anti-British underground organization *Lehi, Israel Freedom Fighters,* and now a leader of the Movement for

Peace and Security in Israel), Mr. Ahmed Hamroush, a former senior Egyptian army officer and long-time editor of the well-known Egyptian weekly *Rose al-Yusif* said: "After the conclusion of peace, nothing will be difficult, nothing will be impossible in relations between the two states, on all levels and in all senses. But as long as the war goes on, as long as there are factors likely to lead to a new war, we are separated by blood, even though there may be the best of intentions and purest of thoughts." [71]

### The Palestinians: Source and Solution

Without recognizing the Arab Palestinian people as a national entity, with a right to self-determination in its part of the common homeland, the state of Israel is faced with two possibilities. One is that Israel will include, along with the Israeli Arabs from before the Six-Day War, nearly 40 percent more "subjects," who may enjoy civic rights but who will be denied their basic rights of national identity, representation, and self-leadership. The other possibility is that Israel will include the above percentage of "non-Jewish citizens," with an increased proportionate representation of Arab Knesset members, which every ensuing Israeli government must take into account. In this case, according to the rate of natural increase among Jews and Arabs (and the expected rate of Jewish immigration), "the Jewish majority in the year 1990 will be in jeopardy." [72] Any thought of "watering down" the Arab population of the areas, which someone may possibly conjure up, means augmenting the number of refugees, with all the terrible hatred and dangers for peace which this involves.

The correct, just, and logical way out of these complex problems is mutual recognition between the state of Israel, within borders substantially those of 4 June 1967 (though this does not rule out reasonable and agreed minor border changes), and the Palestinian Arab people. No problem outstanding between Jews and Arabs, such as the Gaza Strip, the refugee problem, or Jerusalem, should be excluded from the negotiations, and there is no question in dispute which cannot be resolved with mutual goodwill and through a common search for just and honorable solutions.

Every such negotiation must be conducted with the participation of authorized representatives of the Palestinian people, including all its component parts. Israel must support the implementation of this plan insofar as the population of the occupied areas is concerned. If the difficulties involved in establishing democratic and competent Palestinian representation demand this, the United Nations should also be brought in to help (as it did in South Yemen on the eve of that country's independence).

Whatever kind of political regime they have and whatever orientation it assumes is a matter for the Palestinian people to resolve, after a peace agreement has been secured and Israeli forces have been withdrawn from the conquered areas. Similarly, it is the Palestinian people who must determine whether its state will be established on both banks of the Jordan (even in eastern Jordan two-thirds of the population, including the refugees, are originally from west of the Jordan River) or on the West Bank and in the Gaza Strip, and they must decide what connections the new Palestinian state will have with Transjordan or Israel or both of them.

It must be stressed that the test of any solution is its ability to assure simultaneously a satisfactory answer to two basic interconnected questions: Arab recognition of the state of Israel and its integration into the political framework of the region, which is substantially Arab in character, and the granting not only of human rights, but also the realization of the national and political aspirations for the Palestinian Arabs, both settled inhabitants and refugees, through self-determination.

The root of the problem is, therefore, in the dispute between the Jewish people returning to its homeland and the Arab people living there—that is, within the area of Palestine on both sides of the Jordan, as defined by the British mandate after the First World War. The flames of the Israel-Arab conflagration have indeed spread far from its source, but the way to extinguish the flames must start at its source. Just as the dispute began in Palestine, so there it must find its solution. A modus vivendi in Palestine will do away with the main source and focus of the dispute and relations between Israel and her other Arab neighbors can then be satisfactorily settled. No "overall Arab strategy" could then continue a war over a problem which no longer existed.

## The Road to a Political Solution

Many Israelis, including members of the "establishment," are of the opinion that after the June 1967 ceasefire, it would have been possible for Israel to get what it had striven for since its inception: Arab recognition of its sovereignty and right to peace and security within the borders prevailing from 1949 to the Six-Day War. The price Israel would be required to pay was the return of territories in whose conquest much Israeli blood had been shed. Israel's leadership did not adequately evaluate the possibility which had been created and was unwilling to pay the required price. The astonishing results of the June 1967 war cast a spell of intoxication, which distorted in the minds of the great majority of Israelis that very purpose for whose attainment the might of Israel had been marshaled and fostered. Instead, a search for new aims got under way, for which security considerations were more a pretext than the truth. This opinion was shared by some military experts. What had been reiterated on countless occasions, that Israel needed not additional territories but peace, was forgotten. Relatively few continued to think that, given current military technology, the boundary is not the determining factor but what is beyond it—whether feelings for peace or those of hatred and revenge prevail.

The prolonged strategic maneuvering of the Israeli government, which was not without some tactical gains, wound up to all intents and purposes in marking time while disrupting the strategy of peace. The chasm grew deeper. One must not disregard the fact that negotiations with some promise of success can only take place in an atmosphere of good will and some mutual trust. These cannot be attained through one side forcing direct talks on the other against its will, nor through announcements about excluding controversial items from the agenda and confronting the other side with gains converted into established facts.

Nor did the Arab leaders immediately understand the imperative need for eliminating the conflict through a realistic, constructive solution or realize the strength of mind and purpose required for accepting such a decision and implementing it. This failure was dramatized by the widely publicized Khartoum Conference (August–September 1967) with its three well-known negations.

The inertia of the protracted war, the mutual fear and distrust, and also an international constellation which was as yet insufficiently clarified—all these blocked progress on the road to peace.

Even though Resolution 242 of November 1967 laid down lines for a modus vivendi between the superpowers so far as the embroiled Middle East was concerned, the area did not cease to be one of contention. Threats by the Arabs to renew the war and Israeli declarations aimed at deterrence reflected not a little the struggle of the "titans" in the global arena.

However, changes in the global balance of power increasingly cut the ground from under the cold war, which had continued for more than twenty years. Peaceful coexistence between the two chief regimes in our present-day world, without ending the ideological and political conflict between them, has become an objective historical necessity, when the alternative is the destruction of civilization. For anyone with a glimmer of foresight must understand that when the Arab-Israeli dispute increasingly endangers world peace, those responsible for world peace will sooner or later impose a compromise solution, such as Security Council Resolution 242, which was passed unanimously with the support of the United States and the Soviet Union.

It must be acknowledged that in this many-faceted situation so pregnant with danger, the Jewish and Arab political leaders have proved unskilled in finding by themselves a way to each other. Secruity Council Resolution 242 was and remains the fruit of a great effort, serious, resourceful, and fair, to find a peaceful way out of this tragic entanglement. Considering all the circumstances, including the political struggle of global powers, the resolution was and is a real attempt to clear an honorable way to "peace without victors or vanquished." The implementation of this resolution in its entirety, part for part, in letter and spirit, could bring an end to the war and open a road to peace, to normal neighborly relations and, in the course of time, to cooperation and mutual gain.

The real and simple significance of Resolution 242 is that Israel must return to her Arab neighbors the areas conquered in 1967 and the Arabs must recognize Israel's "sovereignty, territorial integrity and right to live in peace, within secure and recognized borders, without threats or acts of force." The weak point in Resolution 242 is that the rights of the Palestinian Arabs are not expressly mentioned—it speaks only (in Article 2b) of "a just settlement of the refugee problem." The gap was closed by the UN resolution of November 1970, which speaks of "equal rights and the right of self-determination for the Palestinian Arab people." This supplementary statement is of great importance, provided that it is clearly understood that self-determination of the Palestinian Arab nation means self-determination in the territory *outside* of Israel's boundaries (the boundaries of 4 June 1967) and not within them. This is the unmistakable content and sense of Resolution 242, and it is similarly the position of those who support the Arab struggle for their legitimate rights.[60] This also found expression in the speech of Soviet Foreign Minister Gromyko at the opening of the Geneva Conference.

The attempt to turn back the wheel of history and to propose *at this juncture* a binational Arab-Jewish state in the common homeland—a concept current among the Palestinian fighting forces—has no prospect of realization. The Jews have paid too costly a price for political sovereignty for them to exchange it for something less clearly defined, less secure. Perhaps, in the course of time, when both peoples are healed of their traumas and mutual fears, new political forms will be found which will be preferable to living side-by-side as two sovereign and separate political entities. At the present stage, historical developments have left both nations with but one choice: joint recognition of the fact that this land, within the framework fixed more than fifty years ago—Palestine on both sides of the Jordan, as turned over to Britain in the mandate by the League of Nations in 1920—is one in which live two nations, of right and not of sufferance, both of which enjoy unequivocal rights. Both, moreover, have vital and just claims and legitimate national aspirations, which must be mutually accommodated. Either this or an endless merciless struggle will ensue which can end only in havoc and ruin for both peoples and the land they cherish.

If this point could be clarified in the position of the Palestinian Arabs, it would take the wind out of the sails of Jewish circles opposing such a compromise or afraid lest a return to the 4 June borders prove to be only a first step, to be followed by a demand to return to the November 1947 borders as set forth in the UN Partition Resolution, and subsequently a demand to return to the 1917 situation . . . all this is accordance with the demands announced by the extremist circles in the Palestinian organizations. Full clarification of this point would create a realistic and constructive basis for the struggle of the Palestinians, as well as a common base for the exertions of all those in both nations who seek understanding and peace.

Regulation of the relations between Israel and the Palestinian Arab nation, inauguration of a common effort to guarantee peace and security, and just settlement of the refugee problem, would all help to remove the thorn which poisons the life of both nations. Even after the thorn is removed, the poison will still remain potent enough to infect mutual relations; yet once the thorn is gone, intelligent and patient treatment will serve to treat the wound and ultimately heal it.

So long as the Arabs refused to recognize Israel's existence and its right to peace within recognized and secure borders, the road to peace was blocked. Once Israel's neighbors agreed to Resolution 242 and once they took on themselves Resolution 338 of October 1973 (whose second article includes "the implementation of Security Council Resolution 242 in all its parts"), the road to peace was open.

These resolutions are a sort of "fixed price." They enjoy strong international backing and rest solidly on the trends in world politics. It is hard to imagine a "reduction" in price, either for the Arabs, who would like to see Israel smaller than it was in the beginning of June 1967, or for Israel, which wants expanded borders. This does not necessarily eliminate reasonable border rectifications, agreed upon in free negotiations. In such a fashion was the border dispute between Egypt and Sudan settled when the Aswan High Dam was being built. Distrust cannot serve as sufficient reason to postpone a possible compromise. This serious obstacle must be overcome through international guarantees by the great powers and the Security Council, in addition to practical security arrangements, such as demilitarized areas, joint Israel-Arab supervision, etc. Nations which have proved brave and daring in battle have the obligation and ability to demonstrate those qualities in making peace.

From the standpoint of their declared policy, Israel's Arab neighbors have covered considerable ground; in fact they have come half the distance separating both sides. Peace with Israel has ceased to be a dirty word in the Arab lexicon. Now Israel must come halfway. "Peace based on justice," as the Arab leaders conceive it, must cease to frighten the Israelis.[73] Details and methods of implementation will certainly require negotiation. Yet these are matters of secondary or tertiary importance compared to agreeing on a way out.

Since the June 1967 war cannot be recorded as the final bloodbath, everything must now be done to make certain that the October 1973 war may be so recorded. The precious men killed in action cannot be restored to life. What we can do and what we have the highest obligation to do is to prevent the sacrifices inevitable in new wars.

As was true twenty-six years ago, when Israel attained statehood with the blessing and joint support of the USSR and the United States, a preciously propitious hour has arrived, when both superpowers, out of global political considerations, want to help end the Arab-Israeli war. This must be utilized without any loss of time. One must conclude that the peace settlement attainable at this stage will fall short of immediately securing a full peace such as that which obtains between Belgium and Holland or between Switzerland and Austria. For this, both peoples must be bold and labor with all their might. But the hour can and must mean removal of the dispute from its dead end and paving the way for the *reconciliation* of the two embroiled peoples, who cannot escape their destiny as neighbors living side by side.

## In Conclusion

Nations must learn from their life experience. The June 1967 war and the October 1973 war, as well as the years in between, have clearly proved that the Arabs cannot destroy Israel and Israel cannot impose peace on the Arabs by force. Two alternatives face these two peoples: either to recognize each other's legitimate rights and aspirations, or to perpetuate an endless and merciless struggle, resulting in death and destruction on both sides.

When one right clashes with another, only a farsighted compromise can avoid mutual disaster. It is vital for both peoples to unravel this Gordian knot by understanding, rather than trying to cut it with the sword. No imposed settlement will benefit both peoples as will a peace won through their own common efforts. A real and lasting peace is impossible without insuring that it is just and honorable for both sides. Force is not, and cannot be, a substitute for this; and a peace that does not take justice and honor into account cannot endure.

After all that has happened, making peace cannot be a short process. The demand for "total and immediate peace" can only block the way forward. There is no direct short cut from the inferno of war to the paradise of peace. Some kind of transitional stage is necessary to reduce hostility, ease the tension, and create a new climate in which peace and coexistence will be feasible.

With the unanimous passage of the Security Council resolution and its acceptance by Israel's Arab neighbors, peace which was always essential becomes also possible. However vital it may be for the parties to the dispute, peace will not come of its own accord: the inertia of prolonged warfare blocks the way. So long as one side considers that the other needs peace more than it does, and that the other side should therefore be left to initiate and pay the price of peace, there will be no peace. The need for and the will to peace are in themselves insufficient to bring it closer, and it may not come at all unless and until people labor and struggle to clear a way for it. The task of every true patriot among both peoples is to work for this noble aim, and every individual among the nations of the world who is concerned for peace and the good of the two peoples should help towards its achievement.

We have referred to the Israeli "earthquake." But there was a certain "earthquake" on the Arab side: the restoration of certain Egyptian territory, the possibility of reconstructing the canal cities, the restoration of Arab honor, economic achievements (the force of oil, reasonable chances for US, European and Japanese investments), and political achievements, both in the international arena and in progress towards the political restoration of the Palestinian Arab people—all these gains are likely to constitute a certain psychological and political balance and to open the way to peace.

It is no easy matter to convince the Israeli public that without a solution to the problem of the Palestinians, there can be no peace. The benefits that Israel may bring to the Palestinians in the areas beyond its 1967 borders will not make them accept Israeli rule. A gilded cage remains a cage, and in our times peoples are no longer prepared to remain in captivity of any sort. It must be shown that Jerusalem could remain united without its Arab sectors necessarily having to be subject to Israeli sovereignty. The axiom "live and let live" is both just and wise for Jews and Arabs alike.

Farsighted Israelis stress day and night that without rehabilitating the Palestinian Arab people and its refugees, and without insuring its political status, there can be no peace; equally it must be understood in the Arab countries that without peace, the rights and status of the Palestinian Arab people cannot be insured. Even the strongest Israeli advocates of peace will not agree to give back the territories conquered at such cost, if they are not assured of peace in return.

There can be no greater mistake than "to let time do its work." Time is not on the side of either party; in fact the opposite is true. Untreated wounds fester and become more dangerous. Only by their own common efforts can the peoples of the region hope to prevent the great powers from foisting their rivalry onto them; only then can the powers be compelled to compete in giving impartial and constructive aid to the people in need of it. Both sides must realize that peace can enable them to call on far greater forces and resources, both local and foreign, than they can attract for their continued war effort. Disputes between states are no rare occurrence in history, but eventually they are overcome when the parties become conscious of the vital need for peace. Surely this time has come in the Arab-Israel conflict.

The people of Israel are in a unique situation in the family of nations. Unlike most other peoples, they still have to struggle for their very existence. Since the terrible holocaust which the Jews suffered during this century, the existence of the Jewish people is unthinkable outside the context of the existence, security, and possibilities of development of the state of Israel. The policies of Israel are a legitimate subject for criticism, but not its existence as a state, whose borders from 1949 until June 1967 were also recognized by the United Nations Security Council Resolution 242. The right to self-determination of the Jewish people is no less legitimate than that of other peoples.

## Notes

1. "East" is nothing but another Europe-centered historiosophic term. World history is viewed in these terms through a European lens (or, more precisely, as seen by some *developed* European countries), as though only European nations created a "real culture" which served as a cultural criterion for other nationalities elsewhere in the world. Because of its proximity to Europe, this region was known as the "Near East" (or, with several other countries such as Iran and Afghanistan, as the "Middle East"), and the countries further east were termed the "Far East." In India and Japan, for instance, the term Western Asia is used.

2. See Aharon Cohen, *Israel and the Arab World* (London: W. H. Allen and New York: Funk and Wagnalls, 1970), chapters 3–5 and 7–8.

3. *Ibid.*, chapter 5, pp. 184ff.

4. "Fasad"—an Arabic term meaning corruption, inciting quarrels, causing friction and divisiveness, hostility.

5. Cohen, *Israel and the Arab World*, chapter 5.

6. From the statement by the League for Jewish-Arab Rapprochement and Cooperation in Palestine on 20 December 1945, following Foreign Minister E. Bevin's statement in the House of Commons on 13 November 1945.

7. For details of this meeting, see Cohen, *Israel and the Arab World*, p. 381.

8. *Ibid.*, pp. 402–403.

9. *Ibid.*, pp. 412–418.

10. According to information gathered by the writer from conversations with Arab personalities closely associated with the Higher Committee.

11. Cohen, *Israel and the Arab World*, p. 423.

12. From the Declaration of Independence, 14 May 1948.

13. *Israel Policy Statements,* published by the Israeli Ministry for Foreign Affairs, Jerusalem, March 1972, p. 5 (hereafter—*Statements*).

14. *Ibid.*

15. *Ibid.,* p. 7.

16. *Ibid.,* p. 8.

17. *Ibid.*

18. Ambassador A. Eban, in the UN General Assembly, 12 November 1953.

19. Foreign Minister M. Sharett, at a press conference in Jerusalem, 11 December 1953.

20. M. Sharett, in the Knesset, 10 May 1954.

21. Julian J. Landau, *Israel and the Arabs, A Handbook of Basic Information* (Jerusalem: July 1971).

22. Interview with M. Sharett by *U.S. News and World Report,* 17 September 1954.

23. M. Comay, leader of the Israel delegation to the United Nations Ad Hoc Political Committee of the General Assembly, 26 November 1954.

24. *The New York Times,* 4 January 1954.

25. *Al-Ahram,* 27 September 1954.

26. Announcement by Prime Minister D. Ben Gurion, in the Knesset, 2 November 1955.

27. Julian J. Landau, *Israel and the Arabs,* p. 70.

28. *Statements,* p. 19.

29. *Ibid.,* p. 21.

30. *Ibid.,* p. 25.

31. Nahum Goldmann, *Memories* (Jerusalem: Weidenfeld and Nicolson, 1972), p. 272. Dr. Goldmann has been president of the World Zionist Organization and president of the World Jewish Congress.

32. Jon Kimche, in the *Jewish Observer,* reported by *Al Hamishmar,* 2 August 1958.

33. For the problems and status of the Arabs in Israel, see Cohen, *Israel and the Arab World,* pp. 491–506.

34. The monthly *Ner* (Candle), Jerusalem, May–June 1953, p. 13.

35. *Al-Ahram,* 20 October 1954.

36. Erskine Childers, "Deadlock in the Holy Land," *Encounter,* August 1958.

37. *Al Hamishmar,* 12 January 1956.

38. *Ibid.,* 4 November 1956.

39. *Ibid.,* 1 November 1956.

40. *Ibid.,* 24 December 1956.

41. For the attempts at mediation, see Cohen, *Israel and the Arab World,* pp. 517–518.

42. For details, see *Newsweek,* 9 January 1954.

43. See note 32.

44. Moshe Sharett, *Mi-shut be-asiah* (*A Journey in Asia*) (Tel Aviv: Davar Publishers, 1958), p. 273.

45. At a meeting at the Jerusalem Press Club, 7 June 1959; *Al Hamishmar,* 8 June 1959.

46. He remained a Knesset member and served as the chairman of the Jewish Agency. He died on 7 July 1965, aged 71.

47. *Daily Mirror,* 9 November 1956.

48. *Al Hamishmar,* 6 March 1964.

49. Ben Gurion, "Our Security and Our Position Before and After the Sinai Campaign," *Israel Government Handbook, 1959–1960,* p. 54.

50. Aharon Cohen, "Israel and the Development of the Region," *Al Hamishmar,* 15 August 1958.

51. *Al Hamishmar,* 31 March 1959.

52. Mapam (the United Workers Party) has as its main slogan: for Zionism, socialism, and the brotherhood of nations ("pioneering Zionism, revolutionary socialism"). Marxism is its declared ideological basis. In the fifth Knesset (1961), Mapam received 9 seats out of a total 120; in the sixth (1965), 8 seats; in the seventh (1969), as part of the alignment with the Israel Labor Party, 7 seats. Its main source was the Hashomer Hatzair youth movement and it is connected with the Kibbutz Artzi Federation of communal settlements, which numbers seventy-five kibbutzim.

53. The Israel Communist Party (founded in 1948) split in August 1965, most of the Jewish members rejecting the policy of the Soviet Union in the Arab-Israel dispute, while all of the Arab members and a small part of the Jewish membership continued to defend this policy, regarding the June 1967 war as "a war of aggression in the service of imperialism." In the first elections after the split (November 1965), the former group, *Maki,* received one seat, and the latter, *Rakah* (the new Communist list), got three seats.

54. The *Haolam Hazeh-Koach Hadash* (New Force) movement was established before the elections to the sixth Knesset (1965) by the editor of the weekly *Haolam Hazeh,* Uri Avneri, who has reservations about the Zionist movement. Avneri was elected to the sixth Knesset and his group won two seats in the elections to the seventh Knesset (1969). The movement backs the integration of Israel into the region, the recognition of a "Palestinian entity," and retreat from all the territories taken by the Israeli army in June 1967, in return for an Arab-Israeli peace. During the seventh Knesset, the second member of this parliamentary list dissociated himself from Avneri (for personal reasons) and set up a separate party called "Black Panthers-Israeli Democrats." Both the Black Panthers and Haolam Hazeh lost their seats in the elections of December 1973.

55. See Cohen, *Israel and the Arab World,* pp. 474–475.

56. A census taken for the army headquarters by the Israeli Central Bureau of Statistics in August–September 1967 revealed a population of 33,411 in northern Sinai, 356,265 in the Gaza Strip, 596,637 on the West Bank, and 65,857 in East Jerusalem (the Old City and other Arab quarters that were annexed to Israeli Jerusalem by special Knesset legislation on 29 June 1967).

57. Foreign Ministry information briefing, 16 January 1972.

58. Statement by the prime minister in the Knesset, 4 August 1970.

59. Foreign Ministry information briefing, 30 April 1972.

60. A commentator in the important Moscow political weekly *New Times* wrote in the 5 February 1970 issue: "In accordance with this

principle [of secure and recognized boundaries] the Soviet Union proposes that the 5 June lines be fixed as permanent and recognized boundaries between Israel and the neighboring countries that took part in the June conflict. The Arab states agree with this proposal, although this solution involves certain concessions by them in Israel's favor, as it is clear that the 5 June borders are better for Israel than those laid down in 1947 by the United Nations Resolution on the establishment of Israel."

61. Syrian President Hafez Asad declared on 9 March 1972: "If the November 1967 Security Council resolution can bring about the return of the territories to the Arabs without war, and ensure the rights of the Palestinian people, then Syria supports it."

62. Mapam participated in the provisional government in 1948–49 and in the governments in 1955–1961 and from 1966 to the present.

63. *Al Hamishmar*, the Mapam newspaper, 2 November 1973.

64. *Davar* [newspaper of the General Federation of Labor], 26 October 1973.

65. Likud (Consolidation)—the parliamentary bloc of rightist parties in the Knesset (Gahal, the Free Center, and the State List, comprising 31 out of the 120 members of the Knesset), which was created for elections to the eighth Knesset, scheduled for 11 October 1973 and rescheduled because of the war and held 31 December 1973.

66. *Yediot Aharonot*, 28 October 1973.

67. The Israel army spokesman, reported in *Haaretz*, 6 June 1972. Nearly all the above casualties fell up to the end of the war of attrition and the start of the ceasefire in August 1970.

68. Cohen, *Israel and the Arab World*, pp. 449, 468.

69. *Davar* [newspaper of the General Federation of Labor], 12 November 1973.

70. As regards the blowing up of houses, arrests, etc., in the occupied areas, one must differentiate between the period of active guerrilla operations, when the Israeli authorities took such measures, and the period following 1970, when the blowing up of houses was stopped.

71. *Haaretz*, Weekly Supplement, 26 February 1971.

72. R. Bachi, Israeli government statistician, as quoted in *Jewish Vanguard* (London), 7 June 1972.

73. "As long as all Arab designs are predicated on the immediate or eventual destruction of Israel, no progress towards peace is possible"— Mrs. Golda Meir, *Foreign Affairs*, April 1973, p. 460.

# Arab Peace Efforts and the Solution of the Arab-Israeli Problem

**George M. Haddad**

## Preliminary Considerations

This study of Arab peace efforts and the search for a solution to the Arab-Israeli conflict will cover three periods: first, the period of the British mandate (1920–1948), when the Arab majority in Palestine was attempting to obtain the independence of the country from Britain and prevent its transformation into a Jewish state; second, the period that followed the proclamation of the state of Israel by the Jewish minority in Palestine in May 1948 until the June 1967 war, during which the Arab states tried to help restore the Palestinians to their homeland in Palestine and contain the expansion and growth of Israel; third, the period since the June 1967 war, during which the Arab states directed

George M. Haddad was born in Syria in 1910 and was educated at the American University of Beirut, the Sorbonne, the École des Langues Orientales Vivantes, and the University of Chicago, receiving his Ph.D. from the latter in 1949. He taught at the University of Damascus from 1949 to 1959 and served for most of that period as Chairman of the Department of History. He was a visiting professor at Bowdoin College, Thiel College, and the University of Michigan, and since 1960 has been Professor of History at the University of California, Santa Barbara.

Dr. Haddad's books in Arabic include *The Arab Conquest of Damascus, 635 A.D.* (Beirut, 1931); *History of Arab Civilization* (Damascus, 1944); *History of Civilization in the Middle East* (3 vols., Damascus, 1953–57); and *Faris al-Khuri: His Life and Times* (Beirut, 1952). In English, he is the author of *Aspects of Social Life in Antioch in the Hellenistic-Roman Period* (University of Chicago Press, 1949); *Fifty Years of Modern Syria and Lebanon* (Beirut, Dar al-Hayat, 1950); and *Revolutions and Military Rule in the Middle East* (3 vols., New York, Robert Speller, 1965–73).

their efforts to securing the withdrawal of Israel from the newly occupied Arab territories and continued, along with the emerging Palestine resistance movement, to defend the rights of the Palestinian Arabs.

One important consideration that should be kept in mind in order to understand how the Arabs view the origins of this conflict and what might contribute to its solution is that Palestine was an Arab country when the struggle began after World War I. Like the other political entities—Syria, Lebanon, and Transjordan—that were created by Britain and France in geographic Syria after the war, Palestine had been a part of the Arab provinces of the Ottoman empire that Britain promised a measure of independence.[1] They all did eventually become independent, but Palestine had a different destiny on account of the international Zionist movement and its drive to establish a Jewish state in Palestine through mass immigration and colonization with the help of foreign powers.

The inhabitants of Palestine at the time the conflict began were 90 percent Arab, and the majority of the remaining Jewish 10 percent were European Jews who had immigrated after 1880. The Arab inhabitants of Palestine did not begin to settle there in the seventh century A.D. as a result of the Muslim-Arab conquests, as it is commonly supposed. They were the descendants of the original and successive settlers, including the Arabs, and they became Arab by language, culture, and tradition after the seventh century. Their obvious and legitimate claim to Palestine is based on the long and continuous occupation and possession of the country, which is the only claim that present peoples have to the countries in which they live. The Zionist claim, on the other hand, is based on the old historic-religious connection of the Jews with Palestine and cannot be equated with the Palestinian Arab claim, even if it could be proved that the Jews of the Diaspora had descended from those Jews who left Palestine between the sixth century B.C. and the first century A.D. Historical connections with lands inhabited today by other peoples cannot justify movements in world populations. The arguments based on the intensity of Jewish religious feeling towards Palestine and on Jewish homelessness are not valid because religious feelings and homelessness—even if it could be said that the Jews were really homeless—do not give a claim to the establishment of an alien state at the expense of the indigenous population. Moreover, the historical plight of the Jews in Europe can not be viewed as a valid reason for their mass immigration into Palestine. The Jewish problems could have been solved by other means, including emigration to the United States, but the Zionists were not interested in this solution, because it would have eradicated the necessity for creating the Jewish state.[2] As a result, the Palestinian Arabs, who were not responsible for the injustices done to the Jews by European intolerance, had to bear the consequences of other peoples' behavior and even became the victims of Jewish intolerance. The claim to Palestine was eventually decided, not by notions of legitimacy and obvious rights, but by power politics in which colonial interests and the capitulation of the big powers to Zionist manipulation and Jewish pressure played a decisive role.

The second important consideration is that the Arab inhabitants of Palestine were not in any way responsible for starting the conflict. It was imposed on them by a succession of resolutions, declarations, and challenges that threatened to deprive them of their homeland. The first challenge was contained in the resolution of the first Zionist Congress of Basel in 1897 to create a home for the Jewish people in Palestine and to promote the colonization of Palestine by agricultural and industrial Jewish workers. The resolution and the efforts that were made later to implement it were in utmost disregard of the already existing Arab population and its interests. Two years earlier Theodor Herzl, the promoter of the congress and the father of political Zionism, had written in his diaries about the need to "spirit the penniless population" of poor Palestinians across the border to the "transit countries" and to expropriate the land of the notables. "Both, the process of expropriation and that of the removal of the poor," Herzl said, "must be carried out discreetly and circumspectly."[3] One of the young Zionists in the Herzlia Gymnasia in Palestine before World War I later wrote, "It was drummed into our young hearts that the fatherland [Palestine] must become ours 'goyim rein' (clean of Gentiles-Arabs)."[4] The father of spiritual Zionism, the poet Ahad Ha'am, later recalled that "the Arab people [have been] regarded by us as non-existent since the beginning of the colonization of Palestine."[5]

The challenge became more real when Britain issued the Balfour Declaration on 2 November 1917, in which it promised to use its "best endeavours" to facilitate "the establishment in Palestine of a national home for the Jewish people." The 90 percent Arab majority was not mentioned by name but only referred to as "the existing non-Jewish communities." The head of the world Zionist organization, Dr. Chaim Weizmann, later spelled out the meaning of the "national home" to Secretary of State Robert Lansing in Paris in February 1919 by saying that his movement intended to "build up gradually in Palestine a nationality which would be as Jewish as the French nation was French and the British nation British." [6] The decisive challenge came on 29 November 1947, when the United Nations partitioned Palestine against the wishes of the Arab two-thirds of the population and under Zionist pressure. In the ensuing conflict the neighboring Arab states became involved when the Palestinians appealed to them for help after the withdrawal of British troops and the subsequent breakdown of security in Palestine. In their conflict with the Zionist forces under the British mandate and with Israel after 1948, the Arabs of Palestine were thus constantly reacting to the challenges, provocations, and injustices that were imposed on them. Their reaction and defensive effort, however, did not regain what they lost, and the hostilities between them and Israel consequently continued and became more serious.

The third important consideration is that the conflict was possible only because the big powers supported the Zionist program. Without this support the realization of the Zionist goals would not have been practicable. The Zionist plan of encouraging Jews to settle in Palestine until they become the majority of the population was not likely to succeed under the Ottoman administration,[7] for the Turks objected to Jewish mass immigration and acquisition of land in Palestine, and the little progress the Zionists made in that direction was mainly with the complicity of corrupt Ottoman officials. The Zionist project, as a result, "stood before a blank wall," as Dr. Weizmann said, until Britain was persuaded to sponsor it in the Balfour Declaration and implement it after it had become the mandatory power in Palestine. The Zionist leaders naturally encouraged Britain to rule the country and emphasized the close relationship between their aims and British imperial interests.[8] Under Britain's protection the Jews were able to increase their numbers from one-tenth to one-third of Palestine's population; they acquired more land, established an autonomous administration of their community, organized and trained a Jewish army, and ensured that Palestine was denied independence as long as the Arabs were the majority. Even though Britain tried after 1939 to restrict Jewish immigration, the fact remains that the creation of a Jewish state would have been inconceivable without the British presence. In the same way, the UN partition of Palestine would have been inconceivable without the unprecedented pressure of American Zionists on the United States government, and the pressure the US exerted on smaller states in order to secure the necessary votes. The struggle between Arabs and Jews in Palestine, therefore, became inevitable only after Britain and the United States had supported a minority that consisted mainly of alien settlers against the indigenous majority. Later Israel was able to disregard various UN resolutions primarily because it felt supported by one or more of the great powers.

The fourth consideration is that while the Arabs of Palestine and the various Arab states have differed on this conflict and its possible solutions, as well as in their regional interests and their attitude toward the great powers, they have all condemned the methods and goals of the Jewish settlement in Palestine, which has resulted in the dispersion and dispossession of the Palestinian Arabs and the conquest of more Arab territories. Individual Arabs, including persons in responsible positions, have criticized the mistakes of their governments and the irresponsible rhetoric that has accompanied the Arab-Israeli conflict,[9] but they have never deviated from the Arab consensus on the righteousness of their claims and the legitimacy of their demands. Their unanimous hostility to Israel is not the product of religious prejudice or of what the Zionists call "anti-Semitism," for the Arabs are themselves Semites, and the Muslims and Christians of the Arab world lived with the Jews in peace for centuries. It was rather the result of the wrongs and sufferings that Zionism inflicted on the Palestinians and other Arabs.

Certain small groups of Jews within and outside Israel have at times raised their voice to criticize Zionist discriminatory, aggressive, and colonizing policies. They have appealed to Israel to curb its territorial ambitions to make a peaceful settlement possible and have expressed regrets for the injuries that the Arabs had to suffer.[10] Some others, like the ultra-Orthodox Jews, have objected from the very beginning to the political and nationalist character of Zionism, and to the return to Zion by political and military action. Others have declared that political Zionism was incompatible with the religious basis of Jewry, and that it was a denial of democracy, because it deprives the people who are in Palestine of the right of self-government.[11] Those who rule Israel, however, have remained insensitive to these declarations and to the plight of the Palestinian Arabs; they have even exploited the Arab refusal to accept injustice in order to give the impression that Israel was willing to end the conflict and the Arabs were not. The great majority of Israeli and other Jews in the world have condoned and supported what Zionism and Israel have done and have continued to ignore the rights of the native Palestinians.

The fifth and last consideration is the various means that the Zionist movement has used to justify its claims to Palestine and enlist the moral and material support of influential members in the world community. They have, first, misrepresented or suppressed the facts relative to the obvious rights of the Arab inhabitants of Palestine. Second, they have tried to justify the creation of the Jewish state on the basis of irrelevant Biblical prophecies and divine promises, and on other narratives in the Bible that were written by those who had developed in exile the nationalist spirit and the chosen-people complex which were bound to have the most serious effects on the destinies of the Jews. Third, they have levelled the charge of anti-Semitism and resorted to threats and blackmail against any person, organization, or publication that criticized Zionist or Israeli policies or dared to suggest a change of attitude that would deal more equitably with the Arabs or would reduce the support given to Israel. Fourth, the Zionists have exploited the sizable Jewish communities in certain countries, particularly in the United States and western Europe, to influence government policy and extract decisions in favor of Israel. Fifth, they have used the plight of the Jews or any restrictions on their freedom in certain countries to draw sympathy to Zionist goals or to justify the emigration of Jews to Israel and reinforce the notion that Israel was the only safe place where the

Jew could live in peace. Sixth, they have invented various slogans and basically inaccurate phrases to justify Zionist plans and claims. They thus have spoken of the "return" to the "homeland" of the Jews and of the "ingathering of the exiles." They portrayed Palestine as a sparsely inhabited country of deserts and swamps and forged the phrase "the people without land to the land without people." They emphasized the backwardness of the Arab inhabitants and boasted the skills of the Jewish immigrant who "made the desert bloom," but they never mentioned Arab accomplishments or their potential for progress, especially if they had the same opportunities or financial support enjoyed by the new Jewish settlers. The Zionists could exploit from the very beginning the advantage of being Europeans, members of a modern industrialized society, while the indigenous Palestinians belonged to an underdeveloped society that was only beginning to modernize. But what Zionism exploited most was the British rule in Palestine.

## Under the British Mandate: How the Opportunities for Peace Were Missed

The transformation of Palestine to a Jewish state which eventually supplanted the indigenous Arab population took place under the British mandate between 1920 and 1948. This process was resisted and opposed by the native Arab population and marked the birth of a conflict that has disturbed the peace in Palestine and the entire Arab world. Conflict between the native Arabs and immigrant Jews could have been avoided, if the latter had been considerate of the interests of the Arab population, and if Britain had fulfilled its promises to both Arabs and Jews in a fair and equitable manner.

In the Balfour Declaration Britain promised support for the establishment in Palestine of a national home for the Jewish people. The Arabs have generally contested Britain's right to make this promise on the grounds that the Arab inhabitants of Palestine were not consulted and that Palestine was a part of the Arab area already promised independence in the British pledge to Sharif Hussein of Mecca in 1915–1916. But even setting this aside, the Balfour Declaration mentioned a "national home," not a national state, for the Jews, and it also contained a restrictive clause that said, "it being clearly understood that nothing shall be done which may prejudice the civil and religious rights of existing non-Jewish communities in Palestine." Moreover, when Sharif Hussein asked for an explanation of the Declaration, because he feared that Palestine was threatened with outside colonization, he was told by Commander D. G. Hogarth of the Arab Bureau in Cairo on instructions from London that "a Jewish settlement in Palestine would only be allowed insofar as would be consistent with the political and economic freedom of the Arab population." Sharif Hussein felt reassured as long as Arab political and economic freedom was safeguarded and he concluded that Jewish settlement must be intended to provide a refuge to Jews from persecution. He consequently promised to further that aim and caused an article to be published in *al-Qibla,* on 23 March 1918 "calling upon the Arab population in Palestine to bear in mind that their sacred books and their traditions enjoined upon them the duties of hospitality and tolerance and exhorting them to welcome the Jews as brethren." [12] When World War I ended, a joint Anglo-French declaration was issued in Palestine, Syria, and Iraq stating that the policy of the two powers in the liberated Arab territories was to set up regimes "that shall derive their authority from the free exercise of the initiative and choice of the indigenous populations."

In January 1919 Prince Faisal, the spokesman for Arab independence at the Paris Peace Conference, gave further proof of how far he—like his father Sharif Hussein—was prepared to assist Arab-Jewish cooperation, as long as it did not conflict with the independence of the Arab countries. In a meeting arranged by the British Foreign Office, he signed an agreement with Dr. Weizmann recognizing such Jewish aspirations in Palestine as immigration and acquisition of land, but he made the agreement conditional upon Britain fulfilling its pledges respecting Arab independence. As the Arabs were not granted independence, the agreement with Weizmann did not acquire any validity.[13] Earlier, in June 1918 in Faisal's camp near Aqaba, Weizmann had assured Faisal that the Zionists did not intend to try establishing a Jewish government in Palestine. On 3 March 1919, shortly after his visit to London, Faisal wrote to the American Zionist leader, Professor Felix Frankfurter, a letter in which he referred to the Arabs and Jews as cousins and stated that there was room for both in geographic Syria. He made it clear, however, that the Arabs would not accept a Jewish state as such but only a possible Jewish province in a larger Arab state.[14]

Faisal had been ruling internal Syria from Damascus since the end of World War I and was working for an independent Arab state in all geographic Syria, including Palestine. The overwhelming majority in Palestine wanted to remain a part of Syria with Faisal as head of state, and they sent representatives to the Syrian Congress, which in March 1920 proclaimed geographic Syria an independent constitutional monarchy with Faisal as its king. Britain and France had already made their own plans, however, and they did not recognize Syrian independence. Instead, in April 1920 Britain was awarded the mandate over Palestine and Iraq and France the mandate over Syria including Lebanon. Palestine thus became a separate entity through no fault of its own; the majority of its people would have preferred to belong to a united Syria. Article 22, paragraph 4 of the League of Nations Covenant said of these former Ottoman communities—Syria-Palestine and Iraq—that they had "reached a stage of development where their existence as independent nations can be provisionally recognized, subject to the rendering of administrative advice and assistance by a Mandatory until such time as they are able to stand alone."

In the course of Faisal's struggle for Arab independence, in accordance with the Allied pledges and the Wilsonian principle of self-determination, the Zionists in the Peace Conference were opposed to self-determination for Palestine because that would make it an Arab state or part of an Arab state. They also objected to President Wilson's proposal to send a joint Allied commission to the Middle East to ascertain the desire of the populations "directly concerned." [15] In August 1919 this purely American commission (Britain and France did not participate because they obviously feared its results) proposed that Palestine become part of a united Syrian state under Faisal, with the United States, or as a second alternative Britain, as the mandatory power. The commission warned against "the extreme Zionist programme for

Palestine of unlimited immigration of Jews looking finally to making Palestine a Jewish state." It told the peace conference that "no British officer consulted by the commission believed that the Zionist programme could be carried out except by force of arms." [16] The report of the King-Crane Commission was ignored by the peace conference, because its frankness did not please Britain and France and President Wilson was no longer there to defend his principle of self-determination.

The Arabs of Palestine expected that the British mandate would only temporarily restrict their free enjoyment of independence despite the incorporation of the Balfour Declaration into the terms of the mandate. They believed, as the League of Nations Covenant said, that the well-being and development of the populations placed under a foreign mandate form a sacred trust of civilization. Although they were aware that Article 6 of the Palestine mandate made Britain responsible for facilitating Jewish immigration, they expected that this would take into consideration the rights and position of other elements of the population. They were bitterly disappointed when they found out that the principles and safeguards contained in the various covenants and declarations were not respected. In sharp contrast to Iraq, Transjordan, Syria, and Lebanon, the Palestine mandate did not lead to independence and Britain never gave Palestine the self-governing institutions that the indigenous population demanded. Even when Britain was inclined to answer Arab demands for a legislative assembly or promised independence, the Zionist forces objected because the Jews were still a minority of the population. The Arabs realized that the Jewish national home mentioned in the Balfour Declaration was neither a mere humanitarian project to protect the persecuted Jews, as Sharif Hussein was told, nor merely the center for the cultural revival and spiritual redemption of the Jews, as some Zionists claimed. The national home was only a screen or an intermediary stage for a Jewish national state, to be established through unlimited immigration and land purchase that could lead—as it actually did—to the displacement of the native Arab population. The Zionists accepted and supported the British mandate as long as it protected these two operations and discriminated against the native Arabs, but the same Zionists rose against the British rulers and accused them of favoring the

Arabs whenever they tried to protect the rights of the Arab population by restricting Jewish immigration and land transfers.

Throughout the British mandate the indigenous Arab majority had to struggle against the Zionist forces because their program meant either the division of Palestine, or the displacement of its Arab population, or both, in order to build their Jewish national state. The Arabs of Palestine had also to struggle against the British because they protected Jewish immigration and land purchase, and because they refused to grant Palestine independence. The struggle was generally peaceful until 1936. Except for a few dispersed clashes in 1920, 1921, and 1929, that resulted from Zionist abuses and provocations, it consisted of protests and demonstrations. Among the major abuses was the Jewish settlers' boycott of Arab labor and the eviction of Arab tenant farmers from the lands purchased by Jewish organizations or transferred to them by the state. The British administration sometimes sent troops to help evict the Arab peasants whose villages were being replaced by Jewish settlements, and Arab riots were often the result.[17]

The Arabs of Palestine resented the development of the Jewish community as a separate, autonomous national entity. They were offended by the aloofness and indifference of the immigrant Jews, who ignored the existence of the Arabs, were insensitive to their interests, and expected privileged favorable treatment from the British rulers. Under the protection of Britain, the Jewish Agency was allowed to become almost a state within a state with its own political institutions, its intelligence service, and its control over Jewish immigration, education, health, social welfare, and the secret Jewish military forces. The Arab majority opposed the steady influx of Jewish immigrants but did not react severely while their average annual number was below 10,000 persons. They became alarmed and provoked, however, during the early years of Nazi rule in Germany, when the numbers rose to 30,000 in 1933, 42,000 in 1934, and more than 62,000 in 1935. It was estimated that if this rate of immigration continued, the Jews would become the majority by 1947. In 1935 they already constituted one-fourth of Palestine's population. The Palestinian Arabs were not ready to become a minority in their own homeland on the pretext that certain European governments were persecuting the Jews. The problem, they said, was the responsibility of the world in general and should not be solved at the expense of the Palestinian Arabs.

The British government sent several commissions to report on the causes of Arab riots and Arab-Jewish clashes. They generally recommended restricting Jewish immigration and land transfers and mentioned that the fears Arabs had about their future and the frustration of their hopes were important factors in the disturbances. The British official statements that followed the reports would include vague promises of self-government and reassurances that the "national home" did not mean a Jewish government to dominate the Arabs, but the British promises and reassurances were regularly disregarded. The admission of more than 130,000 Jews into Palestine between 1933 and 1935 and the continued transfer of land drove the five Arab parties in the country to form the Arab Higher Committee, which in November 1935 petitioned the British High Commissioner for the following: the establishment of a democratic government in Palestine according to the League of Nations Covenant and Article 2 of the Palestine mandate, the prohibition of land transfers, and the stopping of immigration. The High Commissioner rejected the last two demands but agreed to establish a legislative council and presented details for the project. The Arabs expressed their readiness to cooperate, but the Zionists raised an outcry in the House of Commons, and the plans for self-government in Palestine were postponed.

As a result the Arabs of Palestine declared a general strike in April 1936 and decided to rise in an armed insurrection, which took the form of guerrilla warfare between 1936 and 1939. In the course of this insurrection, the British military authorities gave tacit recognition to the Jewish defense force (Haganah) and even cooperated with it against the Arabs, while British officers trained the Jewish soldiers in the art of guerrilla warfare.[18] The Arab Higher Committee, on the other hand, was dissolved by British orders and some of its members were sent into exile. Its head, Haj Amin al-Husseini, had to seek refuge in Lebanon. When the Peel Commission of 1937 recommended partition of Palestine, the Arabs rejected the plan because they opposed the partition of their country on principle, and the Jews rejected it because they thought it did not give them enough territory, although they accepted the principle of partition. After the failure of the February 1939 conference in which Jews, Palestine Arabs, and the Arab states were represented, the British government finally announced its own solution. It is significant because it definitely rejected the establishment of a Jewish state in Palestine. The White Paper of May 1939 explained that a Jewish state in Palestine would be contrary to the Balfour Declaration and to Article 22 of the League of Nations Covenant, but promised that after a transitional period of ten years, Palestine would become an independent state in which Arabs and Jews would share in the government. It limited Jewish immigration to 75,000 persons for the following five years, after which further immigration would be by agreement with the Arabs. It also promised to prohibit the purchase of land by Jews in certain districts.

The White Paper of 1939 was a reasonable and fair solution of the Palestine problem. Had it been accepted by the Arabs and the Jews of Palestine, it would have saved them and the rest of the world from the tensions and wars that later followed the creation of Israel. The Arabs should have accepted it and supported it, because it preserved the integrity of Palestine and avoided a Jewish state. Arab leadership, however, demanded that independence be granted at the beginning of the ten-year transitional period, for they feared that under Zionist pressure Britain might withdraw this project as it had previous promises. The Zionists, on the other hand, condemned the White Paper and fought it both in and outside Palestine. World War II made it difficult for Britain to implement its new policy, and the horrors of the Nazi oppression brought Jewish immigrants to Palestine in numbers far exceeding the limitations of the White Paper, nevertheless the Arabs observed a tacit truce with the Jews and posed no problem to the British, who needed their neutrality.

The Jews had no alternative but to cooperate militarily with the British against Nazi Germany, but they were also preparing to fight a battle with Britain because of the White Paper policy. Their participation in the war gave them the opportunity to equip themselves, with arms which were partly stolen from the Allied forces and smuggled into Palestine. In Palestine itself the British contracted with Jewish concerns to manufacture small arms, many of which went to the Haganah armories.[19] Jewish terrorist activity in Palestine began towards the end of the war. Between 1944 and 1947 terrorists of the Stern Gang and the Irgun, tacitly supported by the Jewish Agency, assassinated Britain's ministers, kidnapped its judges, whipped and hanged its officers, demolished its buildings, and threatened its army's security. But Britain did not deal with the Jewish insurrection in the same harsh manner as it had dealt with the earlier Arab revolt in the previous decade. Illegal Jewish immigration continued along with terrorist action. Jewish troops in the Allied armies and Zionist agents organized escape routes to the Mediterranean and American Zionist organizations purchased or chartered ships for the voyage.[20]

During and after World War II, the United States became the center of world Zionist activity and the source of its financial and moral support. The first open demand for a Jewish state embracing all Palestine was made by an American Zionist conference in New York in May 1942 on the basis of a proposal presented by David Ben Gurion, head of the executive committee of the Jewish Agency in Palestine. The Biltmore conference also asked for unlimited Jewish immigration into Palestine. The plight of the displaced persons was exploited by Zionist organizations, who argued that a recompense should be provided in Palestine for what the Jews were undergoing in Europe—but the interests of the Palestinian Arabs and the victims of the Palestinian tragedy were invisible to most American eyes. Political expediency persuaded certain politicians to support Zionist ambitions, and the leaders of both American political parties began to issue statements in favor of the Biltmore program. President Roosevelt was subjected to enormous Zionist pressure, as was his successor, President Truman. Roosevelt had to abandon his scheme of finding a worldwide asylum for displaced persons, because the Zionists wanted Palestine alone to be the asylum. In his meeting with King Abdul-Aziz al-Saud on 14 February 1945, Roosevelt explained his interest in rescuing the remnant of Jews in Central Europe and said that he counted on Arab hospitality and on the king's help to solve the problem of Zionism. King Abdul-Aziz replied, "Make the enemy and the oppressor pay; that is how we Arabs wage war. Amends should be made by the criminal not by the innocent bystander. What injury have the Arabs done to the

Jews of Europe?" President Roosevelt later told Congress, "I learned more by talking with Ibn-Saud for five minutes than I could have learned in the exchange of two or three dozen letters." In this meeting and a later letter Roosevelt said that he personally as president "would never do anything which might prove hostile to the Arabs" and that "the United States Government would make no change in its basic policy in Palestine without full and prior consultation with both Jews and Arabs." [21]

When Harry Truman became president in 1945, he did not heed his predecessor's promise. At the end of August of the same year he surprised and shocked the Arab and Muslim world by asking the British prime minister to admit 100,000 Jews from Europe into Palestine. Here began the open official American intervention in the Palestine problem in favor of Zionism, a policy which slowly drained the reservoir of Arab good will toward the United States. Truman's "eagerness to combine expediency with charity," as Arnold Toynbee commented, "would appear to have been untempered by any sensitive awareness that he was thereby abetting the infliction of wrongs and sufferings on the Arabs." [22] Although Truman invited his four ministers to the Arab countries to advise him regarding the impact of America's new policy on its interests in the Middle East, he did not receive them until after the November congressional elections. And after he did hear their statement, he replied, "I am sorry gentlemen, but I have to answer to hundreds of thousands who are anxious for the success of Zionism. I do not have hundreds of thousands of Arabs among my constituents." [23]

Britain presented two more projects for solution of the Palestine problem, but both were rejected by both Arabs and Jews. The first, the Morrison-Grady plan of July 1946, provided for a British trusteeship over a federation of two autonomous provinces —one Arab and one Jewish—along with Britain's direct rule over the Jerusalem and Negev districts. The second, the Bevin plan of January 1947, proposed a unified state under a temporary British trusteeship with autonomous Jewish and Arab cantons. The two plans accepted the possibility of admitting 100,000 Jews. The Arabs insisted on an independent unitary state in which the Jews were granted full rights and privileges. The Zionists, encouraged by American support, insisted on Jewish statehood in a partitioned Palestine. On 18 February 1947 British Foreign

Secretary Ernest Bevin announced that Britain was referring the Palestine question to the United Nations. Britain was undoubtedly opposed to Palestine's partition, but it could not force this solution in the face of strong American pressure and escalating Jewish terrorism. Ernest Bevin pointed out that from the Zionist point of view, 100,000 immigrants was only a beginning and that the Jewish Agency talked in terms of millions. He said that the Arabs could be persuaded to accept 100,000 new immigrants on humanitarian grounds, if after that immigration was determined by the elected representatives of the Palestinian people. "The claim made by the Arabs," he added, "is a very difficult one to answer. We here in Great Britain as a House of Commons determine whether people shall be admitted to this country or not. Why should an external agency largely financed from America determine how many people should come into Palestine and interfere with the economy of the Arabs who have been there for 2,000 years?" [24]

The Palestinian Arabs defended their case in the United Nations, as they had done under the British mandate, on the basis of legality and the uncontested material facts, as well as the guarantees of Arab rights that appear even in the documents giving limited support to Zionist goals. They never expected that the United Nations would rashly decide in two short sessions in 1947 what Britain never saw fit to approve in twenty-seven years. The partition of Palestine, as the Arabs viewed it, was the culmination of a series of illegal acts and constituted a denial of peace in Palestine. It was proposed by a majority of the eleven-member UN Special Commission on Palestine (UNSCOP) and approved on 29 November 1947 by the necessary two-thirds majority of the General Assembly, with thirty-three votes in favor, thirteen against, ten abstaining, and one absent. The partition resolution proposed the termination of the British mandate, the creation of a Jewish and an Arab state linked by an economic union, and the internationalization of Jerusalem under United Nations trusteeship. Three members of the UNSCOP proposed, in what is known as the minority plan, the formation of a federal union between two autonomous Arab and Jewish states. The Arabs denounced both proposals, while the Zionists accepted the majority or partition plan.

The Arab UN delegates rejected partition of Palestine because it clearly violated the right of self-determination of the indigenous Arab majority that owned most of the land in Palestine. Second, it violated the United Nations Charter, because the Charter did not confer upon the General Assembly the right to dismember countries and create new states. An Arab proposal to ask the International Court of Justice for an advisory opinion on the competence of the United Nations to enforce any kind of partition without the consent of the majority in Palestine was rejected. Third, the partition scheme was inequitable and unfair in terms of population and land ownership, even if one disregards its juridical and moral deficiencies. It gave 56 percent of Palestine's total area to the proposed Jewish state, although the Jews were one-third of the population and owned only 5.66 percent of the land, or 6.8 percent if one includes the public lands leased to them by the government in the Haifa Bay area.[25] The Arab state was given 43 percent, though the Arabs were two-thirds of the population and owned or held most of the land. Moreover, through a clever process of gerrymandering, the proposed Jewish state was to contain almost all the Jews in Palestine outside Jerusalem, while the Arab state had less than 60 percent of all the Arab inhabitants, the remainder, about half a million, were left in the Jewish state, which therefore would include almost as many Arabs as Jews. Fourth, the resolution was obtained by Zionist pressures and political threats within and outside the United States and through the cooperation of highly placed officials in the White House and some members of Congress who influenced the vote of several states that needed American financial aid.[26] The majority of those who voted for partition did so without much conviction; they were apologetic and did not conceal their apprehensions about the consequences. The Belgian delegate for example said, "We are not certain that it is completely just; we doubt whether it is practical and we are afraid that it involves great risks," and the Canadian delegate declared, "We support the plan with heavy hearts and many misgivings." Moreover, the twenty-four delegations that either did not vote or flatly rejected partition represented two-thirds of the population of the member states. Those who voted in favor belonged mostly to distant states, such as those of Latin America, that had nothing or little to do with the Middle East.

The Arab delegations at the United Nations warned before and after adoption of the partition resolution against its dangerous results. The Syrian delegate, Faris al-Khouri, complained that instead of achieving a workable solution, UNSCOP had simply created a worse situation, while Mahmud Fawzi of Egypt predicted that creating a Jewish state on a religious basis and by force in Palestine would certainly lead to bloody strife whose end no one could foresee.[27] Before the final vote was taken, the Arabs proposed an independent federal state in Palestine, divided into Arab and Jewish cantons, similar to the Bevin plan of 1947 and to the minority UNSCOP plan which they had turned down. In addition they said they would consider other proposals and moved that the Assembly adjourn for a few weeks in order to provide time for conciliation and compromise, but the motion was not even put to a vote and the partition plan went through.[28]

In the Security Council debate in February and March 1948 about whether it should take the necessary measures to implement the partition plan, the Syrian member, warned again that the partition plan threatened the peace and that those who rejected it were those at whose expense it was to be executed. He declared that the General Assembly was exceeding its authority when it recommended partition and asked the Security Council to implement it.[29] On 5 March the Security Council refused the General Assembly request. Violence had already broken out in Palestine between Arabs and Jews following the vote on partition. The Palestine Commission, established by the General Assembly to implement the partition plan under Security Council supervision, found that it could not perform its functions without armed assistance. Since a peaceful implementation was impossible, on 19 March the United States modified its position and recommended a temporary trusteeship under the UN Trusteeship Council. The American delegate asked the Security Council to call for a truce in Palestine and for a special session of the General Assembly in order to consider Palestine's future government.

In the special session of the General Assembly (19 April–15 May 1948), the American trusteeship proposal was discussed, but the deliberations were not conclusive. The Palestinian Arabs accepted the proposal, but the Jewish Agency denounced it vigorously and threatened to use force against its implementation.

Jewish manpower had been already mobilized before the November 1947 partition vote. Even before the British mandate ended and the British troops withdrew, the Jewish Agency was already taking over government functions in the Jewish areas of Palestine and preparing to proclaim the Jewish state. The General Assembly adjourned on the day the mandate ended, without deciding the question of trusteeship and without creating an instrument of government in Palestine. It had voted a partition plan but sent no troops to enforce it. It had, however, appointed on 14 May a mediator, Count Bernadotte of Sweden, to "promote a peaceful adjustment of the future situation in Palestine," and some people thereby assumed that the partition resolution had been abandoned. The mediator at least did not consider himself bound by that resolution. As the Jewish Agency was not ready to retreat before the new developments, it proceeded to "create facts," as Dr. Weizmann said, "and confront the world with these facts." [30] The state of Israel was proclaimed on 14 May. It was immediately recognized by President Truman, although his government had found partition unworkable and its proposal for trusteeship was being debated at the United Nations. The Syrian delegate to the United Nations believed that recognizing the new state was illegal, but drew an angry refusal from the American side when he proposed to ask the International Court of Justice for an opinion.

The birth of the Jewish state was preceded by clashes with irregular Arab forces in Palestine and was followed by hostilities with the regular armies of the neighboring Arab states. The Jewish forces, according to a moderate estimate, counted about 65,000 men—Haganah 55,000, Palmach 4,000, Irgun and Stern band 6,000—and were by far superior in number, equipment, and training to the irregular Palestinian forces supported by the 4,000 Arab volunteers of the "Liberation Army" from outside Palestine.[31] Between the partition resolution of November 1947 and the end of the British mandate the Jewish fighting units tried, first, to confirm their domination over the areas allotted to the Jewish state in the partition plan and to occupy as much additional territory as possible; and, second, to oust by terrorist and psychological means as many Arabs as possible, for they constituted about half the inhabitants of the proposed Jewish state. By the time the Jewish state was proclaimed, about 300,000 Arabs had left not only towns and villages in the "Jewish state," but even such all-Arab towns as Jaffa and Acre that belonged to the "Arab state." The Jewish forces had also expanded their occupation to other Arab areas in western Galilee and took the greater part of Jerusalem, which was supposed to be internationalized. It is believed that they would have overrun all Palestine, if the Arab regular troops had not intervened on 15 May, because of the vacuum left after the British evacuation. Moderate estimates put the Arab forces that entered Palestine at 20,500 men—10,000 Egyptians, 4,500 Jordanians, 3,000 Syrians, 3,000 Iraqis.[32] Their intervention was in response to a Palestinian Arab appeal for protection against Zionist encroachments and massacres. Despite their threats to prevent Palestine's partition, the Arab states made no serious preparations for translating the threats into action, and some, like Egypt and Jordan, intervened with reluctance and had orders not to go beyond the area of the "Arab state."

The violence that accompanied Israel's birth was not unexpected. The Jewish state was the product of an irrational and unjust scheme that did not take the rights or even the existence of the Arab inhabitants of Palestine into consideration. It was, from the Zionist Congress of Basel in 1897 to the Balfour Declaration of 1917 to the UN partition of Palestine in 1947, the result of illegal, unjust, and therefore unworkable resolutions and promises. The Zionist leaders knew that their project could not be imposed on the Arab inhabitants without force, so they obtained colonial protection to help them in the first, or settlement, stage; meantime they prepared the necessary military forces to assure domination by force in the second stage. The Arab inhabitants had full confidence in their obvious and legitimate rights and made no similar preparations; nor would the mandatory power have allowed them to make any preparations, even if they had wanted. Their leaders, moreover, were not as negative or inflexible as they have been portrayed. They accepted the influx of Jewish settlers as long as it was reasonable, and even when the Jews became one-third of the population, they were prepared to live together peacefully in one independent state, or in what they later accepted to be a federal state with autonomous cantons. But their Jewish neighbors wanted an exclusively Jewish state that would have broken up the territorial integrity of the country, appropriated most of its lands, and threatened the existence of the Arab inhabitants. Britain realized, too late, the danger and injustice involved in the Zionist designs and tried rather faintheartedly to restrain them. The United States saw, but only for a short time, that the Zionist scheme was unworkable and then surrendered to the pressures of its Jewish community. It was evidently not aware of the injustice involved, or of the problems, the tensions, and the threats to peace that its encouragement was provoking. The Soviet Union was possibly aware of the tensions and hostilities that the presence of Israel would create and wanted to reap all the benefits that it could from these problems.

In order to have avoided conflict and maintained peace in Palestine during and after the British mandate one of two things should have happened: either the Zionists should have accepted the transformation of Palestine into one united or federal independent state, or the Arabs of Palestine should have accepted the establishment of the Jewish state which the Zionists had been working for with strong determination. The united or federal Palestinian state would have better guaranteed the equal rights of all inhabitants, because it would not have been a racial, or religious state. As later events proved, the Arab inhabitants of the Jewish state, even if they became reconciled to the breakup of their country, would not be able to exercise their national and civil rights on a free and equal basis with the Jews and their mere continued presence in the Jewish state or in the rest of Palestine would scarcely be tolerated.

## Approaches and Obstacles to Peace, 1948–1967

After 1948 the Palestinian Arab struggle became one to resist the new Jewish state and its occupation of Palestine and to regain their lost rights. The Arab states' intervention to prevent Palestine's dismemberment did not succeed. The war lasted about two months (15 May–18 July 1948), interrupted by a first truce of four weeks and followed by a second truce of indefinite duration.

Between October 1948 and March 1949, the Jewish forces resumed fighting despite the second truce and occupied more Arab territory in the Negev and in Galilee. Their last conquest after the truce was the village of Umm al-Rashrash, which they later named Eilat, on the Gulf of Aqaba.

The war of 1948 and the failure of the Arab intervention aggravated Arab-Israeli hostility and created serious obstacles to the restoration of peace. The first result of the war was that Israel continued to expand until the new state included about 78 percent of the entire area of Palestine instead of the 56 percent provided by the UN partition plan. The neighboring Arab states did not lose territory, but they were humiliated by their failure and embittered because an alien state had been imposed on an Arab land in the heart of the Arab world with the support of the great powers. Not only was Israel viewed as an outpost of imperialism, but its territory also disrupted the geographic contiguity between the Arab states. What had been a local confrontation between the indigenous Palestinian Arabs and the Jewish settlers became an Arab-Israeli problem with all its international permutations. Four separate armistice agreements were finally signed between Israel and Egypt, Lebanon, Transjordan, and Syria between February and July 1949. According to the agreements, the armistice demarcation line was not to be construed as a political or territorial boundary and was delineated "without prejudice to rights, claims, and positions of either party to the armistice as regards the ultimate settlement of the Palestine question." [33]

The 1948 war also displaced many Palestinian Arabs, who were denied the right to return to their homes in what became Israel and whose property was eventually confiscated as well. Some Palestinians had left their homes to avoid the dangers of war and naturally expected to return at the end of the hostilities, but the majority of the one million persons who became refugees left under the pressure of terrorism or by outright expulsion. Israel's explanation that the Palestinians were urged by their leaders to leave has been proved unfounded. [34] The Zionists in reality wanted Palestine without its Arab inhabitants, so that they might make room for the new influx of Jews and build up an overwhelming Jewish majority in the new state. A coldly planned operation was expected to terrorize the people out of their homes. The massacre of Deir Yasin on 9 April 1948, in which some 250 persons, mostly old men, women, and children, were killed in cold blood, was most successful in frightening the civilian Arab population. Its effectiveness was described by Menachem Begin, leader of the Irgun and later head of the Herut party; he mentioned that when the Haganah attacked Haifa "the Arabs began fleeing in panic shouting 'Deir Yasin!' " The same leader asserted later that there would have been no Israel without what he called "the victory" at Deir Yasin.[35] Jews and Arabs had agreed that the Arab city of Jaffa should be an open city, but as soon as the British withdrew, Jewish forces began attacking the city with mortars and in the resulting panic, the defenseless population left by boat and by road. These events were repeated in other areas near Lake Tiberias and in Safad before the end of the British mandate, and loud speakers were used in cities such as Haifa, Jerusalem, and Acre to threaten the people with the fate of Deir Yasin if they did not leave. In May–July 1948 Israeli forces occupied several Arab cities and bluntly ordered their inhabitants to leave. As the people left, shots were fired at and over their heads in order to speed their departure.[36] Contrary to what Theodor Herzl had recommended half a century earlier, removal of the native Palestinians was neither discreet nor circumspect.

On 1 August 1948, shortly after the second truce, the foreign minister of Israel informed the UN mediator, Count Bernadotte, that the Palestinian Arabs would not be allowed to return to the Jewish state. Before his assassination at the hands of Jewish terrorists on 17 September, Bernadotte had insisted that the Arab refugees should be able to return to their homes at the earliest possible date. On 11 December 1948 the UN General Assembly adopted a resolution which provided that the refugees should be given permission to return to their homes or receive compensation. Israel refused to implement this and all other pronouncements and United Nations resolutions that upheld the right of the displaced Palestinians to return, even though it agreed to the terms of the 1947 partition resolution which protected the rights of Arab inhabitants in the proposed Jewish state.[37] Moreover, the Israeli proclamation of independence on 14 May 1948 had expressed Israel's readiness to cooperate in implementing the partition resolution.

Israel evidently felt that the war of 1948 released it from the obligations and guarantees contained in the partition resolution. Israeli logic seemed to imply that because the Palestinian Arabs resisted the invasion of their country and failed, they lost the right to live in their country. Israel claimed that the returning Palestinians would be a security risk, and it naturally needed their lands, towns, and homes for housing new Jewish immigrants. It is ironic that the very state which had claimed Jewish homelessness as the primary justification of its existence inaugurated its activity by making other people homeless. Israel's motives were neither morally nor legally valid, because its rule over the major part of Palestine made it automatically responsible for all civilians, including the indigenous inhabitants. Israel, as Arnold Toynbee said, had even less excuse for evicting the Palestinian Arabs than had Nebuchadnezzar, or Titus and Hadrian, or the Spanish and Portuguese Inquisition for uprooting the Jews in Palestine and elsewhere.[88]

Israel's expulsion of the Palestinian Arabs and its refusal to allow their return constituted perhaps the greatest obstacle to Arab acceptance and recognition of the new Jewish state and prevented the creation of that atmosphere necessary to a peaceful settlement. Israel practiced what a French scholar has called "total colonialism," for unlike classical colonialism where the foreign settlers and colonial rulers allowed the native inhabitants to stay on their land and in their country, Israel removed the indigenous population and introduced another people in its place.[39] Israel's action left the Arabs and many non-Arabs with the impression that they were not dealing with a normal government that respects the law and cares to discriminate between right and wrong. This became a certitude when Israel's subsequent behavior never erased that impression. The Arabs cooperated with UN attempts to solve the two standing problems of refugees and boundaries. They participated in the meetings of the Conciliation Commission for Palestine (CCP), and on 12 May 1949 both Arabs and Israelis signed separate protocols at Lausanne in which they accepted the 1947 partition plan as the basis of discussion with the CCP. The Arabs thus indicated for the first time that they would accept the November 1947 partition, but Israel later announced that she would not go back to the partition boundaries and would not accept the December 1948 UN resolution on the repatriation of the refugees.

It soon became clear that Israel had accepted the Lausanne Protocol in order to gain admission to the United Nations. Its first application for membership had been rejected in December 1948, because it was occupying territories that belonged to the proposed "Arab state" and the Jerusalem international zone. When Israel applied again in 1949 and was admitted on 11 May, admission was conditional upon acceptance of the 1947 partition plan and the 1948 repatriation-compensation plan. The United States, who led the move for admission, did not press Israel to implement the two plans or make specific commitments to implement them before being admitted. After it became a United Nations member, Israel refused to abide by these plans, so President Truman made his only attempt to pressure Israel by sending a strong note expressing his disappointment. As a result Israel offered to take back 100,000 refugees under certain conditions, but withdrew the offer when all concerned—CCP, United States, Arabs—found it insufficient. The Arabs, particularly in Egypt and Jordan, had been willing to meet with the Israeli delegations and prepare a peace settlement, but this unique opportunity was lost, because Israel, sure that the Truman administration would never again apply any effective pressure, refused to make the required concessions.[40] Only Jordan, of the Arab states, objected to Jerusalem's internationalization in the spring of 1949, for it had occupied the Arab sector of the Old City since the 1948 war. Israel, which occupied the rest, also opposed internationalization. Israel proclaimed the divided city its capital in 1950 and moved most government offices there, but the UN members did not recognize this action. Originally Israel had claimed that the return of the refugees would be contingent upon concluding a peace treaty with the Arab states, but later it repudiated repatriation and began to insist that the refugees resettle in the neighboring Arab countries.

Between late 1949 and early 1950, because of his long border with Israel and his need for a Mediterranean outlet, King Abdullah of Transjordan entered into separate negotiations with Israel, but found that Israel would only make peace on its own terms.[41] In reaction to this separate negotiation, the Arab League states resolved to expel from the league any member who signed a separate peace with Israel.[42] King Abdullah also incurred the hostility of Egypt, Saudi Arabia, and the former mufti of Palestine and his supporters because he annexed to Transjordan that part of the proposed "Arab state" in Palestine which his army already occupied on the western bank of the Jordan.

The Conciliation Commission for Palestine was not able to solve the refugee problem on the basis of repatriation or compensation in spite of the annual UN resolutions, of various supportive declarations by political leaders like John Foster Dulles, Anthony Eden, and Dag Hammarskjold, and the special mission of Joseph E. Johnson in 1961–1962. It got Israel to accept a very limited reunion-of-families scheme and the release of blocked Arab bank accounts.

Between 1948–1950 Israel took over refugee property in what was called "one of the greatest acts of plunder in the history of Palestine." [43] The property consisted of agricultural land, citrus groves, and thousands of buildings and shops in whole towns or sectors of towns and villages. Arab possessions were placed under an Israeli "Custodian of Absentee Property" who could arbitrarily declare any property vacant. The definition of absentee owner was so unjust that even the Palestinian Arabs who remained in Israel sometimes lost their property because during the fighting they had moved a few miles from their habitual place of residence. In March 1950 a new law allowed the absorption of "absentee property" and gave legal recognition to the de facto takeover.[44] Since the early 1950s the Arab states have tried various times to obtain from the United Nations effective safeguards for the property rights of the Arab refugees, but they were unsuccessful largely because the United States opposed them.[45]

The failure of the world community to bring about repatriation of the Palestinian refugees has produced a Palestinian diaspora and a concomitant "Arab Zionism." While the United Nations Relief and Works Agency and a number of voluntary relief organizations have been providing the refugees with the bare necessities of living and education in the camps, Israel has ignored her victims, admitted no responsibility for their plight, and shown no official sign of repentance. In their diaspora, whether self-supporting and comfortable or living in poverty in the camps, the Palestinian Arabs have carried with them a hatred of Israel and its militancy that eventually produced border incidents and commando raids in which the Arab states became involved. In their diaspora, they have been also "rebuilding the emotional strength" for regaining their homeland, and they have produced a mass of literature—mainly poetry, with some drama and song—and painting on the theme of the refugees, the injustice done to them, and the longing for the return to their homes.[46] The Arab governments, contrary to their critics' claims, have not been holding the refugees as hostages or exploiting them in their struggle against Israel. They have supported the refugees materially and morally and some, especially Syria, Iraq, and Jordan, are ready to resettle those refugees who do not choose to return. The refugee demand for repatriation, however, is genuine, and observers have reported that any action suggesting that their camps were more than a transitory stage was resented. Their close association with the soil where they and their ancestors lived is a part of their national character, and even their children who were born in exile are "instructed in the mystique of the return." Certain American visitors have commented after meeting with them that it is difficult to make the refugees forget in a few years what the Jews did not forget in two thousand years.[47]

The Arab states took several countermeasures when Israel refused to implement the UN resolutions. First, they maintained in principle a state of belligerency with Israel in order to keep the issues alive. Second, they ordered a diplomatic and economic boycott of Israel. The new state was never recognized by any Arab country and its name was banned in books and maps. It was referred to as "occupied Palestine" or the "so-called state of Israel." Third, Israel was denied use of the two waterways that pass through Arab lands, the Suez Canal and the Straits of Tiran. The Security Council attempts in 1951 and again in 1954 to vote a resolution calling on Egypt to allow Israeli ships to pass through the canal were considered unfair, because Israel did not implement several other United Nations resolutions that protected Arab rights. The Arabs could not recognize Israel, because recognition, as a well-known Arab spokesman said, would have meant accepting and respecting its "right to be," although it came into being by making another country "cease to be." [48] Recognition would also have legitimized and perpetuated the dispersion and uprooting of Palestinians. The conflict, according to the same spokesman, was caused by Israel's refusal to recognize the Palestinian people and their right to live in peace in their own country. Arab refusal to recognize Israel was merely a response to Israel's prior refusal to recognize and respect the being of the Palestinian people.

Israel exploited the state of belligerency with its Arab neighbors and took an alarmingly harsh and aggressive attitude towards the Arabs living within and outside its borders. Instead of trying to bring about a reconciliation, it continued to follow a policy of violence and intimidation. The Palestinians who remained in the Jewish state—eventually a minority of about 10 percent—were docile and peaceful after the armistice, but they were nevertheless placed under Israeli military rule and subjected to severe emergency regulations. The military authorities could expel the Arab inhabitants from their villages within what were defined as "defense areas" and "security zones." District commissioners were authorized to take possession of any Arab land, if the action was "in the interest of public safety." Under this pretext about half the lands belonging to the Arab inhabitants were expropriated. The Arab minority was placed in a class "B" category, the movement of its members was restricted, and they were discriminated against in education, employment, political representation, and health facilities. Those Arabs who were born in Israel had to be naturalized—and with difficulty—in order to become citizens, whereas Jews of foreign birth received citizenship the moment they stepped on Palestinian soil. For alleged security reasons certain Arab villages were destroyed and their inhabitants were removed—such as Ikrit and Bir'im in western Galilee—although they were far removed from the armistice line and their people were peaceful law-abiding citizens. [49]

Israel's attitude on these matters produced more Arab hostility and created more obstacles for peacemaking. Although the Mixed Armistice Commissions were present to help settle border disputes and incidents between Israel and its neighbors, the Israeli authorities sometimes crossed the armistice lines into Jordanian territory to destroy villages and kill persons in cold blood in "retaliation" against individual Palestinian infiltrators who committed some vengeful acts in Israel where they had once lived and owned property. The village of Qibya was destroyed on 14 October 1953 by half a battalion of Israeli troops who killed seventy-five persons including women and children. Israel was condemned by the Security Council, but it responded with defiance and self justification. Other villages were attacked in the same way and Israel has accumulated more condemnations than any other state. But Israel no longer heeded what the United Nations decided after it obtained what it wanted in 1947–1948, nor did Israel appreciate the testimony of truce officers that Jordan tried to curb the infiltrators, who usually came from that country.[50]

It is always possible to speculate that the Arab states might have been able to find a solution with Israel shortly after 1948, when the hatreds were not so deep and the positions had not hardened. But Israel's massive retaliatory incursions and the high level of tension it maintained along the borders not only discouraged cooperation but also persuaded the Arabs that Israel was not yet interested in a permanent peace. Many Arabs believed that Israel was planning to acquire more territory, and its Government Yearbook of 1951 and 1952 mentioned that it had been established in only a portion of the land of Israel.[51] The high level of border tension, moreover, and the maintenance of a "situation pregnant with the threat of Arab attack"—as General Carl van Horn, chief of staff of the UN Truce Supervision Organization said—had its manifest advantages for Israel.[52] It strengthened the cohesion and unity of Israeli citizens, ensured a high state of military readiness and efficiency, and produced for Israel a maximum flow of sympathy, aid, and funds, based on the premise that it was threatened by its Arab neighbors. The UN record shows, however, that no Arab state was condemned for any act of aggression against Israel or for violation of the armistice agreements.

The change in Egypt's attitude towards Israel in the mid fifties resulted from Israeli provocation and constant attempts to weaken and humiliate her Arab neighbors. In his early years as leader of the revolutionary regime, Gamal Abdel Nasser was restrained in his public statements and writings on Israel; some believe that he even expressed interest in a peace settlement. It was also reported that Nasser encouraged indirect contacts with Israel's moderate prime minister, Moshe Sharett, and that he actually maintained a secret correspondence with Sharett in 1954–55.[53] The contacts and the correspondence evidently produced no results because Israeli extremists put pressure on Sharett.

The armistice agreement between Egypt and Israel had been already violated in 1953, during Ben Gurion's rule, in the strategic demilitarized zone of El Auja in Sinai, when Israel drove the indigenous Bedouins away, set up a kibbutz, and claimed sovereignty over the whole zone. The Mixed Armistice Commission (MAC) found out in 1954 that the kibbutz was organized as a unit of the Israeli army. In September 1955 Israel took complete military control of the zone and built fortifications, so Egypt responded by moving military forces to the southern area of El Auja. Both sides agreed a month later to obey a request to withdraw their troops from prohibited sectors, but on the night of 1 November 1955 the Israelis attacked the Egyptian forces, killing fifty men. The attack permanently established the Israeli army in El Auja, for Israel refused thereafter UN requests to remove her troops and to allow the Mixed Armistice Commission to meet in that zone.[54]

Adjoining the Gaza Strip, which Egypt had administered since 1949 and where some 300,000 refugees lived, the Israelis set up armed settlements and provoked border incidents. No major assault occurred, however, until 28 February 1955, when the Israelis attacked an Egyptian camp, killing thirty-eight Egyptians and Palestinians and wounding thirty-one. The assault took place eleven days after David Ben Gurion's return to the defense ministry. He followed a tough policy toward the Arabs, but this attack was not warranted by any border incidents, according to UN truce supervisors, and the Security Council condemned Israel for it in late March. The attack was actually a challenge to the rising power of Nasser and to the newly independent Egypt, which no longer had a British buffer in the canal zone. Israel would have preferred the British to stay in that zone. The attack was also intended to tell Egypt to open the waterways for Israeli navigation and to accept Israel's occupation of the Auja demilitarized zone. In addition, Ben Gurion saw the friendly relations of Egypt with the West during the first years of the Eisenhower administration as a threat to Israeli security.[55] In general Israel disliked close or friendly relations between the United States and the Arabs and consistently strove to prove that it was America's only friend in the Arab regions. Ben Gurion was evidently also annoyed by the arrest and trial in Egypt of eleven Israeli agents, two of whom were executed at the end of January 1955. These agents had been charged with placing fire bombs in American and British installations in Cairo and Alexandria in order to damage Egypt's relations with the two Western powers and to prevent the signing of the evacuation agreement with Britain.[56] It was disclosed later, in what came to be known as the Lavon Affair, that the Israeli agents were sent to Egypt in 1954 while Pinhas Lavon was defense minister in the Sharett cabinet, but without his knowledge, by security men who received orders from Ben Gurion.

The attack of 28 February 1955 was a turning point in Egyptian-Israeli relations. The ruling Egyptian officers, who had used the humiliating defeat of 1948 as a pretext for overthrowing the monarchy, became aware of their own military inadequacy and of the humiliation which they would have to endure as a result of Israel's military superiority and aggressiveness. The Israelis had already started in 1954 a large-scale buildup of French weapons. An Egyptian search for weapons ended with the Czech arms deal, which Nasser announced in September 1955. Thus Israel was responsible for starting the arms race and for the dependence of Egypt and other Arab military regimes on Soviet weapons. The continued presence of the Israeli challenge indirectly caused the entrance of the Soviet Union into the Arab area, increased the militancy of Arab radicals, and raised the degree of Arab hostility to the West every time the West gave additional support to Israel. Israeli encroachments and attacks on Egypt's borders, moreover, led to the beginning of Egyptian and Palestinian *fedayeen* or commando raids into Israel, which Nasser reluctantly approved in August 1955.

Israel was not directly involved in the crisis that erupted be-

tween Egypt and the western powers over nationalization of the
Suez Canal Company, but Israel had been entertaining the idea
of a "preventive" war—Moshe Dayan has admitted that Ben
Gurion ordered a Sinai invasion plan a year before the Suez war
of 1956.[57] Ben Gurion wanted to check the growth of Egypt's
military power, diminish the stature of Nasser, who was regarded
as a potentially dangerous leader, open the forbidden waterways,
and expand Israel's borders. Exploiting the Suez crisis for its own
particular goals, Israel joined Britain and France in the attack on
Egypt. It began, in fact, on 29 October 1956 with an Israeli offensive in Sinai and the Gaza Strip—yet another proof to the
Arabs that Israel was ready to serve imperialist designs in the
Arab regions of the Middle East. Israel's success in the war did
not give her the expected fruits of victory. A United States-Soviet
Union effort resulted in a UN resolution that ordered the end of
hostilities and the withdrawal of all foreign troops from Egyptian
territory. Britain and France completed the evacuation of their
forces on 22 December 1956, and though Israel resisted, heavy
pressure from President Eisenhower obliged it to withdraw from
Sinai in January 1957 and from the Gaza Strip in March. No
American president has had so far the courage and the concern
for the international order that Eisenhower had to curb Israel's
appetite for gain at the expense of her neighbors. In his address of
20 February 1957 to the American people he remarked: "Should
a nation which attacks and occupies foreign territory in the face
of United Nations disapproval be allowed to impose conditions
on its withdrawal? If we agree that armed attack can properly
achieve the purposes of the assailant, then I fear we will have
turned back the clock of international order. We will, in effect,
have countenanced the use of force as a means of settling international differences and gaining national advantages." [58]

Egypt made two important concessions—it opened the Straits
of Tiran and the Gulf of Aqaba to Israeli navigation and it accepted the stationing of a UN emergency force on its side of the
border in Sinai, the Gaza Strip, and the Gulf of Aqaba. This
meant the end of incidents and tensions on the Egyptian-Israeli
borders as well as the freedom for Israel to develop her relations
with the nations of Asia and East Africa.

Nasser gained prestige as a world figure and as the undisputed leader of the Arabs when the Suez crisis was turned into a political victory. Inevitably he was expected to play the leading role in restoring Arab rights in Palestine. Although he maneuvered shrewdly to keep control over the Palestine question and preserve his popularity among Palestinians and other Arabs without involving Egypt in military action against Israel, he mostly used the Palestine problem to maintain his Arab leadership and to bargain for international loans and assistance, especially from the United States. He occasionally issued declarations and threats against Israel and spoke of the "holy march" to liberate Palestine. Like the other contemporary Arab military rulers, Nasser mentioned at times the "battle of destiny" with Israel, but he neither prepared seriously for it nor did he have any real commitment or plan for waging it. Nasser was absorbed in revolutionary activity in those Arab countries whose policies did not align with his own. Until Israel imposed the 1967 war on him, Nasser used his Soviet arms against other Arabs, particularly in the Yemen war (1962–1967). Indeed, Imam al-Badr of Yemen had to remind him that "the way to Israel is Sinai, not Yemen." [59] The Arab revolutionaries, including Nasser, sometimes promised that Palestine's turn would come after the conservative Arab rulers were replaced by the socialist transformation, but actually the Arab revolution and cold war diverted them from their professed objective of liberating Palestine. After the Suez crisis the Arabs were mainly preoccupied with one another.[60] In Israel, on the other hand, the overriding preoccupation was to prepare for the day when a confrontation with the Arabs should become necessary. Israel's preparation had to give it such a distinct military superiority as would make possible a decisive victory. This would not only assure Israel's survival, but would also remove the danger of a future attack, thus ending Arab belligerency.

Nasser's role in the Palestine question was passive and peaceful. He succeeded in avoiding a confrontation until 1967, but did nothing positive to reach a satisfactory solution of the problem. His friendship with the Soviet Union assured the flow of arms to Egypt, but the Russians were neither ready to fight for the Arab cause nor anxious to solve the Arab problem with Israel, because that would end Arab dependence on them. Nasser recognized America's interest in Israel's security, so he gave them complete satisfaction in that respect. For this he was rewarded with badly needed American food during the Kennedy and the early Johnson administrations. However, he also attacked and plotted against the Arab friends of the United States and accused them of cooperation with Zionism and imperialism. He further antagonized the US with his abusive criticism of its policy in Vietnam, Cuba, and the Congo and thus lost the material as well as diplomatic aid that he and the Arabs might have expected when they needed it in June 1967. He involuntarily gave Israel a pretext to build up a superior military force on the basis that the Russians were supplying Egypt with arms. Moreover, by emphasizing Egypt's dependence on the Soviet Union and the danger of Soviet expansion in the Middle East, Israel could project itself as the only friend and defender of the West in the Middle East.

Nasser rendered Israel another service by dividing and weakening the Arabs with his conspiratorial activities, his encouragement of military coups against nonsocialist regimes, and even at times against rival socialist or progressive regimes, and his abusive accusations and attacks against Arab leaders. He lowered overall Arab military strength with his military operations against other Arab countries, by the officer purges that followed every military coup or leadership change, by the undermining of army discipline which occurs when the army engages in politics, by diverting part of the armies to protecting the security of the military regimes, and by giving more consideration in promotion and appointments to an officer's loyalty to the ruling leaders than to his military competence.

Among Israel's neighbors, Syria was perhaps the most militantly anti-Israeli. The relative intensity of Arab national feeling in Syria, resentment over the fragmentation of geographic Syria (Palestine had been one of its component parts), the more dangerous and immediate threat of Israeli expansion to Syrian territory, and the special hostile attitude of Israel toward Syria account for this. Syria and Israel disputed the legal status of the demilitarized zone (DMZ), ownership of land within the zone, fishing and irrigation rights on Lake Tiberias, and Israel's diversion of the Jordan River waters. Israel often provoked the incidents in order to have a pretext for massive retaliation that was intended to express disapproval of Syrian policy. Prime Minister

Ben Gurion, who presided over Israel's policy of intimidation, had "little concern" for the legality or illegality of his actions or for world public opinion about them and believed that the Arabs "best understood sharp words and tough actions." [61] In 1956 his moderate foreign affairs minister, Moshe Sharett, was replaced by Golda Meir who, like Ben Gurion, advocated a tough policy. In 1951 the Israelis even destroyed Arab homes in three DMZ villages and on the night of 31 January 1960 they levelled the village of Tawafik. Other clashes in the DMZ were caused by Israeli attempts to drain Lake Huleh and the surrounding swamps.

In an attempt to avoid the incidents of Lake Tiberias between Syria and Israel the United Nations urged Israel not to send its armed patrol boats too close to the shore near the Syrian border, but Israel continued the provocative practice. On 10 December 1955 an exchange of fire was deliberately provoked by Israelis in order to launch an assault on the Syrian positions north of the lake, which killed fifty-six Syrians. The purpose of the attack was to warn Syria against closer ties with Nasser's Egypt.[62] Another such attack occurred on 16–17 March 1962 and the Security Council again condemned Israel.

Israel's diversion of the Jordan River waters was another source of tensions and hostilities with the Arab countries, but it did not lead to war because the Arab states did not want to fight. The diversion operations began in 1953 and were stopped temporarily as a result of pressure by the Security Council and the US government, but they resumed in 1956 when Israel decided to tap Lake Tiberias, which was under its control, and not directly from the Jordan. The Arabs were concerned over the loss of irrigation water, the increased salinity of the remaining waters, and Israel's ability, by bringing more land under cultivation, to absorb more immigrants and increase her potential power.[63] During the period of unity between Egypt and Syria after 1958, Syrian leaders tried to persuade President Nasser to use force to prevent the diversion, but he feared provoking a general war for which the United Arab Republic was not prepared.[64] The Israeli operation was eventually allowed to proceed to its final stage, but Arab pressures were such that Nasser had to call an Arab summit conference in early 1964 to deal with the problem.

Nasser had made it clear on more than one occasion that he

had no intention of taking immediate action to regain Palestine for the Arabs. When a delegation of Palestinian Arabs asked him to save Palestine, he told them with a frankness that shocked and disappointed them that neither he nor any other Arab country had a plan to fight Israel and liberate Palestine and that removing Israel would take a long time and require great preparations. At the January 1964 summit conference the Arab heads of state showed no inclination to use force against the Israeli operation. Instead they decided to divert the tributaries of the Jordan in Lebanon, Syria, and Jordan, and to initiate a hydraulic project for using this water. The conference also created the Unified Arab Command, with an Egyptian general at its head, and the Palestine Liberation Organization (PLO) to represent the Palestine entity. When the Israelis began pumping water to the Negev in May 1964 the Arabs took no action. Egypt was then negotiating to obtain loans and more surplus food from the United States.[65]

At the second summit conference in Alexandria in early September 1964, it was admitted that the decision to divert the tributaries was not being implemented properly. Israel had not only verbally opposed the diversion, but had attacked the diversion area in Syria. The unified command did not react. Nasser tried to justify his failure to support Syria by saying that this would let Israel set the time for any potential battle.[66] The editor of *al-Ahram* developed a rationale for Nasser's decision not to engage in war with Israel and compared the Egyptian policy of not fighting Israel to that of the United States in not fighting Russia or Cuba.[67] The third summit conference, in September 1965 in Casablanca, practically killed the diversion idea. As Ahmad Shuqairi, secretary general of the PLO, commented, "The diversion project has been diverted!" The Arabs who criticized the summit conferences probably did so not because they wanted to fight Israel, but rather because the participating leaders had reached their positions of power partly through their promises to save Palestine.[68]

In the Arab cold war, of which the conferences were only an interlude, Palestine continued to be a handy cause of argument. The Baath rulers of Syria attacked Nasser's moderation, and both Nasser and the Baath of Syria attacked President Bourguiba of Tunisia after he urged the Arabs in April 1965 to accept Palestine's partition and the existence of Israel as outlined in the 1948 UN resolution. When Egypt and Syria signed a mutual defense agreement in November 1966, it was thought Egypt and the Soviet Union intended using the pact to restrain Syria from any rash action against Israel and to coordinate activities of the two revolutionary regimes.[69] In Cairo the head of the PLO spent his time quarreling with the Jordanian government because his organization was not allowed complete freedom of action in Jordan. The Israeli raid on the Jordanian town of Sammu' in November 1966 brought no response from either the Unified Arab Command or from Egypt and Syria. Syria's Baath leader, Nureddin Atassi, was quoted saying that the end of the Jordanian regime should come before the end of Israel.[70]

Tensions on the Syrian and Jordanian borders with Israel increased after the founding, in early January 1965, of the Palestinian commando organization, al Fateh. The new organization, in contrast with the PLO, was independent and not under the wing of the Arab League or any Arab government. Its founder, Yasir Arafat, wanted to keep alive the attachment of young refugees to their national homeland in Palestine. His "armed infiltrators" into Israel entered from either the Syrian or Jordanian borders. Israeli military leaders like Moshe Dayan and Yitzhak Rabin favored immediate military action against the Arabs to prevent diversion of the Jordan tributaries and to disrupt any Arab war plans before the Arabs attained any military strength.[71] The tensions between Syria and Israel over commando infiltration reached their climax in an Israeli air raid on 7 April 1967 in which six Syrian planes were destroyed and Israeli planes flew over Damascus. This test of strength was a sign of things to come. A few days later the Syrian chief of staff accused Israel of massing troops near the Syrian border. It was Egypt's reaction to this accusation, which the Russians had confirmed, that led to the war of June 1967.

It can be emphasized that the Arab states, during the nineteen years that followed the creation of Israel, had neither a real commitment nor a plan to fight the new state. They, however, did have legitimate grievances against Israel and could not recognize its existence unless it was ready to give them satisfaction. But Israel chose to ignore those grievances, even acting with inhuman harshness towards the people it had wronged. It followed, more-over, a policy of provocation and massive retaliation towards its Arab neighbors, who continued to be on the defensive. Israel, the newcomer who sought a refuge from persecution and a place where its people could live in dignity and freedom, took the of-fensive and became the persecutor and the oppressor. As for the world and particularly those who created Israel, they acknowl-edged the Arab rights and Israeli wrongs orally in the form of resolutions, but they failed to restrain their creature and helped it to grow in strength and intransigence. The most prominent Arab leaders during this period were military leaders in an age of revolution, conflicting ideologies, and indecision. They were neither able to build the military strength that was needed to wrest from Israel what it had usurped, nor were they willing to submit to injustice and coercion and accept the dictates of force. Israel could not be expected to make peace when it involved con-cessions and partial loss of what she acquired by force. Peace, therefore, would have had to be imposed by stronger powers. The Arabs would have accepted a peace that redressed some of the grievances, and they would have probably recognized Israel if it had been sensitive and humane, but Israel was not ready to act fairly and kindly, because it was preparing for another "pre-ventive war" and for acquiring more territory.

## The War of June 1967 and the Arab Search for Peace 1967–70

The 1967 war added new problems to those that followed the 1948 war. Israel's growing military power allowed that country not only to ignore the United Nations resolutions, but also to at-tack border villages with impunity, expand in the demilitarized zones, and try intimidating the Arabs with faits accomplis. The Israeli air attack on Syria on 7 April 1967 was followed by offi-cial threats against the Damascus regime. Nasser, when told by official Syrian and Soviet reports that Israel was massing troops on the Syrian border, decided to implement the mutual defense pact of 1966 and ordered a troop buildup in Sinai along the Israeli border. When Egypt requested the removal of the UN emergency forces, its request seems to have applied only to those areas that would have interfered with the Egyptian troop movements. The UN secretary general, however, insisted on a total withdrawal and opposed the temporary restaging of UN forces which Egypt would have preferred.[72] Nasser's crucial decision on 22 May to close the Gulf of Aqaba to Israeli shipping was the direct result of this withdrawal and of the Egyptian occupation of the post of Sharm el-Sheikh.

In order to understand Nasser's action, it is important to realize that the object of his theatrical troop movements and dramatic defiance of Israel was not merely to deter the Israelis from attacking Syria. Nasser wanted also to regain his Arab leadership and prestige which had been impaired by the Yemen civil war, by his allowing UN forces on his borders, and by his failure to help Syria after the 7 April air raid. Had he allowed Israel free access to the Gulf of Aqaba while his forces occupied the area overlooking the Straits of Tiran, he would have certainly been taunted even more severely, thereby defeating the entire purpose of his military buildup. It seems fairly certain that Nasser's basic motives were political and that he did not intend to engage in military action against Israel.[73] Nasser simply wanted a political victory over Israel and both he and the Soviet Union expected that the United States would prevail upon Israel to accept the blockade or a modified version of it, and that it would restrain Israel more than it ultimately did.

The Egyptian blockade gave Israel the pretext, but not the justification, to attack Egypt. The Israeli government declared that the blockade was an act of war and told the world that its "existence was threatened by lawless violence." Unwise statements by some Arab spokesmen and exaggerations in the Arabic press about the coming holy war against Israel, as well as certain of Nasser's phrases that were taken out of context, were widely reproduced and gave the world an untrue picture of a small and helpless state that was about to be destroyed by its numerous heavily armed neighbors. A responsible Israeli admitted later that "this whole story about the threat of extermination of Israel was totally contrived and then elaborated upon to justify the annexation of new Arab territories." Another made it clear that "since 1949 no one dared, or in exact terms, no one was in a position to threaten the very existence of Israel." [74] The blockade did not threaten Israel's existence and war was not inevitable on its account. Israel must have known that Egypt was in no position to attack, because one-third of its troops were in Yemen and the Soviet Union was not prepared to support it militarily even if it were attacked. Israel, moreover, was aware of its own military superiority, as was the United States. CIA and Pentagon reports submitted to President Johnson in late May 1967 are said to have forecast closely the events that unfolded after the war began.[75] Israel did not wish to give a diplomatic victory to its weaker enemy and disliked submitting to a discussion of the Palestine question in exchange for a settlement of the blockade. It was also undoubtedly tempted by the prospect of obtaining better frontiers and destroying the Egyptian military machine in a war which, after careful calculation, it thought it could win.

The Arabs were reassured when President Johnson, 23 May and 3 June 1967, reaffirmed the US commitment to preserving the territorial integrity of all the states in the Middle East and opposing aggression by anyone—a policy the three former presidents had followed since 1950.[76] President Johnson asked Nasser to show restraint, and on 26 May he warned the Egyptian ambassador that for Egypt to fire first would produce grave consequences. Egypt gave assurances that it did not intend to attack and agreed to send Vice President Muhieddin to Washington on 7 June for more discussions. The Israeli offensive began two days before Muhieddin's scheduled arrival, although Defense Minister Moshe Dayan left the impression on the preceding day that Israel would wait for the result of diplomatic efforts.[77] Those Israelis who wanted military action were embarrassed by Pentagon information that belied Israeli reports of an imminent Egyptian attack. What the Israeli preemptive attack of 5 June sought to forestall was not an Egyptian offensive but the attempt to negotiate a compromise that would have killed the opportunity for war.[78] Nasser commented later that Egypt was "the victim of a diplomatic trick played by the United States" in view of Johnson's appeal for restraint but his unwillingness to restrain Israel. He realized that the American guarantee of territorial integrity and opposition to border changes applied only to Israel.[79]

Israel carries the greatest responsibility for the 1967 war, because it deliberately began the offensive without waiting for the results of negotiations. However, Egypt, as a result of several miscalculations, provoked Israel and gave her the pretext for the attack. The Soviet Union had urged Nasser to make a noisy demonstration in favor of Syria, while the United States made it easier for Israel to launch the attack by promising to prevent a defeat of Israel and to deter the Soviet Union from direct military intervention in favor of Egypt.[80] Washington, as the observers noted later, pressed Israel to accept the ceasefire only when victory was assured, and its UN delegates succeeded in keeping the withdrawal of Israeli forces out of the ceasefire resolution.[81] The American chargé d'affaires in Egypt during the months prior to the June war has affirmed, moreover, that the military intelligence Washington wanted from the embassy in Cairo was very largely based on Israel's demands. He concluded that the effectiveness of the 5 June Israeli air strikes "was assured, in part at least, by information on Egyptian airfields and aircraft disposition provided through United States sources." [82]

The war of June 1967 humiliated the Arabs even more than the 1948 and 1956 wars. Israel won in less than six days and inflicted heavy losses in lives and equipment on its three neighbors. For the first time the Israelis held important areas of the belligerent Arab states after the ceasefire, and the Suez Canal remained closed for navigation, not because Egypt wanted it closed as in 1956, but because Israel occupied its eastern bank. Additional territories Israel occupied included the Golan Heights, the West Bank and Arab Jerusalem, Sinai, and the Gaza Strip. Some 300,000 new Palestinians left the Jordanian West Bank, while thousands of Syrians and Egyptians became refugees in their respective countries. Some 400,000 Egyptians had eventually to evacuate the Egyptian Canal Zone because of the irregular warfare that followed the ceasefire.

The military defeat and Israeli occupation of Arab territory did not lead to Arab surrender or to the collapse of any belligerent Arab regime. Nasser was not overthrown, in part precisely because Egyptian and Arab national sentiment refused to give Israel the satisfaction of bringing him down. Nasserist policies, however, underwent a significant change, because Egypt now needed the friendship and the moral and financial support of its former rivals in the Arab cold war, and it was expected to play the key role in the struggle for the liberation of the occupied Arab territories. Nasser himself remained a respected symbol of the Arab revolution, but his responsibilities in the Arab-Israeli problem became more real and urgent in view of the Israeli occupation of Egyptian and other Arab lands. The Baath regime survived in Syria, but its leadership passed gradually to a more moderate and less isolationist group under General Hafez Asad. The Arab defeat even led indirectly to military coups in the Sudan in May 1969 under Colonel Ja'far Numairi and in Libya in September 1969 under Lieutenant Mu'ammar Qaddafi, because the revolutionary officers claimed that the ruling regimes—the constitutional Azhari regime in the Sudan and the Sanusi monarchy in Libya—were not sufficiently involved in the Arab-Israeli conflict.

The defeated Arab regimes not only survived, they refused to negotiate a settlement with Israel. Having reaffirmed their authority at home, they proceeded to replace the military equipment lost in the war with the help of the Soviet Union. They saw clearly that the United States was not cooperating with the Soviet Union, as it did in 1956, in asking Israel to withdraw from the occupied territories, and that the draft resolution of 19 June 1967 which Prime Minister Kosygin presented to the UN General Assembly for that purpose was defeated. They would not negotiate directly with Israel, whom they had never recognized, from a position of weakness, but they were willing to seek a political solution through the United Nations or its leading members. In their summit conference of 29–31 August 1967 at Khartoum the phrases "no recognition, no negotiation, no peace" with regard to Israel were issued largely as a concession to popular Arab feeling and to certain more radical Arab regimes. The conference, however, called for "unified efforts at international and diplomatic levels to . . . assure the withdrawal of the aggressor forces . . . from Arab lands." [83] The resolution clearly sought a political solution and contained no reference to military action. President Nasser showed more moderation than the leaders of Syria, Iraq, and Algeria; indeed he was closer to King Hussein in seeking a peaceful solution.[84]

The significant change in the Arab attitude towards Israel following the 1967 war was the readiness of some Arab governments to accept the existence of the Israeli state. King Hussein, during his first postwar visit to Washington in November 1967, made a peace offer that included recognizing Israel's right to exist in peace and security and ending the state of war on condition that Israel evacuate the newly captured territories. In April 1969, in a more elaborate peace plan, he expressed the same attitude "with the personal authority" of President Nasser. Earlier, in February, Nasser himself presented a five-point peace proposal that promised the end of belligerency and the acceptance of Israel's existence within the borders of 4 June 1967.[85] Israel was not moved by the change of attitude and was unsympathetic to the peace proposals.

The June war also produced a significant change in Israel's position; it became more aware of its strength, and the war modified the strategic situation in its favor. Its new frontiers made it more difficult for the Arabs to defend themselves against Israeli attacks or to initiate an offensive against Israeli territory. Israel's victory, in addition, gave Jews everywhere more confidence and pride in Israel, which in turn produced more generous contributions and a steady increase of immigrants. Now Israel wanted more than Arab acceptance of its existence; it determined on keeping certain areas of the newly occupied territories for strategic and nationalistic reasons, and this determination grew stronger as time passed and hostilities began again along the ceasefire lines.[86]

The UN Security Council succeeded on 22 November 1967 in voting Resolution 242, which became the basis and guideline for subsequent negotiations on the settlement of the Arab-Israeli dispute. Its important principles were "the withdrawal of Israeli armed forces from territories occupied in the recent conflict," termination of the state of belligerency, and acknowledgement of the sovereignty, territorial integrity, and political independence of every state in the area and their right to live in peace within secure and recognized boundaries. Egypt and Jordan accepted the resolution and thereby tacitly agreed to the end of belligerency and to the independence of Israel. They cooperated with the United Nations representative, Swedish Ambassador Gunnar

Jarring, who had been appointed to help achieve a peaceful settlement. Israel also accepted the resolution, as did the Johnson administration, but President Johnson acted in conformity with the Israeli objective that a peace settlement should not be imposed by the great powers but must be arrived at by the parties in the conflict.[87] He also agreed at the end of December 1968 to send Israel the fifty Phantom F-4 jet bombers that Israel's Prime Minister Levi Eshkol had requested earlier in January.

Ambassador Jarring was unable to make progress because Israel wanted direct negotiations and insisted on that part of Resolution 242 that spoke of "secure and recognized boundaries," while Egypt called for indirect negotiations and insisted on the clause that asked for Israeli withdrawal "from territories occupied in the recent conflict." The Nixon administration decided to take new initiatives to end, or at least contain, the explosive Arab-Israeli conflict, so Nixon accepted in February a French proposal for four-power talks to discuss the means of establishing a just peace based on the Security Council resolution of November 1967. The Israeli cabinet rejected this at the end of March, because it feared it might lead to an imposed settlement.

The four-power talks began in New York in early April 1969 between the permanent UN representatives of Britain, France, the Soviet Union, and the United States and continued until the spring of 1970. Bilateral talks had already started in January 1969 between the United States and the Soviet Union. When the bilateral talks ended on 28 October 1969, the United States presented a proposal suggesting restoration of the prewar boundary between Egypt and Israel. The proposal indicated a shift in the US position, but it left for open negotiations the boundaries of Syria and Jordan.

When on 9 December 1969 Secretary of State William Rogers reported on the four-power discussions, he asserted that any changes in the preexisting boundaries between Israel and the Arab states "should not reflect the weight of conquest and should be confined to insubstantial alterations required for mutual security." The Rogers statement added that "we do not support expansionism," and that the United States "cannot accept unilateral actions by any party to decide the final status of Jerusalem." [88] The policy statement was followed on 18 December by an eleven-point proposal for a Jordanian-Israeli peace settlement. The proposal hoped to promote a binding agreement, negotiated under Ambassador Jarring's auspices. It mentioned the withdrawal of Israeli troops from the West Bank and the establishment of permanent frontiers which allowed for minor alterations of the former boundaries. The problem of control over Jerusalem was to be negotiated, but the city was to be unified, with Israel and Jordan sharing in the civic and economic responsibilities of city government. Both countries were to work out arrangements for administering the Gaza Strip and delimiting demilitarized zones. Dr. Jarring was to establish an international commission which would determine the choice of the Palestinian refugees and the implementation of their gradual return on the basis of yearly quotas to be worked out in cooperation with Israel.[89]

For the first time the United States spelled out publicly the importance of Israeli withdrawal from occupied Arab territory as a prerequisite for a peace settlement. As editorialists pointed out at the time, the proposals also attempted to disengage US policy from that of Israel and to dramatize that the national interests of the two countries were not identical.[90]

Israel rejected the Rogers statement of 9 December and the 18 December proposals immediately, and its leaders began to speak of the erosion of American-Israeli relations. They charged that the withdrawal provisions were concessions to the Arabs and their Soviet backers. Secretary of State Rogers explained that his proposals required concessions from both Arabs and Israelis. He rejected Mrs. Meir's charge of appeasement, because the term suggested that the Arabs were enemies of the United States and this was not true. While understanding that Israel might not agree with all US policy, he said, "we have to conduct our foreign policy in a way that we think is best for our national interests." [91]

The American supporters of Israel based their arguments against the proposals on two assumptions: first, that the strength of the United States in the Middle East depended on the security of Israel, and second, that the American concessions to the Arab states threatened Israel's security and hence American national interest.[92] Other Americans and even some Israelis have challenged these assumptions by pointing out that "the American connection with Israel is a liability, not an asset" and that the real American interests lie distinctly elsewhere.[93] Soviet involvement in the Arab world, they said, was actually "the ripe fruit of Israeli policy since 1956," for Israel, in its search for support and guarantees, had escalated military activity and driven Nasser into greater dependence on the Russians.[94] Senator J. William Fulbright rejected as "myths" the "obsessive Israeli fears that the Arabs were still determined to destroy Israel" and he denounced the spheres-of-influence psychology "which causes a nation to believe that it can have no security at all until it has robbed its neighbors of all semblance of security." [95]

The United States did not press for the implementation of its proposals and promised Israel that the territorial provisions would not be publicly reiterated.[96] President Nixon and Secretary of State Rogers also reassured Zionist leaders, the national emergency conference of major Jewish organizations that met in Washington on 25 January 1970, and interested congressmen that the United States would impose no settlement on Israel and would maintain the arms balance between it and the Arab states.

Egypt tried to impress the four-power group with the urgency of imposing a settlement based on Resolution 242. In the spring of 1969 it initiated what was called the war of attrition. The Egyptian artillery attacks and commando raids on the eastern side of the canal brought immediate Israeli retaliation that showed the inadequacy of the Egyptian defense system. Soon the artillery battles escalated into air raids launched by both sides. Israel began a systematic bombing of Egyptian artillery and missile sites near the canal in August and continued its daily strikes through September. Another phase began in January 1970 when low-flying Israeli planes struck against military installations in the Cairo region and penetrated deep into other areas of the Egyptian heartland. The war of attrition was thus turned against Egypt and its victims included scores of Egyptian school children and factory workers. Israel's purpose was to limit Egypt's capacity for war, give the Egyptians a proof of their country's vulnerability, and humiliate and discredit Nasser and the Egyptian leadership. In addition, Israel was probably reacting against the December 1969 Rogers proposals.

The deep-penetration raids forced Nasser to seek and obtain

modern air-defense equipment including SAM-3 missiles from the Soviet Union. Egypt rebuilt its defenses in the Cairo region and near the canal front with the help of Soviet military experts, who remained to man some of the missile sites for several months. Israel ended the deep air raids at the end of April, but began continuous massive strikes in late May against Egyptian positions along the canal. Chief of Staff Haim Bar-Lev now defined Israel's policy not as retaliation but as continuous military activity.[97] To avert further escalation, Secretary of State Rogers proposed on 19 June 1970 that Egypt, Jordan, and Israel accept a ninety-day ceasefire and work under Ambassador Jarring's auspices to carry out the Security Council resolution of November 1967. The Rogers Plan was intended, in his own words, "to encourage the parties to stop shooting and start talking." [98]

President Nasser accepted the new American proposal on 23 July 1970 after his return from a three-week visit to Moscow, and King Hussein gave his approval three days later. Israel reluctantly accepted on 4 August following American entreaties and more reassurances on maintaining the balance of power in the Middle East. The Gahal party, which wanted to maintain Israeli rule over the occupied territories, withdrew from Mrs. Meir's national coalition cabinet.[99] On this, as on several other occasions, Israel opposed or obstructed any proposal that involved Resolution 242, because it could result in her withdrawal from the occupied territories. By the same token, Israel accepted the proposal only after it obtained certain concessions or guarantees or promises of aid and arms deliveries, and later found an excuse to evade whatever action it was expected to take as a result of acceptance.

In accepting the Rogers Plan Egypt and Jordan committed themselves again to making peace with Israel and recognizing its 1967 borders, while Israel accepted indirect negotiations. The attrition war had impressed the powers with the need for a settlement, but it did not inspire them actually to impose a settlement. On 1 July 1970 President Nixon compared the Middle East situation to that of the Balkans before World War I, but he emphasized the need to maintain Israel's military superiority, thus almost destroying the Rogers Plan, because his statements were viewed in Arab circles as the bluntest expression of American support for Israel and discrimination against the Arabs.

The ninety-day ceasefire went into effect on 7 August 1970 and peace talks were initiated on 25 August. Israel, however, withdrew from the talks after one procedural session, charging that Egypt had been violating the ceasefire by moving missiles to new sites in the ceasefire zone near the Suez Canal. The Egyptians may have tried to complete the antiaircraft missile network which they had started before the ceasefire arrangements, but this was probably not the basic reason for Israel's reaction. Essentially Israel refused to accept what was about to happen, namely the withdrawal from occupied Arab territory. It also hoped to obtain more Phantom jets and electronic equipment from the United States as an inducement to return to the negotiating table and in order to offset Egypt's improved air defense system.[100] In September 1969 Prime Minister Golda Meir had sought to buy fifty Phantom jets and fifty-five or more Skyhawks, but the request was not answered immediately because Israel's air capacity, as Mr. Rogers said in late March 1970, was sufficient to meet its current needs. In September 1970, partly as a result of the alleged ceasefire violation and the pressure of American congressmen, Israel obtained a pledge from Mr. Nixon to supply her with $500 million in arms including eighteen new Phantoms and $250 million in economic aid. It was decided also to sell Israel 200 M-60 tanks. Mr. Roger's even-handed policy had been abandoned by the White House.

At the end of 1970 the search for peace was still fruitless. Israel was under no overwhelming pressure to withdraw, but the Arab states had changed from refusing to admit Israel's existence to accepting Israel as a reality and attempting to stop its territorial expansion. Those in the United States who sought to equate American interests with those of Israel by emphasizing the danger of Soviet advances in the Arab countries seemed to have won. In December 1970 Charles Yost, the American ambassador to the United Nations, was replaced, reportedly because he advised Mr. Nixon that the best way to expel the Russians from the Middle East was not to arm Israel and alienate the Arabs, but to reach a settlement in accordance with Resolution 242.[101]

By the end of 1970 Israel had been able, mainly through American support, to prevent the imposition of a peace settlement. It was also assured a constant flow of American credit and sophisticated weapons. Finally, it had drawn the United States into a closer relationship and projected itself as the defender of American interests against Soviet ambitions in the Middle East. It is noteworthy that Soviet advances in the Arab world did not lead to the establishment of any communist satellite regime, and the image of the United States as the stronghold of Zionism and supporter of Israel did not prevent most Arab countries from maintaining more or less friendly relations with Washington. The 1967 war did not hurt basic American economic interests in the Arab world, especially in the oil-producing states, but those interests were threatened by increasing American arms shipments to Israel. Arab moderates, including the Egyptian ruling elite, have continued to hold that the United States could bring peace to the region because of its special relation with Israel and its concern with stability in the Arab countries.[102] They accepted the Rogers Plan as an expression of American impartiality. Nasser died while the Rogers Plan was encountering difficulties. His successor, President Anwar Sadat, went far beyond him in depending on the United States for reaching a peaceful settlement.

Other significant developments following the 1967 war were the emergence of the Palestine resistance movement as a force in Arab politics and the growing divergence of Arab views on the question of peace with Israel. The inability of the Arab states to work effectively for the liberation of Palestine before the 1967 war, and the additional losses suffered by the Arabs in that war persuaded the Palestinian leaders that they should take the initiative for the defense of their cause. Palestinian concern was further aroused when Egypt and Jordan accepted Resolution 242, which the Palestinian resistance groups rejected because it dealt with the 1967 occupation only and ignored that of 1948. The Palestinians wanted to liberate all Palestine and "refused the position that occupation, like wine, improves with age."[103] The Palestinians were also alarmed by the annexation of Arab Jerusalem, the establishment of permanent settlements in the newly occupied territory, the campaign for increased Jewish immigration, and Prime Minister Levi Eshkol's talk of consolidating Israel's position in the conquered territory.

Among the dozen Palestinian resistance groups, the two most active were al Fateh, under Yasir Arafat, and the Popular Front for the Liberation of Palestine (PFLP), which appeared in December 1967 under the leadership of George Habash, a leftist Palestinian physician from Lydda. The common goal of all the resistance groups was the establishment of a secular democratic state in Palestine in which Arabs (Muslims and Christians) and Jews could live in equality and peace.[104] This meant the dissolution of the exclusive Jewish sovereignty in an exclusive Jewish state. The guerrilla organizations knew that they could reach their goal only after a long struggle against Israel and only by transforming their guerrilla movement into a popular revolutionary one.[105]

The Palestinian resistance groups did, however, act independently and they differed in size, ideology, and tactics. The relatively older and less active Palestine Liberation Organization (PLO), which the Arab League had created and financed, was eclipsed by the new militant groups. In February 1969, al Fateh leader Yasir Arafat was elected chairman of the PLO executive committee, thus gaining control of its various facilities. He could now take advantage of its position as the official representative of the Palestinian people and participate in Arab deliberations and conferences. The guerrilla organizations remained dependent on the Arab states in many ways in spite of their apparent independence. Since the guerrillas operated mainly out of the Arab states adjacent to Israel, they needed the cooperation and good will of these states. Their activities had to be reduced whenever they became an undesirable burden for the host countries either as a result of Israeli retaliation or of clashes with the local security forces. In addition, guerrilla operations were possible largely because of the continued state of belligerency between the Arab states and Israel, and they were usually weakened by the interruption of formal Arab military action or by the prospect of any political settlement that dealt merely with the territories occupied in 1967.

The guerrilla groups tried to disrupt Israeli life by shelling and rocketing Israeli territory, damaging railway tracks, telephone wires and other public utilities, mining roads, and attacking military camps and patrols. However this activity was unable to create an insurrectionary movement among the Arabs of the occupied areas or within Israel. Israeli forces moved directly against the guerrillas—whom they called terrorists and infiltrators—and sent large numbers of them and of those who were suspected of cooperating with them to jail.[106] It also moved against the host countries, particularly Jordan, Syria, and Lebanon.

On 21 March 1968 Israel invaded Jordanian territory to attack the guerrilla camp at Karameh. The raid met with stiff resistance from the guerrillas and Jordanian troops. The camp was partly destroyed but the raid failed to stop guerrilla activity, rather it gave al Fateh and the guerrilla movement additional prestige. King Hussein, commenting on Premier Levi Eshkol's threat to invade the land east of the Jordan again if the guerrillas continued their operations, said, "we are in the ridiculous position of being blamed for not assuring Israel's safety." [107] Hussein, however, was anxious to control guerrilla activity and avoid being dragged to a war for which he and the other Arabs were not prepared. He was also afraid that the guerrilla organizations might become a state within his state and that their popularity might erode his control. Indeed, in the three years that followed Karameh, the guerrillas often clashed with Jordanian troops. These conflicts climaxed in the ten-day battle of 17–26 September 1970 that weakened the guerrilla movement, almost stopped its activity in Jordan, and forced most of its members out of the country.

The different attitudes of the Arab countries towards the Palestinian resistance often provoked inter-Arab tensions, particularly in Jordan and Lebanon where the governments had to restrain guerrilla activities for fear of Israeli retaliation. Arab states sometimes broke relations with Jordan or closed their borders with it or Lebanon on account of the guerrillas. Nasser's policy toward them was ambivalent. He sometimes protected them and tried to gain their good will in order to retain his prestige among the Arab masses, and at times he feared their extremism and the threat they posed to existing governments and to the envisaged political settlement. He often acted as mediator in their quarrels with Lebanon and Jordan, especially in the bloody civil war that followed the Rogers Plan ceasefire. Since the Rogers Plan contained no provision for Palestinian participation in the discussions or for self-determination, the Palestinian national council decided not to lay down arms until Palestine was liberated. The hijacking of planes on 6 and 9 September and the Jordanian civil war that followed were partly attempts to undermine the cease-fire.

Israeli action against Lebanon on account of the guerrillas was often brutal and irrational and only helped deepen the hatreds and increase the obstacles that stood in the way of a peace settlement. Israel held the Lebanese government responsible for any Palestinian or Arab guerrilla action against Israeli citizens and property even if it occurred outside Lebanon. The Israeli commando attack on 28 December 1968 on the Beirut airport that destroyed thirteen planes on the ground was an unwarranted act of retaliation for an Arab commando attack on an Israeli airliner in Athens. It only played into the hands of Lebanese and other Arab militants and led to a sharp increase in the number of Arab guerrillas in Southern Lebanon. On 4 September 1969 Israeli infantry penetrated into Lebanese territory for the first time to attack a guerrilla position. The "search and destroy" operation of 12 May 1970 that lasted thirty-six hours was of such magnitude that it drew a condemnation of Israel by the Security Council.

## Arab Peace Efforts in the Post-Nasser Years 1970–1973

When President Nasser died on 28 September 1970, one day after ending the ten-day fighting between Jordanian troops and Palestinian guerrillas, foreign observers expressed their pessimism about the prospects for peace. They spoke of him as the only Arab leader who had enough strength and prestige to make peace with Israel.[108] His acceptance of the Rogers Plan had been criticized by Palestinian guerrillas and several Iraqis made strong statements against him, but he scornfully told his critics that "those who want to fight should send us their troops and take part in our struggle." [109] A bloodless coup in Syria by General Hafez Asad removed the radical faction of the Baath party from office on 13 November 1970 because of its role in the Syrian military intervention in the Jordanian civil war that almost precipitated a coordinated American-Israeli military reaction. In the meeting that followed Nasser's funeral on 1 October 1970 the delegates of ten Arab states pledged full support for the new Egyptian leaders and urged them to pursue Nasser's intentions of liberating the Arab territories occupied by Israel in 1967.

Sadat not only adhered to the ceasefire agreement, he went beyond Nasser in trying to elicit American support for a political settlement. But his efforts ended in disappointment and frustration, because the United States refused to help overcome Israel's intransigence and in certain ways even contributed to it.

On 5 November 1970 the UN General Assembly voted to extend the ceasefire for three months and asked for the resumption of the peace talks under Ambassador Jarring's auspices. After a boycott of four months Israel was induced by the Nixon administration to return to the talks, but not without obtaining promises of military and economic aid, assurances that Russia would not be allowed to interfere directly in a future conflict, and promises that the United States would veto any Security Council resolution against Israel.[110] The ceasefire was later extended until 5 February 1971, and it continued de facto until October 1973.

Ambassador Jarring tried to break the deadlock between Israel and Egypt by giving each side identical aide-memoires in which he requested certain prior commitments that he thought were inevitable prerequisites for an eventual settlement. He asked Israel to give a commitment to withdraw its forces from occupied Egyptian territory and Egypt to enter into a peace agreement with Israel and make explicitly, on a reciprocal basis, various undertakings arising from Security Council Resolution 242.[111] Egypt indicated that it would accept the requested commitments, but Israel's answer made no specific reference to the commitment which Jarring had sought. It welcomed the Egyptian "readiness to enter into a peace agreement with Israel" and stated that it was prepared for meaningful negotiations on all subjects relevant to a settlement. On the crucial question of withdrawal, however, Israel said that it would undertake to withdraw "to the secure, recognized, and agreed boundaries to be established in the peace agreement," but it would "not withdraw to the pre-June 5, 1967 lines." [112] Israel has repeatedly stated since then that it would negotiate without conditions, but would not withdraw to the prewar lines. In order to make a peace settlement acceptable to Egypt and the Arabs, Secretary of State Rogers

stated that alterations in the prewar borders should be insubstantial. Israel, on the other hand, has made it clear that some modi-
fications must be major ones.[113] The areas which Israeli leaders
said they would retain are the Golan Heights, a large part
of the West Bank, East Jerusalem, the Gaza Strip, Sharm
el-Sheikh, and a broad strip of Sinai connecting it with Israel
proper.[114]

The indirect talks under Dr. Jarring's auspices ended in March
1971 when Israel refused to make a commitment to withdraw
from Sinai and Egypt refused to enter into detailed discussions
before such a commitment. Egypt's attitude was generally thought
reasonable and conciliatory. It responded positively to Jarring's
proposals for entering into a peace agreement and recognizing
Israel, and by so doing it put Israel on the spot. The editor of
al-Ahram commented that Egypt's diplomacy "has stripped the
Israeli position of all cover, including the fig leaf." Israel was
criticized for preferring territory to its long-sought peace and security guarantees. Israel was reminded that security depends not
on geography but on a genuine political settlement accepted by
all parties and guaranteed by international backing.[115] Secretary
of State Rogers told the Senate Foreign Relations Committee on
12 March that the United States would be willing to provide
troops as part of a Big Four police force under United Nations
auspices and that, unlike the situation after 1956, the peacekeeping force would be withdrawn only by a Security Council vote.
Prime Minister Golda Meir answered, "We do not trust Rogers'
offer even if it is proposed in good faith."[116] Senator Fulbright
had already offered, after the ceasefire of August 1970, to support a treaty between the United States and Israel to guarantee
Israel's independence within the borders of 1967 and to oblige
Israel not to violate these borders, but the offer was coldly received in Jerusalem because it could restrict Israel's ultimate freedom of action.[117]

In his report of 5 March 1971 UN Secretary General U Thant
appealed to Israel to respond favorably to Jarring's initiative.
The deputy prime minister of Israel, Yigal Allon, resented
U Thant's appeal and comments on the "positive" response of
Egypt and the "negative" response of Israel, and the Israeli em-
bassy in Washington issued a statement that Israel would resist

all pressures from whatever source that aimed at resurrecting its past vulnerability. Foreign Minister Abba Eban admitted that his country stood alone in a "tenacious solitude" on the key terms of a settlement.

The search for peace took another turn when President Sadat suggested on 4 February 1971 that Israel partially withdraw its forces from the eastern bank of the Suez Canal, which he promised to open for navigation. The United States encouraged this initiative and undertook to help the parties reach an interim agreement. Israel accepted negotiations for the opening of the canal but rejected the Egyptian view that the partial pullback would be the first stage in a complete withdrawal from Sinai, and it wanted no Egyptian troops on the eastern bank of the canal. Israel demanded an unlimited ceasefire after the partial pullback, whereas Egypt wanted one of six months or more, until a peace settlement was reached. In early May 1971 Mr. Rogers visited the Middle East "to discuss ways in which the United States can help Jarring promote an Arab-Israeli settlement." Sadat later related that while in Cairo Rogers said he had nothing more to ask of Sadat because Sadat had done his utmost.[118] Sadat received other US assurances about his position and he, in turn, assured them that his 27 May 1971 treaty with the Soviet Union was only a new frame for existing relations, that it brought nothing new. American assurances, however, and the eight-day mission of Assistant Secretary of State Joseph Sisco to Israel in late July 1971 brought no breakthrough in modifying Israel's conditions for an interim agreement. Secretary of State Rogers's speech to the UN General Assembly on 4 October and his six principles for the desired agreement had the same result.[119]

Israel was able to maintain its stand because it believed that Egypt was militarily incapable of forcing its way into Sinai and that the Russians were opposed to a renewal of fighting. In December 1971 the United States abandoned the temporary, but never complete, withholding of Phantoms as a means for obtaining concessions from Israel. Israel's air force was already superior to that of Egypt and the other Arab states, and President Nixon constantly reassured Israel that its military superiority would be maintained. The Israeli lobby in Congress and at the White House had considerable influence on American policy as the presidential elections of 1972 approached.

When Nixon approved in January 1972 the sale of the additional Phantoms and Skyhawks that Israel wanted, observers viewed it as retreat from the position that Israel should withdraw from Sinai and as an indication that Sadat's policy of relying on the United States to pressure Israel had failed. Sadat's policy had been based on three considerations: first, the United States had clearly supported the idea of Israeli withdrawal from Egyptian territory; second, Israel was dependent on the United States for military equipment and for economic aid; third, the United States needed Arab friendship for economic and strategic reasons and was interested in peace and stability in the Arab area. Sadat was bitterly disappointed when the United States did not obtain the needed concessions and refused to impose a settlement on Israel. Sadat had hoped that the other great powers would put pressure on Israel either directly or through the United States, but the world community was content to express their displeasure through ineffective United Nations resolutions which Israel disregarded, as in the case of the Security Council resolution of 25 September 1971 that asked Israel to halt changes in the occupied Arab sector of Jerusalem.

President Sadat made several speeches in the summer and fall of 1971 about the inevitability of war, because "there was no longer hope for a peaceful solution," but he always kept the door open for a peaceful settlement in spite of his war rhetoric. On 5 November 1971 he assumed command of the armed forces and moved his office to the military general headquarters to emphasize the preparation for war. Sadat wanted some pressure on Israel's eastern flank, but the eastern command of Syria, Jordan, Iraq, and the guerrillas had ceased to exist in August 1971. The Arab position had been further weakened by dissension following the Jordanian civil war, the attempted coups in Morocco and Sudan in July 1971, the breaking of relations between several Arab states, and the strain in Soviet-Arab relations because of the suspicion of Soviet connivance in the pro-Communist Sudan coup and the crackdown on the Communists in Egypt and the Sudan.

Sadat's war talk was partly intended to create a crisis atmosphere prior to the United Nations debate, but Israel used Sadat's threats to press for more Phantoms, although its own former air force commander said Israel had "enough equipment to defeat the Arabs in battle." [120] On 3 December Egyptian Foreign Minister Mahmud Riad asked the General Assembly to take enforced measures against Israel to compel it to withdraw from occupied territory. Abba Eban promised that Israel would negotiate either an interim or a general settlement, if no prior conditions were fixed, and pleaded that sanctions not be applied against his country. On 13 December 1971 the General Assembly voted a resolution urging renewal of the talks and calling on Israel to respond favorably to Jarring's appeal of 8 February 1971, but no sanctions were applied.

The Nixon administration's decision to deliver Phantoms and Skyhawks to Israel was regarded by Egypt as a betrayal and an affront. Students demonstrated for a whole week in Cairo and asked their government to fight American interests and to make serious preparations for war. Sadat had staked his policy for almost a year on the American proposals; he had even won the internal showdown against Ali Sabri and his group in May 1971. But now he no longer wanted American mediation and preferred the return of Jarring's mission. Egypt was put on a war footing, and Sadat declared that "the battle is now with Israel and the United States, her ally, who authorizes her to make American weapons." [121] On 2 February 1972 Sadat again went to Moscow, because he needed long-range offensive weapons to match what Israel already possessed, but he was unable to obtain them.

On 9 February 1972 President Nixon reported that no progress had been made toward the essential requirement of peace which he defined as "an arrangement which rests the security of all on something more reliable than the good will of a nation's adversaries." He thereby seemed to adopt Israel's view on the importance of "defensible" boundaries and to undercut the State Department view that international guarantees of future borders could serve as a substitute for additional territory and buffer zones.[122] Israel felt more confident following the new expressions of President Nixon's support and Golda Meir, while she remained suspicious of the "Arabists" of the state department, was grateful to Mr. Nixon because "he kept every promise he ever made to me." [123] Israel no longer feared that the United States might make an accommodation with the Soviet Union or other powers at her expense as in the alarming cases of Nationalist

China and Pakistan at the end of 1971. The communiqué following Nixon's visit to Moscow in May 1972 indicated that the superpowers did not wish to impose a solution and demonstrated their desire to avoid a confrontation in the Middle East. No further efforts were made to end the no war-no peace situation, and on 15 June the United States told Russia that it would not undertake any new peace initiative until after the November elections.[124]

After his return from Moscow, President Nixon multiplied the instances of his solicitude for Israel. Israel's ambassador in Washington, Yitzhak Rabin, described Nixon as "the best president Israel ever had in the White House." [125] Governor Nelson Rockefeller disclosed later on 13 August 1972 that Nixon won an agreement from the Soviet leaders permitting the emigration of 35,000 Jews a year to Israel,[126] and the Senate Foreign Relations Committee approved the allocation of $85 million for the resettlement of Soviet Jews in Israel. In the Security Council the United States abstained from voting on the resolution of 26 June 1972 that condemned the Israeli invasion of Lebanon on 21 and 23 June. The resolution was sponsored by Britain, France, and Belgium and passed thirteen to nothing. On 10 September the Nixon administration vetoed a resolution that called for the immediate cessation of military operations following an Israeli air attack on ten guerrilla targets deep inside Syria and Lebanon two days earlier. The Israeli attack was intended to avenge the athletes killed by Palestinian terrorists in Munich on 5 September 1972.

The Nixon administration's unprecedented support of Israel constantly irritated and frustrated Egypt and the other Arab states and it made a peaceful solution more difficult. In the five years that followed the 1967 war, Israel established forty settlements in the occupied areas.[127] Her action violated the Fourth Geneva Convention of 1949 that prohibits occupying powers from transferring part of their population into occupied territories. Israel also refused to discuss with an appointed UN committee the Security Council resolution that asked Israel to rescind all measures taken to alter the status of Jerusalem. The Christian world expressed its concern about official Israeli declarations on "reinforcing the Jewish character of the City" and about the expropriation of Arab land, the diminishing number of Christian inhabitants, and the possible elimination of the Christian presence in Jerusalem.[128]

The evident motives behind President Nixon's extensive support of Israel were, first, the pressures of Jewish organizations on the White House during an election year. Second, the Nixon administration assumed that Israel's military superiority would deter Egypt from resuming the war and would help restrict Arab revolutionary activity. Third, the administration hoped to contain the expansion of Soviet political influence and naval power in Egypt and the eastern Mediterranean and to assert the American presence in the Middle East through continued support of a militarily strong Israel.[129] The reasoning underlying the last two motives has been proved wrong by events, for outright support of Israel and Israeli military superiority has not helped the cause of peace nor contained Soviet influence or presence in the area.

Although the Arabs were disappointed that the United States did not apply significant pressure on Israel, they saw, nevertheless, that the American stand was the significant one, for the Russians were not prepared to take any major step that might displease the United States. On 18 July 1972 President Sadat surprised the world by announcing that he had decided to wind up the functions of the Soviet military advisers. Sadat's action was a show of dissatisfaction with the Russian refusal to deliver the advanced weapons Egypt sought and with the limitations the Russians set on the use of other modern weapons. It was also the result of friction between Egyptian and Russian officers and of patriotic discontent with the Soviet presence in Egypt. There was a general feeling that the Russians had a vested interest in maintaining the status quo and had no intention of helping Egypt regain its occupied territory. Sadat may also have wanted to ward off American concern about Soviet influence in Egypt and encourage a more balanced US policy. The Nixon administration, however, refrained from making any official comment in order not to disturb the new detente with the Soviet Union or to provoke any suspicions and fears in Israel or the American Jewish community. Observers within and outside Israel agreed that his decision freed Sadat from the restraining action of the Soviet Union and removed the screen that separated the two opposing sides on the canal, but at the same time it weakened Egypt militarily. The Soviet departure also ruled out the possibility, long feared by Israel, of a direct encounter with the Soviet Union in any new outbreak of combat. However, it weakened the Israeli argument about Egypt's "client" status and the threat this posed to western interests and thus undermined the rationale for supplying modern weapons to Israel to maintain the military balance.

Prime Minister Meir viewed Sadat's decision as highly significant and appealed to him to meet with her as equals to arrive at an agreed solution to all the outstanding problems.[130] Sadat rejected the concept of direct negotiations implied in the appeal, because negotiations while one's land is occupied, as he often explained, amounted to surrender. Israel, nevertheless, decided to make a peace offensive rather than wait for international pressure to withdraw from the occupied territory. According to a *Time* magazine report in September 1972, Israel made a secret peace offer to Cairo with a map describing the proposed new borders.[131] The offer suggested immediate secret negotiations and was allegedly transmitted to Cairo by American intermediaries, but the State Department disclaimed knowledge of it. Israel would retain, according to the proposal, the southern third of Sinai from a line north of Eilat in the east to the oil fields of Abu-Rudeis on the Gulf of Suez in the west, and the rest of Sinai from Rafah to the Suez Canal would be returned to Egypt and demilitarized, while the Suez Canal would be reopened. Israel would keep the Gaza Strip.

Another approach was made to Jordan, according to the same report, in a meeting between Yigal Allon and King Hussein in the Eilat-Aqaba area. The offer was based on the old Allon plan which would return most of the West Bank to Jordan but would retain a band of territory with its armed Israeli settlements along the River Jordan. The West Bank would be demilitarized and the frontier would be pushed back in the vicinity of Latrun, but no compromise was made on the status of Jerusalem or on Syria's Golan Heights. Sadat's response to the reported offer was not disclosed, but his statement to an interviewer in early October suggested that he would make peace only under terms laid down by the United Nations.[132] King Hussein, on the other hand, declared in early November 1972 that he was ready to conclude a total peace through direct negotiations if necessary on the basis of minor frontier adjustments, but he would reject any Israeli annexation of Jordanian territory including the Arab sector of Jerusalem. He warned that any permanent annexation of territory by Israel would never be accepted by the Arab masses and would sow the seeds of new conflict and violence.[133]

The relatively relaxed atmosphere of Arab-Israeli relations that followed the Russian exodus from Egypt was suddenly inflamed when Palestinian terrorists of the Black September group attacked the Israeli Olympic athletes in Munich on 5 September 1972. The action was partly intended to put an end to the peace feelers between Israel and its Egyptian and Jordanian neighbors and to prove the impossibility of reaching a peace settlement without taking account of the Palestinian problem. Since then Israel has concentrated on eradicating terrorism by fighting the Palestine guerrilla organizations and attacking their Syrian and Lebanese bases. Israel's aircraft bombardment of guerrilla targets in Lebanon and Syria on 8 September 1972 and its thirty-six-hour invasion of southern Lebanon by mechanized troops and aircraft on 16–17 September were particularly destructive and were followed by a new policy of "preventive" rather than reprisal strikes. Israeli forces struck whenever and wherever they wanted and provoked more Arab hostility without discouraging terrorism. On 9–10 April 1973 they attacked in the heart of Beirut, the capital of Lebanon, and killed three top Palestinian leaders in their apartments,[134] and on 10 August 1973 the Israeli air force jets "hijacked" an Iraqi airliner within the Lebanese air space, because the leaders of the Popular Front for the Liberation of Palestine were expected to be on it, but they had evidently changed their plans.[135] Israel was condemned by the Security Council in the two cases. The shooting down on 21 February 1973 of a Libyan civilian airliner that lost its way to Cairo and passed the Suez Canal into Sinai by mistake raised an outcry against Israel in the Arab world, because 106 passengers died in the shooting.

Israel's policy of "creating facts" and "putting down roots" in the conquered or administered territories, as Israel officially calls them, clearly showed its determination to stay. Defense

Minister Moshe Dayan was quoted saying in 1971: "Any place where we establish an inhabited settlement we will not give up either the settlement or the place it is in." [136] He favored giving Israelis the right to buy Arab land in the occupied territory and obtained the approval of the Cabinet and the Labor Party that dominates it in early September 1973 in preparation for the approaching elections. Dayan also declared that if confronted with the choice between peace and Sharm el-Sheikh (renamed Ophira by the Israelis) he would choose Sharm el-Sheikh.[137] The Israelis, moreover, incorporated land adjacent to Jerusalem into the unified city, and thousands of apartments were built on the areas encircling its Arab sector. Scores of Syrian villages were bulldozed in order to build Jewish settlements. In the village of Akraba in the West Bank the army of occupation sprayed destructive chemicals over the fields because the farmers refused to sell their land.[138] These harsh measures moved the chairman of the Israeli league of human and civil rights to declare, "we are beginning to do what others have tried to do to us." [139]

The Arab states expected that the United States would take some new initiatives after the elections of November 1972 to end the dangerous no-war, no-peace situation, but no initiatives were made following Nixon's reelection. President Nixon ended the efforts to reach an equitable settlement when he opened the weapons pipeline to Israel in December 1971 and undercut the patient policy of Secretary of State Rogers and damaged his prestige and credibility.[140] Nixon actually was satisfied with the expulsion of the Russian advisers from Egypt in July 1972 and with the detente that followed the Moscow summit meeting, and he saw that the Israelis were militarily superior and self-confident. In February 1973 President Sadat decided to reopen the diplomatic channels with the United States and sent his presidential adviser Hafez Ismail to Washington, but the talks on 22 February produced no positive results. Three weeks later, following Mrs. Meir's visit to Washington, Israel was given twenty-four more Phantoms and twenty-four Skyhawks over two years and a General Electric jet engine for producing super-Mirage planes.[141] Nixon, nevertheless, was able to claim in his unbelievable declaration of 5 September 1973 that "we are not pro-Israel or pro-Arab, but pro-peace." On 26 July 1973 his UN ambassador cast another veto in favor of Israel against a Security Council resolution at the end of a long debate on the Middle East crisis that began in June. The resolution called for Israeli withdrawal from occupied Arab territory and the votes were thirteen to one (US), with China abstaining, as usual, because the text was not strong enough.

During the discussions about the oil shortages in the United States in the spring and summer of 1973, President Nixon's unwavering support of Israel began to be explained in a new light. Israel's military power and her occupation of strategic areas in the Middle East, it was supposed, could be used to threaten and coerce those oil-producing Arab states that might follow an unfriendly oil policy towards the United States. Israel, some mentioned, could cooperate or act alone in any military operation that the American government undertook against those who used the oil weapon to influence American policy.[142] On 5 September 1973 Nixon warned the Arab oil producers who raised their prices or expropriated American oil interests without compensation that they would lose their markets, and he reminded them of the fate of Prime Minister Mossadegh of Iran. The military training given to the marines in the Mojave Desert in California gave credence to the belief that Mr. Nixon was preparing for the possibility of a war in Arab lands.[143]

Although President Sadat spoke of 1973 as the "year of total confrontation," his real intentions were peaceful. He had struggled for a political settlement for three years and everyone was growing restless. It is possible that out of frustration and indignation, the cautious Sadat became determined to fight, not because he expected to win a decisive victory, but because, as his friend Ihsan Abdul-Quddus wrote in March 1973, "peace cannot be sought unless there is fighting," and in order to compel the United States to impose its will on Israel, "the dialogue must begin under the pressure of a new situation." [144] Sadat hoped that the new war would put pressure on the United States and Europe to start talks, because the talks had to be started by military action.[145] Sadat declared himself military governor of Egypt on 28 March and thus held the three positions of president, prime minister, and military governor. His new cabinet submitted to the People's Assembly a program calling for "full and complete" mobilization of the nation's material and human resources, and the Arab chiefs of staff met to coordinate their military efforts.

King Faisal of Saudi Arabia was always considered a friend of the United States but his friendship and prestige as a Muslim leader did not contribute to any change in President Nixon's pro-Israeli actions. The king was also a close friend of Sadat, who went far beyond Nasser in espousing Faisal's Islamic orientation. The Saudi king was growing impatient with the excessive American support for Israel and, as a fervent Muslim, was incensed over the continued Judaization of Jerusalem. He talked to the board chairman of the Arabian American Oil Company (ARAMCO) about the situation in May 1973 and evidently made it clear that he could not continue to act as a friend of the United States under these conditions, not only because of pressure from the other Arab states, but because of his personal convictions.[146]

In Jordan, King Hussein had to face two challenges: first, that of Israel, which was unwilling to leave the West Bank and the Arab sector of Jerusalem; second, that of the Palestine Liberation Organization (PLO) which considered itself responsible for all Palestinian interests and recognized neither Hussein's claim to the West Bank, nor Israel's existence. On 15 March 1972 King Hussein announced a unilateral plan for the establishment of an autonomous Palestinian state on the West Bank of the Jordan after Israeli troops withdrew from that area. The Palestinian state would be included in a federal union called the United Arab Kingdom, whose capital would be Amman. Hussein thereby ensured that any future Palestinian state would be a part of his kingdom. The plan was denounced by the PLO and the revolutionary Arab states, because it ignored the right of the Palestinians to decide their own destiny and it recognized Israel's presence in the other part of Palestine. President Sadat joined the Palestinians in denouncing it, and on 6 April 1972 he announced that Egypt would break its relations with Jordan. Hussein was thus ostracized by the PLO, Egypt, Syria, Libya, and Iraq, and his subsidies from Kuwait and Libya were suspended. Sadat was probably influenced by the more drastic attitude of his two partners in the "federation of Arab republics"—Syria and Libya —that was proclaimed on 1 September 1971, but he later drifted away from Qaddafi of Libya in 1973 and preferred the moderation and financial support of King Faisal. Syria under General Asad inclined more to Sadat's moderation than to Qaddafi's extremism and it gradually accepted the idea of a political settlement based on Israel's existence.

Jordan came out of isolation following the conference of Egypt, Syria, and Jordan on 10–12 September 1973 in Cairo. Egypt and Syria agreed to resume diplomatic relations with Jordan, and Jordan agreed to release 700 political prisoners, mostly Palestinians. The reconciliation was intended to revive the old Eastern Command and to insure the cooperation of Syria and Jordan in the event of a new war. Israel lost no time and responded by sending its planes to provoke an air battle with Syria more than 100 miles north of its borders. It claimed that it shot down thirteen Syrian planes in the engagement and lost one.

The period that followed the war of June 1967 was thus a period of violence in which the guerrillas and the Arab states participated and the Israelis retaliated heavily. The search for peace reached a stalemate in 1972 because Israel in reality was not willing to relinquish her conquests, and the United States was unwilling to impose a settlement on the basis of Security Council Resolution 242 and did what it could to assure the military superiority of Israel. The Arab states, on the other hand, made a major concession in accepting the existence of Israel and promising to end the state of belligerence, but they also wanted back their lands. Because of the stalemate and the prolongation of the no-war, no-peace situation, Sadat and other leaders thought that a new war was necessary in order to create a new situation from which the peace talks could resume.

## The War of October 1973 and the Prospects for Peace: The Obstacles and the Solutions

The war that Egypt and Syria started on Saturday, 6 October 1973 was not one of aggression or conquest; its objective was limited to breaking the stalemate in the peace talks. It was the result of Arab frustration with Israel's policy of "creeping annexation" in the occupied territories, and the product of the evident satisfaction of both Israel and the Nixon administration with the status quo, as well as their miscalculations about the Arab's ability to fight.

The war shattered certain assumptions about Israeli invincibility, Arab military ineptitude, and Arab disunity. It also proved that the extended Israeli borders did not deter an Arab attack. The Egyptians were able to cross the Suez Canal and smash the Bar Lev line, while the Syrians overran a major part of the occupied Golan Heights. Their initial success did not give them a military victory, but it proved that they "were battling as hard as the Israelis," [147] and it gave them a new sense of pride after the humiliation of 1967. By the third day of fighting, Israel had to request urgent replacement of war materiel and the American government began on 13 October a massive airlift of equipment that enabled the Israelis to mount their counteroffensive. Even so, the estimate of Secretary of State Henry Kissinger that the Israelis would need no more than three days—later revised to five days—to seize the offensive and defeat the Arabs did not materialize.[148]

The fighting ended with the 25 October 1973 Security Council ceasefire resolution, but not without bringing the United States and Soviet Union to the brink of confrontation. The war, moreover, precipitated the Arab oil embargo. The embargo had been preceded by a decision of most of the Arab oil producers to reduce their output by 5 percent each month until Israel withdrew from the occupied territories. Then on 18 October 1973 King Faisal of Saudi Arabia declared a total ban on oil shipments to the United States, in which the other Arab producers soon joined. Several American oil companies had tried prior to the 1973 war to emphasize the American stake in Middle East peace and to create an understanding of Arab aspirations, but their statements were vigorously assailed by Jewish organizations, and the headquarters of one of the companies—Standard Oil of California—were splashed with red paint and its credit cards were burned or returned by their pro-Israeli holders.[149] The Nixon administration ignored warnings about the impending crisis, while Moshe Dayan, Israel's defense minister, gave assurances that there would be no war and no oil embargo due to Israel's overwhelming military strength.

The Arab oil producers repeatedly declared that the oil weapon was intended to put the Arab case to the people of the world as effectively as possible and that the embargo was by no means directed against the American people but was "rather prompted by their government's massive arms deliveries to the Israelis during the recent war to help them remain in Arab lands." [150] The Arabs emphasized that they had been provoked into the embargo decision and that the United States on more than one occasion had also resorted to economic boycott when its national interests so demanded.

Pro-Zionist writers and public figures, however, tried to ignore the relation between the boycott and American-Israeli policies and used the embargo to promote anti-Arab feeling and speak of Arab blackmail.[151] The question of using force against the Arab oil producers was raised by Defense Secretary James Schlesinger on 6 January 1974 and has been raised since then on various occasions by newspaper columnists and by President Ford and Secretary of State Kissinger.[152] The Arabs and many non-Arabs tried to explain that the oil producers, in refusing to let their oil fuel American plants that turn out war machines to kill their people, or in trying to persuade Americans not to underwrite the Israeli occupation of their lands with billions of dollars, were not practicing blackmail.[153] When the embargo ended on 18 March 1974, it was still very uncertain whether the Arabs would obtain the satisfaction of their basic goals.

The war of October 1973 significantly ended the stalemate in the search for a peace settlement. The sense of urgency the events in October created led to an Arab-Israeli conference in Geneva on 21 December 1973 under US-USSR auspices with a minor role for the United Nations. The conference was to disengage the forces, establish ceasefire lines, and find a path to peace. It was the first meeting, since the creation of Israel, where Arabs and Israelis sat face to face to discuss their problems. Israel attended only at Secretary Kissinger's insistence, while the Palestinians were not invited at all. Three weeks earlier in Algiers, the Arab states tacitly endorsed the idea of a permanent peace settlement with Israel.[154] At the same time they acknowledged the Palestine Liberation Organization under the leadership of Yasir Arafat as the sole representative of the Palestinian people. The Geneva conference recessed two days after it met and while it was to resume serious work after the disengagement of forces had been accomplished, by the end of 1974 it had not reconvened.

With Secretary Kissinger playing a leading role in negotiations, a disengagement agreement between Israel and Egypt was concluded on 18 January 1974, which established a buffer zone in Sinai under UN supervision. Between Syria and Israel, it was not until 29 May that the agreement was reached. The Israelis agreed to return Kuneitra, which they destroyed before leaving, and a buffer zone was set up under UN supervision in the Golan Heights. The prominent US role and close relations between Kissinger and Sadat displeased the Soviet Union, especially as its position in Egypt eroded. President Nixon's trip to the Arab countries underscored the changed US position and, at the same time, gave the Arab rulers the occasion to remind the American leaders that peace in the Middle East could not be attained unless the Palestinians were given the right of self-determination.

Disengagement, however, and the Israeli pullback of a few miles in Sinai and a few hundred yards in the Golan were not what the Arab states fought for in October 1973. The disengagement agreements were preliminary arrangements or, as their text stipulated, they were only a step toward a just and durable peace based on Resolution 242. By the end of 1974, there was still no positive agreement on the basic issues. During the oil embargo, the highest American authority told the Arabs their boycott would slow down peace efforts.[155] Although the embargo was lifted in March 1974, Kissinger's step-by-step diplomacy has shown no positive results. Israel has been concentrating on getting all the arms and money it can get from the United States, while its lobbyists and supporters in Congress were trying to increase its manpower by bringing more Jews from the Soviet Union.

The October war produced no perceptible change in Israel's policies regarding the conquered Arab territories and the Palestinian people, but it did cost Israel unprecedented losses in human lives and war materiel. A ruinous rise in taxes and the cost of living followed as well as an enormous increase of the national debt and the military budget. Disillusionment with the leadership on account of the initial setbacks in the war weakened the ruling Labor Alignment. The number of Jewish immigrants from the Soviet Union decreased from 34,000 in 1973 to 21,000 in 1974, and more than 10 percent of the Israelis interviewed in an opinion poll thought of emigrating for economic and security reasons.[156]

Israel, nevertheless, would make no moves toward a peaceful settlement. In fact, the opposition Likud coalition insists that Israel should keep all the occupied territories, while the Labor coalition cabinets of Mrs. Meir and General Rabin, who in principle have favored partial withdrawal, had made several declarations that show a lack of readiness to withdraw. At the height of Secretary Kissinger's visits to Israel and Syria in May 1974 for the disengagement agreement, construction activity in the Golan did not stop and the Israeli settlements were building and expanding as though there was no Kissinger mission.[157]

In the months that followed the disengagement agreements of January and May 1974, the Israeli leaders occasionally talked about the second disengagement step, but they concentrated their talk on Egypt and ruled out any simultaneous negotiations with the other parties. No definite proposals, however, were presented and President Sadat declared on 9 January 1975 that he had "not received a new offer from Israel on any withdrawal." [158]

Israel's attitude towards Syria and the Palestinians has been completely negative. In mid-November 1974, there were apprehensions that Israel might attack Syria. Secretary Kissinger himself was reported to have predicted in early September 1974 that war might break out in six to eight months, and he cited the possibility of a preemptive Israeli strike. The same warnings were made by Defense Minister Shimon Peres and his chief of staff Mordechai Gur in early August 1974.[159]

The questions of who speaks for the Palestinians and whether there should be a separate Palestinian state have provided Israel with a constant pretext for delaying the peace negotiations, particularly those that bear on the Israeli withdrawal from the occupied West Bank. The right of the Palestinian people to national self-determination has been recognized by several United Nations resolutions, the most recent of which was the General

Assembly resolution of 22 November 1974 that reaffirmed their right to national independence and sovereignty and the "inalienable right to return to their homes and property."[160] The Palestine Liberation Organization and its chairman, Yasir Arafat, have been gaining recognition as the dominant voice of the Palestinians. The seventh Arab summit conference in Rabat (26–29 October 1974) again recognized the PLO as the sole and legitimate representative of the Palestinian people, as it had done before in Algiers, and King Hussein of Jordan joined this time in supporting the resolution. On 13 November 1974 Arafat participated in the UN General Assembly debate on Palestine to which the PLO was invited by a large majority of UN members, and on 22 November the PLO was given permanent observer status in the United Nations. Palestinian leaders in the Israel-occupied West Bank, moreover, have admitted that no leader can negotiate with Israel without the approval of the PLO and that they cannot stand against the Rabat resolution.[161]

The Israelis, however, have repeatedly rejected the idea of an independent Palestinian state and have declared that they would not negotiate with the "so-called Palestine Liberation Organization" at Geneva or anywhere else.[162] They have mentioned on various occasions that they would discuss peace with Jordan on the basis of a Jordanian-Palestinian state in which the identity of the Palestinian and Jordanian Arabs can find expression. Israel's position was reenforced by Secretary Kissinger's reported opposition to such a Palestinian state on the West Bank on the ground that it would be against American interests and by his insistence that negotiations relative to the West Bank should start first between Israel and Jordan.[163] The American government has constantly spoken of Palestinian "interests," but not of Palestinian "rights," and has supported the Israeli concept that distinguishes between the Palestinian guerrilla movement and the Palestine question. The Palestine resistance organizations that are included in the PLO have refused to recognize Israel precisely because of its opposition to an independent Palestinian state. The PLO and the entire Palestine National Council have nevertheless left the door open for their possible participation in the Geneva conference, if and when they are invited, and have often suggested that they would moderate their position.[164]

The war of October 1973 broke the stalemate in the search

for a peace settlement, but it has only succeeded in establishing new ceasefire lines on the Egyptian and Syrian borders of Israel. The dangerous no-war, no-peace situation that prevailed before the October war seems to be returning, and the arms race has resumed at an alarming rate.[165]

Two fundamental obstacles have caused the peace efforts since 1967 to fail: first, Israel's continued refusal to return to the Arabs what belongs to the Arabs, including the Palestinians; second, the large-scale American military and political support that has enabled and encouraged Israel to maintain its negative and defiant attitude. Secretary Kissinger's policy has been, in what relates to the Arab-Israeli conflict and the peace efforts, sluggish, contradictory, and self-defeating. He has undoubtedly tried to promote a peaceful settlement, but he has also been willing to give Israel the military means of rejecting the basic concessions needed for that settlement. Kissinger, moreover, has assumed that if he strengthened Israel militarily by maintaining a balance of power between it and its neighbors or by insuring its military superiority, the Arabs would be deterred from fighting. The war of October 1973 has disproved this assumption, but even if it were proved to be correct, nothing would be gained except a dangerous prolongation of the status quo. Kissinger has, furthermore, wanted to retain the friendship and good will of the Arab world and keep the Arab oil flowing to the western world at reasonable prices. But, at the same time, he gave Israel the devastating arms that it used to kill more Arabs and occupy more Arab lands and thus provoked the Arab states into using their oil weapon against the American unfriendly action. The Arab oil producers, moreover, were driven to seek in the raised price of their commodity the means of paying the billions of dollars needed to purchase weapons in order to meet the Israeli challenge. The question of whether the United States would use military force to occupy the Arab oil fields in order to prevent the so-called "strangulation" of its economy, therefore, amounts in reality to whether the United States would support Israel militarily in another war, because there would be no oil embargo and no "strangulation" except as a result of such support.[166] Moreover, the talk about using force against the oil-rich Arab countries has strengthened Israel's view that it could be used as the spearhead against those countries in any military solution of the oil crisis. This, of course, has done nothing to promote peace efforts.

Another mistaken assumption is that Israel acts as a bulwark against the extension of Soviet influence in the Middle East.[167] Soviet penetration *resulted* from western support of Israel in the Arab-Israeli conflict and from the Arab need for Soviet weapons to face Israel's military power and territorial ambitions. The best way, therefore, to weaken Soviet influence is to get Israel out of Arab lands, and the surest way to maintain and defend American interests in the area is to stop underwriting Israeli wars and conquests.

The removal of the two obstacles that have caused peace efforts to fail demands a drastic change in the attitude of Israel towards the Palestinians and the Arab neighbors and a similar change in the attitude of American political leaders and supporters of Israel. Israel will have to start recognizing some of the basic Arab rights that it has disregarded, and the Arabs, including those who have not explicitly declared their position, would respond by accepting Israel's existence. The recognition of Arab rights would include Israeli withdrawal from the Syrian and Egyptian territories that it occupied in 1967 in the Golan and Sinai, and the acceptance of a Palestinian state in the areas that it would evacuate on the West Bank and the Gaza Strip. Jerusalem would either be internationalized or it would revert to its pre-1967 condition with the Arab sector as a part of the Palestinian state. The form of government and the choice of the rulers in the Palestinian state would be for the Palestinians alone to decide. Israel would contribute to removing the stigma of Palestinian hostility by admitting a certain annual quota of Arab refugees whose homes were in the Israel of 1948, while the remaining refugees would be compensated for their property loss. The provisions of Security Council Resolution 242 of November 1967 guaranteeing the territory and independence of every state in the area can be reinforced by great-power guarantees through the United Nations for Israel and the Palestinian state.

Several considerations should help the Israelis as well as the American supporters of Israel to accept the withdrawal of Israel from the conquered territories and the establishment of a Palestinian state. They should realize, first, that the present state of Israel is completely different from that which the United Nations created in 1947 and that its withdrawal to the 4 June 1967 borders would still leave it in possession of more land than the United Nations resolution originally awarded it.

Second, the establishment of a Palestinian Arab state was an integral part of the 1947 partition resolution, and its area was almost double the size of what was left after the Zionist conquests of 1948. That the Palestinian leaders refused the partition of their country in 1947 does not mean that the Palestinian people should be deprived forever of a state in a much smaller part of their country. It is, moreover, not for Israel or any other state to define the way in which the independent identity of the Palestinian Arabs could find expression.

Third, the Jewish state was established as a haven in which the Zionist founders thought the Jews would live in peace and dignity, but Israel brought neither peace nor dignity, because it dealt unjustly and aggressively with its civilian Arab population and its Arab neighbors.

Fourth, the emotional concern over Israel's survival, should it withdraw from the conquered territories, is unfounded, because the issue for Israel has not been one of survival, but of expansion. The basic condition for Israel's existence would have to be its willingness to live on good terms with its neighbors. Israel could make itself more acceptable by modifying its discriminatory "law of return" in a way that would create an Israeli-world-Jewish relationship similar, for example, to that between Greece and its emigrant Greek-American community.

The Israelis and their American supporters will have to realize that Israel can no longer afford to finance the wars that are needed to keep its conquests and that its dependence on the United States for financing its wars is hurting the Americans in many ways. They have also to realize that the Arabs are determined not to abandon their rights and would continue to fight for them while time is on their side in what relates to the growth of their financial and military power. Consequently, it serves neither Israeli nor American interests to persist in denying justice to the Palestinians and the other neighbors of Israel. The Jews within and outside Israel should be encouraged to read such writers as

Judah Magnes (d. 1948), former president of the Hebrew University, who favored peace and Jewish-Arab cooperation. He said:

> If we have a just cause, so have they [the Arabs of Palestine]. If promises were made to us, so were they to the Arabs. If we love the land and have a historical connection with it, so too the Arabs. Even more realistic than the ugly realities of imperialism is the fact that the Arabs live here and in this part of the world and will probably be here long after the collapse of one imperialism and the rise of another. If we too wish to live in this living space, we must live with the Arabs.[168]

## Notes

1. The portions of Syria "lying to the west of the districts of Damascus, Homs, Hama, and Aleppo" mentioned in McMahon's letter of 24 October 1915 to Sharif Hussein did not include Palestine and lie to the north of Palestine. The British wanted their exclusion from the independent Arab state because France was interested in them; they include the present coast of Lebanon and Syria.

2. The publisher of the *New York Times,* Arthur Sulzberger, wrote on 27 October 1946 that "the unfortunate Jews of Europe's D.P. camps were helpless hostages for whom statehood has been made the only ransom." Quoted in Alfred M. Lilienthal, *What Price Israel?* (Chicago, Regnery, 1953), p. 37.

3. Theodor Herzl, *Complete Diaries,* ed. Raphael Patai, 5 vols. (New York: Herzl Press, 1960), vol. 1, p. 88.

4. See Moshe Menuhin, *The Decadence of Judaism in Our Time* (New York: Exposition Press, 1965), p. 52.

5. Hans Kohn, "Zion and the Jewish National Idea," *Menorah Journal,* XLVI (1958), 38.

6. U.S. Department of State, *Papers Relating to the Foreign Relations of the United States: The Paris Peace Conference, 1919,* Vol. IV, Publication No. 1963 (Washington, D.C.: Government Printing Office, 1943), p. 169. Quoted in Walid Khalidi, editor, *From Haven to Conquest; Readings in Zionism and the Palestine Problem until 1948* (Beirut: Institute for Palestine Studies, 1971), pp. 190–191.

7. See A. L. Tibawi, "Syria in War Time Agreements and Disagreements," *Middle East Forum* (Beirut), 43, 2 (1967): 86.

8. See Erskine Childers, "The Wordless Wish: From Citizens to Refugees" in Ibrahim Abu-Lughod, editor, *The Transformation of Palestine; Essays on the Origin and Development of the Arab-Israeli Conflict*

(Evanston, Ill.: Northwestern University Press, 1971), p. 170, on Dr. Weizmann's talk with Lord Cecil in April 1917 about a Jewish Palestine under a British protectorate.

9. As for example Bourguiba of Tunisia in his speech at Kef on 24 August 1967; Muhammad Hassanein Haikal's articles in *al-Ahram,* October 1967.

10. As for example Amos Kenan in *The Los Angeles Times,* 6 May 1973, section IX, p. 4; Israel Shahak in *Action* (New York), 30 April 1973.

11. See various anti-Zionist opinions and protests in Joseph Mary Nagle Jeffries, *Palestine: The Reality* (London, New York: Longmans, Green, 1939); George Lenczowski, *The Middle East in World Affairs,* 3rd ed. (Ithaca, N.Y.: Cornell University Press, 1962), pp. 374ff; and the two works of A. Lilienthal and Moshe Menuhin already cited and that of Elmer Berger, *Judaism or Jewish Nationalism: the Alternative to Zionism* (New York, Bookman Associates, 1957).

12. Cited in George Antonius, *The Arab Awakening; The Story of the Arab National Movement* (New York: Putnam's, 1946), p. 269; see also Anthony Nutting, *The Arabs; A Narrative History from Mohammed to the Present* (New York: Potter, 1964), p. 293.

13. Details on the meeting and the agreement and Faisal's conditional note on the agreement in A. L. Tibawi, "T. E. Lawrence, Faisal and Weizmann: The 1919 Attempt to Secure an Arab Balfour Declaration," *Royal Central Asian Journal,* 56, 2 (June 1969): 156–163.

14. Fred John Khouri, *The Arab-Israeli Dilemma* (Syracuse, N.Y.: Syracuse University Press, 1968), p. 12.

15. Lenczowski, *The Middle East in World Affairs,* pp. 85–88.

16. See text of the recommendations of the Commission in Antonius, *Arab Awakening,* Appendix H.

17. John Ruedy, "Dynamics of Land Alienation in Palestine," in Abu-Lughod, *Transformation of Palestine,* pp. 127–131.

18. See David Ben Gurion, "Britain's Contribution to Arming the Hagana," and "Our Friend: What Wingate Did for Us," in *Jewish Observer* and *Middle Eastern Review,* 20 and 27 September 1963, quoted in Khalidi, *From Haven to Conquest,* pp. 373, 382; Leonard Mosley, *Gideon Goes to War: Story of Orde Wingate* (London: Barker, 1955), Chapter 4; Maurice Pearlman, *The Army of Israel* (New York: Philosophical Library, 1950), pp. 29ff.

19. George Eden Kirk, *A Short History of the Middle East, from the Rise of Islam to Modern Times,* 2nd ed. (London: Methuen, 1952), p. 205; Lenczowski, *The Middle East in World Affairs,* p. 388.

20. Kirk, *Short History,* p. 215; Sydney Nettleton Fisher, *The Middle East, a History,* 2nd ed. (New York: Knopf, 1968), p. 641.

21. William Alfred Eddy, *F.D.R. Meets Ibn Saud* (New York: American Friends of the Middle East, 1954), p. 35.

22. Arnold Joseph Toynbee, *A Study of History* (New York: Oxford University Press, 1962), Vol. 8, p. 308.

23. Eddy, *F.D.R.,* pp. 36ff.

24. Quoted in Lawrence Griswold, *This Sword for Allah* (Washington D.C., Graphic Arts Press, 1952), pp. 49ff.

25. Henry Cattan, *Palestine: The Road to Peace* (London: Harlow, Longman, 1971), p. 18, gives figures of population and land ownership based on publications of the government of Palestine and UN documents.

26. The pressures and American influence have been described fully in several books such as Harry S. Truman, *Memoirs* (Garden City, N.Y.: Doubleday, 1955–56); James Vincent Forrestal, *The Forrestal Diaries,* Walter Millis, editor (New York: Viking, 1951); Millar Burrows, *Palestine Is Our Business* (Philadelphia: Westminster Press, 1949); and Lilienthal, *What Price Israel.*

27. For details of declarations by Arab delegates in the General Assembly, see Hanna Khabbaz and George Haddad, *Faris al-Khouri: Hayatuhu wa 'Asruhu* ("Faris al-Khouri: His Life and Times"), (Beirut: Sadir Rihani, 1952), pp. 207ff.

28. Khabbaz and Haddad, *Faris al-Khouri,* p. 214; Fred Khouri, *Arab-Israeli Dilemma,* pp. 55ff.

29. For Faris al-Khouri's statements in the Security Council on 24 February and 2 March 1948, see Khabbaz and Haddad, *Faris al-Khouri,* pp. 219–221.

30. Quoted from Fayez A. Sayegh, *A Palestinian View* (Amman: 2nd World Conference on Palestine, 1970), p. 4.

31. Estimate of the Jewish forces in Sir John Glubb, "The Battle for Jerusalem," *Middle East International* (London) (May 1973): 6.

32. Glubb, "Battle for Jerusalem."

33. Text and details on the armistice agreements in Sami Hadawi, *Bitter Harvest; Palestine Between 1914–1967* (New York: New World Press, 1967), pp. 116ff.

34. Childers, "The Wordless Wish," pp. 182ff; Cattan, *Palestine,* p. 24.

35. Menachem Begin, *The Revolt, Story of the Irgun* (New York: Schuman, 1951), p. 165; Hadawi, *Bitter Harvest,* p. 105.

36. Childers, "The Wordless Wish," p. 194; Cattan, *Palestine,* pp. 23–24; George Eden Kirk, *Survey of International Affairs: The Middle East, 1945–1950* (London, New York: Oxford University Press, 1954), pp. 262, 282; Edgar O'Ballance, *The Arab-Israeli War, 1948* (New York: Praeger, 1957), p. 209; John Bagot Glubb, *A Soldier with the Arabs* (New York: Harper, 1957), p. 81.

37. Mentioned in Hadawi, *Bitter Harvest,* pp. 187, 211 and in Ahmad Shuqairi, *Liberation—Not Negotiation* (Beirut, 1966), p. 137, in a speech before the Special Political Committee of the UN, 19 November 1963.

38. Toynbee, *A Study of History,* vol. 8, p. 290.

39. Jacques Berque, "Predicament and Perspectives of the Arab World," in Edward Said and Fuad Suleiman, *The Arabs Today: Alternatives for Tomorrow* (Columbus, Ohio: Forum Associates, 1973), p. 13.

40. See the section on the Palestine Conciliation Commission in Fred Khouri's chapter in this volume; Hadawi, *Bitter Harvest,* pp. 159, 165; David P. Forsythe, *United Nations Peacemaking: The Conciliation Commission for Palestine* (Baltimore: Johns Hopkins University Press, 1972), p. 159, quoting Ralph Bunche on the possibility of a settlement in 1949; Rony E. Gabbay, *A Political Study of the Arab-Jewish Conflict: the Arab Refugee Problem: A Case Study* (Geneva: E. Droz, 1959), p. 322.

41. Glubb, *A Soldier with the Arabs,* pp. 256, 341; Kirk, *The Middle East 1945–1950,* pp. 309ff; Walter Eytan, *The First Ten Years; A Diplomatic History of Israel* (New York: Simon and Schuster, 1958), pp. 42–43.

42. George M. Haddad, *Revolutions and Military Rule in the Middle East,* Vol. II, Part I: *The Arab States: Iraq, Syria, Lebanon, and Jordan* (New York: Robert Speller, 1971), p. 486.

43. Cattan, *Palestine,* p. 28.

44. See Ruedy, "Dynamics of Land Alienation," p. 137; Fayez A. Sayegh, *Arab Property in Israeli-Controlled Territories* (New York: Arab Information Center, 1956); Don Peretz, *Israel and the Palestine Arabs* (Washington, D.C.: Middle East Institute, 1958), p. 148.

45. Hadawi, *Bitter Harvest,* p. 253.

46. See A. L. Tibawi, "Visions of the Return: The Palestine Arab Refugees in Arab Poetry and Art," *Middle East Journal* 17, 5 (Late Autumn, 1963): 507–526.

47. Tibawi, "Visions of the Return," pp. 508–511; Hadawi, *Bitter Harvest,* pp. 170ff.

48. Sayegh, *A Palestinian View,* p. 11.

49. Hadawi, *Bitter Harvest,* pp. 195ff.; Peretz, *Israel and the Palestine Arabs,* pp. 95ff.

50. See Lieutenant-General Edson Louis Millard Burns, *Between Arab and Israeli* (New York: I. Obolensky, 1963), pp. 33–68.

51. Mentioned in Shuqairi, *Liberation,* pp. 38–40.

52. Quoted by Hadawi, *Bitter Harvest,* pp. 237–238.

53. Gamal Abdel Nasser, "The Egyptian Revolution," *Foreign Affairs,* 33, 2 (January 1955); Michael Hudson, "Arab States' Policies toward Israel," in Abu-Lughod, ed., *The Transformation of Palestine,* p. 322; Jean and Simonne Lacouture, *Egypt in Transition* (London: Methuen, 1958), p. 233; Uri Avnery, *Israel without Zionists* (New York: Macmillan, 1968), pp. 100–113.

54. Khouri, *The Arab-Israeli Dilemma,* p. 199.

55. Michael Hudson, "Arab States' Policies," p. 324; Kennett Love, "The Other Nasser: Profile of a Bogeyman," *Mid East* (December 1970): 9; Khouri, *The Arab-Israeli Dilemma,* p. 201.

56. Harry Hopkins, *Egypt, the Crucible; the Unfinished Revolution in the Arab World* (Boston: Houghton Mifflin, 1969), p. 169ff; K. Love, 9.

57. Major General Moshe Dayan, *Diary of the Sinai Campaign* (New York: Harper & Row, 1966), p. 12; Love, "The Other Nasser," p. 10.

58. *The New York Times,* 21 February 1957.

59. See George M. Haddad, *Revolutions and Military Rule in the Middle East,* Vol. II, Part II: *The Arab States: Egypt, the Sudan, Yemen, and Libya* (New York: Robert Speller, 1973), p. 278; and for Nasserism and the Palestine question during this period, pp. 96–114.

60. On the cold war, see Malcolm H. Kerr, *The Arab Cold War; Gamal 'Abd al-Nasir and His Rivals, 1958–1970,* 3rd ed. (London, New York: Oxford University Press for the Royal Institute of International Affairs, 1971).

61. Robert St. John, *Ben-Gurion; the Biography of an Extraordinary Man* (Garden City, N.Y.: Doubleday, 1959), quoted in Fred J. Khouri,

"The Policy of Retaliation in Arab-Israeli Relations," *Middle East Journal*, 20, 4 (Autumn 1966) : 437.

62. Fred John Khouri, "Friction and Conflict on the Israeli-Syrian Front," *Middle East Journal*, 17, 1 and 2 (Winter-Spring 1963) : 24ff; Burns, *Between Arab and Israeli*, pp. 118ff.

63. Khouri, "Friction and Conflict," p. 32.

64. For the discussions in the meeting of Nasser and the Syrian leaders on 29 November 1959 in al-Qubba Palace in Cairo, see *Al-Nasr* (Damascus), 13 June 1962.

65. Tewfik Moussa, *Al-ishtirakiya al-misriya wa al-qadiya al-filistiniya* ("Egyptian Socialism and the Palestine Question") (No place or publisher; 1966), pp. 106ff.

66. Text of Nasser's speech in *Arab Political Documents, 1965*, eds. W. Khalidi and Y. Ibish (American University of Beirut, Department of Political Studies and Public Administration, 1965), pp. 220–229; *Time*, 11 June 1965.

67. Haikal's article quoted in *The New York Times*, 27 September 1964.

68. *The Heritage* (New York), 25 September 1965, quoting Michel Abu-Jawdeh in *al-Nahar* (Beirut).

69. *Le Monde* (Paris), 7 November 1966.

70. Quoted by *L'Orient* (Beirut), 8 December 1966.

71. Khouri, "The Policy of Retaliation," p. 454; *The New York Times*, 14 March 1965; *Life*, 18 June 1965.

72. See Henry G. Fischer, review of Abdullah Schleifer, *The Fall of Jerusalem* (New York: Monthly Review Press, 1972), in *The Link* (New York) (September-October 1973) : 6.

73. See text of Nasser's speeches of 22, 25, and 26 May and 9 June 1967 in Walter Laqueur, editor, *The Israel-Arab Reader; a Documentary History of the Middle East Conflict* (New York: Citadel Press, 1969); claims of Defense Minister Shamseddin Badran in *The Los Angeles Times*, 25 February 1968; and of other officers in *New Outlook* (Tel Aviv) (September-October 1967), quoting *al-Hawadith* (Beirut).

74. Quoted by Amnon Kapeliouk, "Israel était-il réellement menacé d'extermination?" *Le Monde*, 3 June 1972, p. 4; translated in *Middle East Newsletter* (Beirut) (January-February 1973) : 10.

75. Lyndon Baines Johnson, *The Vantage Point: Perspectives of the Presidency 1963–69* (New York: Holt, Rinehart and Winston 1971), pp. 293, 296.

76. Kemal Abu Jaber, "United States Policy Towards the June Conflict," in I. Abu-Lughod, ed. *The Arab-Israeli Confrontation of June 1967: An Arab Perspective* (Evanston, Ill.: Northwestern University Press, 1970), p. 159.

77. Mentioned in *Middle East Newsletter*, special supplement, 21 February 1973.

78. See review by Henry Fischer in *The Link*, p. 6.

79. Nasser's speeches of 9 June and 23 July 1967 in Laqueur, *Reader*, p. 190.

80. *Le Journal de Dimanche* (Paris), 28 May 1967; Hopkins, *Egypt*, p. 483.

81. Hopkins, *Egypt,* pp. 483ff; *The Times* (London), 12 June 1967; Abba Eban's declarations reported by Louis B. Fleming in *The Los Angeles Times,* 9 June 1969.

82. David G. Nes, "Our Relations with Israel and the Arabs" (Boulder, Colorado: American Committee for Justice in the Middle East), p. 5.

83. Quoted by Khouri, *The Arab-Israeli Dilemma,* p. 313.

84. Kerr, *The Arab Cold War,* pp. 129ff, refers to this cooperation as the "Nasser-Hussein Axis."

85. *The New York Times,* 9 November 1967 and 3 February 1969 commented on the proposals of Hussein and Nasser and described them as "positive."

86. See Nadav Safran, "Israeli Politics since the 1967 War," *Current History* (January, 1971): 23.

87. Johnson's speech at B'nai B'rith convention in Washington on 10 September 1968.

88. William P. Rogers, "A Lasting Peace in The Middle East: An American View," Department of State, Washington, 1970; Harry Howard, "Recent American Policy in the Middle East," *Middle East Forum* (Summer 1971): 15.

89. *The New York Times,* 20, 22 December; *The Los Angeles Times,* 22 December 1969; *Department of State Bulletin,* 12 January 1970, pp. 21ff.

90. *The New York Times,* 24 December; *The Los Angeles Times,* editorial, 24 December 1969; James Reston column, *Santa Barbara News-Press,* 11 January 1970; Nick Thimmisch column, *The Los Angeles Times,* 31 December 1969.

91. *The New York Times,* 24 December 1969.

92. See *ibid.,* for what the "Boston group" said during its visit to the White House; Max Lerner column, *The Los Angeles Times,* 26 December 1969; Senator Henry Jackson in his report to the Senate Armed Services Committee, December 1970.

93. Former Ambassador John Badeau, quoted in Harry Howard, "Recent American Policy," p. 13.

94. Amos Kenan, *Middle East Newsletter* (Beirut) (August-September 1970): 4; Zeev Schiff in *Haaretz,* 4 July 1971.

95. J. William Fulbright, "Old Myths and New Realities: The Middle East," *Congressional Record,* 24 August 1970.

96. Parker T. Hart in *Middle East International* (April, 1971): 8–9; James Reston, *The New York Times,* 23 December 1970.

97. *Time,* 15 June 1970.

98. The initiative was announced on 25 June; see text of the announcement and of Rogers's letter of 19 June to the Egyptian foreign minister in *Current History* (January 1971): 46, 50–51.

99. *The New York Times,* 24 July and 5 August 1970 mentioned US pressure on Israel; see also Bernard Reich, "United States Policy in the Middle East," *Current History* (January, 1971): 5; Nadav Safran, "Israeli Politics," p. 21 on the Rogers Plan and the Israeli cabinet.

100. *The Los Angeles Times,* 19 August 1970; Evans and Novak column, 22 August 1970.

101. Evans and Novak column, 15 December 1970; for a sample of

Ambassador Yost's opinion, see his "Last Chance for Peace in The Middle East," *Life*, 9 April 1971.

102. See conclusion of George Lenczowski in *Soviet Advances in the Middle East* (Washington, D.C.: American Enterprise Institute for Public Policy Research, 1972), 161; George Lenczowski, "Arab Radicalism: Problems and Prospects," *Current History* (January, 1971): 52; Richard Cottam, "American Policy and the Arab World" in *The Arab World: From Nationalism to Revolution,* eds. A. Jabara and Janice Terry (Wilmette, Ill.: Medina University Press International, 1971), p. 126.

103. Yusif A. Sayigh on Palestine peace in *Middle East Newsletter* (Beirut, Americans for Justice in the Middle East) (June-July 1970).

104. See *Towards a Democratic State in Palestine* (Fateh contribution to the 2nd World Conference on Palestine, Amman, 2–6 September 1970); Sayegh, *A Palestinian View,* pp. 12–13, for a description of the projected "new Palestine."

105. See Hisham Sharabi, "Palestine Guerillas: Their Credibility and Effectiveness," *Middle East Forum,* 46, 2–3 (1970): 44ff.

106. *Haaretz* (Jerusalem), 21 July 1971 estimated that there were 3600 guerrillas in Israeli prisons.

107. *The New York Times,* 25 March 1968; estimates on Karameh battle losses in *The New York Times,* 23 March.

108. See, for example, Lawrence Mosher, *The National Observer,* 5 October 1970 and the quotations in his article.

109. *The New York Times,* 27 July 1970.

110. Nixon's promises were included in a letter to Golda Meir according to a report by United Press International mentioned in *Santa Barbara News-Press,* 12 December 1970.

111. See the report of UN Secretary-General U Thant of 30 November 1971 on the activities of Dr. Jarring and the text of the two memoranda and of Israel's answer in *Middle East Journal,* 26, 1 (Winter 1972): 69–77.

112. *Ibid.,* pp. 71, 76; Bernard Reich, "Israel's Quest for Security," *Current History* (January, 1972): 5.

113. Golda Meir's interview with Ma'ariv of 3 September 1972 quoted in *Middle East Monitor,* 1 October 1972.

114. Moshe Dayan in *Jewish Telegraphic Agency, Daily News Bulletin* (New York), 15 February 1972; the often-quoted Allon Plan for the West Bank; Golda Meir in *The Times* quoted in *The Los Angeles Times,* 3 March 1971; *Time,* 11 September 1972 report on Israeli offer to Egypt and Jordan; *Time,* 10 August 1971, interview with Mrs. Meir.

115. James Reston column, 14 March 1971; Charles Yost, "Last Chance for Peace in the Middle East," *Life,* 9 April 1971.

116. See *The New York Times,* 17, 18 March 1971; *The Los Angeles Times,* 13 March 1971.

117. *The New York Times,* 23 August 1970; Parker T. Hart, "U.S. Middle East Policy in 1971," *Middle East International* (London) (April 1971): 9.

118. Sadat's account of Rogers's visit and his relations with the US diplomats including the memorandum of Donald Bergus that was disowned by the State Department was related in his speech of 16 Septem-

ber 1971 and in his interview with *Newsweek* 13 December 1971, 43, 47; see also Joseph Kraft report in *The Los Angeles Times*, 29 June 1971.

119. Text of Rogers's speech and six points for the agreement in *Current History* (January 1972): 44, 47; see also reaction of Israel and comments in *The Los Angeles Times*, 7 October, 26 November, 3 December 1971.

120. General Ezer Weizman quoted in *The Los Angeles Times*, 22 November 1971.

121. *The Los Angeles Times*, 19 January 1972.

122. Speech and comment in *The New York Times* and *The Los Angeles Times*, 10 February 1972.

123. James Reston, report from Jerusalem in *Santa Barbara News-Press*, 29 March 1972.

124. *The Los Angeles Times*, 16 June 1972.

125. *The Los Angeles Times*, 11, 20 June 1972 on the criticism of Rabin's comments on Nixon by Democratic leaders who considered them inappropriate political propaganda in the election campaign by a foreign diplomat.

126. *The News* (Mexico City), 15 August 1972.

127. According to Minister of State Israel Galili, in *Middle East Monitor*, 1 August 1972.

128. See declarations of Israeli ministers and reactions of Christian religious leaders including Pope Paul in "Some Thoughts on Jerusalem" by Archbishop Joseph T. Ryan, *The Link* (New York) (September–October 1972): 3ff.; "Jerusalem: City of Peace or War?" (Boulder, Colo., 17 March 1922): 1–4; Malcolm H. Kerr, "The Changing Political Status of Jerusalem," in Abu-Lughod, *The Transformation of Palestine*, pp. 361ff; *The New York Times*, editorial 17 February 1971; statement by George Bush, US ambassador to the UN, in Security Council, 25 September 1971.

129. See Naseer Aruri, "The Nixon Doctrine and the Mideast," *The New York Times*, 20 May 1972; Amnon Rubinstein in *The New York Times*, 17 June 1972.

130. *Let Us Meet as Equals*, statement by Mrs. Meir in the Knesset on 26 July 1972 (Washington D.C., Embassy of Israel), pp. 6–9.

131. *Time*, 11 September 1972.

132. Interview with *al-Hawadith* (Beirut).

133. Reported by Eric Rouleau in *Le Monde*, 3 November 1972, in interview with King Hussein; see *The Los Angeles Times*, 4 November 1972.

134. *Time*, 23 April 1973, p. 23.

135. Report by Peter Chew in the *National Observer*, 25 August 1973.

136. John K. Cooley, "Israelis Put down Roots in Arab Soil," *Christian Science Monitor*, 30 May 1973, p. 7, quoted by *Palestine Digest*, July 1973, pp. 5–7.

137. Mentioned in Elias Sam'o and Cyrus Elahi, "Resolution 242 and Beyond," in *Controversy in the Middle East* (New York: IDOC-North America, September 1973), p. 15.

138. Report by Rev. Joseph L. Ryan, *Action*, 2 July 1973.

139. *Action,* 30 April 1973 for what Dr. Israel Shahak said.

140. See Evans and Novak column, 3 February 1973; Lawrence Mosher, "Israel or Arab Oil: U.S. May Face a Choice," *National Observer,* 16 June 1973, p. 3.

141. *The Los Angeles Times,* 20 March 1973.

142. See *Middle East Monitor,* 15 June 1973, for Senator J. William Fulbright's speech in the Senate on 21 May 1973 on the dangers of American pro-Israel policy; Ernest Conine's column on the new era of big-power imperialism to meet the oil crisis, in *The Los Angeles Times,* 23 March 1973.

143. John Peterson, "Jungle-Weary Marines Go to War, Stress Desert Combat," *National Observer,* 25 August 1973, p. 4; "Why Marines Are Training in the Desert," *U.S. News and World Report,* 27 August 1973.

144. Quoted from *Akhbar al-Yom* (Cairo), 24 March in *Brief* (Tel Aviv), 16–31 March 1973.

145. *Newsweek,* 9 April 1973.

146. See the article about Frank Jungers and his meeting in May with King Faisal, *The Los Angeles Times,* 4 September 1973; see also Lawrence Mosher in *National Observer,* 16 June 1973.

147. *Time,* 22 October 1973 quoting Aharon Yariv, former intelligence chief of Israel.

148. On Kissinger's estimate and his role in carrying out the airlift, see Marvin and Bernard Kalb, "Twenty Days in October," *Palestine Digest* (Washington, D.C., September 1974): 18–20; E. Luttwak and W. Laqueur, "Kissinger and the Yom Kippur War," *Commentary* (September 1974): 39.

149. See *The Los Angeles Times,* 3 August 1973; Jack Forsyth, "Arab Oil and the Zionist Connection" in *The Link* (January–February 1974); Ray Vicker, *The Kingdom of Oil; the Middle East: Its People and Its Power* (New York: Scribner, 1974), pp. 10–11.

150. See the page-long "open letter to the American people" by the government of Kuwait in *The Los Angeles Times,* 19 November 1973, and by the government of Saudi Arabia in *ibid.,* 31 December 1973.

151. See, for example, the columns of Max Lerner of 22 December 1973 and 16 February 1974; Joseph Alsop column on 8 November 1974.

152. *The Los Angeles Times,* 7 January 1974 for Schlesinger's remarks and the headline "Arabs Risk U.S. Public Demand for the Use of Force"; speeches of President Ford on 18 and 23 September 1974 and of Kissinger on 23 September in news releases of Bureau of Public Affairs, Department of State; Kissinger's interview in *Business Week,* 13 January 1975.

153. See William Raspberry, "Blackmail or Diplomacy," in *Washington Post,* 23 November 1973, p. A31.

154. *The Los Angeles Times,* 29 November 1973.

155. President Nixon's press conference on 26 February 1974; Nixon's speech in Chicago on 15 March 1974.

156. On this opinion poll, *The Los Angeles Times,* 27 March 1974. The figure was more than 20 percent among the 18–29 age group.

157. *The Los Angeles Times,* 8 May 1974.

158. *The Los Angeles Times,* 10 January 1975.

159. *Daily Star* (Beirut), 4 August, and *Herald Tribune* (Paris), 8 August 1974.

160. See text of the resolutions in *Middle East Monitor,* 1 December 1974.

161. Report by Bernard Rossiter in *The Washington Post,* 19 November 1974, on what the mayor of Hebron, Sheikh Ja'bari, said.

162. Premier Rabin's declaration in the Knesset on 3 June 1974, in the *Middle East Monitor,* 15 June 1974; official decision of the Rabin cabinet on 21 July 1974; Foreign Minister Yigal Allon's declaration in Washington, in *The Los Angeles Times,* 18 January 1975.

163. See *Daily Star* (Beirut), 26 July 1974 quoting *Ma'ariv; Herald Tribune,* 15 July 1974; *The Los Angeles Times,* 15 October 1974 on his talks with Arab leaders in mid-October before the Rabat summit.

164. See the resolutions of the Palestine National Council in Cairo in early June 1974 in *Middle East Intelligence Survey,* 15 June, 1974; Eric Rouleau, "The Palestinian Quest," *Foreign Affairs* (January, 1975): 280–283; Arafat's declarations in *Le Monde,* 7 January 1975.

165. See Fuad Jabber, "Curbing the Arab-Israeli Arms Race," *The Link* (New York) (November–December 1974): 1–7.

166. The mention of "strangulation" as a cause of using force was made by Secretary Kissinger in interview published by *Business Week,* 13 January 1975.

167. See President Ford's declaration about Israel as a bulwark, *Middle East Monitor,* 15 September 1974, in his interview with *The Economist.*

168. Quoted in Alan Taylor, "Zionism's Dilemma," *Middle East International* (London) (May 1973): 13.

# American Efforts for Peace

John C. Campbell

EVER since the Palestine crisis arose at the end of the Second World War the United States has seen itself as an advocate and promoter of peace in the Middle East. It is not necessary to ascribe this view to a special missionary feeling of the American people, some Wilsonian impulse to settle other peoples quarrels by the application of American wisdom and practicality, although that is one aspect of it. It also grew out of events for which the United States itself was in part responsible. Even more, it grew out of concern for national interests. In the latter respect the United States was not different from any other power, and it goes without saying that other nations did not share the Americans' view of themselves. The fact remains that for over twenty years a peaceful Arab-Israeli settlement has been a primary aim of American policy.

The story of American efforts for peace is thus another way of describing the history of American policy toward Palestine and

John C. Campbell has been, since 1955, Director of Political Studies and Senior Research Fellow at the Council on Foreign Relations, New York. Educated at Harvard University (A.B. 1933, Ph.D. 1940), he served for twelve years in the Department of State in the Bureau of European Affairs and the Policy Planning Staff. Since joining the Council on Foreign Relations he has continued to serve as a consultant to the State Department, as well as a member of the associated staff of the Brookings Institution; North American Rapporteur for Energy of The Trilateral Commission; and Vice President and Member of the Board of Governors of the Middle East Institute.

Dr. Campbell is the author of three volumes of *The United States in World Affairs* (Harper & Bros., 1947–49); *Defense of the Middle East: Problems of American Policy* (Harper, 1958 and 1960); a monograph, *The West and the Middle East* (with Helen Caruso) (Council on Foreign Relations, 1972); and numerous articles. In addition, he has written extensively on non-Middle Eastern subjects.

the Arab-Israeli conflict. But it is a way, depending on the narrator's objectivity or lack of it, which carries an element of judgment. How far did American policies actually promote peace? What were the motives behind them, and what have been the effects?

It is manifestly impossible to tell that history, even with the strictest economy of detail, in one chapter of this book. A narrative proceeding month by month or year by year—studded with pleas for peace, warnings against war, armistice agreements and their violation, UN resolutions and negotiations about negotiation —would produce too much and too little. Too much because the story is so long and has been told in whole or in part by so many books already published. Too little because in the absence of essential source material, mainly diplomatic documents which are still inaccessible, the full history cannot yet be written.

The device attempted here is to choose certain themes and episodes which illustrate American efforts for peace and security in the Middle East. They are not cut into neat time periods, or precise patterns. Nor are they selected to prove virtue or vice, honesty or hypocrisy, single-mindedness or inconsistency. The purpose is to deal with critical points and periods, to show the whys and hows of the decisions taken, and to relate what was done to our general subject of the promotion of peace. The case studies range from the establishment of an independent Israel in 1948 to the attempts to arrange an interim settlement between Israel and Egypt in the period before the war of 1973.

The story, carried through 1972, does not include the dramatic changes brought about by the fourth round of Arab-Israel war in October 1973. The initiatives taken by the United States in bringing about a ceasefire and later detailed agreements on military disengagement on both Egyptian and Syrian fronts obviously represent a new and even spectacular phase of American efforts for peace. The war, though at heavy cost, brought into being new prospects for peace through its political and psychological impact. It offered an opportunity for imaginative diplomacy which Secretary Kissinger boldly seized. His enterprise was favored by the absence of opposition from Moscow, the availability of UN forces and observers, and especially the willingness of both sides to negotiate seriously. The disengagement agreements of 1974 were no guarantee that a peace could be achieved, but as the first negotiated agreements between Israel and any Arab states since 1949 they were a remarkable achievement, and one which would have been impossible without the intermediary role of the American secretary of state.

With due respect to the talents of Henry Kissinger, his achievement was not just a personal triumph. It was the logical continuation, in new circumstances, of a policy followed in greater or less degree, albeit with very little success, over a period of many years through four rounds of war and the intervening periods of uneasy truce.

## The Decision to Support an Independent Jewish State

As the Second World War drew to a close, the United States had no aspiration to the role of arbiter or peacemaker in the Middle East. It had made no decision to support or to oppose the Zionist idea. Palestine was in the area of British responsibility, and President Roosevelt was content to leave it that way. Yet he was aware of trouble ahead which the United States could hardly ignore. The tragic fate of European Jewry was generating pressure for a massive movement of its remnants to find refuge and a new life in Palestine; the world Zionist organizations, with strong support from the American Jewish community, had in 1942 declared as an immediate goal the establishment of a Jewish state in Palestine and urged American pressure on Britain to bring it about; Arab leaders in and outside Palestine made plain their insistence on its character as an Arab country and their opposition to any further influx of Jews; the British were tired and not in full control of events.

Roosevelt straddled the issue. He showed sensitivity to Jewish appeals, which were reinforced by Congressional resolutions, and to the plight of Jews of Europe, but he did not ignore the Arabs. On returning from Yalta in February 1945 he met King Ibn Saud and gave him two assurances, later specifically confirmed by letter: that he personally, as president, "would do nothing to assist the Jews against the Arabs and would make no move hostile to the Arab people," and that the United States government would make no change in its basic policy in Palestine without full consultation with both Jews and Arabs.[1] The assurance of full consultation, following a formula used many times since 1943, was also given to other Arab governments. Roosevelt knew that relations with the Arab world would come under stress because the American public sympathized with Jewish aims in Palestine. How he would have dealt with the problem no one can say. On several occasions during the war he endorsed the view that a Jewish state could be established and maintained in Palestine only through the use of force; but on another (in a letter to Senator Wagner in 1944) he supported the idea of such a state. He gave some thought to the concept of a trusteeship for Palestine and seemed confident that after the war he could bring about a settlement between Arabs and Jews.[2]

The importance of Harry Truman's ideas about Palestine can hardly be exaggerated, for he had the final word on American policy. He was continually reminded by his principal advisers on defense and foreign policy that it was important not to jeopardize relations with the Arab states, which were so important for strategic reasons and for their immense petroleum resources. He disregarded this advice on two critical occasions: in 1947, when he decided to support in the United Nations the partition of Palestine into independent Jewish and Arab states; and in May 1948, when he recognized the state of Israel a few minutes after it was proclaimed.

The barest outline of developments between 1945–1948 is necessary to show the influences, the conflicting views and shifting currents, not to speak of the confusion, through which the president had to cut to make his decisions. At the end of the war the British, pressed insistently by Jewish refugees and their backers to open the gates of Palestine to massive immigration, had the impossible task of keeping order in a situation where active elements of the Jewish population had turned to violence and the Palestine Arabs to sullen noncooperation. Foreign Secretary Ernest Bevin, concerned about the security of the empire and incensed by what he thought were irresponsible American demands for the admission of large numbers of Jews to Palestine, felt compelled to seek American cooperation as the only way of getting a temporary or more lasting solution. It was then up to the United States to decide on the relative importance of several conflicting interests: cooperation with the British for the common security, the good will of Arab governments, the urgency of seeking Jewish-Arab agreement on the future of Palestine, and the need to use Palestine to reduce the agony of Europe's remaining Jews.

The period 1945 through 1946 was one of much Anglo-American talk and of continuing deterioration of the situation in Palestine. President Truman took two positions which illustrated his own approach and helped to make agreement with the British impossible. He picked out one specific point from the many under discussion—the immediate admission of 100,000 Jewish refugees to Palestine—and insisted on it unconditionally. Refusing to accept as a whole the carefully balanced report of the Anglo-American Committee of Inquiry which recommended a binational Palestine, he singled out for endorsement the proposal on Jewish immigration. Bevin apparently would have accepted the entire report if the United States had done so.[3] Truman also rejected the recommendation of American and British representatives at the subcabinet level, the Morrison-Grady Plan, for a federal Palestine with a Jewish province, an Arab province, and separate districts of Jerusalem and Negev, under a trusteeship with a British high commissioner. Not that he was alone in rejecting these proposals, or that they would have worked. But his position made sure that the attempt to find a common Anglo-American approach would fail. It degenerated into bitter public exchanges between Bevin and Truman and left things worse than they had been before.[4]

This fact was evident in Britain's decision to give up the mandate and throw Palestine's future into the lap of the United Nations. The United States welcomed the opportunity for the world organization to find a solution. With the British out of the picture and refusing to take any responsibility even for helping to enforce a UN decision, the main question was how to balance the conflicting rights and interests of the two communities, Arab and Jewish. From this moment the United States assumed an active role in the search for such a balance, and at a time, the spring of 1947, when the general lines of American foreign policy were being set for years to come. By assuming responsibility for supporting Greece and Turkey and by declaring the Truman doctrine, the United States took on the task of defending the Middle East against Soviet expansion. At the Council of Foreign Ministers in Moscow the big four agreed on nothing, and the lines of the cold war in Europe were drawn. Acting Secretary Acheson pointed out to Congress that if Greece and Turkey lost their independence, other states would soon lose theirs and the West would then lose the strategic bases, lines of communication, and resources of the Middle East.[5] This was the wider context of seeking a solution in Palestine. And so it continued to be down the years as the smaller problem became ever more intertwined with the larger.

The United Nations Special Commission on Palestine, of which the United States was not a member, produced a majority report recommending partition of Palestine into an Arab and a Jewish state plus an international territory of Jerusalem, and a minority report favoring a single federal state of Palestine. The United States decided to support the majority report, stating that it seemed the only practical way out. The desire of the Jewish community in Palestine for statehood had become so strong that it could hardly be denied without the use of force. Arab-Jewish relations in Palestine, moreover, had reached the point where the degree of cooperation necessary to a common state was missing. True, the partition proposal could be faulted on the same ground, for it drew the boundaries of the new states in such a bizarre way that they could not exist without freedom of movement and economic unity; and although such unity was indeed specified as part of the proposal itself, it was questionable whether it could ever work. Moreover, if the Jews were certain to oppose by force any solution other than partition, the Arabs were as adamant in their intention to use force to prevent partition.

Truman himself was well informed on that point. He states bluntly in his memoirs that, knowing it, "I instructed the State Department to support the partition plan." [6] But he was "not committed to any particular formula of statehood in Palestine." That was for the United Nations to work out. Here he showed a rather naive conception of the United Nations as a body which somehow could find solutions where the responsible states could not, even when those states in their wisdom added new complications to the problem before handing it to the world organization.

The US government did indeed support the partition plan as the crucial UN vote approached. Prominent American citizens and organizations, in line with an active Zionist campaign, were even more pressing in trying to influence the votes of some states.[7] In any event, the combination of American and Soviet support for partition virtually assured the necessary two-thirds majority.

What happened after the UN voted for partition in November 1947 confirmed the prophecies of those who had predicted trouble and also the president's determination to continue his historic role. As expected, fighting in Palestine started immediately, the British did absolutely nothing to prepare the way for the two new states, no member states were of a mind to provide the force necessary to enforce the UN decision, and the Arab states were preparing to invade Palestine as soon as the British left. In March the US Ambassador to the United Nations proposed placing Palestine under a temporary UN trusteeship with a force to keep order until an agreement could be hammered out between Arabs and Jews.

How much this was a desperate measure to avoid chaos, how much an attempt to reverse the partition decision and save US influence with the Arab states, is a matter of conjecture. That Truman approved it in its full implications seems highly unlikely.[8] He defended it publicly at the time as a postponement, not a reversal, of policy,[9] even though privately he felt he had been double-crossed by the striped-pants conspirators in the lower levels of the State Department. In any case, time ran out on that particular proposal, for on 14 May the Jewish leaders in Palestine declared the independence of the state of Israel, within the borders of the partition resolution. Within a few minutes the president gave de facto recognition. News of what happened was passed to US delegate Philip Jessup as he was presenting the trusteeship plan to the General Assembly.

Objections to the president's position were much in evidence in his own official family during this whole period. Secretary of Defense Forrestal's opposition was sincere, intense, and squarely based on the danger he saw to vital American interests in strategic positions and oil.[10] At the State Department, with Secretary

Byrnes and later Marshall largely engaged in negotiations in Europe, Under Secretaries Acheson and Lovett bore the brunt of the Palestine affair, and they too had reservations about declarations and policies which cut off the possibilities of a solution the Arabs could accept. The department's Middle East experts were strongly of the opinion that the establishment of a Jewish state would store up unending trouble in American-Arab relations.

The inability of these people to be more effective was not due simply to the president's stubbornness; rather, they lacked an alternative which took sufficient account of the totality of factors in Palestine, in Europe, and in the United States itself. On occasion they could turn or temporarily reverse American policy—they could steer it toward a trusteeship plan in 1947 or a Bernadotte plan (which redrew the partition map) in 1948—but the president always had the last word. As J. C. Hurewitz has said, "the Department had never developed an integrated American policy toward the Near East, into which Zionism, not in its most extreme form to be sure, could fit." [11]

Truman, however, did not support partition merely because he saw no alternative. He favored it positively. He had stated publicly in 1946 that partition "would command the support of public opinion in the United States." [12] His decision to support it in the 1947 UN vote was virtually automatic. His rapid recognition of Israel was quite in character with his convictions. He later described his purpose as "to help bring about the redemption of the pledge of the Balfour Declaration and the rescue of at least some of the victims of Nazism."

How much were these decisions the result of Zionist pressure or of domestic politics and the "Jewish vote"? Some members of the cabinet were cognizant of the importance the president gave to Jewish influence and Jewish financial support of the Democratic Party.[13] Dean Acheson, however, who worked closely with Truman on Palestine from 1945 to mid-1947, states flatly that the president's support of Jewish immigration and of a Jewish state was not inspired by domestic political opportunism.[14] He saw the issue as a moral one, requiring a historic act of justice; indeed, he had public support for that view going far beyond the American Jewish community. The president himself defended his positions as "an American policy," not a Zionist or Jewish one. He has described his annoyance at the "constant barrage" of pressure and propaganda aimed at the White House by extreme Zionists.[15]

This was not a simple conflict of presidental "idealism" on the Zionist side versus the "realism" of those more concerned about strategy, oil, and relations with the Arab world. A man like Sumner Welles supported the creation of a Jewish state on the ground that it was not only morally right but would provide a fair and lasting settlement which would keep the Russians out of the area.[16] That it would be a lasting settlement and keep out the Russians was bad prophecy. That it was fair is a matter for argument; certainly the Arabs did not so regard it.

In a sense the professional foreign service officers who predicted that the Arab reaction, over the years, would present the world with an insoluble problem and a source of continuing crisis have been proved right. Israel became and has remained a bone in the throat of the Arab world. On the other hand, suppose that partition had not been supported by the United States and voted by the United Nations. Would the Jews of Palestine have accepted any other solution, such as a single binational state in Palestine? Could it have worked if they did? Would not a test of strength have come anyway, with the same results as in 1948?

The fighting, not a considered international decision, finally determined how Palestine was divided. The UN truces in 1948 merely interrupted the fighting, they did not provide for a return to former positions. And the hasty attempts at revision of the partition terms through Count Bernadotte's plan assigning Galilee to Israel and the Negev to the Arabs foundered. Britain accepted the plan in principle and Secretary Marshall endorsed it as "a generally fair basis for settlement" and "the best possible basis for bringing peace to a distracted land," [17] but it found favor with neither Jews nor Arabs.

Marshall's endorsement had no echo in the White House. Truman was urged by close political advisors and by American Jewish leaders to repudiate it, but not wanting to disagree publicly with his secretary of state or to be charged with injecting partisan positions on foreign policy into the current presidential campaign, he remained silent. However, after Governor Dewey announced he was supporting the borders for Israel designated by the UN resolution on partition, the president was persuaded to issue a statement saying that he felt no changes unacceptable to Israel should be made in those borders, a position already stated in the platform of the Democratic Party.[18] On 28 October, in a fighting campaign speech in New York, Truman spoke out for an Israel "large enough, free enough and strong enough to make its people self-supporting and secure." Nothing further was heard of the Bernadotte plan. At the UN the American position was stated in the president's terms, with the addition that if there were changes in Israel's favor there should be equivalent changes in favor of the Arabs.[19] Whether the United States would ever enforce that principle against Israel was questionable, to say the least.

It is impossible to say whether the president's negative attitude toward the Bernadotte proposal was a missed opportunity for peace. It was difficult to see any disposition for compromise on the part of Israel or the Arab governments. Marshall had wanted to keep the door open, but the president was more concerned with taking a position on the merits in support of Israel.

The armistice lines, negotiated early in 1949, reflected Israel's military victories. Israel had proved itself a political reality, but so had Arab nonacceptance and sense of injustice, heightened by the humiliation of defeat, loss of territory, and the flight of hundreds of thousands of Palestine Arabs from their homes.

The conclusion of the Armistice agreements began a new period. The United States welcomed the establishment of agreed truce lines with UN supervisory institutions as a contribution to peace. But two main problems remained. The first was how to keep the peace the armistice had established. The second was how to promote an agreed peace settlement. These had been American aims before, pursued without great success. Now the scene had changed. The sovereign state of Israel was there, but the state of Arab Palestine envisaged by the UN partition resolution had not been born. Two pieces remained: the West Bank area, soon to be annexed by King Abdullah of Transjordan, and the Gaza Strip, turned over to the administration of Egypt. So the problem now went far beyond Palestine. While the fate of the Palestine Arabs remained at the heart of the matter, Israel and the neighboring Arab states were the main actors who had to be persuaded, or coerced, not to break the peace. They were the ones who alone could make a real peace based on agreement.

## Support for a Negotiated Peace

### The Conciliation Commission for Palestine, 1949

Creation of the Conciliation Commission for Palestine (CCP) by the UN General Assembly in December 1948 [20] gave the United States an unanticipated opportunity to play the peace-maker.

It was clear from the start that, although the United States had not sought membership, the American representative, Mark Ethridge, would have a more prominent and influential role than his colleagues from France and Turkey because of the power his country had in world affairs and its relations with the parties to the dispute. Ethridge did not confine himself to trying to bring the parties together. From the start he plunged right into the substance and took the CCP and the disputants along with him.

Both Arab and Israeli negotiators were willing to come to Lausanne, where the CCP set up shop in April 1949, after preliminary meetings with Arab and Israeli leaders in their own countries. When early efforts to find a starting point on the refugee question failed, the CCP took a bolder course and attacked the territorial question itself. It asked the parties to sign a protocol accepting "as a basis for discussion with the Commission" a map setting forth the boundaries of Arab and Jewish states according to the UN resolution of November 1947, with the understanding that the exchange of views "with the two parties" would "bear upon the territorial adjustments necessary to the indicated objectives." [21] To persuade both sides to sign this protocol was a major accomplishment. But after the protocol was signed on 12 May, in separate rooms and in separate copies, the two sides then began making specific proposals quite unacceptable to each other. The negotiations broke down, and the

Lausanne protocol remained as a lonely monument, the high point of agreement never reached again over the next quarter-century.[22]

Washington, however, encouraged by this limited success and not wanting to lose any momentum, decided to bring its own influence to bear on the situation more directly. The chosen point was Tel Aviv.

In a diplomatic note delivered two weeks later the United States asked Israel to reconsider its policies on boundaries, refugees, and Jerusalem, taking as its guidelines the existing UN resolutions. There was an implied threat that refusal might cause the United States to alter its attitude toward Israel. The note came as a shock both to Israel's leaders and to Ambassador McDonald, a firm friend of their cause, who had to present it.[23] Firmly believing their current policies, some of which were at odds with those resolutions, to be essential to their country's security, the Israelis rejected the American suggestions and then put out a press release criticizing foreign pressure. If the purpose was to test their American support, it was a shrewd move. Washington backed down and gave up the idea of exerting pressure on the parties or identifying itself with specific proposals.[24] Did the White House intervene to change the line? Whatever the reason, the abrupt approach had merely antagonized Israel, and the hasty retreat did no credit to the United States. The lessons which each, and the Arabs as well, could draw from the affair were scarcely conductive to the success of future American attempts to bring about a settlement. An American suggestion later in the year that Israel give up part of Galilee and the southern Negev in return for the Gaza Strip was summarily rejected by Israel.[25]

Meanwhile Mark Ethridge, a prominent publisher who had no desire to make a career in diplomacy or to prolong this particular assignment, had learned enough about the problem to make a realistic estimate of the prospects for settlement. He withdrew in mid-1949, to be replaced by Paul A. Porter.

For Israel the entire activity of the CCP, and of the United States as its leading member, had fortified the distrust felt for third-party mediation and for the United Nations. Because this was a body with a mandate tied to UN resolutions that the Israeli leaders regarded as outdated or one-sided, it was no wonder that they preferred direct negotiation with individual Arab states. The Arab states, for their part, clung to the UN involvement and especially to the General Assembly's resolution of December 1948 on refugees. Nonrecognition of Israel and insistence on the right of repatriation, with diplomatic support from outside, were the only means they had to keep open the territorial question and eventually reverse the verdict of 1948–1949. Neither the CCP nor the United States had the power to change those deeply held views on both sides.

The empty outcome of this laborious peacemaking effort provided a kind of preview of later efforts. Israel, with a strong position on the ground, did not have to concern itself much with UN resolutions. Even at this time before the Soviet Union had any position in the Arab states, Israel discovered it could easily make good its unwillingness to submit to American persuasion. Another factor was the Arab leaders' inflexibility, their inability to accept the kinds of compromise solution that the United States might have been more willing to press on Israel.

By the fall of 1949 the CCP was already being overshadowed by its own Economic Survey Mission, which sought by a regional economic approach to appease the Arab-Israel conflict and cope with the immediate demands of the refugee problem. Paul Porter, in a realistic appraisal of the lack of progress toward a political settlement, helped to direct Washington's attention toward economic action as the only alternative and one which might in due course make the political situation more tractable.

## Anglo-American Efforts at Settlement, 1953–1956

The advent of a Republican administration in Washington provided a test between innovation and continuity in foreign policy. The Middle East was one of a number of laboratories. That John Foster Dulles, a few months after taking office, took off on an extensive tour of that region was a sign that he saw it as one of the most important. This was no special mission for peace. Primarily it was a quest to see what the practical prospects were for building a regional defense system to keep the Russians out. But the Arab-Israel question had a prominent place in Dulles's calculations, for it had been a major obstacle to the efforts of America and Britain to bring Arab states into such a regional system.

The earlier efforts for an Allied Middle East Command and a Middle East Defense Organization had got nowhere with the Arabs, Egypt's opposition being crucial. The secretary wanted to get something started immediately, so he turned to that "northern tier" of states which feared the Soviet Union and had no complex about alignment with the West. Turkey, Iran, and Pakistan were prospective candidates, plus Iraq, the only Arab state so inclined; other Arab states might come in later. As to Egypt, Dulles wanted a friendly and cooperative relationship with the new revolutionary regime which could become a defense arrangement when the time was ripe, presumably after Anglo-Egyptian differences were settled. Raising the question of Israel would not be helpful to those enterprises, but Dulles knew well enough that he could not avoid it, either in his diplomatic endeavors or in explaining and defending his policy at home.

The counterpart of the northern-tier strategy was a more "impartial" American stance on the Arab-Israel conflict. Dulles's public report on his trip not only restated American willingness to help in promoting a settlement but added that "the United States should seek to allay the resentment against it that has resulted from the creation of Israel." He noted that the Arabs were "more fearful of Zionism than of communism" and were concerned "lest the United States become the backer of expansionist Zionism." To this he added, "We cannot afford to be distrusted by millions who should be the sturdy friends of freedom. . . . Israel should become a part of the Near East community and cease to look upon itself, or be looked upon by others, as alien to this community." [26]

Ultimate American aims might be the same, but this was hardly the language of Harry Truman. It was rather the voice of those in the Departments of State and Defense who had opposed the creation of Israel in the first place and now wanted to limit the damage. To Israelis, the advice to become a part of the Near East community was familiar Arab terminology for ceasing to be a Jewish state. It was no wonder that they felt a cooler wind blowing from Washington. And that feeling worsened Dulles's chances for getting Israeli cooperation in peacemaking endeavors without assuring him any greater flexibility on the Arab side.

Secretary Dulles, like his predecessor, pledged that the United States would use its influence to promote reduction of tension and the conclusion of ultimate peace. But far from registering progress toward reconciliation or settlement, the year 1953 witnessed heightened tension, a succession of border incidents, the temporary suspension of an American loan to Israel when it attempted to divert the waters of the upper Jordan River, and a stinging censure of Israel by the UN Security Council (in a resolution sponsored by the United States, among others) for its heavy raid on Qibya, a Jordanian border village.

In 1954, as border raids and retaliatory strikes continued, the United States took to lecturing the two sides, telling them to change their attitudes. Assistant Secretary of State Henry A. Byroade bluntly told the Arabs in a public speech that they were attempting to maintain a state of affairs suspended between peace and war while desiring neither, a dangerous policy which world opinion would increasingly condemn. They should accept the state of Israel as an accomplished fact and move toward a modus vivendi with it. For Israelis he had even stronger words: "I say that you should come to truly look upon yourselves as a Middle Eastern State and seek your own future in that context rather than as a headquarters, or nucleus so to speak, of worldwide groupings of peoples of a particular religious faith who must have special rights within and obligations to the Israeli state." He also told them to drop the attitude of conqueror, give up the policy of force and retaliatory killings, and make their deeds conform to their frequent utterances of the desire for peace.[27] A later speech, which Byroade pointedly chose to deliver before the anti-Zionist American Council for Judaism, called attention to Israel's policy of unlimited immigration and to Arab fears of Israeli expansion, urging that Israel find some way to lay those fears to rest.[28]

These were certainly things that needed saying if the idea was to show that the United States knew what some of the fundamental problems were. But they were hardly conducive to bringing the parties closer together through effective diplomacy, although Byroade offered to assist in arriving at any arrangement both sides would accept. His advice to the Israelis appeared to strike at their concept of statehood: that Israel was and could only be a Jewish state, and that its very character required unrestricted immigration of Jews. Israel might explain these convictions as unrelated to expansion or to war and peace, but would not change them in order to allay Arab fears or meet American criticism. This was true even though the more moderate Moshe Sharett, not Ben Gurion, was serving as prime minister at the time.

It was in 1954 that the Soviet Union began to give full diplomatic support to the Arab side in issues involving Israel which came before the United Nations.[29] So Israel, which had already found its attempt to establish a relatively neutral position unrewarding, now turned toward closer alignment with the West, although the United States was at this very time openly trying to improve its relations with the Arab states. Israel's weakened international position, however, was reflected not in conciliatory moves but in greater militancy toward the Arabs, particularly after Ben Gurion returned as minister of defense in February 1955, and in a turn to France for arms.

Later in 1954, after Anglo-American diplomacy helped Italy and Yugoslavia settle their dispute over Trieste, Secretary Dulles hit upon the idea of applying the same technique to the Arab-Israel conflict. In a series of negotiations on Trieste at London, in which diplomats from the United States and Britain conferred first with one side and then with the other, the two parties were finally brought together in an agreement both were able to accept and to defend before their own peoples. Could it work for Palestine? Aside from the obvious need for a similar procedure in which the two parties would not negotiate directly, the differences were considerable. The political atmosphere was not nearly so favorable, and the problems were much more difficult. Yet Dulles thought it worth a try.

He gave to Francis H. Russell, a diplomat with recent experience in Israel, the assignment of reviewing the situation and working with the British on proposals which could be put before the parties. Russell and a high British official, Evelyn Shuckburgh, worked out detailed tentative solutions to a number of

the problems: frontier adjustments, repatriation and resettlement of refugees, the status of Jerusalem, and draft security
treaties. This was the first real effort since 1949 to put possible
terms of settlement on paper. But no new technique of diplomacy
could bring the parties closer to agreement; they could not even
be brought to consider the idea. Israel's large-scale attack on
Gaza in February 1955, one week after Ben Gurion returned to
the government, virtually precluded the possibility that the two
powers could bring Nasser into any kind of negotiation for settlement.[30] His concentration was on getting arms so that, for
peace or for war, Egypt would not deal from weakness.

The continuing deterioration of the situation and the appearance of the Soviet Union on the scene brought the Americans and British out into the open. Drawing on the Russell-
Shuckburgh studies, Dulles delivered a speech containing the
most far-reaching proposals that Washington had made to date.
He said the United States would enter into formal treaty en-
gagements (with other states and under UN auspices if possible) to guarantee the permanent frontiers agreed upon by the
parties; it would help financially in the repatriation or resettlement of refugees if Israel itself could not take the entire burden;
and it would aid Israel and the Arab states economically through
a regional plan such as that proposed by Eric Johnston for the
sharing of Jordan waters.[31]

The day after the Dulles speech the British Foreign Office repeated a British offer of the previous April to guarantee by treaty
any territorial settlement made by the parties themselves. American and British representatives in the Arab states followed up
these initiatives, but they got no positive reactions at all.[32] It was
the same story in Israel, which had little confidence in Anglo-
American promises and preferred to rely on its own policies and
strength.

Two months later Prime Minister Anthony Eden made a major
speech,[33] in which he warned of the acute dangers of the un-
settled situation and the growing Soviet threat in the Middle
East. He walked right into the thicket of the territorial question,
as Dulles had not, to stress the need for a compromise somewhere
between the existing armistice lines and the boundaries set by
the UN resolution of November 1947. The latter had scarcely

been mentioned since the Lausanne Protocol of 1949, and this was the first time in years that a western leader had spoken of them in connection with a peace settlement. The Arab reaction took account of Eden's gesture, and Nasser credited him with "trying to be fair." But Israel, having no intention of giving up territory, protested Eden's speech even more loudly than it had that of Dulles.

Following up the initiative, British diplomats talked in Cairo and Tel Aviv about arrangements for negotiation. Egypt responded positively, stating its willingness to negotiate through an intermediary. Muhammad Hassanein Haikal, who was close to Nasser, is reported to have said privately at the time that there was "a strong possibility of settlement" in the near future.[34] However, the British ambassador to Cairo at that time reports in his memoirs that "in all the various attempts made at this time to get negotiations started, Nasser was careful not to commit himself; the others sometimes interpreted him in a sense more favorable than he intended."[35] In any case, Israel was not interested in the kind of compromise the British were talking about. Nothing else at the time improved the atmosphere for negotiation. Israel and Syria had a major armed clash in December 1955, and British attempts to bring Jordan into the Baghdad Pact had led to riots in Amman.

In a parallel American effort, early in 1956, Washington sent Robert B. Anderson, a former secretary of the navy then in private business, on a secret mission to Israel and to Cairo. He made several trips between the two countries, discussing with Ben Gurion and Nasser such matters as requirements for security, possible declaration of a ceasefire, boundaries, and freedom of choice and compensation for the Arab refugees. Ben Gurion stuck to the line that he was ready to negotiate with Egypt directly, preferably at the highest level. Nasser said he was willing to work out a framework for peace in the area but could not speak for other Arab states without consulting them, nor could he begin by direct talks with Ben Gurion, Sharett, or another Israeli. He was willing to continue communication, but only indirectly through the United States. Neither Anderson nor the US government could give either side an assurance of a real will to peace on the part of the other.[36]

An interesting and obscure aspect of the Anderson mission is the question of US pressure on Egypt. The only public indication to that effect was an unsigned "random note" from Washington in *The New York Times* stating that "the U.S. government is tying its proposals for a ten-year program to build the high Aswan Dam in Egypt to a settlement of the Egyptian-Israeli dispute." [37] If that was the purpose, the failure was complete, for the continued drift toward violence in the Arab-Israel conflict and the breakdown of the deal on the high dam unleashed the chain of events which produced the 1956 crisis.[38]

Would the United States have done better to apply pressure to Israel? There was pressure of a sort in Washington's unwillingness to meet Israel's request for arms. Ben Gurion was interested first of all in arms, at a time when Soviet arms were pouring into Egypt, and only secondarily in moves toward detente, for he put no trust at all in Nasser and did not believe in appeasement but in deterrence and reprisal.[39] America's refusal to provide arms only strengthened his resolve to get them elsewhere and did not serve as pressure to seek a settlement.

In retrospect one is struck by the persistence of American endeavors to promote peace negotiations during these years when there was so little basis for it in the attitudes and policies of Israel or the Arab states. Perhaps the signs that Eric Johnston might succeed with his Jordan waters plan generated false optimism. The fact is that Israel, with Ben Gurion in command, was not looking for compromise; he was not prepared to pay for recognition with territory or with concessions on the refugee question. The more moderate line represented by Moshe Sharett, whom Ben Gurion retained as foreign minister after replacing him in the top spot, was not a difference in fundamental positions. Israel found no strong reasons to put faith in the United States; indeed it was during the first Eisenhower administration that Israeli leaders became more convinced than ever that in making peace or in making war they had to depend on themselves alone.

On the Arab side, proclaimed US impartiality did not produce compensating gains. Relations with the Nasser regime were relatively good in 1954, when American influence was used to bring about the Anglo-Egyptian agreement on British withdrawal from the Suez military base. But the relationship came to grief in the following year on the question of military aid, for which Nasser finally turned to the Russians. At the same time Syria and Israel were engaged in many hostile encounters, culminating in the heavy Israeli raid in December 1955.[40] Israel was unanimously condemned by a Security Council resolution, but that was the extent of outside restraint. American declarations of impartiality did not impress Arab leaders when it became apparent that the United States would not fill their military needs and would make no attempt to coerce Israel on major questions or deprive it of American financial support.

It was quite plain to the US government, even before Soviet penetration of the area in 1955, that the deteriorating Middle East situation was harmful to American interests. It was all very well to talk about the need for a diplomacy of peaceful settlement, but the United States, though its naval power dominated the Mediterranean by this time, did not have the political weight and flexibility to bring it about. Once the Soviets appeared on the scene, what weight America had was drastically reduced.

In 1955 and 1956 Israel and its Arab neighbors were moving toward war. There was no golden moment for peace which outside powers failed to seize. The positive idea of settlement had to give way to the other and more negative aspect of American policy: how to prevent the use of force and keep the fragile status quo intact.

### The Sanctity of the Status Quo

One of the recurrent dilemmas of American policy over the years was when to stress peacemaking, which meant change, and when to concentrate on peacekeeping, which meant upholding the status quo. Sometimes the two were pursued simultaneously, sometimes one overshadowed the other. The general tendency in time of peace was to prevent the use of violence and the outbreak of war; unsatisfactory as the status quo might be in many respects, it was preferable to a new round of war and all its unknown consequences.

Hence the sanctity which the armistice lines of 1949 inevitably attained. They were provisional, as the agreements themselves stated, but with the failure to achieve a peace settlement they became part of the natural order of things. The continued UN supervision of the armistice agreements, imperfect as it was, tended to give additional sanction to that order of things, despite the attempts both sides made to interpret the agreements in their own way.

In the spring of 1950 the United States took an initiative toward putting a western guarantee behind the status quo. A paper drafted by an American diplomat for discussion with his British colleagues, then belatedly submitted to France as the third partner, became on 25 May 1950 a tripartite declaration.[41] It stated the intention of the three governments to reduce violence and enhance stability in the Arab-Israel area. One point had to do with maintenance of the armistice lines. The three powers placed the weight of their influence behind the territorial status quo, saying that in case any state were preparing to violate it, they would immediately take action, both within and outside the United Nations, to prevent such violation. This was close to a guarantee, although no formal obligation to any state was undertaken.

The other main point covered the level of armed forces and the supply of arms. The three powers recognized that Israel and the Arab states needed to maintain a certain level of force for internal security, legitimate self-defense, and defense of the area as a whole. Applications for arms would be "considered in the light of these principles." What levels the three powers proposed to maintain was certainly not apparent. They could not bind other suppliers, but they happened to be the principal ones and therefore could substantially control the arms traffic so long as they worked together.

For a while the tripartite declaration worked as its authors intended. Border forays and other violations of the armistice were frequent, but no state mounted a major attack against the territorial status quo. Israel occasionally crossed the armistice lines in force to strike at targets in Syria, Jordan, or Egypt, for which it was generally censured by the Security Council. But the Israeli forces always returned immediately, thus there was no occasion for the three powers to take action to prevent an alteration of the borders. As for the control of arms supplies, the three powers acted through a committee to keep matters in hand, at least for a few years.

Toward the mid-1950s the aims of the tripartite declaration became harder to attain. The Arab governments could not or would not control infiltration of armed Palestinians into Israel, and Israel's retaliatory raids grew more severe. Each side began to think seriously of larger-scale military operations: Syria, especially after an election in 1954 started a drift toward the parties of the left, took a harder line in its acts and its pronouncements; Egypt, after the 1954 agreement with Britain opened the way to the withdrawal of British troops from the Suez base, had forces free to move eastward and confront Israel; and Israel, under Ben Gurion's driving leadership, looked increasingly to offensive military action as the only reliable defense against continuing Arab hostility. Not unexpectedly, students of these developments differ on the degree of each side's responsibility. Some stress Ben Gurion's disdain for talk of compromise, his deliberate practice of massive reprisals,[42] and his conviction that a test of arms must come.[43] Others maintain that Nasser, as soon as he was in control at home and had settled with the British on Sudan and the Suez base, contemplated a war-oriented policy and sought arms to make it possible.[44]

Other and larger changes involving the outside powers combined to break down the effectiveness of the tripartite declaration. France, annoyed by American and British maneuvers leading to the Baghdad Pact and their apparent disdain for French interests in Syria and in North Africa, ceased to work closely with its western partners. The Russians began to support the Arab cause against Israel. After February 1955, a month in which the Egyptian regime was humiliated and angered by the conclusion of the Baghdad Pact and by the Israeli raid on Gaza, Nasser turned to Russia for arms, got them in large quantities, and publicly took pride at the rebuff he had administered to America.

The Soviet-Egyptian arms deal, announced in September 1955, was of transcendent importance in marking Russia's entry into the power politics of the Middle East. It put an end to American hopes that Egypt might eventually be lured into cooperation or association with the western alliance. It broke the western monopoly of arms supply and thus nullified that part of the tripartite declaration directed at arms control. Did it also nullify the western guarantee of the armistice borders? The status quo was now more precarious than ever, and no one in the West knew what hand Moscow was going to play. As Soviet arms poured into Egypt, Israel naturally pleaded for western arms to keep the balance. The United States, clinging to its desire not to become a primary supplier, would not itself meet Israel's request, but it encouraged its allies, mainly France and Canada, to do so. The French, meanwhile, had adopted a policy of heavy arms deliveries to Israel for reasons having little to do with the Soviet incursion or with stabilizing the status quo. Nasser was supporting the Algerian revolt, and the French therefore decided to support Nasser's main enemy, Israel.

It was at this juncture, early in 1956, that Anthony Eden came to Washington with the express purpose of reviving the tripartite declaration and putting teeth into it. Hoping for a clear statement that would prevent a war, he ran into American caution and hesitation that limited the agreement to the estab- lishment of a tripartite working group—the French were still going through the motions—to plan military measures in case of a crisis. The lack of action was bound to cast doubt on whether the western powers could or would do anything.[45]

The drift toward an Arab-Israel war continued through 1956 with the United States little more than a spectator, occasionally urging the parties not to resort to force and to settle their differences in a peaceful manner. When Secretary General Ham- marskjold made a hurried visit to the area in May to calm things down, the United States backed his advice with its own. Actually, Britain was more involved than America because of its treaty obligations to Jordan and its ties with Iraq. The possibility that Iraqi troops would be sent to Jordan, an act which Israel said it would not tolerate, threatened to involve the British in military action against Israel. Then with Nasser's seizure of the Suez Canal Company in July the dangers to the peace took on a new complexity and higher tension, for Britain and France were now themselves considering military action against Egypt.

The United States, agreeing with its allies on the merits of the case against Nasser but trying to restrain them from using force to uphold it, could exercise no restraining hand on anybody. It tried hard to keep the Suez Canal dispute from becoming enmeshed with the Arab-Israel conflict. France, however, was busy tying them together. All during the year it was furnishing arms to Israel on an urgent basis, and Nasser's move at the canal was a heaven-sent opportunity for collusion. The British came along reluctantly, but they came, and thus the plans were laid for a course of action in which two signatories of the tripartite declaration encouraged and collaborated in its violation by Israel.

The Israeli attack of 29 October 1956 was obviously more than a large-scale retaliatory raid, although there was no doubt that recent raids of Arab *fedayeen* had caused fear and rage in Israel. It was an attempt to break the back of Egypt's army, to seize territory either for bargaining purposes or permanently, and to dictate conditions of coexistence more tolerable to Israel. The United States did not hesitate in condemning the attack as aggression or in going before the UN Security Council to call for Israel's immediate withdrawal, a proposal which Britain and France promptly vetoed. By the time Secretary Dulles came before the General Assembly, "with a heavy heart," his allies had joined the attack on Egypt. The combined opposition of the United States and the Soviet Union, however, spelled doom for the Anglo-French enterprise, and also for that of Israel. Although Moscow made some blood-curdling threats, it was the cold and remorseless role of the United States and a run on the pound presaging economic disaster that were decisive in causing Anthony Eden to give up,[46] and when he did so, the French could not carry on by themselves. Israel was left alone.

The American decision to take the pure and holy line against aggression and for the principles of the UN Charter was in large part the result of its concern for a viable world order for which the United Nations stood despite its weaknesses. But American motivation was not all purity and holiness. Eisenhower and Dulles were smarting from the deception they felt their European allies had practiced on them. They did not want America to be associated with what seemed like the worst form of colonialism. They did not want to alienate the Arab countries beyond recall, leaving the Middle East and perhaps the whole third world open to the blandishments of the Soviet Union. This was a clearly seen

American interest against which close ties with historic allies and with Israel were not allowed to prevail.

The United States, with majority support in the United Nations, insisted that Israel's forces go back, out of Sinai, out of the Gaza Strip, all the way to the armistice lines from which their offensive had begun. Lester Pearson and Dag Hammarskjold, to their great credit, worked out with remarkable speed the formation of the international force which followed the Israeli forces as they moved back. But the power behind them was the United States. Ben Gurion said that the armistice no longer existed and must be replaced by a negotiated peace. He argued strongly with Eisenhower that Israel should at least stay in Gaza and at Sharm el-Sheikh, but in the end he gave in. Given Israel's position in the world and its dependence on American economic aid, he knew how important it was to maintain cooperation with Washington. The president did not threaten sanctions (which he could hardly have put through Congress anyway), but he spoke publicly of "pressure" which ". . . the United Nations has no choice but to exert," and sanctions were about to be proposed by others at the UN. It was enough that the firmness of his friendly persuasion conveyed an implacable will that the territorial *status quo ante* be restored.[47] In return, Israel got very little. It had greater security against attack or blockade thanks to the presence of UN instead of Egyptian forces on the border and at Sharm el-Sheikh. It had a document committing the United States to support the right of free passage through the Straits of Tiran. And Ben Gurion had a letter from President Eisenhower saying that Israel would have "no cause to regret" its compliance.[48]

America's policy in the crisis of 1956, in contrast to 1948–49 and 1967, was notable for putting first and foremost a return to previously existing borders. It was not a decision universally applauded in America. Some maintained that the United States should have stood by its European friends when their vital interests were challenged or at least left them alone to dispose of Nasser and Soviet influence in Egypt; others, that Israel's military action was not an isolated and unprovoked aggression but the culmination of a series of actions and reactions for which both sides bore responsibility. Even without passing such judgments, one could argue that the armistice obviously had broken down and events had created the opportunity to grasp the real nettles of the Arab-Israel problem and establish a more secure peace.

It was an attractive idea. Dulles himself had stressed the importance of making progress toward permanent settlements, and the United States had put before the United Nations the idea of special committees to work on the basic problems of the Suez Canal and Palestine.[49] But this initiative was never followed up or linked to the process of Israeli withdrawal. Under the rigid legal approach the United States had taken, it was not possible to use, or appear to use, bargaining power created by military action to compel Egypt to accept solutions that it had previously found unacceptable. Conceivably the presence of UNEF could have induced Egypt to be more amenable to negotiations and new solutions, but that did not prove to be the case. Secretary Dulles, meanwhile, lost any interest he may have had in a basic approach to the issues of the Arab-Israel conflict and turned his attention to filling the Middle East "vacuum" by means of the new "Eisenhower doctrine."

It was ironic that the United States, in the aftermath of the Suez crisis, lost influence with the Arabs as well as with Israel. The credit gained in the Arab world by its stand against aggression and retention of conquered territory was largely dissipated within a year by its own political decisions and diplomacy. The Nasser regime and indeed the Egyptian people were alienated by the continued freezing of Egyptian funds and the denial of aid in food. The attempt to build up King Saud as a rival to Nasser did not succeed, and the new Eisenhower doctrine, which in effect told Arab states to stand up and be counted on the American or Communist side, completed the demolition of US prestige in Egypt and impaired it elsewhere.

## The Economic Approach

The belief that economic means hold the key to political problems has infused American foreign policy since the time of the Marshall Plan. On a global scale the foreign aid program rested on the general proposition that economic progress in the receiving states would give them a greater stake in the future, enhance stability, and reduce the twin threats of war and Communism. In the Middle East when problems resisted political and diplomatic solutions, it stood to reason—American reason—that if Arabs and Israelis could see the prospect of a brighter economic future, they might concentrate less on fighting each other.

Such an approach had too much to overcome, both in the conditions of the conflict and the mentality of the contestants. The original UN partition plan of 1947 had optimistically envisioned close economic ties between the two states to be created in Palestine, but that idea could not be put to the test because the prospective Arab state never came into being. Israel, after the armistice agreements in 1949, would have welcomed economic cooperation with its Arab neighbors, but that would have presupposed something like normal relations. The Arab governments, though they had to accept Israel's existence de facto and deal with it through the Mixed Armistice Commissions, otherwise shunned Israel like the plague. Their choice was for economic warfare, not cooperation, not only to weaken the enemy but also to protect themselves; normal contact struck them as a formula for their own subordination to Israel's more advanced society.

The United States thus found little opportunity to use economic largesse as an inducement to peace, but it did see an immediate need to provide for the Palestinian Arab refugees, the chief losers of the war in Palestine. The UN Economic Survey Mission, which assessed the problem in 1949, was created in response to a primarily American initiative and was headed by an American, Gordon Clapp. Its work and its recommendations resulted in the establishment of UNRWA, the organization which fed, housed, and educated the refugees from that time onward. Its work went on year after year, as no agreement could be reached on repatriating the refugees in Israel or resettling them elsewhere. Their numbers grew, and so did the costs. More than two-thirds of UNRWA's funds were provided by the United States.[50]

The history of the refugee question was punctuated by periodic American efforts to attack it anew. The continuing waste of human lives and the unending annual appropriations were reasons enough for trying to do something. In addition, there was always the hope that somehow a breakthrough on refugees could lead to a wider political settlement. In 1951 the United States persuaded the CCP to propose that Israel take back specified numbers of refugees in categories which could be integrated into its economy and pay a lump sum to the others, who would be resettled in the Arab world. Both sides rejected it.[51]

A decade later, the CCP appointed Joseph E. Johnson as a special representative to explore what might be done. Again this was an international enterprise, but the initiative came from the US government, and the mission was widely regarded as an American show. Johnson recommended a solution of which the centerpiece was the right of individual refugees to express their choice for repatriation or resettlement; Israel would take back the former (with some exceptions) and would contribute to compensating the latter. The approach gained a persisting place in American thinking, but Washington refrained from a positive endorsement of Johnson's plan, which had only partial acceptance among the Arabs and none on the part of Israel.[52]

American support of UNRWA can be explained on numerous grounds. It was eminently humanitarian. It reflected, perhaps, a feeling of guilt that Palestine Arabs were refugees partly because the United States had done so much to make Palestine a haven for Jewish refugees. There was also the obvious explanation that if the United States did not help to support UNRWA, neither would others, and such stability as existed in the area would vanish. This policy even survived the Six-Day War, which transformed the refugee problem but did not end it, and the events that saw many of the refugee camps become strongholds of Palestinian guerrilla movements.

Hope remained alive in Washington that the refugee problem could somehow be solved either by itself or as part of a broader settlement. In either case a central idea would be to open up economic opportunities for the refugees in Arab countries or elsewhere, the assumption being that only a small fraction of them would want to live in Israel. Meanwhile, the US aid program to Jordan, beside its main purpose of strengthening and stabilizing Hussein's regime, had an additional aim of absorbing more and more the refugees into the economy there. In the years following the Six-Day War, official Washington had surprisingly little to propose along these lines, but private American organizations did undertake research on economic development in the Middle East,[53] keeping an eye on opportunities for the resettlement of refugees. Israel proposed an international conference to consider the problem and also took its own measures to deal with the refugees (and with UNRWA) in the newly occupied territories. The United States, however, was looking toward an Israeli-Egyptian settlement, and there the refugee question, like the broader question of the political future of the Palestine Arabs, was a complicating and incendiary factor best left aside.

To go backward in time again, it is worth looking at some specific economic proposals of the 1950s, for it was in the Eisenhower administration that the idea of regional economic development as a foundation for peace began. In 1953 President Eisenhower named Eric Johnston as his special representative to work out with the states in the Jordan basin a plan for sharing the water resources to promote over-all development without involving direct cooperation of Arab states with Israel. Johnston's first visit came at a time of high tension: Israel had begun a diversion of Jordan water in the demilitarized zone north of Lake Tiberias —earning thereby a cease-and-desist order from the UN Truce Supervisor and a temporary cutoff of US aid until it did so—and border raids had come to a climax in the massive Israeli attack on the village of Qibya. He achieved a limited success, however, in getting Syria, Lebanon, Jordan, and Israel to consider his plan, which was based on engineering surveys done for UNRWA by the Tennessee Valley Authority and would be expected to have outside financing.

Johnston's proposals stimulated counterplans from Israel and the Arab League, and the following year he got all the governments to cooperate in arriving at an agreement on the basis of his own plan. In 1955 he succeeded in bridging a number of technical gaps, but technical agreement did not mean political agreement. Israel was not really happy with the plan, regarding the proposed "neutral" (probably UN) supervision as an impairment of its sovereignty, but it saw the benefits of even indirect cooperation. On the Arab side, although Egypt was relatively favorable, Syria denounced the plan at a meeting of the Political

Committee of the Arab League. No other Arab state would then defend it. The reluctance to avoid anything that looked like formal acceptance of Israel's existence, even at the cost of their own economic interests, was decisive in killing the Johnston plan and with it American hopes for a bright new beginning.[54]

Thereafter each country went its separate way. Israel built its own national water conduit from Lake Tiberias to the south, which the Arab states, particularly Syria, threatened to prevent by force, but failed to do. In the mid-1960s the Arab League decided to divert the upper Jordan tributaries in order to deprive Israel of water, but Israeli armed intervention put the construction works out of commission, to the point of permanently discouraging the constructors. In 1967 Israel "solved" the Jordan waters question to its satisfaction when, with the occupation of the Golan Heights, most of the Jordan's headwaters were securely in its own control.

At times the economic approach cast its net more widely. The political crisis of 1958, which comprised a civil war in Lebanon, the dispatch of a UN mission there, a violent revolution in Iraq, and the landing of American and British forces in Lebanon and Jordan respectively, gave birth to a final effort by the Eisenhower administration to turn the energies of the Middle East toward regional economic development. Addressing the UN General Assembly, Eisenhower proposed a program of six points as "integral elements of a single concerted effort for peace." Five points had to do with security measures and the control of inflammatory propaganda, but the sixth was a pledge of US support to a soundly based regional development institution for the Arab states to accelerate progress in industry, agriculture, water supply, health, and education. Israel had not been involved in the crisis of 1958 and went unmentioned in the president's proposal.[55]

The rest of the story is anticlimax. The Arab governments were concentrating on getting western troops out of Lebanon and Jordan, so the vista opened up by the president did not stir their imagination. They had discussed similar plans in the Arab League and these they preferred to anything proposed from outside, despite the League's dismal record of accomplishment.

A central element in Eisenhower's thinking about the Middle

East was the development of water resources by new scientific methods, especially nuclear technology, an idea strongly advocated by Lewis Strauss, Chairman of the Atomic Energy Commission. Neither of them forgot it after leaving office.

Shortly after the Six-Day War, Eisenhower personally recommended to President Johnson a memorandum of Strauss's which argued that two elements underlay the whole trouble in the Middle East: water and the displaced Palestinian population. The heart of his plan was construction of three large nuclear plants for desalting and for producing power, two on the Mediterranean coast and one at the northern end of the Gulf of Aqaba. One plant alone could produce as much fresh water as the entire Jordan River system. This was a way, Strauss argued, out of "the morass in which the powers are floundering." Unlike earlier plans, this one could be started in individual countries without the requirement of Arab-Israeli agreement. The completed project could irrigate barren areas from Egypt to northern Jordan, opening to settlement enough area to sustain all the Palestinian refugees.[56]

Using the same arguments, Senator Howard Baker of Tennessee proposed a resolution which the Senate adopted in December 1967 by an overwhelming vote.[57] Its preamble stated flatly that "the greatest bar to a long-term settlement of the differences between the Arab and Israeli people is the chronic shortage of fresh water, useful work, and an adequate food supply," and its operative recommendation urged the executive branch to take the necessary action for the construction of nuclear desalting plants. The reasoning was naive, to put it mildly, but because the Senate had spoken, the agencies of the executive branch had to take the recommendation seriously. They did a lot of studying of the possibilities, as did the World Bank, but without generating much enthusiasm. One factor was financing. The foreign aid program was already committed elsewhere, and the administration was not of a mind to make a special request to Congress for funds to finance nuclear desalting plants, even for Israel, which had asked for help on a project of its own. There were many unanswered questions about economic feasibility and on the political side the State Department had found nothing in the atmosphere of the Arab world that was receptive to another grandiose American scheme. In the end, nothing much came of the Strauss plan or the Baker Resolution, although American help to individual Middle Eastern states in modest desalting enterprises continued without fanfare, and detailed public and private studies continued with the cooperation of the Atomic Energy Commission. For once the US government was going slowly, very slowly, on regional economic projects bearing road signs to Arab-Israeli peace, especially those which had as a magic corollary the final solution to the Arab refugee problem.

## Preventive Diplomacy: The Wooing of Nasser

In January 1961 John F. Kennedy came into office with a promise of dynamic action on behalf of peace and freedom in the world. What would that promise mean for America's role in the Middle East? In essence, it meant a not very spectacular attempt to prevent Soviet gains and to retrieve lost influence in the Arab world, without changing the basis of the American relationship with Israel. Because the Democratic party was by tradition and inclination more favorably disposed than the Republican to Israel, it seemed desirable to make a special effort to show concern and understanding for Arab views. As Nasser was the most influential spokesman for those views, it was symbolic of a new approach that President Kennedy's ambassador to the UAR was John Badeau, a former president of the American University in Cairo and of the Near East Foundation.

Actually, the new approach was not so new. During its last two years the Eisenhower administration had tried, largely through quiet diplomacy in Cairo, to work its way back to a more normal relationship. In the troubles which arose at that time between the UAR and Iraq, and between the Arab governments and Moscow, the United States wisely remained a spectator and let the other parties learn some lessons for themselves.

The Kennedy administration's policy was founded on a number of propositions: that Nasser and the radical Arab nationalism which he represented were a growing force and that it was a mistake to try to combat it or assume it was controlled by or sold to Moscow; that polarization of alignments in the Middle East, leaving the United States tied only to the conservative regimes in the Arab world, and to Israel, would advance Soviet rather than American interests; that Nasser might be persuaded to concentrate more on his domestic problems, and for that task American help would be available. Washington had no idea of persuading him to settle the conflict with Israel, but it hoped that a cooperative relationship might help restrain both sides.

In May 1961 Kennedy sent personal letters to Nasser and other heads of Arab states, assuring them of the friendship of the United States and its desire to help the Arab peoples in their struggle for self-realization. He said that the US government would use its influence toward a just and honorable solution to the Arab-Israeli dispute, and gave particular emphasis to American support of past UN resolutions on the Palestine refugees, thus leaning to the Arab side on that key problem.[58] The Arab replies were not uniform—and Nasser's might even have cut off the dialogue then and there with its long denunciation of Israel and its challenge to Kennedy to prove that US policy was not inspired by internal political considerations. Nevertheless, the exchange continued and had some effect on the attitudes of both sides. Badeau describes the Kennedy letters as clear and frank, never condescending or peremptory.[59] But if relations were bouyed somewhat by the greater civility in official communication, they remained subject to the strain of divergent interests and policies, especially as Arab-Israeli tension continued unabated.

Kennedy made his major statement on the Arab-Israel conflict at a press conference in May 1963. It was a unilateral replay of the tripartite declaration, which had not survived the war of 1956. Avoiding a specific pledge to Israel, such as Ben Gurion had wanted, he reaffirmed the basic US opposition to the threat or use of force anywhere in the Near East: "In the event of aggression, or preparation for aggression, whether direct or indirect, we would support appropriate measures in the United Nations and adopt other courses of action on our own to prevent or to put a stop to such aggression. . . ."[60] The statement, broad enough to cover an aggression by one Arab state against another, seemed like a declaration of Pax Americana. In the following January, Deputy Under Secretary U. Alexis Johnson reaffirmed it, saying that "any intended victim of any would-be aggression can count on our support." [61]

The Arab states were not, in fact, counting on US support against Israel as a result of these statements. They paid more attention to the American decision in 1962 to provide Hawk missiles to Israel.[62] The Arab summit conference in January 1964, called for the very purpose of doing something about Israel, decided to take counteraction to Israel's diversion of Jordan River waters and to support a "Palestine entity," one step short of a government-in-exile. But Nasser made it clear to the more hotheaded Arab leaders that the time had not come for war. Bogged down in the Yemen, his army was in no shape to take on Israel. And he was not ready to break with America, which was providing much needed food aid and loans amounting to over $1 billion by mid-1956.[63] For Egypt this was the golden age of nonalignment, with the Soviets supplying quantities of arms and the Americans providing quantities of food.

In the end, however, the US-Egyptian rapprochement fell victim to events. The war in Yemen, Nasser's threat to Saudi Arabia, the stepped-up arms race, and friction over various crises in Africa all contributed to the breakdown. It was the affairs of the Congo, hardly a vital Egyptian interest, that provoked Nasser's advice to Americans to drink up the Red Sea. Inevitably the US Congress, never enthusiastic about the "appeasement" of Nasser, began to show its reluctance to continue aid to a leader whose verbal attacks on America made him seem an ingrate for past largesse. After a Cairo mob burned the USIA offices in November 1964, the Johnson administration had little chance to carry on the aid program at the existing levels and did not really try.

By the middle of 1965 the policy of courting Nasser had obviously failed. From then on the United States was not taking the lead but following events in the Middle East, as the conflict of Israel and the Arab states moved to a higher stage of violence. The Pax Americana was reduced to urging both sides to show restraint. By 1967 the United States did not have enough influence with either to halt the drift toward war.

### War as a Breakthrough to Settlement?

The end of the Six-Day War brought to Washington a feeling of great relief. The fumbling in dealing with the crisis as it arose, the inability to make good on commitments to Israel, the failure of American restraint to keep Israel from going to war, the danger that Russia and America might be drawn in—all this had disappeared in the thunderstorm of Israel's rapid and decisive military victory. Perhaps the storm had cleared the air for a real peace.

Who would take the initiative? It is a matter for speculation whether a generous peace offer by Israel when the Arab governments were under the immediate shock of defeat could have opened the way. Probably not. In any case the Israelis sat down on their new ceasefire lines and offered negotiations from that position of strength. The Arab governments were intent, first of all, on securing their authority at home and then on getting new arms and other support from outside. The Russians almost immediately decided to rearm Egypt massively and to call a special session of the UN General Assembly to give the Arabs political support. By the time of the Arab summit conference at Khartoum in late summer 1967, there was enough restored confidence for unanimous adoption of the three noes: no recognition of Israel, no negotiation with Israel, no peace with Israel—although Egypt and Jordan were given approval to seek a political settlement of the war.

The United States did not even consider repeating the course taken in 1956, for a number of good reasons. The war had been no clear case of aggression by Israel. By demanding recall of the UN Emergency Force, declaring a blockade of the Straits of Tiran, and moving his army into Sinai, Nasser had made "the war nobody wanted" almost inevitable. As Secretary of State Dean Rusk saw it, he had deliberately put his hand in a rattlesnake's nest. Israel had moved to avert what it took to be a mortal peril and was determined that such a situation should never arise again. Hence its absolute refusal to go back to a system (the old armistice lines, the UN peacekeeping forces, and the flimsy outside guarantees) which had produced war instead of peace. Hence also the American acceptance of that viewpoint, at least to the extent that demanding Israeli withdrawal to the old lines was the wrong way to begin. The American failure, in the weeks of crisis preceding the war, to make good on its commitment to freedom of navigation through the Tiran Straits was another factor inhibiting a tough and "principled" stand on Israeli withdrawal.

Washington favored beginning with a set of principles on which an agreed settlement could rest. President Johnson proposed five points on 19 June,[64] all but one of which later found their way into the UN Security Council resolution which provided the basis for the entire UN peace effort. They were: the recognized right of national life; political independence and territorial integrity for all; justice for the Palestinian refugees; the right of innocent maritime passage; limits on the wasteful and destructive arms race in the area, a proposal which had never evoked Soviet interest. He ruled out Israeli withdrawal as "a single, simple solution"; troops must be withdrawn but only in the context of the five points. Of course the points were general, but the idea was to get negotiations started, not to determine their outcome.

First the UN special session had to be got through without spoiling the chances for further negotiation. The United States managed to beat back Soviet and other proposals to force Israel's unconditional withdrawal to the old armistice lines. But the Soviet performance was not entirely negative or inimical in the impression it made on American representatives. There was a brief moment when a Soviet-American compromise appeared out of the blue and failed only because it was too strong medicine for the more belligerent Arabs. The issue then went to the Security Council, which on 22 November finally reached unanimous agreement on Resolution 242, a carefully worded British draft which took refuge in ambiguity at some points as the only way to make agreement possible. In addition to the principles set forth, the resolution called for one specific action: the naming of a UN representative to help the parties come to a settlement.

Everything was in place: the general principles were accepted by the world organization and a respected and skillful Swedish diplomat, Gunnar Jarring, was ready to act as middleman. The

US government regarded the state of affairs as the best that could be expected in the circumstances and stepped into the background so that Jarring could make his run. He was neutral, not tainted in the eyes of either party as the great powers were. All he had to do was perform the kind of miracle that Ralph Bunche had wrought in 1949. He could presumably draw upon the lessons of that successful experience (Bunche was still at the UN) and also of the unsuccessful CCP experience. But the intervening years, it seemed, had only made the problems more difficult.

The idea that the Six-Day War could lead to a breakthrough to peace was an attractive one to the United States. Defeat had brought Arab leaders and peoples closer to facing reality. Despite the incantations of Khartoum, the more responsible Arabs knew they could not ignore Israel. Israel controlled all of Palestine, plus Egyptian and Syrian territory beyond the borders of Palestine. Unlike 1956, there was no effective international pressure to get the Israeli forces out. If they really wanted them out, the Arab governments might be persuaded to make a formal contractual peace, one that would provide security for them as well as for Israel. Perhaps they would begin to pay more heed to political realities. This was a vain hope, however. Israel's military superiority was not the only political reality affecting the chances for peace, and in some ways the magnitude of the Arab's defeat made it more difficult for them to contemplate a settlement. The idea that somehow a new atmosphere could break Arab-Israeli relations out of the old mold may have had some justification immediately after the war. But it could never have survived the hardening of positions in debate and on the ground or the laborious process of putting together Resolution 242, with its set of far from clear rules for solving the problems resulting from twenty years of struggle. By the time Jarring began his quest in November 1967, with very little weight to back up his powers of persuasion, both sides had settled into an uncompromising mood.

Israel's government was intent on keeping the new strategic borders until it got, signed and sealed, the kind of peace it wanted. Where the "secure and recognized boundaries" which were to be a part of that peace settlement would be located was not to be revealed until the Arab states sat down to negotiate seriously and directly. There was no doubt that Israel intended to keep some of the occupied territory, and that fact alone made it difficult for any Arab leader to talk about negotiation and peace. Meanwhile, the Arab governments, Egypt in particular, were finding that they could live with the *status quo,* for a while anyway, as they tried to build up their military strength and mobilize diplomatic support. Jordan had little flexibility. King Hussein might be ready for peace with Israel, but he could not move ahead of Nasser. At the other end of the spectrum, the fiery intransigence of Syria, in its refusal to accept UN Resolution 242, was a sign to Nasser that he had better not sacrifice the Palestine Arabs or the general Arab cause for a deal that might benefit Egypt alone.

American diplomacy had not remained entirely inactive. Closely following Jarring's efforts, it had on occasion urged both sides to be more flexible and forthcoming in dealing with him. It had tried, in continuing military aid to Jordan, to keep in being a government favorable to settlement and to discourage a turn to Russia. Influential officials in the State Department tended to blame Nasser for blocking productive negotiations.[65] On the other hand, the United States had dallied during 1967 and most of 1968 in meeting Israel's request for Phantom planes to show Jerusalem and Cairo and Moscow that the primary American objective was a negotiated settlement and not an arms race. On the whole, however, the American role was relatively passive, and deliberately so. The desire to have Jarring try it on his own, the absence of a crisis compelling action, and absorption in the Vietnam war combined to explain it.

By the autumn of 1968 Jarring's mission, after nearly a year of effort, was getting nowhere. The question arose whether anything could be gained by an American initiative. Or had Jarring's experience shown that nothing could be accomplished by anybody? The Soviet government was talking about the need of great-power agreement on the terms of an Arab-Israel settlement. Secretary Rusk decided that a discreet push of both Egypt and Israel might at least give the Jarring Mission a new lease on life. He met the two foreign ministers, Mahmud Riad and Abba Eban, for separate private and informal talks in November 1968, when the General Assembly was in session in New York.

Rusk's proposals have not been published, but apparently he listed a number of points that the United States regarded as a fair basis for settlement. The main point he wished to clarify with Riad was that the United States was prepared to back a full withdrawal of Israeli forces from Sinai and restoration of Egyptian sovereignty over it, in exchange for a signed peace agreement embodying the obligations of each side to the other. Other points included stationing of UN forces at Sharm el-Sheikh on a permanent basis, not subject to recall on demand by Egypt; acceptance by Egypt of freedom of navigation through the Suez Canal and the Straits of Tiran for ships of all nations including Israel; and movement toward resolution of the refugee problem by allowing the refugees themselves to state their preferences on repatriation or resettlement. The peace agreement might be buttressed by an agreement by the United States and the USSR to limit their shipments of arms to Israel and the Arab states.[66]

Egypt's reaction was no real acceptance, but it was not entirely negative. It stated that upon the withdrawal of Israeli forces from all Arab territories taken in 1967, including Arab Jerusalem (and presumably the Gaza Strip as well), Egypt would end its state of belligerency with Israel. That was encouraging, although it also meant that Egypt would not separate itself from the other Arab states in a settlement with Israel. As before, Egypt wanted the refugee question settled in accordance with past UN resolutions, but no longer linked it directly with the Suez Canal question. Freedom of navigation for Israel through the canal and through the Straits of Tiran would be acceptable in the context of a total settlement. The Egyptian note said nothing about demilitarization or a UN force. On the question of an agreement signed by both parties, it said that Egypt would give the Security Council a statement of the obligations it would fulfill and that Israel should do the same.[67]

Israel's response to Rusk indicated no basic change in the "nine precepts of peace" which Abba Eban had presented to the General Assembly on 8 October: a durable peace, duly negotiated and contractually expressed; secure and recognized boundaries agreed through negotiation; security arrangements; open frontiers; precise and concrete guarantees of freedom of navigation; an international conference on the refugee problem; Jerusalem to remain in Israel, but with a special status for the holy places; recognition of sovereignty, integrity, and right to national life; and regional cooperation.

The parties were still far apart, despite the signs of flexibility. The United States could not really find enough in their responses to help carry the conversations to a higher stage. The basic difference, full withdrawal versus negotiation of new boundaries, remained; and Rusk was not ready to try pushing the parties toward a point of compromise which apparently did not exist. Yet it was a significant initiative. It showed that the United States had not washed its hands of the affair and left everything to Jarring. It was willing to state some specific points of its own on the terms of a settlement. In doing so the expiring Johnson administration laid the groundwork for further efforts.

## Search for Settlement through the Powers

As the Nixon administration took office, it undertook a review of all major aspects of foreign policy and in the Middle East tried to put efforts for peace in the context of global policy. As before, the United States genuinely wanted an Arab-Israel settlement for the sake of bringing peace to those peoples. It wanted a settlement even more, however, because of the Soviet-American relationship in the Middle East and elsewhere. Two major concerns—they could even be called vital interests—were at stake: the need to prevent a military confrontation and clash between the two powers and the need to prevent a growth of Soviet power and influence in the Middle East that would seriously shift the global balance.

So long as the climate of East-West detente was absent in the Middle East the rivalry of the two superpowers continued to fuel the Arab-Israel conflict and was in turn intensified by it. Neither power was willing to stop the flow of arms, lest its own clients be put at an intolerable disadvantage. And as long as the local conflict continued, the Soviets were almost certain to consolidate and expand their positions in the Arab world, pushing the United States toward reliance on Israel alone.

The United States had several possible ways of meeting this

dangerous and deteriorating situation. It could try global bargaining with Moscow, linking the Near East to other areas of
conflict; it could seek a strengthening of the western military
presence in the Mediterranean; it could pour more arms into
Israel. But one logical answer was still an Arab-Israel settlement.
If a settlement could be reached without directly involving the
Russians, well and good. But Jarring's mission was becalmed and
Rusk's initiative had failed. There remained the possibility that
the two big powers could work together. After all, Moscow had
supported UN Resolution 242 and still professed its desire for a
political settlement.

In September 1968 the Soviet Union had sent a note to Washington with some general suggestions on terms of settlement and
a request for American views. In December came another note,
to which Washington replied with some rather comprehensive
proposals. After stressing the need to deal with Arab terrorism,
then in a virulent phase, the American proposal went on to
recommend a package deal based on Resolution 242, including
withdrawal of Israeli forces from occupied Arab territories to
secure and recognized frontiers "which should not reflect the
weight of conquest." The package deal would have to be agreed
between the parties in its entirety before any part of it would be
put into effect.[68] By this time the Nixon administration had come
in, claiming that an era of negotiation was at hand. Here was a
place to start, and a new, activist Assistant Secretary of State for
Near Eastern Affairs, Joseph J. Sisco, started.

The year 1969 witnessed a serious attempt—serious on the
American side at any rate—to establish Soviet-American agreement. The idea was that if those two powers could agree on the
basic terms of a settlement, Britain and France would join in
recommending those terms to the Security Council, which in
turn could invite Jarring to put them before the parties.

Israel did not like this prospect one bit, fearing an imposed
solution. The Israeli government considered the Soviet Union as
its enemy, France as sold to the Arabs, Britain as dubious, and
the United States as an uncertain friend. In any four-power conference, the line-up would be two and a half or three to one; in a
two-power negotiation it would be an uneven contest between
Soviet firmness and American flexibility. Israel anticipated that

an agreement emerging from any of these outside efforts would be reached at Israel's expense.

Regardless of Israel's objections, the United States thought the time ripe to undertake direct talks with the Russians. The four-power talks at the United Nations, begun at the original suggestions of France and U Thant and carried on under the aegis of the Security Council, were distinctly secondary in American eyes, although they were useful in keeping the British and French involved in the responsibility for peace. French participation was based on de Gaulle's conviction that France must assert its independent position in the world generally and in the Mediterranean and Middle East in particular. Both Moscow and Washington were willing to indulge France, and perhaps to gain something besides, by engaging in four-power discussions. But the real possibilities for opening the way to a settlement lay in the bilateral Soviet-American talks.

By general agreement of the two powers the talks focused on the issues between Israel and Egypt, leaving aside for the time being the Israel-Jordan relationship, the position of Syria, and the problem of the Palestine Arabs. The Soviet government could not undertake to speak for Jordan's interests; presumably the US government would have to talk to itself on that phase of the settlement. Anyway, the major danger was war between Israel and Egypt, and the main settlement, if there was to be one, would be between those two countries.

The story of the Soviet-American talks has not been officially told. What is publicly known comes from a few remarks dropped by officials into their speeches or statements to the press and from the reports of enterprising newspaper correspondents who did their best to find out what was going on. The stated purpose was to explore and widen the area of Soviet-American agreement on the outlines of an Israel-Egyptian settlement in line with UN Resolution 242. The agenda included withdrawal of forces, permanent frontiers, the end of belligerency, the rights of states to exist, freedom of navigation, peacekeeping arrangements, international guarantees, and such matters of procedure as the nature of negotiation and the documents constituting the settlement.

The salient fact about these talks is that they were conducted directly and informally, with no propaganda or statements for the public record, and with an apparently serious intent on both sides to reach an agreement if possible. The procedure was a succession of working sessions between Assistant Secretary Sisco and Anatoli Dobrynin, Soviet ambassador in Washington, with occasional recourse to the Rogers-Gromyko level. The American side kept in close touch with Jerusalem, the Soviet side with Cairo. Perhaps this constant reference to friends and allies inhibited greater progress, but it also provided some guidance on whether what came out of the talks would stand a chance of acceptance by Israel and Egypt. Besides, neither Moscow nor Washington wished to leave its protégé in the dark, imagining that its doom was being sealed in a secret bargain between its fair-weather friends and its declared enemies.

The question of the final frontier did not cause great controversy between the American and Soviet negotiators. The status of the Gaza Strip was left in the air. As to Sinai, the United States had never felt that Israel had a case for annexation of any part of it; thus the obvious border was the old line between Egypt and Palestine. The only points that had to be made on the territorial issue were that withdrawal of Israeli forces must be part of the settlement, not a condition precedent to it, and that the total package should contain measures of demilitarization and international guarantees providing security to both sides. The Soviets did not quarrel with these general propositions, although some differences existed and agreed positions on them were never nailed down. The character of the document or documents which would embody the settlement was not an easy subject because of the Soviet Union's concern for Arab sensitivity. The phrase "peace treaty" was too blunt to be considered. The Americans held to the concept of a contractual agreement which would bind each party in specific obligations to the other, and this the Soviets seemed to accept. The related question of how to arrive at the point of having a contractual agreement on the table to be signed was also troublesome, but here again the Soviet negotiators appeared to find the "Rhodes formula" acceptable.

There was no attempt to work out precise wording on such matters as freedom of navigation, refugees, or international peacekeeping arrangements, as both Americans and Russians were talking only about the outlines of a settlement, something more specific than UN Resolution 242 but not the text of an agreement; that would have been too much to expect the parties to swallow.

In the end, it turned out that the Soviets themselves had not swallowed as much as the Americans thought they had. The argument that agreement on any part was subject to final agreement on the whole could hardly be refuted. Nevertheless, the Americans definitely felt that the Soviets, at a given point, began to enlarge the area of disagreement by throwing back into it items already agreed. Whether a new turn in Soviet-Egyptian relations was responsible for what happened is not clear. But one could not easily avoid the conclusion that Moscow was not going to stray very far, if any distance at all, beyond the limits of concession set by Nasser.

The four-power talks going on simultaneously in New York had not accomplished much and obviously would not unless real progress was made by the two big powers. France kept trying to bridge the differences, but even the task of putting down on paper the agreed and unagreed points proved onerous and eventually fruitless. The lesson of these talks was that no four-power authority could be effective in the absence of concord between the United States and the Soviet Union. Those two had first to establish the necessary minimum of reconciliation of their own interests and to make corresponding readjustments in their respective relations with Israel and the Arab states before any outside persuasion by two or by four could bring results.

The failure of the 1969 talks meant that these conditions did not yet exist. It left the United States in an uncomfortable position. Israel felt relieved that the United States had not given anything away, but the Arabs tended to be confirmed in their conclusion that the Americans had merely pushed Israel's interests and had been repulsed by the Soviets. The time was ripe for the US government to make a public statement of where it stood on the more important terms of settlement. Secretary Rogers did so in a speech on 9 December 1969, implying that these were the positions taken by the United States in the negotiations with the Soviets.[69]

The most important item had to do with the permanent boundaries. The United States made known for the first time its view that the best new border to separate Israel and Egypt was the old border, the one that had run between Egypt and the British mandate of Palestine. As for Israel's other boundaries, the United States favored the 1949 armistice lines, with the proviso that changes in them should not reflect the weight of conquest and should be confined to insubstantial alterations required for mutual security. Presumably this statement applied to Israel's border with Syria as well as with Jordan, although the refusal of the Syrian government to accept UN Resolution 242 left that question in limbo. Between Israel and Lebanon there was no dispute: the old international border, the armistice line of 1949, and the existing de facto border were all the same.

Other points in the Rogers speech mentioned the Arab refugees, with only vague language on what to do about them, and the status of Jerusalem, without saying where sovereignty over it should lie. In any case it should be a unified city, with open access to it by persons of all faiths and with roles for both Israel and Jordan in its civic, economic, and religious life. On sovereignty, peacekeeping arrangements, and future security, the secretary did little more than cite Resolution 242 and state that these matters would have to be worked out in specific detail by the parties with the help of Ambassador Jarring. The main theme was that "our policy is and will continue to be a *balanced* one." There should be no withdrawal without agreement on peace, and no peace not including withdrawal.

This was not a speech which could please Israel, but it contained significant points calculated to impress the Arabs, whether they admitted it or not. The first public responses of their governments were negative, the standard reflex reaction to any American statement of policy. But there were items in the speech for them to ponder, especially on boundaries and on refugees, and the hope in Washington was that these points would finally sink in. The real import of the speech was that it established a position from which the United States could by itself exert greater influence on both parties. Within months it proved its value in a critical situation requiring an ability to get cooperation from both sides. The proposed terms, moreover, stood as a reasonable basis for settlement: at least the United States was betting that this was how the world community, and eventually the parties themselves, would see it.

## Coping with the Conflict on the Ground

By design or coincidence, as the big-power negotiations on terms of comprehensive settlement sank into the doldrums, the need to do something to control the situation on the ground increased. The year 1969 had seen Nasser's proclaimed war of attrition turn more and more against him as Israel's air force pounded his troops on the Suez front and ranged far and wide to flaunt their capacity to wreak destruction in the middle Nile valley and the environs of Cairo itself. By 1970 Nasser, his regime and his country in danger, pleaded for Soviet help and got it in the form of more surface-to-air missiles, with Soviet crews to shoot them, and more fighter aircraft, with Soviet pilots to fly them.

The balance on the Suez front took on a whole new dimension. Israel had to decide whether to risk a clash with the Russians, and the United States had to decide how to meet this obvious raising of the stakes, which seemed to give dramatic confirmation to Israel's thesis that its own armed forces were significant not only in the local balance with the Arabs but also in the larger balance of the two superpowers. The Nixon administration sought ways to deal with the situation. It could try to force Moscow to pull the Soviet military out of Egypt; it could increase its own strength in the area; it could step up arms deliveries to Israel; or it could take a diplomatic initiative. Various officials talked rather boldly and seriously about the first three possibilities, but the main effort went into diplomacy.

The so-called Rogers Plan, which emerged in June 1970, was a proposal of strictly American origin aimed at doing three things: getting a ceasefire between Egypt and Israel in order to end a dangerous state of open warfare; forestalling development of a situation in which Soviet and possibly American forces were likely to be engaged in that warfare; and reviving the moribund peace mission of Gunnar Jarring. Fortunately, the situation was such that both Egypt and Israel were impressed with the desirability of calling a halt. The Israeli government accepted in the knowledge that the right-wing parties (Gahal) would leave the coalition government in protest. Nasser accepted knowing that the militant Palestinian organizations would denounce him for it. Moscow, brought in on the plan, had no objection. And so a ninety-day ceasefire went into effect on 7 August 1970.

The dispute that broke out almost immediately over Egyptian and Soviet movement of missiles in the canal zone nearly killed the whole arrangement. Washington filled the air with charges of Soviet bad faith, but not being able to enforce compliance with the agreement (which did not commit the Soviets in writing), it ultimately compensated Israel by extending half a billion dollars in new credits, largely for Phantom aircraft. Although Israel would not resume talks with Jarring, the ceasefire held and in November was prolonged for another ninety days.

In December Israel was prepared once again to take up the talks with Jarring, but when his mission finally got into action the negotiation was a short one. It consisted of two similar notes sent by him to Egypt and to Israel on 8 February 1971, asking them to pledge their acceptance of a number of points as a necessary preliminary to negotiations, and their replies delivered later in the same month.[70] The key points were a pledge by Egypt to sign a "peace agreement" with Israel embodying the final settlement, and agreement by Israel that the settlement would include Israeli withdrawal to the old Egypt-Palestine line, which would be the final frontier. On the first point the Egyptians said yes. On the second the Israelis said no, and they gave their answer special emphasis by adding gratuitously and bluntly, ignoring American advice, that Israel would not return to the armistice lines that existed before the Six-Day War. The Jarring Mission was stuck again.

In a sense Egypt had scored a diplomatic success. Anwar Sadat had done what Nasser had never done: whatever his unrevealed intentions may have been, he had met Israel's most substantial argument by declaring his willingness to sign a contractual agreement with Israel on terms of peace. Henceforth the would-be peacemakers, including the United States, could be expected to put less heat on Egypt and more on Israel, and on the one point which was most important to the Arabs and generally deemed reasonable by the rest of the world, Israel's withdrawal to the old frontier. It was a good diplomatic position. Its weakness was that a favorable world opinion, a new UN resolution, or a pat on the back from the United States would not end the Israeli occupation of Sinai.

From the Rogers speech of December 1969 through the ceasefire proposals of June 1970 and thereafter, the United States had been moving to the forefront of the efforts to avert war and move toward peace. As the ceasefire held, extended by agreement for a final thirty days to March 1971 and continuing thereafter as a de facto truce observed by both sides, American diplomacy had the field largely to itself. Jarring was out of the picture; the Soviet Union kept its own counsel; Britain and France remained passive; and the European Economic Community was taking only the first steps toward developing a common policy in the Mediterranean and Middle East. The United States, in contrast, was trying simultaneously to revive the Jarring Mission and to promote a partial interim settlement on the Suez Canal front.

For some time the idea of such a partial settlement including a reopening of the canal and a withdrawal of Israeli forces some distance from its east bank had had fleeting attention in Washington,[71] but the aim of getting a comprehensive package took precedence. In the fall of 1970 it had been raised as a trial balloon by Moshe Dayan, and early in the following year favorable comments began to come from Cairo. In another departure from Nasser's line, Sadat took up the idea and made it his own.[72] American diplomacy went on from there. Secretary Rogers made an unprecedented visit to Cairo in May—unprecedented because there were no normal diplomatic relations between the two countries.

These negotiations, which continued through the remainder of 1971, were a prime example of the hazards of seeking settlements in the Middle East. Here was a seemingly reasonable proposition of benefit to both sides, but it was not a simple matter such as accepting a temporary truce or exchanging prisoners. On each of the terms that had to be worked out a gap existed between Israeli and Egyptian positions, and even if some gaps could be bridged, both sides would have to be convinced

in the end that the total package offered greater advantage than
no agreement at all. How far were Israeli troops to be pulled
back? Was the fixing of a new line to stand on its own or be but
a stage to an agreed total withdrawal? Were Egyptian forces to
cross the canal into the territory evacuated by Israeli troops and
if so, in what permissible strength? What new arrangements for
security and for policing the agreement were required? What
was the relationship, if any, between the interim agreement and
a final settlement?

Into every one of these issues crept the larger ones which had
made a comprehensive settlement impossible: withdrawal, boundaries, security requirements, guarantees, modes of negotiation.
Only the United States kept the idea of agreement alive by refusing to accept defeat. Whether American diplomats gave Sadat
to understand that they could persuade Israel to accept something close to the positions he took on their urging is a debatable
question.[73] Whether they misunderstood or misread the tough-
ness of the Israeli positions is another. In any event the gaps
were not closed, and by the end of summer 1971 the American
hand was played out.[74] Rogers's speech at the United Nations in
October, listing six points on which he saw agreement as attainable,[75] was an exercise in optimism which had no echoes and
raised no hopes in Jerusalem or Cairo. The American effort went
on but registered no progress by the end of the year.

Once again an attempt from outside had failed for lack of effective bargaining power sufficient to bring the parties together
even on a limited arrangement. At least two essentials were
missing: Soviet cooperation, which could have increased the
pressure on Egypt, and American influence exerted to modify
Israeli policy. The Soviets, at this point unsure of their relations
with Egypt, especially after Sadat removed the Moscow-oriented
Ali Sabri and others from the government, were more interested
in preserving and strengthening the bilateral Soviet-Egyptian ties
(as they did through the treaty signed in May 1971) than in convincing Sadat he should make more concessions to get an Amer-
ican-sponsored agreement with Israel. As for American influence
on Israel, Washington would have had to face, as the price of
exerting real pressure by economic measures or by cutting down
on the supply of arms, a row which would disrupt hitherto har-

monious relations with Israel and stir up trouble at home; moreover, there was an American as well as an Israeli interest in keeping up the flow of arms to counterbalance Soviet arms going to Arab states. The State Department might have been willing to think seriously about paying such a price, but the White House and the Pentagon were not. Besides, Israel was not in a mood to compromise and would probably have defied any measures of pressure the United States could bring itself to take. The question for Washington would be: what then?

Sadat's proclaimed "year of decision," 1971, came to an end without war and without any progress toward peace. The following year, 1972, was one of political and diplomatic maneuver, as Egypt tried to strengthen its international position by recourse to the United Nations and Israel continued to cultivate the United States. American peace efforts followed well established lines, with periodic proposals for "proximity talks," in which Egyptian and Israeli delegations might inhabit the same hotel somewhere, with Assistant Secretary Sisco shuttling between them. In default of new attitudes on both sides the chances of progress were minimal. Israel, as always, was ready to negotiate "without conditions" and was otherwise content to stay with things as they were. Sadat could not talk about an interim settlement without tying it to the ultimate demand for full Israeli withdrawal. He also felt that he had been deceived by the Americans in the 1971 negotiations and was saying so loudly in public.

Because Sadat did not act during his "year of decision," it was natural for outsiders to believe he would not act at all; it was also easy to underestimate the depth of his and his country's frustration. Unexpectedly, at least for the Americans, it was the Soviet Union that found itself the target of that frustration. A number of minor irritations and some real conflicts of interest, primarily the Soviet Union's unwillingness to provide Egypt with the offensive weapons Sadat wanted and its apparent collusion with the United States to keep the Middle East *in statu quo,* led to Sadat's sudden demand in July 1972 for the recall of the thousands of Soviet military "advisers," including combat pilots and missile crews, then stationed in Egypt. From the standpoint of American diplomacy the crucial question was whether Sadat's coldness toward Moscow offered an opportunity for a new initiative. Cut off from his supplies of Soviet weapons, for how long he did not know, Sadat was looking elsewhere for arms and greater political support. In Cairo, officials and the press spoke of Egypt's return to real nonalignment, meaning that it would seek a western weight in the scales to balance the Soviet connection. Saudi Arabia, it was evident, had encouraged the Egyptians to get rid of the Soviet military presence on the assumption that the United States would then be ready to reduce its support of Israel.

Some American officials thought the time ripe to approach both Egypt and Israel again. The United States was in no position to try to replace the USSR as arms supplier to Egypt, but it might encourage European states to do so and find other ways to regain lost credit in Cairo. The key to accomplishing anything in this direction, of course, was the ability to produce movement on the Israeli side. But 1972 was a presidential election year. Neither in the White House nor in Jerusalem was there a disposition to rock the boat. The upsurge of Palestinian terrorism and counterviolence by Israel, leading to debates and votes in the United Nations in which the United States found itself alone in standing with Israel, diminished still further the scope for American diplomacy. President Nixon, whose policies in the Middle East had been generally applauded by the American Jewish community, was not going to ruffle the smooth state of US-Israeli relations before the November election. Nor, it turned out, was there to be any appreciable change in American policy after the president was overwhelmingly reelected. But there was an awareness of the dangers of the situation and a declared intention to do something about it.

With the settlement of the Vietnam war in January 1973 and the consolidation of relations with China and Russia following the president's spectacular visits to Peking and Moscow, word went out that the administration would now turn its attention to the Middle East. But how? In the disposition of Israel and the Arab states toward serious negotiation there was no change.

In the absence of a climate for such negotiations the United States turned to the more practical problem of containment of the conflict on the ground. As American officials were fond of saying, peace may not have broken out, but war had not broken out either. The ceasefire had held for more than two years. The United States, in its growing detente with the Soviet Union, stressed the interest the two powers had in seeing that the ceasefire continued to hold, and indeed the Soviets did not disagree. They did not relish facing again the dilemma of 1967, seeing their Arab allies go down to defeat or intervening to help them at great risk of war with the United States. The Soviet government did, however, accompany its support of the ceasefire with constant reiteration of the theme that there could be no respite from the peril of war until Israel withdrew from all the occupied Arab territories.

The course of 1973 until October illustrated the limited chance outside powers have to control a dynamic local situation or even to judge it correctly. New elements began to appear on the Arab side—changed political alignments, the assumption by King Faisal of Saudi Arabia of a more prominent role in Arab councils and his decision to use "oil power" for political ends, and the eventual determination by Egypt and Syria that a military gamble was preferable to going on with the status quo. The United States was not successful in keeping the peace. It did not even suspect that war was coming. The Soviet leaders knew it (although just when they learned has not been revealed), did not like it, but decided against trying to stop it.

Yet what the small powers started on their own, they could not finish without the intervention of the big powers, and the overall result—both of the war itself and of the way in which it was handled by the big powers, especially the United States— was to enhance greatly the role which Henry Kissinger could and did play. When, after the war, he brought the parties together on truce lines and disengagement of forces, he opened up for the first time a serious negotiation for peace.

## Conclusions

A number of subtitles might be appropriate for this chronicle: the limitations of power; the futility of diplomacy; or perhaps the myth of the impartial peacemaker. Has it been a self-perpetuating folly of American political leaders and diplomats, this continuing endeavor to help bring peace to the Middle East? Looking at the mournful record as a whole, one might be impelled to say, "Yes, the conflict goes too deep for settlement by the parties, and the advice and help of an outside power will not make any difference." Looking at that same record at each phase along the way, from the contemporary view of responsible individuals in the White House and the State Department, the answer has to be different. As long as there was a possible opportunity to reduce the prospects for a local or wider war, the world and especially the great powers had an interest in exploring that opportunity to the utmost. By holding to the validity of that proposition, even at times when it seemed hopeless, the United States could move forward when conditions became more favorable.

The obstacles were formidable from the start. Even in the time when the United States had no active competitor in the area, in the first few years after the armistice agreements of 1949, the limitations on its ability to bring about a settlement were amply demonstrated. In those years the Soviet Union, having joined the United States in supporting Israel's independence, had not yet turned to the Arab side; Britain was trying to develop a partnership with the United States and joined in proposals for an Arab-Israel settlement; France was relatively passive, not yet striking out on a policy of its own. But the parties were not ready to negotiate. From 1955 onward, Soviet-American rivalry was actively projected into the local conflict, with the result that America's influence with both sides was reduced. Peacemaking moves had to be carefully considered in the light of their effect on the global balance; to put it more bluntly, cold-war factors pushed American policy sometimes in one direction, sometimes in the other and largely determined what was done, or not done, in the pursuit of peace between the Arab states and Israel.

Perhaps a greater obstacle to effective diplomacy was the qualitative difference in America's relations and commitments to the two sides. Despite the absence of a treaty obligation, the Executive and the Congress have felt a moral commitment to the survival of Israel. For various reasons—historical, emotional, political—a special relationship exists. No matter how many US official statements pointedly proclaim support of the independence of *all* the states in the area, no Arab government has felt itself on an equal basis with Israel in the enjoyment of American favor and protection.[76] Over the years there have been precious few occasions when the Arab side felt sufficient confidence in American objectivity to give the United States a chance to work constructively for a peace of reconciliation.

These two factors, the cold war and the intimate relationship with Israel, contributed to a third: the direct involvement of the United States in the local arms race as Israel's only outside supplier of advanced aircraft and other weapons. Assurances that the United States would not permit the arms balance to be tipped against Israel, which in fact meant maintaining Israel's superiority over its Arab neighbors, virtually committed Washington to match every major delivery of Soviet equipment to the Arabs. And each new commitment of American arms to Israel made it all the more difficult to play the mediator's role. In the absence of Soviet restraint in arming Egypt, it became all the more difficult for the United States to overcome Israeli arguments that the vital interests of both countries against combined Arab-Soviet encroachment required that Israel have secure geographical positions and the necessary arms to defend them. All the more difficult, as well, to convince Arab leaders that the United States would ever make Israel modify its policies.

The war of October 1973, by the very fact that it happened, exposed the futility of years of effort to bring peace to the area. At the same time it exploded the theory that there was some kind of stability and permanence in the status quo, buttressed as it appeared to be by Israel's recognized military superiority and the unwillingness of outside powers to back military action by either side. Appearances were deceptive. Egypt and Syria dared to choose war, with all its risks, because they decided that the alternative was worse. Although they did not win the war, they did not lose it either, and they came out of it with better political and diplomatic prospects than when they went in.

The United States, unlike the situation in 1967, had something to say about the course of the war, through its airlift of arms to Israel, and about how it ended, through its agreement with Moscow on a ceasefire and its support of the resulting resolutions of 22 and 24 October in the United Nations. In the period immediately after hostilities the United States, again in contrast to 1967, was able to maintain an appreciable influence with both Israel and Egypt. The events of the war, moreover, had broken old modes of thought and brought both countries to think seriously about negotiation on front-line disengagement and on a peace settlement. In these new conditions Secretary of State Henry Kissinger was able to bring the parties together on arrangements for new truce lines, disengagement of forces, and UN-patrolled buffer zones, and for moving on from there into negotiations for peace.

That Kissinger was able to achieve that much was due in no small measure to his own talents in negotiation and in retaining the confidence of both parties. It was due also to the new element of realism in the outlook of Arab and Israeli leaders and to Moscow's relatively benevolent noninterference. But this was not the whole story. The factor of continuity in American policy was not negligible. Kissinger followed a line which Marshall and Acheson, Dulles and Rusk and Rogers had followed before him, with the benefit of experience and staff from those earlier years. In moving on toward political settlements, moreover, he would be subject to the many obstacles which handicapped and frustrated his predecessors. Somehow the parties to the conflict would have to want peace enough to give the middleman, through his position of influence and confidence with both sides, room to find points of agreement. The Soviet Union would have to substantiate in fact its professed desire to see settlements reached between Israel and its Arab neighbors. And the United States might have to associate the Soviets, in one way or another, with its own efforts for peace.

Experience holds many lessons, most of them negative. Some past failures stem from the nature of the conflict and the manner of trying to resolve it. The Western powers recognized that the gulf between Arabs and Israelis was wide, perhaps unbridgeable. But they, and especially the United States, persisted in trying to bridge it by ways in which controversies are settled in western democratic societies. They have assumed that differences are subject to compromise, that the parties can be brought by bargaining and diplomacy from their extreme positions to a point of agreement somewhere in the middle. Hence the search for formulas, for words that both sides can be induced to accept. But when the "extreme positions" are seen as absolutes, as principles which cannot be given up, the words of compromise have no meaning.

The illusion is maintained because so many times the happy combination of words seemed to be within reach. The real gap has been the one between the words on paper, as those of UN Resolution 242, and the thoughts and emotions of the leaders on both sides, the psychological drives within their societies which sharply limit their choices. Time and again American diplomats have warned that a particular time was the best possible opportunity or the last clear chance for a negotiated peace. One wonders. The profound mutual distrust was never dissipated. If by some miracle agreement had been reached on terms of peace, even a formal treaty, could it have lasted? Could the Arab states really accept Israel as a sovereign state with which they could have normal relations? Could Israel ever give up its reliance on military superiority to maintain its independence in a hostile environment? We do not know the answers to those questions. The fourth round of war in 1973 may have shattered some illusions and brought a new realism. But it may have created some new illusions too.

Finally, there is a great void in all the attempts to reach a settlement: the real interests of the Palestine Arab community. For twenty years following the armistice agreements of 1949 the problem was approached as one between Israel and the neighboring Arab states. They were to be the parties to any peace agreement. The Palestine Arabs had no territory, no government, no leaders who could take responsibility for negotiations. When they were given an institutional base, the Palestine Liberation Organization created by the Arab League in 1964, the purpose was not peace with Israel but war. Not even the Arab governments, much less the United States or Israel, could talk of peace or compromise with the PLO leader, Ahmed Shukairy.

The problem of the Arab refugees was on everyone's agenda. But talk of repatriation and compensation or reiteration of UN resolutions in that vein, commendable as the humanitarian motive might be, could not melt the coldly political positions taken by Israel and the Arab governments. The essence of the problem was that nobody tackled the question of the future of these people, not as individual refugees to be given a home or a job but as Palestine Arabs with rights and interests as a community.[77] After the Six-Day War, which greatly increased the number of refugees and brought a million Palestine Arabs under direct Israeli control, the approach in President Johnson's peace proposals and in UN Resolution 242 was still "justice for refugees."

The exploits of the *fedayeen* in 1969 and 1970, above all the extraordinary publicity which accompanied them, made it seem as if Yasir Arafat, more than Nasser or Hussein, was the man to reckon with in dealing with the Arab-Israel conflict. The United States took cognizance of the Palestine Arab community when Assistant Secretary Sisco stated in June 1970 that they had become "a formidable political force in the area." [78] But when the *fedayeen* failed totally in Israel and were smashed in Jordan by Hussein's army in 1970 and 1971, all concerned were relieved, although some of the Arab governments said the opposite.

Yet if the *fedayeen* were a nuisance, disrupting the effort for settlement by negotiations among governments, the Palestine Arab community was not to be so easily dismissed. The heart of the Arab-Israel problem is not the frontier with Egypt or with Syria but how the Israelis and the Palestine Arabs on both sides of the River Jordan are to find a relationship which gives to both the right to live in freedom. They are going to have to work it out for themselves. Outside powers, including the United States, will not be able to do much about it. They had better be aware, however, that "the question of Palestine," the term under which the Arab-Israel conflict first came before the United Nations in 1947, will remain, even though other aspects of the conflict may somehow be settled.

All in all, history counsels modesty to American governments in their quest for peace in the Middle East. There are many other governments with a finger in the pie, each defining peace in terms of its own national interests—and in this the United States is no exception. In a situation of danger to the world we may expect American diplomacy to try to reduce the danger, as it has in the past. That task is necessary for its own sake, whether the goal of an Arab-Israeli settlement appears to be within reach, or whether it remains visible only on an ever-receding horizon.

## Notes

1. William Alfred Eddy, *F.D.R. Meets Ibn Saud* (New York: American Friends of the Middle East, 1954), pp. 35–36; *Foreign Relations of the United States, 1945,* Vol. 8, pp. 2–3.

2. *Foreign Relations of the United States, 1945,* Vol. 8, pp. 690–691; Harry S. Truman, *Memoirs* (New York: Doubleday, 1956), vol. 2, p. 133; Evan M. Wilson, "The Palestine Papers, 1943–1947," *Journal of Palestine Studies* (Summer 1973): 37–44.

3. *Foreign Relations of the United States, 1947,* Vol. 5, p. 1020.

4. Jacob Coleman Hurewitz, *The Struggle for Palestine* (New York: W.W. Norton, 1950), pp. 244–259; Christopher Sykes, *Cross Roads to Israel* (London: Collins, 1967), pp. 337–371.

5. U.S. Congress, 80th Congress. 1st session. Senate. Committee on Foreign Relations. *Assistance to Greece and Turkey* (Hearings on S. 938) (Washington, D.C.: GPO, 1947), pp. 9–10; 24; 39.

6. Truman, *Memoirs,* p. 155.

7. This story of the politics of pressure is told by an American who was critical of the resolution (Kermit Roosevelt, "The Partition of Palestine: A Lesson in Pressure Politics," *Middle East Journal* [January 1948]: 14–15), and by another who supported it (Sumner Welles, *We Need Not Fail* [Boston: Houghton Mifflin, 1948], p. 63).

8. According to his daughter, he wrote on his calendar, "The State Dept. pulled the rug from under me today. I didn't expect that would happen. . . . I approved the speech and statement of policy by Senator Austin to the U.N. meeting. This morning I find that the State Dept. has reversed my Palestine policy. The first I know about it is what I see in the papers. Isn't that hell?" Margaret Truman, *Harry S. Truman* (New York: William Morrow, 1973), p. 388.

9. See White House statement of 26 March 1948 (*The New York Times,* 27 March 1948, and Truman, *Memoirs,* Vol. 2, pp. 161–164).

10. James Vincent Forrestal, *The Forrestal Diaries,* ed. by Walter Millis (New York: The Viking Press, 1951), pp. 323–24; 357–59; 365.

11. Hurewitz, *The Struggle for Palestine,* p. 265.

12. *Public Papers of the Presidents of the United States: Harry S. Truman, 1946* (Washington: GPO, 1962), p. 444.

13. Forrestal, *The Forrestal Diaries,* p. 309.

14. Dean Acheson, *Present at the Creation: My Years in the State Department* (New York: W. W. Norton, 1969), pp. 169–182.

15. Truman, *Memoirs,* Vol. 2, p. 158; Margaret Truman, *Harry S. Truman,* pp. 299–300, 386–391.

16. Sumner Welles, *We Need Not Fail,* pp. 79–80.

17. Hurewitz, *The Struggle for Palestine,* pp. 322–323.

18. Statement of 24 October 1948, *Public Papers of the Presidents of the United States: Harry S. Truman, 1948* (Washington: GPO, 1964), p. 844; Truman, *Memoirs,* Vol. 2, pp. 166–169. For background, see John Snetsinger, *Truman, the Jewish Vote, and the Creation of Israel* (Stanford: Hoover Institution Press, 1974), pp. 124–132.

19. John Coert Campbell, *The United States in World Affairs, 1948–1949* (New York: Harper, 1949), p. 396.

20. The story of the CCP is told by Fred Khouri on pp. 31–50 of this volume. This account is concerned only with the US role.

21. UN Document A/927, 21 June 1949, Annex B.

22. For further information on the American part in the work of the CCP, see David P. Forsythe, *United Nations Peacemaking: The Conciliation Commission for Palestine* (Baltimore: Johns Hopkins University Press, 1972).

23. James Grover McDonald, *My Mission in Israel, 1948–1951* (New York: Simon and Shuster, 1951), pp. 181–183.

24. Forsythe, *United Nations Peacemaking,* p. 53.

25. Don Peretz, *Israel and the Palestine Arabs* (Washington: Middle East Institute, 1958), pp. 64–65.

26. U.S. Department of State, *Department of State Bulletin,* 15 June 1953, pp. 831–5.

27. *Ibid.,* 26 April 1954, pp. 628–633.

28. *Ibid.,* 10 May 1954, pp. 708–711.

29. Avigdor Dagan, *Moscow and Jerusalem: Twenty Years of Relations between Israel and the Soviet Union* (London-New York-Toronto: Abelard-Schuman, 1970), pp. 80–91.

30. See John Coert Campbell, *Defense of the Middle East: Problems of American Policy,* 2nd edition (New York: Harper, 1960), pp. 87–88; Kennett Love, *Suez, The Twice-Fought War* (New York: McGraw-Hill, 1969), pp. 303ff.

31. U.S. Department of State, *Department of State Bulletin,* 5 September 1955, pp. 378–380.

32. Humphrey Trevelyan, *The Middle East in Revolution* (London: Macmillan, 1970), p. 41.

33. *The Times,* 10 November 1955.

34. Love, *Suez,* pp. 306–307; see also Wilton Wynn, *Nasser of Egypt* (Cambridge: Arlington Books, Inc., 1959), pp. 129–131.

35. Trevelyan, *The Middle East in Revolution,* pp. 42–43.

36. An extensive summary of Anderson's conversations with Ben Gurion is given in the latter's *My Talks with Arab Leaders* (New York: The Third Press, 1973), pp. 274–325, presumably taken from his papers.

37. *The New York Times,* 12 December 1955. Anthony Nutting's *Nasser* (New York: E.P. Dutton, 1972), pp. 127–128, refers to Dulles's hope that US aid for the dam would act as a sweetener for an Arab-Israeli settlement.

38. Kennett Love, who made as thorough an investigation as he could, is "persuaded by the evidence" that peace and the dam were tied together in Washington and that Nasser was so informed. He cites a "party to the

secret" as saying that Under Secretary of State Herbert Hoover, Jr., one of the main sponsors of the original western offer of support for the high dam, "wanted out of Aswan the moment he couldn't buy Egyptian-Israeli peace with it." (See Love, *Suez*, pp. 303–310.)

39. See Michael Brecher, *The Foreign Policy System of Israel* (New Haven: Yale University Press, 1972), pp. 282–285.

40. Edson Louis Millard Burns, *Between Arab and Israeli* (London: George G. Harrap, 1962), pp. 107–120.

41. Text in U.S. Department of State, *Department of State Bulletin,* 5 June 1950, p. 886.

42. Burns, *Between Arab and Israeli,* pp. 62–64, 82.

43. For example, Love, *Suez,* pp. 52–53, 102–105.

44. For example, Nadav Safran, *From War to War: The Arab-Israeli Confrontation, 1948–1967* (New York: Pegasus, 1969), pp. 48ff.

45. Anthony Eden, *Full Circle* (Boston: Houghton Mifflin, 1960), p. 372; Safran, *From War to War,* pp. 50–51.

46. Eden, *Full Circle,* pp. 620–624; Love, *Suez,* pp. 622–626.

47. Love, *Suez,* pp. 662–667. See also Brecher, *The Foreign Policy System of Israel,* pp. 135–136.

48. For the set of understandings and commitments given by the United States, see aide-memoire handed to Ambassador Eban by Secretary Dulles on 11 February 1957 (in *Department of State Bulletin,* 11 March 1957, pp. 392–393). Clarified by agreed statement between the two on 24 February 1957 (*ibid.,* 11 March 1957, p. 394); statement by Ambassador Lodge to the UN General Assembly, 1 March 1957, and Eisenhower letter to Ben Gurion (*ibid.,* 18 March 1957, pp. 431–434.)

49. UN General Assembly, First Emergency Special Session, Documents A/3272, 3273, 3 November 1956.

50. UNRWA's total contributions from governments from 1950 through 1969 were $667 million, of which the United States contributed $456 million. See Edward H. Buehrig, *The U.N. and the Palestinian Refugees* (Bloomington: Indiana University Press, 1971), pp. 167–168.

51. Rony E. Gabbay, *A Political Study of the Arab-Jewish Conflict: The Arab Refugee Problem (A Case Study)* (Geneva: Librairie E. Droz, 1959), pp. 333–337.

52. Dr. Johnson gave a summary account of his mission in a speech before the 24th American Assembly, 24 October 1963 (Text in *Middle East Journal* [Winter 1964]: 1–13). His complete official report to the CCP was not published.

53. Notably a study sponsored by The RAND Corporation and Resources for the Future, Inc., and directed by Sidney S. Alexander, resulting in volumes on agricultural potential, economic development and population growth, water supply, oil, and political dynamics, published by American Elsevier, New York, 1970–72.

54. See Georgiana G. Stevens, *Jordan River Partition* (Stanford: Hoover Institution, 1965); Kathryn B. Doherty, "Jordan Waters Conflict," *International Conciliation,* No. 553, May 1965.

55. UN General Assembly, *Official Records,* 3rd Emergency Special Session, A/PV 733, 13 August 1958, pp. 7–10.

56. U.S. Congress, 90th Congress. 1st Session. Senate Committee on Foreign Relations. *Hearings before the Committee on Foreign Relations on S. Res. 155* (Washington, D.C.: GPO, 1967), pp. 60–61.

57. S. Res. 155, adopted 12 December 1967.

58. Text of the letter to King Hussein of Jordan, *The New York Times,* 27 June 1961. *Al-Ahram* (Cairo), 21 June 1962, published the text of Kennedy's letter to Nasser and the latter's reply (see *Middle East Record 1961,* Jerusalem: Israel Program for Scientific Translations, n.d., pp. 197–200).

59. John Stothoff Badeau, *The American Approach to the Arab World* (New York: Harper & Row, 1968), p. 136.

60. Richard Poate Stebbins (ed.), *Documents on American Foreign Relations, 1963* (New York: Harper & Row, 1964), p. 268.

61. U.S. Department of State, *Department of State Bulletin,* 10 February 1964, pp. 208–211.

62. Jacob Coleman Hurewitz, *Middle East Politics: The Military Dimension* (New York: Praeger, 1969), pp. 478–479.

63. From mid-1961 through mid-1965, grants from the United States totalled $102 million; deliveries under the Food for Freedom program, $525 million; and loans, $519 million. See: Agency for International Development, *U.S. Overseas Loans and Grants and Assistance from International Organizations: Obligations and Loan Authorizations July 1, 1945–June 30, 1968,* Special Report prepared for the House Foreign Affairs Committee, p. 59.

64. U.S. Department of State, Department of State Bulletin, 10 July 1967, pp. 31–34.

65. Eugene V. Rostow, "The Middle East Crisis in the Perspective of World Politics," *International Affairs* (April 1971): 283–284.

66. Peter Grose in *The New York Times,* 5 December 1968.

67. Reports from Arab press sources, reported in U.S. House of Representatives, Committee on Foreign Affairs, "Background Information Prepared for the Subcommittee on the Near East," 10 January 1969 (Washington: G.P.O., 1969), pp. 19–20. See also *The New York Times,* 10 December 1968.

68. *Al-Ahram* of Cairo published on 19 January 1969 the purported text of the American note, commenting editorially that it was a literal representation of the Israeli view and extremely hostile to the Arabs. US officials later confirmed the accuracy of the *Al-Ahram* version. See *The New York Times,* 20, 21 January 1969.

69. U.S. Department of State, *Department of State Bulletin,* 5 January 1970, pp. 7–11.

70. The Jarring memorandum, the Egyptian reply of 15 February, and the Israeli reply of 26 February are all published in *The New Middle East* (April 1971): 44–45. See Fred Khouri's account (pp. 70–79) for a discussion of Jarring's proposals.

71. John Coert Campbell, "The Middle East," in Kermit Gordon (ed.), *Agenda for the Nation* (Washington: The Brookings Institution, 1968), pp. 467–471.

72. He first stated it publicly in an interview with Arnaud de Borchgrave in *Newsweek,* 22 February 1971.

73. Sadat himself said that they did (interview in *Newsweek,* 13 December 1971).

74. John Coert Campbell, "Is America's Lone Hand Played Out?", *New Middle East* (September 1971): 11–15.

75. Address to the General Assembly, 4 October 1971.

76. It apparently did not strike members of Congress as out of proportion when in 1970 they authorized a program of additional military aid which provided, inter alia, $500 million for Israel and $5 million for Lebanon (U.S. Congress. 91st Congress, 2nd Session. Senate. Supplemental Foreign Assistance Authorization, Senate Report, No. 91–1437, 14 December 1970; Public Law 91–652, 5 January 1971).

77. See Don Peretz, "The Arab Refugees: A Changing Problem," *Foreign Affairs* 41, 3 (April 1963): 558–570.

78. U.S. Department of State, *Department of State Bulletin,* 10 August 1970, p. 176.

# Peace in the Middle East

E. L. M. Burns

THIS concluding chapter will not attempt to review the several proposals for making peace, and the attitudes towards them, which have been already set out. Rather than try to judge whether Arabs, Israelis, and outside parties were just or unjust in the past, it seems more useful to examine present possibilities for a settlement, beginning with the passing of Security Council Resolution 242 of 22 November 1967 and following with the negotiations based on it, particularly those conducted by Ambassador Jarring and those under the authority of Secretary of State Rogers.

Lieutenant-General E. L. M. Burns (Canadian Army, retired) was born in 1897 and attended the Royal Military College in Kingston from 1914 to 1915 when he received a special wartime commission. After combat service in both world wars, he was Deputy Minister of Veterans' Affairs from 1950 to 1954. In August 1954 he became Chief of Staff of the United Nations Truce Supervision Organization in Palestine. From November 1956 to the end of 1959 he commanded the United Nations Emergency Force which helped secure the withdrawal of the invading British, French, and Israeli forces from Egypt and subsequently was stationed along the Armistice Demarcation Line between Egypt and Israel.

From 1960 to 1968 General Burns served as Adviser on Disarmament to the Government of Canada, and led the Canadian delegations to the Ten-Nation and Eighteen-Nation Conferences on Disarmament. Since 1971 he has been Visiting Professor of Strategic Studies at Carleton University, Ottawa.

General Burns is the author of the following books, all published in Toronto by Clarke, Irwin:

*Manpower in the Canadian Army, 1939–1945* (1956);

*Between Arab and Israeli* (1962; also published in New York by Obolensky);

*Megamurder* (1966; New York, Pantheon, 1967);

*General Mud; Memoirs of Two World Wars* (1970);

*A Seat at the Table* (1972).

The conflict has deep historical roots, and the attempts to find solutions and their failure are a part of history. The present situation and the prospects for a peaceful outcome cannot possibly be understood without a knowledge of how the problems of borders and of refugees originated, and what the several parties thought about them. This the authors of the preceding chapters have supplied.

As Professor Khouri described it in the chapter on UN peace efforts, the Security Council on 22 November 1967 passed Resolution 242, setting out two principles and three necessary conditions for establishing a "just and lasting peace" in the Middle East, a peace in accordance with the tenets of the United Nations Charter. The secretary general was requested to designate a special representative to establish and maintain contacts with the states concerned in order to achieve a peaceful and agreed settlement. Ambassador Gunnar Jarring of Sweden was appointed and has pursued his task patiently and skillfully, but, for reasons to be described, with small progress.

Israel, Egypt, and Jordan agreed to the terms of the resolution,[1] but this was agreement in principle, and as is well-known, it is a long way from agreement in principle to obtaining concurrence on substantive, concrete terms of a treaty or convention which can be put into effect. In the case of Resolution 242, the agreement in principle obtained by Ambassador Jarring was for practical purposes nullified by disagreement over the meaning and mode of application of its terms.

In November 1968 Secretary of State Dean Rusk put certain proposals to the foreign ministers of Israel and Egypt[2] for a settlement under the general terms of Resolution 242. Mr. Rusk's suggestions were:

> Withdrawal of Israeli forces from the Sinai and restoration of Egyptian sovereignty in it;
>
> status of Gaza Strip to be determined later;
>
> declarations ending state of belligerency;
>
> stationing of a UN force at Sharm el-Sheikh, not subject to withdrawal on Egyptian demand;
>
> Egypt to allow freedom of navigation through the Suez Canal and Straits of Tiran, including Israeli vessels;

move towards solution of refugee problem by allowing
them to state their preference for repatriation or
resettlement;
a signed contractual agreement embodying the obligations
of the parties;
a supplementary proposal was for the USA and the USSR
to limit provision of arms to Israel and the Arab states.

The initiative was significant, although the responses of the parties were not such as to encourage further diplomatic action by the United States at the time. (The Nixon administration would soon take over from President Johnson, and the invasion of Czechoslovakia by its Warsaw Pact partners inhibited diplomacy.) Then, in a speech on 9 December 1969, Secretary Rogers announced proposals which were basically the same as Secretary Rusk's.[3]

Some of the more important passages in this speech follow.

When this administration took office, one of our first
actions in foreign affairs was to examine carefully the
entire situation in the Middle East. It was obvious that a
continuation of the unresolved conflict there would be
extremely dangerous; that the parties to the conflict alone
would not be able to overcome their legacy of suspicion to
achieve a political settlement; and that international
efforts to help needed support. . . .
We accepted a suggestion put forward both by the French
Government and the Secretary-General of the United
Nations. We agreed that the major powers—the United
States, the Soviet Union, the United Kingdom and France
—should co-operate to assist the Secretary-General's
representative, Ambassador Jarring, in working out a
settlement in accordance with the resolution of the Security
Council of November, 1967. We also decided to consult
directly with the Soviet Union, hoping to achieve as wide an
area of agreement as possible between us.

Mr. Rogers went on to cite and comment upon the several principles and conditions set out in Resolution 242 and had this to say about the refugee question:

There can be no lasting peace without a just settlement of the problem of those Palestinians whom the wars of 1948 and 1967 have made homeless. . . . The United States has contributed about 500 million dollars for the support and education of the Palestine Refugees. We are prepared to contribute generously along with others to solve this problem. . . . The problem posed by the refugees will become increasingly serious if their future is not resolved. There is a new consciousness among the young Palestinians who have grown up since 1948 which needs to be channeled away from bitterness and frustration towards hope and justice.

After dealing with the problem of Jerusalem in an un-specific way, Mr. Rogers went on,

We started with the Israeli-United Arab Republic aspect because of its inherent importance for future stability in the area and because one must start somewhere.

We are also ready to pursue the Jordanian aspect of a settlement—in fact the powers in New York have begun such discussions.

In our recent meetings with the Soviets, we have discussed some new formulas in an attempt to find common positions. They consist of three principal elements:

First, there should be a binding commitment by Israel and the United Arab Republic to peace with each other, with all the specific obligations of peace spelled out, including the obligation to prevent hostile acts originating from their respective territories.

Second, the detailed provisions of peace relating to security safeguards on the ground should be worked out between the parties, under Ambassador Jarring's auspices. . . . These safeguards relate primarily to the area of Sharm Al Shaykh controlling access to the Gulf of Aqaba, the need for demilitarized zones as foreseen in the Security Council resolution, and final arrangements in the Gaza Strip.

Such an agreement . . . would require the UAR to agree to a binding and specific commitment to peace. It would require withdrawal of Israeli armed forces from UAR territory to the international border between Israel and Egypt which had been in existence for over half a century.[4]

These US policy guidelines had not changed up to the spring of 1973, when optimists hoped that a renewed effort would be made to reach a settlement. However, as will be mentioned later, a variation was tried—a partial withdrawal of the Israeli forces from the Sinai, far enough to allow the reopening of the Suez Canal to traffic, including Israeli rights of passage.

In 1969 [5] the Egyptians ill-advisedly carried on a "war of attrition" which had only increased the dangers of superpower involvement and made impossible negotiation to put the principles of Resolution 242 into effect.

In June 1970 the United States intervened with proposals [6] whose aims were to get a ceasefire between Egypt and Israel; prevent further involvement of Soviet military personnel and equipment, which might induce an American countermove, bringing about increased possibility of an armed encounter between the superpowers; and revive Ambassador Jarring's stalled negotiating mission.

A ceasefire was brought about on 7 August 1970. The United States and the Soviet Union both had a hand in achieving it. However, there was no written agreement, and hardly had 7 August passed when Israel accused Egypt of violating its terms, with the complicity of the USSR, by moving SAMs (antiaircraft missiles) into and about the purported ceasefire zone, where the parties were not supposed to do anything to improve their military positions. There was apparently some justification for this accusation, but with no written agreement and no impartial observers (such as the UNTSO) to determine what had actually happened, there was no decision whether in fact a breach had been committed; the dispute simmered down, and the ceasefire remained in effect.

Following the establishment of the ceasefire and the UN General Assembly of 1970, the secretary general reactivated the Jarring Mission. Ambassador Jarring began to hold meetings with the parties in January 1971 and continued them through February. The questions he put in identical aide-memoires to Egypt and Israel and the answers received, together with a general account of his proceedings during 1971, are set out in a report by the secretary general.[7] A summary of Ambassador Jarring's questions and the replies of Egypt and Israel is appended to this chapter.[8]

The two principles set out in the first operative paragraph of Resolution 242 are:

> Withdrawal of Israel armed forces from territories occupied in the recent conflict;
> Termination of all claims or states of belligerency and respect for and acknowledgement of the sovereignty, territorial integrity and political independence of every State in the area and their right to live in peace within secure and recognized boundaries free from threats of acts of force.

The first dispute over interpretation is whether the meaning of the first principle is withdrawal of Israel armed forces from *all* territories occupied in the 1967 war, as the Arabs claim, or whether, as the Israelis read it, it only calls for the withdrawal from "territories," but not all the territories. In any case, the Israelis stated in their reply to Jarring's questions that they did not intend to withdraw from *all* the territory they occupied following their June 1967 victory, but only to "secure and recognized boundaries," which would not be precisely those of the 1949 Armistice Demarcation Lines, from which the Israeli offensives had started. The government of Israel has not specified any boundaries which they would regard as "secure," stating that this is a matter on which they cannot be expected to give their position before negotiations commence.[9]

In approaches to peacemaking since 1967, it has been the trend to treat the issues of Egypt-Israel, Jordan-Israel, and Israel-Syria separately, following the precedent of the successful armistice negotiations of 1948–49. The several cases are all different to a degree, as are certainly the questions of where the boundary should lie and matters affecting the Arab and Israeli people contiguous to them.

## Egypt and Israel

The two principles of Resolution 242 quoted above have to be examined with reference to the three necessary conditions which read as follows:

(a)  Guaranteeing freedom of navigation through international waterways in the area;
(b)  Achieving a just settlement of the refugee problem;
(c)  Guaranteeing the territorial inviolability and political independence of every State in the area, through measures including the establishment of demilitarized zones. . . .

Bearing this in mind, let us first examine the possible "secure and recognized boundaries" between Egypt and Israel, behind which Israel could withdraw its forces now occupying the Sinai. A return to the armistice demarcation lines of 5 June 1967 has been refused by Israel. The second alternative would be a return to the old boundary between Egypt and Palestine, running from south of Rafah on the Mediterranean to the head of the Gulf of Aqaba, south of Eilat, in accordance with the Rusk suggestion. This would leave the Gaza Strip [10] under Israel's control.

The Palestinian inhabitants and refugees presently in the Strip under Israeli control would remain so, and this raises the question of the "just settlement of the refugee problem." It will be more convenient to leave this until we examine the situation of the Palestinian refugees and inhabitants in the so-called West Bank of Jordan.

However, Israeli leaders have said publicly that they must retain control of the Sharm el-Sheikh area and a corridor to the north.[11] In his statement in the UNGA plenary on 29 November 1972, Foreign Minister Zayyat of Egypt, quoted from an interview given by Mrs. Meir to a correspondent of the Italian magazine *L'Europeo,* which appeared in the 23 November 1972 issue,

With regard to the Egyptian peninsula of Sinai Mrs. Meir said in this interview, only six days ago, that Israel only wanted control of Sharm el-Sheikh and a stretch of desert linking Israel with Sharm el-Sheikh.[12]

Up to the end of 1974 the government of Israel had not shown any intention to abandon this territorial condition, which it presumably justifies as necessary to establish "secure and recognized boundaries."

An article in *The Economist* of 30 December 1972 told of the Israeli government's decision to create a new Israeli town, Yamit, in the Sinai to the west of the old Egypt-Palestine border, between Rafah and El Arish. This suggests, *The Economist* writes, that

> "the land bridge" which Israeli leaders say should connect Israel to Sharm el Shaikh is envisaged, at least by the Minister of Defence [General Dayan] as a great chunk of Sinai from Yamit in the north to the Straits of Tiran to the south.

The reason for the claim to Sharm el-Sheikh—or the indefinite presence of an Israeli garrison there—is that if the area were handed back to the Egyptians, they could at any time close the Straits of Tiran and the route to Eilat, through which the bulk of Israel's essential oil supply from Iran comes. Closing the straits had been a *casus belli* in 1956 and 1967.

Egypt will certainly refuse to cede any portion of the territory which has been recognized as belonging to it for very many years —although the slice of Sinai which Israelis propose to annex must be next door to hell in its climate and topography, with no compensating advantages. If Egypt refused to cede territory, it would be supported by the very great majority of United Nations members. The General Assembly resolution of 8 December 1972, in its fourth operative paragraph,

> *Declares once more* that the acquisition of territories by force is inadmissible and that, consequently, territories thus occupied must be restored.[13]

This resolution was passed with eighty-six in favour, seven against, thirty-one abstaining, and eight absent. The only countries voting with Israel against the resolution were Bolivia, Colombia, Costa Rica, the Dominican Republic, Nicaragua, and

Uruguay—a curious flocking of Latin American states to the Israeli side.

Among the more important countries abstaining for various reasons were Australia, Brazil, Canada, China, Denmark, New Zealand, Norway, South Africa, Sweden, and the United States.

Apart from the legal and political objections to annexation of Sharm el-Sheikh and the corridor to it, would the acquisition of this territory really give Israel greater security than a boundary coinciding with the old Egypt-Palestine one?

It should be obvious that no kind of geographical feature as a boundary can give security in itself. There must be adequate armed forces to defend it, if we consider military factors alone. Of course, some boundaries are more defensible than others, for example a mountain range, an important river, a desert. The Sinai desert, up to the time of the first World War, constituted a boundary area which gave a considerable degree of security to the states situated on either side of it, as the chronicles of the millennia of warfare in the area show. But with the mobility conferred by tanks and other tracked vehicles and with the great power of strike aircraft in the coverless desert, conditions have changed.

The history of the 1956 and 1967 Sinai campaigns shows clearly that even behind the demarcation lines of 1967 Israel can easily repulse an attempted invasion from Egypt, provided that its air force remains strong enough to maintain control of the air over the desert and that there is a reasonable balance in armored force. If control of the air were lost, any force Israel might have in Sharm el-Sheikh could be cut off.

It must be agreed that Israel's security requires free passage for shipping through the Gulf of Aqaba and up to Eilat. But is it necessary that there should be an Israeli garrison at Sharm el-Sheikh to guarantee this?

The third condition which Ambassador Jarring proposed, if Israel were to withdraw its forces from occupied Egyptian territory, was freedom of navigation through the Suez Canal and the Tiran Straits into the Gulf of Aqaba. Free passage in the Straits would be maintained by "practical security arrangements," which he interpreted as the stationing of a United Nations force in the area. Egypt in its reply to Jarring of 15 February 1971 said it

would give a commitment to ensure freedom of navigation in the
Suez Canal in accordance with the 1888 Constantinople Convention. Egypt was also prepared to accept the establishment of a
UN peacekeeping force, in which the four permanent members [14]
of the Security Council would participate, and the stationing of
part of this force at Sharm el-Sheikh.

Israel, in its reply to Jarring of 26 February 1971, made no
mention of this proposal for "practical security arrangements in
the Sharm el-Sheikh area." It is understandable, though regret-
table, that Israel would not trust a United Nations force to provide safe passage of its commerce, because of the withdrawal of
UNEF with no warning in 1967 on Egypt's request. Even if a
new UN force with contingents from the permanent members
were set up under Security Council authority, which would not
be subject to withdrawal by unilateral request of any "host country," it is unlikely that Israel would accept the solution. The reasons for Israel's distrust of the United Nations will be discussed
below.

But the whole question of possession and garrisoning of Sharm
el-Sheikh may have been rendered irrelevant by the fact that the
Arab states after 6 October 1973 established a blockade of Is-
rael-directed shipping at the Straits of Bab el Mandeb, where the
Red Sea opens into the Indian Ocean. This is 1200 miles south
of Sharm el-Sheikh, beyond the reach of Israel's armed forces.
Particulars are lacking on the mode of the blockade and of instances where Israeli-bound shipping has been stopped. But if a
blockade can be established at that point, what importance has
Sharm el-Sheikh?

During part of 1970 and 1971, as Mr. Campbell recounts,[15]
the United States tried to negotiate a partial settlement, which
would have comprised an Israeli withdrawal from part of the
Sinai, leaving the Suez Canal free to be opened for navigation.
However in spite of encouraging but cautious initial reactions
from both sides, it proved impossible to put an acceptable package together. The Egyptians wanted an assurance that the partial
withdrawal would be a stage to complete withdrawal, and they
wanted to be allowed to move their armed forces across the canal
to the vacated area. Israel was not prepared to concede either of

the terms, and there was no further progress on these lines until 1974.

Let us look again at the feasibility of the idea that Israel should maintain a garrison at Sharm el-Sheikh and continue to occupy sufficient of the Sinai to provide a land corridor to it.

Suppose that Egypt agreed to this proposition as a tactical move to regain possession of the rest of the Sinai. What would be the military status in this recovered part? Could armored and other formations be stationed in it, fortifications and other military installations be constructed? If so, presumably Israel would have to keep forces in readiness to counter the threat, that is to say, considerable parts of the armed forces of both states might be within cannon-shot of each other—an explosive situation.

Israel might expect the peace settlement to provide that Egypt should not move any troops into the Sinai, other than perhaps something like the Camel Corps, which before 1948 was the only force there, with the duty of keeping order among the widely scattered Bedouin groups. Even if such peace terms were accepted by Egypt, it would seem that there should be a guarantee that they were being observed. Perhaps some Israeli hawks would feel that the threat of Israel again resorting to armed action would prevent the terms being breached. But what kind of a peace would that be?

A second possibility would be to set up a corps of UN observers based at the Suez Canal crossings, with liberty of movement in the Sinai itself. These could report any infractions of the terms demilitarizing the Egyptian part of the Sinai to the Security Council. But the record shows that the Security Council failed to take any effective action when faced with reports from the UNTSO that the 1949 Armistice Agreements were being broken.

If the above objections to the first two alternatives are valid, we come back to the essence of the proposal implied in Ambassador Jarring's questions to Egypt and Israel—and this would seem applicable to either a complete withdrawal to the old Egypt-Palestine boundary, or a partial one. This proposal, to repeat, would be to station an armed UN force at Sharm el-Sheikh, and by implication along the Suez Canal, with the mission to ensure that the demilitarization terms were kept and that international shipping, including Israeli ships and cargoes, would have free passage. The force should include contingents from the permanent members of the Security Council. Of course this solution would only be possible if the permanent members were in agreement on the other terms of the peace settlement, in particular the interpretations of Resolution 242, as propounded by Ambassador Jarring.

Egypt's reply to Jarring's memorandum [16] accepts the solution, but would it also accept a limitation of sovereignty over the Sinai, a limitation of the kind of armed forces that could be sent into the territory? In the Armistice Agreements of 1949 there is a precedent for such a limitation on the kinds of forces and armaments that could be in certain areas on both sides of the demarcation line. This never worked very well, as neither party, due to mutual suspicion, would cooperate with the UNTSO to verify or disprove complaints that these provisions of the agreements were being violated.

Israel's position has been *not* to accept Jarring's proposal,[17] under which it would be agreeing to a guarantee by the Security Council. Israel has had little reason to trust in a United Nations guarantee. There are several bases for its misgivings. One is the evidence of General Assembly resolutions, in which large majorities have voted in favor of the Arab case.[18] However, these majorities testify more to the emotional support of the Third World than to the attitudes which the great and middle powers would assume if there were a reasonable chance of a settlement which would provide a lasting peace in the Middle East.

The record shows that the Security Council, in dealing with threats to the peace in the region, is generally paralyzed by the veto, or the threat of its use. How does Israel assess the feelings of the permanent members of the Security Council towards it? The Soviet Union has been hostile to Israel's interests, as Israel conceives them, since soon after the foundation of the state. Relations have been prevented from improving in recent years by the agitation to allow Jews to emigrate freely from the Soviet Union to Israel. The United Kingdom can hardly be considered a reliable friend. The attitudes of many Israeli political leaders towards Britain have been colored by her policy of restricting Jewish immigration in the years before 1948. France's attitude became hostile on de Gaulle's decision to suspend arms supply when the 1967 war broke out, and it has not changed greatly under the Pompidou and Giscard regimes. China is still an unknown quantity on the Security Council, but might be expected to take the side of the Arabs in any dispute. That leaves the United States, which up to the present, with few exceptions, has acted in the United Nations to protect Israel's interests. Could US influence counterbalance the generally adverse attitudes of the other permanent members? Could the US be always counted on as "a present help in time of trouble"?

The Israelis would weigh the worth of any American guarantee in the light of the US promises they thought they had in March 1957 regarding the Gulf of Aqaba, when they finally agreed to withdraw from the Sharm el-Sheikh area and the Gaza Strip.

On 11 February 1957 Secretary Dulles handed an aide-memoire to Ambassador Abba Eban in which the following position was stated:

> With respect to the Gulf of Aqaba and access thereto—the United States believes that the Gulf comprehends international waters and that no nation has the right to prevent free and innocent passage in the Gulf and through the Straits giving access thereto.
>
> The United States recalls that on January 28, 1950, the Egyptian Ministry of Foreign Affairs informed the United States that the Egyptian occupation of the two islands of Tiran and Senafir at the entrance of the Gulf of Aqaba was only to protect the islands themselves against possible damage or violation and that this occupation being in no way conceived in a spirit of obstructing in any way innocent passage through the stretch of water separating these two islands from the Egyptian coast of Sinai, it follows that this passage, the only practicable one, will remain free as in the past, in conformity with international practice and the recognized principles of the law of nations.
>
> In the absence of some overriding decision to the contrary, as by the International Court of Justice, the United States, on behalf of vessels of United States registry, is prepared to

exercise the right of free and innocent passage and to join with others to secure general recognition of this right.

It is of course clear that the enjoyment of a right of free and innocent passage by Israel would depend upon its prior withdrawal in accordance with the United Nations Resolutions. The United States has no reason to assume that any littoral state would under the circumstances obstruct the right of free and innocent passage.

The United States believes that the United Nations General Assembly and the Secretary-General should, as a precautionary measure, seek that the United Nations Emergency Force move into the Straits area as the Israeli forces are withdrawn. . . .

The United States is prepared publicly to declare that it will use its influence, in concert with other United Nations members, to the end that, following Israel's withdrawal, these other measures will be implemented.

We believe that our views and purposes in this respect are shared by many other nations and that a tranquil future for Israel is best assured by reliance on the fact, rather than by an occupation in defiance of the overwhelming judgement of the world community.[19]

Ambassador Eban went to Israel, consulted with his government, and returned for further discussions in Washington, during which "the Secretary of State clarified certain points regarding the attitude and intent of the United States on matters discussed in the US memorandum of 11 February." These clarifications were presumably reported to Tel Aviv.

In a plenary session of the UN General Assembly on 1 March 1957, Mrs. Golda Meir, then foreign minister of Israel, announced that Israel would withdraw its forces from Egyptian territory.

In making her announcement, she said:

My Government has noted the assurance embodied in the Secretary-General's note of 26 February 1957 (A/3563, annex) that any proposal for the withdrawal of the United Nations Emergency Force from the Gulf of Aqaba area would first come to the Advisory Committee for the United Nations Emergency Force, which represents the General Assembly in the implementation of its Resolution 997 (ES I) of 2 November 1956. This procedure will give the General Assembly an opportunity to ensure that no precipitate changes are made which would have the effect of increasing the possibility of belligerent acts. We have reason to believe that in such a discussion many members of the United Nations would be guided by the views expressed by Mr. Lodge, representative of the United States, on 2 February in favour of maintaining the United Nations Emergency Force in the Straits of Tiran until peaceful conditions were in practice assured.

In the light of these doctrines, policies and arrangements by the United Nations and the maritime powers, my Government is confident that free and innocent passage for international and Israeli shipping will continue to be fully maintained after Israel's withdrawal.

After giving Israel's views on the legal status of the Straits of Tiran, Mrs. Meir continued:

Interference by armed forces with ships of Israel exercising free and innocent passage through the Straits of Tiran will be regarded by Israel as an attack entitling it to use its inherent right of self-defence under Article 51 of the United Nations Charter and to take all such measures as are necessary to ensure the free and innocent passage of its ships in the Gulf and Straits.

We make this announcement in accordance with the accepted principle of international law under which all States have an inherent right to use force to protect their ships against interference by armed force. My government naturally hopes this contingency will not occur. . . .

In a public address on 20 February 1957 President Eisenhower stated: "We should not assume that, if Israel withdraws, Egypt will prevent Israel shipping from using the Suez Canal or the Gulf of Aqaba." This declaration weighed heavily with my Government in determining its action today.

Mr. Henry Cabot Lodge, then the US permanent representative to the UN, followed with a statement which included the following passages:

> The United States takes note of the declarations made in the statement of the representative of Israel. We do not consider that these declarations make Israel's withdrawal "conditional." For the most part the declarations constitute, as we understand, restatements of what has already been said by this Assembly or by the Secretary-General in his reports, or hopes and expectations which seem to us not unreasonable in the light of the prior actions of this Assembly.
>
> It is essential that units of the United Nations Emergency Force be stationed at the Straits of Tiran in order to achieve there the separation of Egyptian and Israeli land and sea forces. This separation is essential until it is clear that the non-exercise of any claimed belligerent rights has established in practice the peaceful conditions which must govern navigation in waters having such an international interest. . . .

Mr. Lodge then repeated the first three paragraphs set out above from Secretary Dulles' aide-memoire of 11 February.[20]

The Israeli government seemed at the time disappointed that Mr. Lodge did not announce a more specific and positive US engagement to intervene if an attempt were made to close the Straits of Tiran to Israeli or international shipping. Whether, in the negotiations between Secretary Dulles and Ambassador Eban, the Israeli government had been given the impression that such a stronger guarantee would be forthcoming if Israel announced that it would withdraw from the occupied territories does not appear in the public record. If the Israelis did believe that there had been such a promise, they would have felt that they had been diplomatically outmanoeuvred by Secretary Dulles (to put it politely). And Mrs. Meir, if the above is true, would not forget it, nor place a very high value in 1973 on United States assurances in regard to freedom of navigation into the Gulf of Aqaba.

Whether the Straits of Tiran are international waters is a question of international law which has not been determined until now. The majority of maritime nations hold that they are, and should be free for innocent passage. But in a statement in the debate following Mrs. Meir's announcement, Mr. Sobolev stated that in the USSR view, they were not international waters. This was notable, in view of what happened in 1967. Mr. Sobolev also said that Egypt had territorial rights in the Gaza Strip, which was not so. He accused the western powers of attempting to use UNEF to keep a foothold in the Middle East in accordance with the intent of the "Eisenhower Doctrine." [21] He said the UN force should leave Egyptian territory immediately after the Israelis evacuated it.

The representatives of India, Mr. Krishna Menon and Mr. Arthur Lall, also supported the position that the Straits of Tiran were Egyptian territorial waters. Whatever decision may eventually be made on this point, it is clear that from the time Egypt occupied the Island of Tiran, its only interest in the Gulf or the territory on its western shore was for blockading Israel. Therefore, as Egypt insisted on maintaining that a state of belligerency existed, the Soviet Union and India were supporting Egypt's right to impose a blockade in the Straits.

In 1967, when President Nasser announced the closing of the Straits of Tiran, after the expulsion of the UNEF and the deployment of large Egyptian forces in the Sinai, what did the US do to make good the assurances to Israel given or implied in the passages quoted above?

The Israeli Cabinet decided on 23 May 1967 that diplomatic action should be taken to try to get the United States and its allies to act according to the understood assurances. Even if the Straits were not reopened by this means, an attempt to solve the problem peacefully would put Israel in a better position in the eyes of the world if eventually it had to take a military offensive.

But events moved too fast for the diplomatic moves to have any effect. Mr. Abba Eban was dispatched on a mission to Paris, London, and Washington. In Paris he got a frosty answer from General de Gaulle, who would not commit his government to diplomatic moves to reopen the Straits and further warned Israel not to begin a war, on penalty of losing French political support (and presumably armaments)—which threat he carried into execution.

In London, Prime Minister Wilson told Mr. Eban that Britain

would act, along with the United States, in order to secure free navigation. Mr. Eban got to Washington on 26 May. As well as sounding President Johnson on the question of reopening the Straits, he asked about the United States' position in case hostilities broke out, the Israel government having become increasingly apprehensive of Egyptian attack as a result of military deployments made by Jordan, Iraq, and Syria.

It is understood that President Johnson told Mr. Eban that the United States intended to force President Nasser to rescind his blockade. The United States would organize a group of maritime nations to send ships to pass through the Straits, using force if necessary, ensuring also the passage of Israeli shipping. But this would take some time, and President Johnson hoped that Israel would not find it necessary to take military action before the necessary moves had been made. He took the attitude that Israel had nothing to fear if the Egyptians attacked—such was the Pentagon estimate of Israel's clear military superiority.

But this cool attitude did not and could not prevail in Tel Aviv. The Cabinet was divided between those who wanted to wait and see and those who thought Israel must strike at once, or give Egypt and her allies the advantage of opening hostilities when their deployment was completed. Time was not on Israel's side. Mr. Eshkol, the prime minister, was indecisive, and appeared so to his people. But with the appointment of General Dayan as defense minister, the die was cast for war.

Seeing the lack of firmness and despatch in Washington and London, and the adverse position of de Gaulle, it is no wonder that the Israeli government decided to rely on its own military power to open the Straits—and to strike down the menace of invasion by Egypt and the other Arab forces. And it is no wonder that this attitude should still prevail, as is implied by the insistence on keeping a garrison at Sharm el-Sheikh, and a corridor to it, as a condition for peaceful settlement.

While this position is not surprising, is it the best policy for Israel in the long run, if it means rejecting the possibility of a negotiated peace, on the lines of the conditions accepted by Egypt?

If Israel does not wish to continue in a state of suspended warfare, its alternative would be to agree, in spite of misgivings, to the guarantee of a UN force set up with participation of the superpowers, on the canal and at Sharm.[22] Israel would probably look on this as an exercise of superpower condominion in this corner of the world, and hence a restriction on its unfettered sovereignty—and that of its Arab neighbors, of course. But is not perhaps the choice of Israel and the Arab states alike between such a limitation of sovereignty and a never-ending state of war —if not the ultimate catastrophe of a war between the super-powers arising out of the conflict of their interests in the Middle East?

Any answer to this question must be conjectural, and at the end of this chapter we shall speculate on the political purposes of the superpowers in the Middle East, the strategic implications, the tenacity and force with which they will pursue their policies, and the risks they may be prepared to accept in doing so.

If the "secure and recognized boundary" were determined to be the old line between Egypt and mandated Palestine, this would leave the Gaza Strip and roughly 300,000 Palestinian inhabitants and refugees within Israel. What would be the status of these people, and how could a "just settlement" be devised for them?

As a result of the 1967 war, they are at present the inhabitants of an occupied country. The government of Israel, in reply to Jarring's questions, said it would be prepared, if other conditions for peace were met, to negotiate with the governments directly concerned on the payment of compensation for abandoned lands and property and to participate in the planning for rehabilitation of the refugees in the region.

There have been conflicting stories about the living conditions of the Palestinians in the Strip. Reports of Arab origin accuse the Israeli police and guard troops of atrocities and the general oppression associated with the concentration camps of World War II. The Israeli version is of benevolent, though firm—even occasionally stern—guardianship; they assert that conditions in the camps are better than in 1967. The refugees have been allowed to enter Israeli territory, to visit relatives in Jerusalem and the West Bank, and to some extent have been encouraged to transfer themselves and their families to the latter area. Some have been given employment in agriculture and construction, which has enabled them to improve their living over the subsistence level afforded by UNRWA.[23]

Allowing movement between the Strip and the West Bank would follow logically if the Israelis believe that what to do with the Palestinians in the two occupied territories forms a single problem. It would have to be allowed, to some degree, in any peace settlement.

## Jordan and Israel

The dilemma which faces Israel in devising a policy for peace with its Arab neighbours and moving towards what would seem a just settlement with the Palestinians has been set out in Aharon Cohen's chapter.[24]

Unless Israel decides to keep possession of all the West Bank territory it now occupies—a solution which is generally rejected —there will have to be some kind of "secure and recognized boundary" between Israeli territory and the lands occupied by the Palestine Arabs, whatever the legal status of these lands may be. The boundary and the circumstances of the people living beyond it are obviously two parts of one problem.

There has not been the same clarification of what this eastern boundary of Israel might be as has been achieved with regard to the Israel-Egypt border. Secret negotiations between King Hussein of Jordan and emissaries of the government of Israel have been reported many times. However, King Hussein has been eliminated as an Arab spokesman, at least temporarily, since the October 1974 Rabat conference of Arab states decided that the Palestine Liberation Organization (PLO) should be the representative of the Palestinian people in the settlement of their claims to self-determination and the right to return to their former homes in what is now Israel. While Israel had given signs of being disposed to deal with King Hussein, it has vehemently refused to negotiate with the PLO "gang of terrorists."

Israel has made it clear that it will not withdraw its troops from the West Bank area to the 1949 Armistice Demarcation Lines with Jordan (which still existed in 1967), but has not indicated where a "secure and recognized boundary" could lie. Israel has stated firmly that a return to the pre-1967 status of Jerusalem is not negotiable. In other words, it intends to maintain control over the entire area of the Holy City and has made this intention literally concrete by building apartment blocks in the open areas round the ancient walls and on the adjoining heights and filling them with Jewish immigrants. There have, however, been vague statements about allowing the Arab inhabitants of the Old City to participate in the government of the region above the municipal level and to allow freedom of access and religious practice to the Christian and Muslim holy places.

Apart from the matter of Jerusalem, no policy or opening negotiating position on territorial division has been announced. The 1949 Armistice Demarcation Line was anything but a clearly recognizable boundary, let alone a secure one. It was just a line on the map (made with a thick pencil at that) indicating where the fighting had left the opposing forces facing each other at the time of the 1949 armistice. Furthermore, it would hardly be possible to find any easily recognizable boundary line based on topographical features between the 1949 armistice line and the Jordan River.

The Jordan River is the present ceasefire line. As Aharon Cohen informs us,[25] the chauvinistically inclined political and intellectual circles grouped in the "Greater Israel" movement have demanded that this should be the boundary, whether agreed to in an eventual peace treaty or not. Although it creates a seemingly clear boundary, this would entail disadvantages to Israel which would rule the solution out.

What appears to find general agreement in Israel is that even if the West Bank (less Jerusalem and environs) is returned to Jordanian sovereignty, no Jordanian military forces should be allowed west of the river. This would make it a demilitarized zone, which would require enforcement either by Israel itself or by a United Nations force.

Some years ago, Yigal Allon proposed that a chain of Israeli garrisoned villages should be established along the river. This policy is apparently being brought into effect by the unpublicized establishment of Nahal villages. More recently, in February 1973, General Dayan said to the World Assembly of Jewish

Agencies that Israeli troops should continue to be stationed along the Jordan and that no other force should be allowed to cross the river.[26]

Whether the West Bank could be made a demilitarized zone under a United Nations force, which Resolution 242 could be interpreted to suggest, is discussed later.

As Aharon Cohen has put it:

> The root of the problem is, therefore, in the dispute between the Jewish people returning to its homeland and the Arab people living there. . . . Just as the dispute began in Palestine, so there must it find its solution.[27]

Mr. Cohen says the policy of the "Movement for Peace and Security"[28] includes the provision "to incorporate the residents of the occupied areas as a factor in and party to the efforts to achieve peace, while recognizing the right of the Palestinian Arab people to self-determination."

He then[29] discusses two alternative solutions to the problem of the Palestinian Arabs—including the refugees, supposing that Israel refuses "[to recognize] the Arab Palestinian people as a national entity, with a right to self-determination in its part of the common homeland."

The difference between the alternatives is whether the Arabs in the occupied territories should be given citizenship rights in Israel—as the minority of Palestinian Arabs who remained in Israeli-held territory after the 1948 war have been—or whether they should remain as at present, resident in the occupied territories, but without political rights, other than in municipal and strictly local affairs. Liberal Israeli opinion rejects the latter as unjust and unrighteous and as tending to project a world view of Israel as a nation of colonialist oppressors.

The objection to the first alternative is that if the Palestinian Arabs in the occupied territories were granted citizenship, the ratio of Jews to Arabs in Israel would immediately become sixty to forty. Since the Arabs would increase at a higher rate biologically than the Jews, even adding the expected number of Jewish immigrants, the Jewish citizens of the state might no longer be in a majority sometime after 1990. An Arab majority would mean, sooner or later, that Israel would no longer retain its essential character as a Jewish state. So in the long run this alternative would mean an abandonment of the Zionist ideals, whose realization in Israel has entailed such labor, sacrifice, and devotion over nearly a century. This is unthinkable to Israelis of nearly every shade of opinion. In fact, this alternative, over the long run, would accomplish what has been proposed by al Fateh as an immediate solution: a secular state of Palestine/Israel, where Jews and Arabs would have the same rights—including the right of immigration. The al Fateh proposal of course has never been accorded any serious attention by Israel.

The solution which Mr. Cohen regards as the best [30] is ". . . mutual recognition between the state of Israel, within borders substantially those of 4 June 1967 (though this does not rule out reasonable and agreed minor border changes), and the Palestinian Arab people." The latter would have the right to self-determination, which would in effect mean whether to be joined with Jordan, or to create a "state of Palestine," consisting of the truncated West Bank, with or without the Gaza Strip.

But would such a state of Palestine be economically and politically viable? Experience has shown that a state consisting of two separated pieces—*vide* Pakistan-Bangladesh—is not a practicable form of political and economic organization. And more apposite is the fate of the 1947 UNSCOP ideas for dividing Palestine between Jews and Arabs.

All things considered, the solution of rejoining the West Bank to Jordan, combined with a gradual transfer of the surplus Arab population of the Gaza Strip to this area on both sides of the Jordan, would seem to offer the best chances of enduring.

But neither the West Bank nor the rest of Jordan has sufficient natural resources to support the Arab population which would inhabit it, and it would not be a good solution to set up a state which would be a charity ward of the world—with an indefinite continuation of payments to the refugees through the United Nations or subventions from the oil-rich Arab states. The only reasonable prospect of economic viability would be if the Israelis continued to allow Arabs to take employment within Israel and permitted a free exchange of agricultural and perhaps other goods across the frontier between the eventual state of Palestine and Israel as it exists.

Whatever the solution, to satisfy Israel and to reduce the danger of future armed conflict, it must be one which will allow for effective control to prevent guerrilla or terrorist Arab attacks on Israelis. Within al Fateh and other groups devoted to the liberation of Palestine are many irreconcilables. The Israelis have been able to reduce their actions within Israel and the occupied territories to a level which leaves them as not much more than a minor nuisance. Terrorist action from outside the occupied territories is confined to raiding across the Lebanese border, against which Israel retaliates with violence.

The mention of demilitarized zones in paragraph 2C of Resolution 242 may be taken to mean that the West Bank, formerly held by Jordan, is to be a demilitarized zone. Presumably it is thought that part of the UN force required on the Suez Canal and at Sharm el-Sheikh could be stationed on the Jordan River and could act to prevent armed military formations from crossing. But the problem would be to prevent the actions of terrorists. From experience in the Gaza Strip, 1957 to 1960, I would say that this has to be a task for police. Furthermore, a strong intelligence organization is essential to control and prevent terrorism, as is recognized in all recent work on the subject throughout the world. The police and intelligence organization, and the judicial power to impose penalities on terroristic acts or conspiracy to commit them, has to be Arab. It is not conceivable that the United Nations would take on the responsibility of governing this area under some kind of trusteeship—as was contemplated for a while in regard to the Gaza Strip in 1957.

So it would be left to the Palestine/Jordan authorities to control the elements in the Palestinian population which might resort to terrorism to gain their ends. This is by no means impossible, as King Hussein has shown in his 1970 action against the would-be guerrillas in Jordan. During the period 1954–55, while Glubb Pasha commanded the then Arab Legion, "infiltration" of Palestinians to attack Israelis was held in check. Israeli success in suppressing terrorism has been possible because intelligence of terrorist activity, past or mooted, is relatively easy to obtain—because of the indiscretions of the "fedayeen" in boasting of their exploits and the vulnerability to bribery of the poor Arab refugees.

## Lebanon, Syria, and Israel

It is generally believed that if the more difficult questions of peace between Israel and Egypt and Israel and Jordan were settled, peace terms between Lebanon and Israel could be quickly arranged. There is no border problem; the old Lebanon-Palestine border, the Lebanon-Israel Armistice Demaraction line, and the present ceasefire line are all the same. Lebanese forces were not engaged in either the 1956 or 1967 wars. The difficulties between the two countries since 1967 have been owing to the Palestinian guerrilla activities already mentioned, especially since Jordan suppressed its guerrilla groups. Such groups in Lebanon could be suppressed too, if peace were in the offing. A problem which has disturbed the Lebanese since the main ingress of Palestinian refugees in 1948 is that they are mostly Muslims, and their presence, if they become citizens, would upset the delicate Muslim-Christian balance in the population, on which the elaborate constitutional arrangements are based. But this would not be an insurmountable obstacle to a peace agreement.

Syria was the last of the neighboring Arab states to negotiate an armistice agreement with Israel in 1949, and at first it refused to agree to Resolution 242 as a basis for negotiating a "just and lasting peace." But if the other Arab neighbors made peace, it would be difficult for Syria to remain at war, however irreconcilable her leaders may seem to be now. If there is to be a negotiated peace on this frontier, the Israelis would have to abandon their hold on the Golan Heights and the part of Syrian territory beyond. Generous compensation for the Arab lands taken over in the Huleh and Jordan valleys could remove one main reason that caused the Syrians to harass Israeli settlements along the Syrian border before June 1967.

Syria, alone of the Arab states surrounding Israel, has the land capacity to absorb the Palestinian refugees within her borders, and perhaps others from outside. This is owing to the development of the Gezirah, long-delayed, but getting nearer with completion of the great dam on the Euphrates.

The renewal of hostilities by Egypt and Syria in the Yom Kippur War beginning 6 October 1973 took Israel and the western world by surprise. The general opinion had been that

Sadat was unlikely to make good his vague threats to lead Egypt into a fourth round. But it happened, and Middle East "experts" have expended many words in print and on the air waves in speculating just exactly why it did. But now there are more important speculations: what are the chances for peace, a real negotiated and stable peace? Can the progress achieved through Secretary Kissinger's adroit negotiations in 1974 be maintained, and the hostile parties be convoked in a forum, for example in Geneva, as has been tentatively agreed?

The Arab and Israeli viewpoints have been so contradictory for so long that if there is to be a settlement guaranteeing the "peace with justice" envisaged in Resolution 242, the great powers must intervene to persuade or pressure them into it. The wars in the Middle East came about because of great-power intervention, by the creation of Israel in the first instance and more recently by the provision of great quantities of armaments. The great powers, particularly the superpowers, have a major responsibility for the situation. They must take firm action to settle it and to ensure peace and security in the region, if they are to honour their obligations under the Charter of the United Nations.

However, a cynical world may not trust greatly to the super-powers' sense of obligation. More to the point, are their interests in the region such as would be served by a true peace, rather than by a state of affairs similar to that before the October war or as it is now? Are American and Soviet motives and policies sufficiently compatible for them to press their respective client states to accept a peace settlement on the lines of Resolution 242, ironing out their differences of interpretation to arrive at a solution which will have a reasonable prospect of remaining stable?

When the United States armed power was first extended to the Middle East, it was in accordance with the Truman doctrine of 1947, for the support of Greece and Turkey against Communist pressure, subversion, and possible takeover. After NATO was extended to take in Greece and Turkey, this American interest has usually been conceived as protecting the southern flank of the alliance.

In the 1950s came the Dulles policy of containing the advance of Communist power, in this region through the Central Treaty

Organization, of which the "northern tier" countries, Pakistan, Iran, and Turkey are members. The United States is not formally a member, but stands behind the organization, and the credibility of US support depends on its maintaining an effective strategic presence in the eastern Mediterranean—the Sixth Fleet and associated bases.

This is the United States' purpose in geopolitical terms; more specific and regional purposes are the protection of American interests in the Persian Gulf oilfields and the maintenance of Israel's right to exist as a sovereign state. It has always been evident that these two interests are contradictory, with critical impact since October 1973.

The Soviet Union's interest in maintaining a strong presence in the Middle East and eastern Mediterranean will be discussed more fully later, but here it may be remarked that it is clearly and directly opposed to the worldwide strategic purposes of the United States.

The Middle East is traditionally the gateway from the West to the Orient, more particularly to the countries surrounding the Indian Ocean. It is obvious that if Soviet Union influence blankets all the Arab countries eventually, as it now does Iraq, Syria, South Yemen, and Egypt (with limitations), and if western influence and strategic presence is at the same time reduced to a minimum, the Soviet Union will have gained a very great advantage in power to exercise control throughout Asia and Africa.

The stronger the Soviet military presence from the Suez area to the Persian Gulf, the less possible it will be to apply any sort of military pressure on the oil-producing countries to prevent a boycott or slowdown in production, such as was put into effect in the early days of November 1973. It is commonplace to say that the days of gunboat diplomacy are gone forever; but apparently people still exist in the United States (as suggested by Senator Fulbright [31]) who think it would be possible for force to be applied in the interests of the United States by a "surrogate"—Israel or Iran. More recently, Senator Fulbright warned the Arab oil producers that the United States "is a superpower which can get away with the use of economic pressure however unwise it may be. The Arab oil producers are militarily insignificant—gazelles, as I suggested before, in a world of lions." [32]

In January 1975, Secretary Kissinger said that the possibility of military intervention to assure oil supplies in the face of a threat of "strangulation" could not be excluded. This statement more or less coincided with the move of a large US aircraft carrier and supporting vessels into the Indian Ocean, with unspecified destination and purpose.

It is beyond the scope of this chapter to speculate on the strategic possibility of using military force, or threatening to do so, against the oil-rich states of the Persian Gulf. But it must be obvious that such a move by western powers would entail the greatest risk of USSR intervention and a direct military confrontation of the superpowers.

If the Suez Canal were opened, and Egypt were again in close relations with the USSR, this would make it easier for the Soviet Union to extend its increasing global naval strength to the Persian Gulf and the Indian Ocean. As it is, the West has an advantage, as it is a shorter voyage to the Persian Gulf from American Atlantic naval bases than it is for Soviet Union vessels, which must come out of the Black Sea, through the Mediterranean, and round the Cape of Good Hope—a route flanked throughout by western air and naval bases.

However, the policies put forward by Secretary of State Rogers in 1970 and 1971 aimed at the opening of the canal, so evidently this possible USSR strategic advantage did not weigh sufficiently against the need to make a start at settlement between Israel and Egypt and to eliminate the inconvenience to world trade. The additional costs of the longer voyages between the Orient and western Europe and America has been estimated at $4 billion over the five years after 1967.

It was as a defense against the US Sixth Fleet, with its ballistic-missile-launching submarines and aircraft carriers, that Soviet naval forces were sent into the Mediterranean. That is, their primary task was to defend the southern part of the USSR. The first Soviet strategic interest in the area is that it should not serve as an approach route for forces threatening its southern industrial and population centers. While inferior in numbers and power to the US and allied naval forces in the east Mediterranean, the Soviet fleet has been increasing year by year, and this strengthens the Soviet influence vis-à-vis the United States. Until the bulk of Soviet military personnel were withdrawn from Egypt, on President Sadat's request in July 1972, the naval force could benefit from the possibility of air cover based in Egypt. Whether relations with Egypt will recover sufficiently for the USSR to regain use of the air and naval bases which it formerly had is uncertain. It could definitely come about if there is no move toward a peace satisfactory and acceptable to the Arabs.

The Soviet fleet, incidentally, has recently acquired the ability to intervene on land through use of specially organized and trained troops—"naval infantry," a sort of counterpart to the US Marines, who landed in Lebanon in 1958.

But in citing these military buildups, and the tensions and divergent interests which are their cause, we should also remember that since 1967 it has been clear that neither the US nor the USSR wishes to be driven into war because their respective client states behave recklessly. It would seem that these reciprocal policies have stood the test of the events since 6 October 1973 in spite of the alarm caused by President Nixon's placing of the US armed forces—including an ICBM complex—on alert. As yet, there is insufficient independent evidence to enable the world to decide whether it was necessary or not.

## Israel and the United States

The US concern for Israel's survival could be said to be reflected in Resolution 242, which states that there should be

> . . . respect for and acknowledgement of the sovereignty,
> territorial integrity and political independence of every State
> in the area and their right to live in peace within secure and
> recognized boundaries free from threats or acts of force. . . .

The American interest since the 1967 war has been shown by the provision of modern weaponry on favorable terms, most notably many Phantom strike aircraft, with the purpose, as President Nixon announced of "not allowing the balance of power to be tilted against Israel." The Congress has voted $2.2 billion to pay for the supply of armaments and munitions to Israel, including replacements for losses in the October war. In January 1975, Israel asked for a further $2.2 billion in armaments and financial support to be provided through the US financial year 1976.

The policy of supporting Israel diplomatically and with arms and financial aid is generally favored in the United States, not merely by the very influential Jewish part of the population, but also by the majority of Americans. It is not only that the presentation of the Israeli case in the American media is much more skillful and effective than any communication by the Arabs, but because the seeds of pro-Israel propaganda have fallen on fertile ground. Protestant Christians, in particular, greatly influenced in their youth by the Bible as presented in churches and Sunday schools, found it fitting that the Jews should return to the home of their ancestors after nearly two thousand years. And the American stereotype of the Arabs was of nomadic groups wandering around the deserts on camels. More important in influencing acceptance of the Israeli cause was the Nazis' terrible slaughter of European Jews and the guilt feelings that aroused, in that the United States had seemingly done nothing to prevent it. Any American who had harbored anti-Semitic prejudices was liable to feel doubly guilty.

The common idea abroad that the "Jewish vote" handcuffs US policy in respect to the Middle East is too simple. Nevertheless its importance cannot be ignored. During the presidential election campaign of 1972, both candidates took pains to tell the electorate that they were favorable to the interests of Israel.[33] The attitudes of senators and representatives in the October-November crisis reveals this influence on the outlook of American politicians. Senator Fulbright said on 21 May 1973:

> Neither a voluntary nor an imposed solution is likely to come about in the foreseeable future, owing primarily to the refusal of the U.S. administration, backed by heavy congressional majorities, to modify its commitment to the present policy of Israel.[34]

In the months following the Yom Kippur War, in spite of increasing concern over oil supplies and the possibility that a continued impasse in Middle East peace negotiations may lead to a crisis between the superpowers, it does not appear that the attitude of the US administration or Congress has substantially changed.

Having reviewed the US attitude toward Israel, we must consider the Soviet Union's attitude toward the Arab states. One Russian objective in the Middle East is to gain influence in the Arab countries and to prevent the United States from assuming the predominant authority formerly exercised by Britain and France. As well as reducing or eliminating US and western European influence, the Soviet Union probably hopes to prevent China from acquiring more than the minimum it presently has.

The question which Arabs, Israelis, and the West have been asking is: does the Soviet Union want to continue the present state of "no-war, no-peace"? If they do, no negotiated stable peace is possible; if they do not, there is a chance for it.

Probably the Soviet Union would be happy to see the condition of no peace, no war ended, if it could be done with advantage to the Arab states, which would then tend to regard the USSR as a good and powerful friend. But, taking another viewpoint, would the Soviet Union wish to see a state of affairs in which the Arab states, freed of the threat of an expanding Israel, would come together in an effectively integrated group, capable of acting within the region in ways which might be contrary to USSR interests? The USSR governing circles are foresighted enough to see the possibility of a strong coalition of Arab states, immune to threats of military coercion by either side, continuing to enjoy the game which Egypt itself—or India, for another example—has played, that is, setting one superpower off against the other in a mild blackmail for getting more favorable military or economic aid.[35] So we are left with yes and no possibilities; real answers will have to wait on future events.

Another question on Soviet-Arab relations will probably have to wait for a long time before it is answered. And that is why Sadat invited the Russian military technicians and advisers to depart so hastily from Egypt in July 1972. Evidently Sadat, and perhaps the Soviet leaders, reconsidered positions during 1973. That the Kremlin knew beforehand of Sadat's intention to launch the Egyptian army across the Suez Canal is evident, as indicated by the hasty exodus of many Russians only a day or so before the event. It has been assumed that in 1972 the Soviet authorities may have counselled Sadat against going to war again, and that this, coupled with their refusal to supply certain advanced military offensive armament, may have been part of the reason for Sadat's request that they withdraw. But when he made up his mind that the Egyptian army must move, if the Sinai was to be regained, and if the Arab oil countries were to bring their boycott into play, the Russians must have acquiesced. In any case, immediately after hostilities began, arms lifts from the Soviet Union to Egypt and Syria began to make good the expenditure of munitions and loss of equipment.

The Soviet Union's position in Security Council debates on ending the hostilities certainly shows no lessening of support for the Arabs. Their reluctance to countenance a cease fire resolution in the early days of October may be interpreted as preventing interference while the Egyptians and Syrians were making gains against the Israeli forces. When the tide of battle began to turn, they became willing to join the call for a ceasefire and to take part in the arrangements for a UN observation group (or the strengthening of the still existing UNTSO), followed by the complicated question of setting up another UN peacekeeping force.

The attitudes which the Soviet Union will take if the belligerents are brought to a negotiating table remains to be seen. They did vote for and accept Resolution 242, agreeing with the Arab interpretation that withdrawal of Israeli forces should be from *all* the territories occupied since 5 June 1967. They emphasized this stand in the discussions calling for ceasefire and withdrawal. But there would not appear to be any obstacle, from the USSR positions so far disclosed, to a settlement on the lines proposed by Secretary Rogers, if Egypt will accept them, as it appeared to do in its replies to the January 1971 Jarring memorandum.

The new, and perhaps decisive, factor in the Middle East is the power of oil-producing Arab states to exercise pressure on the western world. This was brought home to the average American citizen by shortages of heating oil and gasoline, following the relatively brief oil embargoes imposed in the autumn of 1973. Since then, the states in the Organization of Petroleum Exporting Countries have proved their power by extracting very much higher prices for their oil and by imposing conditions which give them much greater control over the whole industry.

In April 1973 the situation was serious enough for President Nixon to issue a special message to Congress. In it he looked to measures which might be taken over several years to reduce US vulnerability to a cut in oil imports. As he said in a press conference on 8 September 1973,[36] US energy resources must be fully developed, because "no industrial nation must be in the position of being at the mercy of any other nation by having its energy supply suddenly cut off." The measures his administration had in mind were reduction of controls on coal strip mining, the exploitation of oil-bearing shale deposits, increased use of nuclear power to generate electricity, and the completion of the Alaska pipeline.

It will be several years before these measures will have any impact on the foreseen energy shortage. In the meantime, American citizens may suffer sufficient discomfort as to reduce their enthusiasm for maintaining Israel's right to garrison the Egyptian territory of Sharm el-Sheikh and the Syrian territory on and beyond the Golan Heights. This is not to suggest that the US government will be turned aside from a policy it believes to be right and *vital to its own interests* by an oil squeeze. But it is not a matter of acquiescing in Israel's destruction, but only of persuading Israel's rulers to withdraw its forces from the territories occupied since 5 June 1967 to within "secure and recognized boundaries," not far from the 1949 armistice demarcation lines.

By the third week in November 1973, a ceasefire was established, and elements of a new United Nations Emergency Force were deployed in the Suez area. During the first part of 1974, Secretary Kissinger scored memorable successes in persuading the Israelis and Egyptians to agree to a ceasefire line some ten miles to the east of the Canal, with a buffer zone occupied by the new UNEF between them. Then the more difficult withdrawal of Israeli forces to a new line on the Golan Heights, again with UNEF buffering, was achieved. As 1975 began, Egypt and Syria demanded further withdrawals from their occupied territory and a promise of withdrawal from all of it. Israel is unwilling to concede this, failing much more convincing evidence than has yet been offered that Egypt and Syria will sign a peace treaty, and sincerely fulfill it, in return for such withdrawals.

What will happen? Are the pressures for peace stronger than they were in 1949, in 1956, and in 1967? Are they sufficiently strong for Israelis, Egyptians, and Syrians to accept peace terms based on Resolution 242, the Rogers Plan, and the clarifications obtained by Ambassador Jarring in 1971? Will these nations opt for peace, even if it is a peace which will not give any of them all the conditions they have been demanding?

Perhaps even more important, are the superpowers ready for a peace in this area leaving neither one dominant and neither one obliged to pour armaments into the region to meet the demands of their client states?

No one can answer these questions now. The world can only wait, hoping that it is true, as many observers have said, that the chance for a real peace is greater now than it has been since the Arab-Israeli wars began in 1948.

Without a solution to the Palestinian refugee problem, there can be no durable peace. A solution requires some kind of program which can be initiated soon and which will hold the promise of restoring a feeling of community, freedom, and of economic opportunity to a people now displaced and subject.

Will the mooted peace conference in Geneva take place? Who will be there to negotiate with Israel on behalf of the Palestinians? What will be the end to this warring of peoples, semitic cousins, both claiming rights to the same territory? What will be the next phase in the quarrel? More war, or an agreement under which they can live together?

The lands of Israel and the Arabs have formerly abounded in prophets. It would be presumptuous for a foreigner to intrude on their domain.

## Appendix

*Summary of Proposals in Jarring Memorandum of 8 February 1971, and Replies by Israel (26 February) and Egypt (15 February).*

1.  Israel is to give commitment to withdraw forces from occupied Egyptian territory to old Egypt-Palestine boundary.

    Israel replied that she would not withdraw them to the pre-June 1967 lines, but to secure, recognized, and agreed boundaries to be established in a peace agreement.

Egypt replied that Israel should withdraw her forces from the Sinai and the Gaza Strip.

2. Israel's commitment to withdraw to be contingent on the establishment of demilitarized zones.

   Israel made no comment on this proposal.

   Egypt would accept demilitarized zones astride the borders to equal distances and would agree to the establishment of a UN peacekeeping force in which the four permanent members of the Security Council would participate.

3. Egypt's commitment to accept practical security arrangements in Sharm el-Sheikh for guaranteeing freedom of navigation through the Straits of Tiran and to allow freedom of navigation through the Suez Canal.

   Egypt would accept this and would ensure freedom of navigation in the Suez Canal in accordance with the 1888 Constantinople Convention.

4. Egypt to agree, on a reciprocal basis,
   (a) to terminate all claims or states of belligerency;
   (b) to respect the territorial sovereignty and political independence of all states in the Middle East and their right to live in peace within secure and recognized boundaries;
   (c) to do all in its power to prevent hostile acts from or within its own territory against the population, citizens, or property of the other party;
   (d) not to interfere in another country's domestic affairs.

   Egypt would agree to commit itself as above, on condition that Israel would commit itself to complete withdrawal and to a "just settlement of refugee problems" in accordance with UN resolutions.

   Israel agreed that she would negotiate with the governments directly involved on:
   (a) payment of compensation for abandoned lands and projects,
   (b) participation in planning of rehabilitation of refugees in the region.

   Israel also called for a peace agreement to be expressed in a binding treaty and believed that "parties should pursue their negotiations in a detailed and concrete manner, without prior conditions."

## Notes

1. Khouri, supra, pp. 69–70.
2. Campbell, supra, p. 286.
3. *Ibid.*, pp. 292–293.
4. Department of State Bulletin, 9 December 1969.
5. Campbell, supra, p. 294.
6. *Ibid.*
7. UN Document A/8541; 30 November 1971.
8. Khouri, supra, pp. 75–76.
9. Campbell, supra, pp. 285–286.
10. Legally the Gaza Strip is a remnant of the mandated territory of Palestine, and so not Egyptian territory, if there is any point of mentioning legality in this connection.
11. Kerr, supra, p. 4.
12. UN Document A/PV 2092, p. 7.
13. UN Document A/L686, rev. I.
14. The People's Republic of China had not at that time taken its place in the United Nations and the Security Council.
15. Campbell, supra, pp. 296–297; Khouri, supra, p. 77.
16. Khouri, supra, pp. 75–76.
17. *Ibid.*, p. 76.
18. *Ibid.*, pp. 74, 77–80, 85.
19. Department of State Bulletin, 11 March 1957.
20. Statements from UNGA report A/PV 666, 1 March 1957.
21. The Eisenhower Doctrine, generally speaking, promised that the United States would come to the aid of any country threatened by aggression from another country under international Communist control. It was intended as an assurance to those Middle East countries which might be threatened by another Arab country (in particular Egypt) which had come under USSR influence, and thus which might be used as a proxy for moving against those Middle East Arab countries which were favorable to the West, or even neutral. It also implied an assurance to Israel of United States support—even armed support—if it should suffer aggression from a "communist-controlled country." The formula was ingenious, but it was too vague to reassure any potential beneficiary. Little effective action followed the proclaiming of the doctrine; the exception was in the case of the Lebanese troubles in 1958, when a US Marine force was landed and helped, together with the operation of the UN observer mission in Lebanon (UNOGIL) to defuse the internal crisis and the threat from Syria.
22. See pp. 319–320, Burns, supra, regarding possible reduced importance of Sharm el-Sheikh.

23. "Improved New Conditions in West Bank," *Newsweek*, 26 June 1972; also Dayan interview, The New York Times News Service, reprinted in Toronto *Globe and Mail*, 14 December 1972.

24. Cohen, supra, pp. 155–159.

25. *Ibid.*, p. 142.

26. The New York Times News Service, reprinted Toronto *Globe and Mail*, 5 February 1973.

27. Cohen, supra, p. 154.

28. *Ibid.*, pp. 142–143.

29. *Ibid.*, p. 153.

30. *Ibid.*

31. See *Congressional Record*, 21 May 1973.

32. *The Economist*, 17 November 1973.

33. *Newsweek*, 21 August 1972.

34. *Congressional Record*, 21 May 1973.

35. See extracts from article by M. Hassanein Haikal, editor of *Al-Ahram*, printed in *Survival*, International Institute of Strategic Studies, London. His observations were used in this chapter to represent Egyptian views of Soviet aims.

36. AP dispatch, Washington, published Toronto *Globe and Mail*, 10 September 1973.

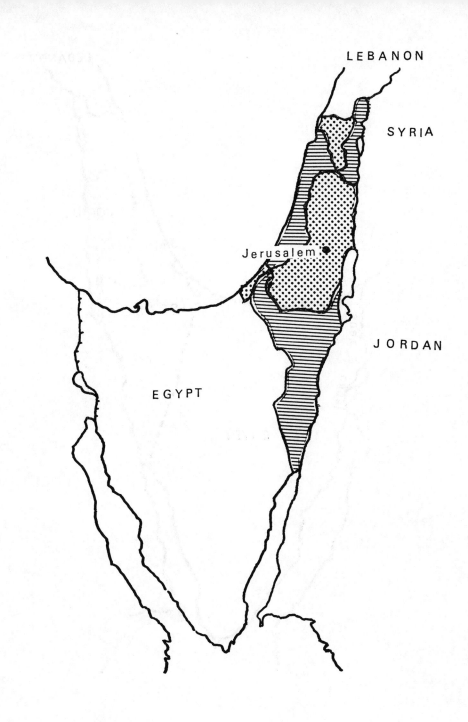

LEBANON

SYRIA

Jerusalem •

JORDAN

EGYPT

1947  UN  PARTITION  PLAN

JEWISH  STATE  ▤  ARAB  STATE

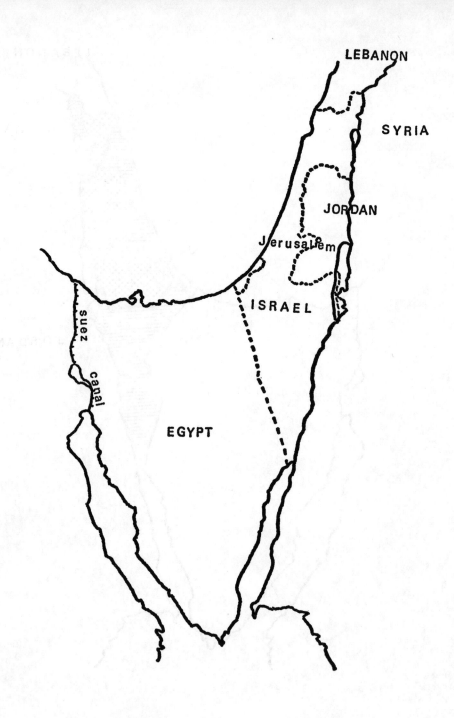

LEBANON

SYRIA

JORDAN

Jerusalem

ISRAEL

suez

canal

EGYPT

ISRAEL BEFORE 1967

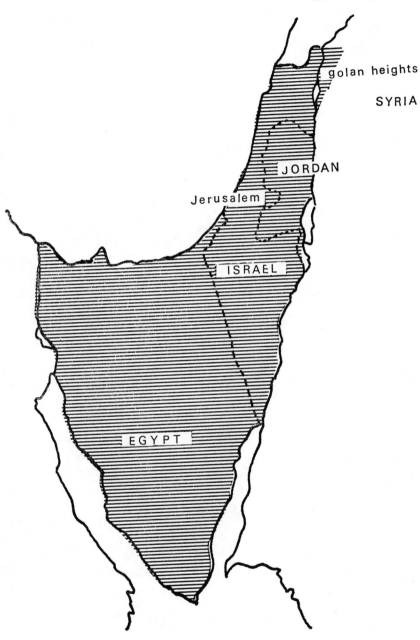

LEBANON

golan heights

SYRIA

JORDAN

Jerusalem

ISRAEL

EGYPT

ISRAEL & OCCUPIED TERRITORIES
1967 – 1973